THE MIND
OF THE
TERRORIST

The Psychology of Terrorism
from the IRA to al-Qaeda

Jerrold M. Post

palgrave
macmillan

First published in 2007 by
PALGRAVE MACMILLAN™
175 Fifth Avenue, New York, N.Y. 10010 and
Houndmills, Basingstoke, Hampshire, England RG21 6XS
Companies and representatives throughout the world.

PALGRAVE MACMILLAN is the global academic imprint of the Palgrave Macmillan division of St. Martin's Press, LLC and of Palgrave Macmillan Ltd. Macmillan® is a registered trademark in the United States, United Kingdom and other countries. Palgrave is a registered trademark in the European Union and other countries.

ISBN -13: 978–1–4039–6611–7
ISBN-10: 1–4039–6611–7

Library of Congress Cataloging-in-Publication Data

Post, Jerrold M.
    The mind of the terrorist : the psychology of terrorism from the IRA to al-Qaeda / Jerrold M. Post.
        p. cm.
    Includes bibliographical references and index.
    ISBN 1–4039–6611–7 (alk. paper)
        1. Terrorism—Psychological aspects. 2. Terrorists—Psychology.
    3. Terrorism—History—20th century. 4. Terrorism—History—
    21st century. I. Title.

HV6431P669 2007
363.3250199—dc22   2007014258

A catalogue record for this book is available from the British Library.

Design by Newgen Imaging Systems (P) Ltd., Chennai, India.

First edition: December 2007

10 9 8 7 6 5 4 3 2 1

Printed in the United States of America.

To my three wonderful daughters, Cindy, Merrie, and Kirsten:
May the cloud of terrorism that shadows our lives
be lightened by better understanding man's inhumanity to man,

and to

Ehud Sprinzak, a pioneer in terrorism research, who has helped
illuminate the psychology of terrorism and political extremism.

CONTENTS

ACKNOWLEDGMENTS

There is a small band of intrepid terrorism researchers whose work has been particularly valuable. This book has been enriched by primary source material from interviews conducted by Farhana Ali, Nicole Argo, Mia Bloom, Mohammad Hafez, Nasra Hassan, Ariel Merari, Fernando Reinares, Ann Speckhard, Ehud Sprinzak, and Jessica Stern.

Colleagues who have provided valuable commentary on draft chapters include John Cope, Dogu Ergil, Michael Gunter, John Horgan, Martin Kramer, Chris Kutschera, Thomas Marks, Ariel Merari, David Scott Palmer, Dennis Pluchinsky, Fernando Reinares, and Goldie Shabad.

I have had the benefit of research contributions by a remarkable group of assistants and interns whose contributions to this effort have been indispensable. I want to single out in particular Brooke Sweet, Lara Panis, and Laurita Denny, treasures beyond compare, without whose devotion, dedication, and persistence this project could not have been completed. Valuable contributions were made by Neil Aggarwal, Jorge Aguilar, Daniel McFadden, Saray Mendoza, Keven Ruby, Ahren Shaffer, Jessica Souder, Inna Taller, Rebekah Vogel, and Peter Zemenides.

And I wish to express special thanks to my family, particularly my wife, Carolyn, always my strong supporter, who patiently endured long hours of isolation as I was closeted with my computer.

CHAPTER 1

TERRORISMS AND TERRORIST PSYCHOLOGIES: AN INTRODUCTION

When the hijacked American and United Airlines planes struck the World Trade Center towers and the Pentagon on 9/11 with concussive force, America's perceived shield of invulnerability was irrevocably shattered. No longer would the insular American nation look on at the conflict-ridden world believing itself safe from danger. The searing images of the two hijacked planes striking that symbol of U.S. economic might, the World Trade Center towers, of their collapse, and of smoke billowing out of the symbol of U.S. military might, the Pentagon, would be engraved on international consciousness. When we learned that the fourth hijacked plane, which was brought down in a field outside of Pittsburgh, Pennsylvania, was bound for Washington, D.C., believed to be targeted against the Capitol or the White House, symbols of American political might, the fear grew further. The scope of the coordinated attacks, on symbols of the three pillars of America's stature as the world's remaining superpower—economic, military, and political—was unprecedented, and breathtakingly audacious. The previous feelings of invulnerability were at once replaced by feelings of vulnerability and fear. Who were the unknown attackers? Why would they hate us so? What would be the next target? Fear gripped the nation and the civilized world.

On September 13, 2001, President George W. Bush addressed the nation. This was, he declared, "the first war of the 21st century." On September 20, he went on to declare "Either you are with us, or you are with the terrorists. From this day forward, any nation that continues to harbor or support terrorism will be regarded by the United States as a hostile regime."

Bold words, valiant words, words of resolve and determination that rallied the nation. But historically inaccurate words. For the history of terrorism is as old as the history of humankind. And the modern era of terrorism is usually dated back to the late 1960s–early 1970s, with the iconic event being the Black September terrorist in a ski mask, patrolling outside of the seized Israeli Olympic village at the 1972 Munich Olympics. Two years earlier, on September 6, 1970, the dramatic coordinated hijacking of four U.S.-bound airliners by Palestinian Front for the Liberation of Palestine (PFLP) terrorists first drew the world's attention to the Palestinian cause.[1] But it was the effrontery of the terrorist event at the Munich Olympics that transfixed the world. It marked the forcible intersection of political terrorism with the information revolution, ushering in what was to be known as the age of terrorism. An estimated international television audience of some 900 million from more than 100 countries looked on, transfixed, as the violent drama played out, culminating with the botched German police team attack. Eleven Israeli Olympic athletes and five Palestinian terrorists were killed. The Palestinian cause was squarely on the map, demonstrating the power of the media to propagate the terrorists' violent message to a worldwide audience. It was violence as communication writ large.

This spectacular event emphasizes a feature of terrorism to which Alex Schmid, in his painstaking examination of terrorist definitions, has called attention: the distinction between the target of violence and the targets of attention.[2] The target of violence is the innocent victims or noncombatants: the workers in the World Trade Center, the teenagers in a Tel Aviv disco. There are three targets of attention: the target of terror, the target of demands, and the target of influence. The target of terror refers to the members of the class of the victims of violence. Emphasizing that the goal of terrorism is to terrorize, when Sulaiman Abu Ghaith, a spokesman for Osama bin Laden, after 9/11 famously offered advice to "*those who reject the unjust U.S. policy*" to not live or work in high-rise buildings or travel by plane, because there were "*thousands of Muslim youths who are eager to die and that the aircraft storm will not stop, God willing,*" his target audience was not observant Muslims but the American public, and his goal was to continue to propagate the terror caused by the attacks of 9/11.[3]

The target of demands, sometimes referred to as extortionate terrorism, is well illustrated by the wave of kidnappings and threatened beheadings in Iraq, such as British contractor Kenneth Bigley and U.S. contractors Eugene Armstrong and Jack Hensley. Displaying a terrified weeping Philippine contractor, Angelo de la Cruz, pleading for his life, the message was conveyed by

Abu Musab Al-Zarqawi, the terrorist leader of al-Qaeda in Mesopotamia, that unless the Philippine government withdrew its troops from Iraq by the end of the month, de la Cruz would be beheaded. The fragile government yielded, and de la Cruz was released.

The target of influence is usually the West or the establishment, calling attention, for example, to the cause of the Palestinian people. But an additional audience is the audience of constituents and potential recruits, demonstrating the ability of the group to strike out powerfully at its enemies. Not everyone who watched the coordinated attacks of 9/11 was horrified; some were exultant at the ability of the powerless to strike a blow at the powerful.

Thus, violence against victims is intended to convey a message to the audiences of attention. And it is the fact that the victims are unarmed and the randomness of the act that could occur to anyone, at any time, anywhere—the *extranormality* of the act—that so compels horrified attention.

Terrorism then is a particular species of political violence. It is violence or the threat of violence against noncombatants or property in order to gain a political, ideological, or religious goal through fear and intimidation. Usually symbolic in nature, the act is designed to have an impact on an audience that differs from the immediate target of the violence. It will be noted that this definition is value free. It says nothing about the goodness or badness of the cause, in the name of which these acts are being committed. One can strongly favor, for example, an independent Palestinian state but still deplore the taking of innocent life in pursuit of that goal. Thus terrorism is a behavior, a strategy adopted by groups with widely differing goals and constituencies. While the 9/11 terrorist spectacular and its aftermath has tended to focus international attention on radical Islamist terrorism, the spectrum of terrorism is broad and diverse, as illustrated in figure 1.1.

At the top tier, we have the three major divisions of political, criminal, and pathological terrorism or, in the marvelously alliterative title of an early work on terrorism by the psychiatrist Frederick Hacker, *Crusaders, Criminals, and Crazies.*[4]

There is a widespread assumption in the lay community that groups and individuals who kill innocent victims to accomplish their political goals must be crazed fanatics. Surely no psychologically "normal" individual could perpetrate wanton violence against innocent women and children.

In fact, those of us who have studied terrorist psychology have concluded that most terrorists are "normal" in the sense of not suffering from psychotic disorders. Martha Crenshaw, a prominent international terrorism expert, has observed that "the outstanding common characteristic of terrorists is their

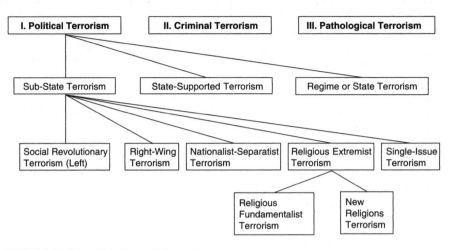

FIGURE 1.1 New Typology of Terrorism.

Source: This graphic is adapted from a typology introduced by Alex P. Schmid, *Political Terrorism: A Research Guided* (New Brunswick, NJ: Transaction Books, 1983).

normality."[5] McCauley and Segal, in a major review of the social psychology of terrorist groups, found that "the best documented generalization is negative; terrorists do not show any striking psychopathology."[6] In his recent book, *The Psychology of Terrorism*, John Horgan has emphasized that there are no individual psychological traits that distinguish terrorists from the general population.[7]

A consensus conclusion of the Committee on the Psychological Roots of Terrorism for the Madrid Summit on Terrorism, Security and Democracy, held in Madrid on the first anniversary of the 2004 bombing of the Madrid train station bombing, was that "[e]xplanations at the level of individual psychology are insufficient in trying to understand why people become involved in terrorism. The concepts of abnormality or psychopathology are not useful in understanding terrorism."[8] Rather, we concluded that "[g]roup, organizational and social psychology, with a particular emphasis on 'collective identity,' provides the most constructive framework for understanding terrorist psychology and behavior."

While, to be sure, some emotionally disturbed individuals have carried out acts of violence in the name of a cause, severe psychopathology is incompatible with being a member of a terrorist group. Indeed, terrorist groups regularly screen out individuals who are emotionally unstable. Just as the British Special Air Service (SAS) commandos would not wish to have an emotionally unstable individual in their ranks because they would pose a security risk, for the same reason neither would a terrorist action cell wish to have an emotionally unstable member in its ranks.

"Criminal terrorism" refers to acts of terrorism by a criminal enterprise in order to further its goals. So, when the narco-terrorists in Colombia assassinate a judge, the goal is not merely eliminating a judge who has threatened their enterprise, it is also to intimidate other judges in order to give the terrorists the freedom to operate they desire.

For "political terrorism," the subject of this book, there are two main subdivisions represented in the graphic: the middle tier, the level of the state, and the lower tier, sub-state terrorism. "State terrorism" refers to when the state turns it own resources—the courts, the police, the military—against its own citizens. Argentina during the "dirty wars" is a prime example, when citizens opposed to the state were "disappeared." Another example of terror by the state would be Saddam Hussein using chemical weapons and aerial bombings against his own Kurdish citizens in the al-Anfal campaign in the late 1980s; more than 100,000 Kurdish Iraqi citizens were killed.[9] "State-supported terrorism," a matter of great concern to the United States, refers to the circumstance when a state covertly provides support to a terrorist group or organization to further its own national goals. This guidance and support can be doctrinal, financial, tactical, and logistical, including providing training, and the degree of control and influence by the state will vary. The usual suspects on the annual State Department list of state supporters of terrorism have included: Iran, Iraq, Syria, Libya, Sudan, North Korea, and Cuba. Iraq has been removed from this list since the overthrow of Saddam Hussein's regime, and in return for ceasing its program of developing weapons of mass destruction Libya's name was removed in May 2006.

"Sub-state terrorism" represents terrorism from below. In the beginning of the modern era of terrorism, two types predominated: social revolutionary terrorism and nationalist-separatist terrorism, also known as ethnic-nationalist terrorism. Steeped in Marxist-Leninism, the social revolutionary terrorists, represented by such groups as the Red Army Faction in Germany, the Red Brigades in Italy, and the Weather Underground in the United States, seek to overthrow the capitalist order. These groups have significantly declined since the end of the Cold War and the dissolution of the Soviet empire, although Latin American social revolutionary groups, especially the Revolutionary Armed Forces of Colombia (FARC), remain a significant security threat. The nationalist-separatist terrorists, represented by such groups as the Provisional Irish Republican Army (PIRA) in Northern Ireland; Fatah, Palestinian Front for the Liberation of Palestine (PFLP), and other secular Palestinian groups; and Euskadi ta Askatasuna (ETA—Basque Fatherland and Liberty), seek to establish a separate nation for their minority group.

In the beginnings of the modern era of terrorism, these groups regularly sought to call public attention to their cause. There were often competing claims of responsibility for their terrorist acts. Then in the late 1980s and early 1990s, the situation gradually changed; no responsibility was claimed for upward of 40 percent of terrorist acts. These were the acts of religious fundamentalist terrorists. They were not trying to influence the West but to expel the West, with its secular, modernizing values. And they did not need a *New York Times* headline or a CNN story to claim responsibility, for they were "killing in the name of God," and God already knew. In addition to religious fundamentalist terrorists, the category of religious extremist terrorists also includes millenarian or new religions terrorists, exemplified by the Aum Shinrikyo terrorists responsible for the first major chemical weapons terrorist attack, the sarin gas attack on the Tokyo subways in 1995.

With the decline in social revolutionary terrorism at the end of the Cold War, there was a concomitant rise in right-wing terrorist groups pursuing racist, anti-Semitic, and "survivalist" ideologies. The same groups that used to warn against the communist menace that had invaded the United States now turned their venom against what they characterized as the illegitimate federal government. Timothy McVeigh and Terry Nichols, responsible for the destruction of the Alfred P. Murrah Federal Building in Oklahoma City, were right-wing terrorists. It is widely believed by security officials that the wave of anthrax letters in the fall of 2001 was perpetrated by an unknown right-wing extremist.

And finally, single-issue terrorism refers to terrorism in pursuit of causes, such as the environment and animal rights. That groups, such as the Animal Liberation Front (ALF), would be motivated to commit criminal acts of violence in order to preserve animal life or, as in the case of the Earth Liberation Front (ELF), to preserve the environment suggests that *the cause is not the cause*. Rather it is the justification, the rationale for frustrated, alienated individuals who have had their frustration channeled against a particular group.

Given how different their causes and their perspectives, nationalist-separatist, social revolutionary, religious fundamentalist, right-wing, and single-issue terrorists would be expected to differ markedly in psychology. We can distinguish among terrorist organizations with broad social support, terrorism arising from diaspora/émigré populations, anti-regime terrorism within a society, and the global Salafi jihad. Given the diversity of these causes, there is no reason to believe that there is one terrorist mind-set, one overarching terrorist psychology. Why should we assume that the motivations and attitudes of individuals and groups who are pursuing such diverse causes are the same? Thus, to explain the otherwise mysterious title of this introductory chapter, we should be considering terrorisms—plural—and terrorist psychologies—plural.

As there is a diversity of terrorist causes, the typology of terrorist groups also reflects a diversity of generational provenance. The X in the upper-left-hand cell of figure 1.2 indicates that individuals who are at one with families who are at one with the regime do not become terrorists. Generational issues are particularly prominent for the two types of terrorism that dominated the scene at the onset of the modern era of terrorism: social revolutionary terrorism and nationalist-separatist terrorism.

As reflected in figure 1.2, in many ways the generational dynamics of social revolutionary terrorists and nationalist-separatist terrorists are mirror images. The social revolutionary terrorists, whose generational dynamics are represented in the lower-left cell, are striking out against the generation of their parents that is loyal to the regime. Their acts of terrorism are acts of revenge for hurts, real and imagined. A member of the German terrorist group Red Army Faction declared, "These are the corrupt old men who gave us Auschwitz and Hiroshima." Jillian Becker addresses this dynamic with the German social revolutionary terrorists in her aptly titled book, *Hitler's Children*.[10]

In contrast, the nationalist-separatist terrorists, represented in the upper-right-hand cell, are loyal to parents and grandparents who are disloyal to the regime because they were damaged by the regime. They are carrying on the mission. Whether in the pubs of Northern Ireland or the coffeehouses in Gaza and the occupied territories, they have heard of the social injustice visited upon

Youths' Relationship to Parents	Parents' Relationship to the Regime	
	L oyal	**D** isloyal / amaged / issident
L oyal	✕	Nationalist-Separatist Terrorism
D isloyal	Social Revolutionary Terrorism	

FIGURE 1.2 Generational Pathways to Terrorism.

Source: This generational matrix was first introduced by the author in Jerrold M. Post, "Notes on a Psychodynamic Theory of Terrorism," *Terrorism* 7, no. 3 (1984).

their parents and grandparents, they have heard their parents complaining of the lands stolen from them and have been raised on this bitter gruel of victimhood. It is time to stop talking and start acting.

The variation in the generational dynamics described above emphasizes the importance of understanding the historical/cultural/political/economic context in which terrorism develops and terrorist identities are shaped. A review of the differing provenances of the variety of terrorist groups portrayed in Crenshaw's (1995) major volume *Terrorism in Context*[11] demonstrates how strikingly different are the backgrounds that shaped the youth attracted to the path of terrorism.

But if there is a broad range of terrorist psychologies and motivations, there are some general conclusions that contradict lay assumptions. Explanations of terrorism at the level of individual psychology are insufficient in trying to understand why people become involved in terrorism. As observed, terrorists are not depressed, severely emotionally disturbed, or crazed fanatics. It is not individual psychopathology, but group, organizational, and social psychology, with a particular emphasis on "collective identity," that provides the most powerful lens through which to understand terrorist psychology and behavior. For some groups, especially nationalist-seperatist terrorist groups, this collective identity is established extremely early, so that from childhood on, "hatred is bred in the bone." The importance of collective identity and the processes of forming and transforming collective identities cannot be overemphasized. This fact in turn emphasizes the sociocultural context, which determines the balance between collective identity and individual identity. Terrorists have subordinated their individual identity to the collective identity, so that what serves the group, organization, or network is of primary importance.

This subordination to the cause, in turn, gives the leaders of these terrorist groups who frame the cause a major role in creating the dominant terrorist psychology. As my committee at the Madrid summit on terrorism noted: "It is important to distinguish leaders from followers. The role of the leader is crucial in drawing together alienated, frustrated individuals into a coherent organization. The leader provides a 'sense-making' unifying message that conveys a religious, political or ideological justification to their disparate followers."[12] Portraits of terrorist leaders, as a result, offer windows into the psychology and motivations of the followers who are attracted to their hate-mongering messages.

The following chapters attempt to peer into and illuminate the minds of the terrorists who belong to the diverse spectrum of terrorist groups sketched out above. All too many terrorist experts have never laid eyes upon a terrorist, much less spoken with one. It may be that the gravest threat to international security is not the proliferation of weapons of mass destruction but the proliferation of terrorism experts. If one really wants to understand "what makes terrorists tick," the best way is to ask them. As a result, I try to lead the reader into the minds of the terrorists by drawing on their own words—those I have gathered from an interview project with incarcerated Middle Eastern terrorists, from my experiences and in-depth interviews with terrorists during my service as an expert witness in terrorist trials, from terrorist memoirs and biographies of terrorist leaders and their followers, as well as from other terrorist scholars who have interviewed terrorists. When it is the written or spoken words of the terrorists or their supporters, they are italicized for emphasis.

In separate sections, we consider nationalist-separatist terrorism, social revolutionary terrorism, and religious extremist terrorism. The intent is not to publish an encyclopedia of terrorism. With no attempt to be comprehensive, I present major exemplars of these terrorist types to convey the psychological world of people in these groups and organizations. The intent is specifically not to be objective but to be subjective, which is the only effective pathway into the minds of the terrorists.

We cannot deter an adversary that we do not understand. An optimal understanding of the psychology and motivations of the terrorists is crucial to developing optimal strategies to deter these violent actors. Moreover, each terrorism must be understood in its own unique context, and the counterterrorism strategy tailored to that context.

The volume concludes with a psychological strategy for countering terrorism that draws on these understandings of terrorist psychologies. The strategy focuses on the life course of terrorists, suggesting interventions at key stages of the terrorist life cycle: inhibiting alienated youth from joining the group, creating tension within the group, facilitating exit from the group, and reducing support for the group and its leaders.

NATIONALIST-SEPARATIST TERRORISM: CARRYING ON THE MISSION OF THEIR PARENTS

The beginning of the modern era of terrorism is usually dated to the late 1960s when a wave of urban terrorism converged with the age of media. Two types of terrorism—nationalist-separatist, exemplified by the Palestinian terrorists of Fatah, and social revolutionary terrorists of the New Left, exemplified by the Red Brigades in Italy—dominated the political landscape. The origins of the struggle by the Palestinian diaspora to establish a separate Palestinian state long preceded the dramatic skyjackings orchestrated by Leila Khaled in 1970 and the seizure of the Israeli Olympic village by radical Palestinian terrorists at the 1972 Munich Olympics, but these acts, presented to a broad international audience through the relatively new medium of television, emphasized to minority groups how they could call attention to their cause through acts of terrorism.

This section covers terrorism inspired by five separatist causes—Palestinian, Northern Irish, Basque, Kurdish, and Tamil. Each of these groups was carrying on the cause, the mission of their parents and grandparents (and, for the IRA of Northern Ireland and the Basque separatist terrorists ETA, their great-grandparents and great-great-grandparents as well); as reflected in the generational matrix in the introductory chapter, they were loyal to parents who were damaged by and disloyal to the regime. They were carrying on acts of vengeance against the regime. The oppression by the dominant group and the government led to a defensive intensification of the identity of the minority group. Powerful writers helped develop and propagate an inspiring ideology, justifying their violence against the oppressors, who sought to eliminate their culture, their history, their language, their very identity. Just as they felt dehumanized by the dominant group, so too they dehumanized "the enemy," justifying their violence as required by "the other." Often members were influenced to join by a close relative; some joined to avenge the death of a relative killed in the name of the cause. Each of these groups was fighting for a mission that, at the onset at least, expressed the goals of the people. The sociopolitical environment was accepting and supporting, with members winning praise for their service and dedication to the cause. Their prestige was enhanced by the membership in these separatist organizations.

First, secular Palestinian terrorism is discussed, with exemplars of three different groups operating under that nationalist-separatist banner, Omar Rezaq, a member of the Abu Nidal Organization (ANO) whom I had the opportunity of interviewing in connection with his federal trial in Washington, D.C.; Leila Khaled of the Palestinian Front for the Liberation of Palestine (PFLP), a Palestinian heroine for her role in hijacking airliners in 1970; and Yasser Arafat, founding leader of Fatah, the dominant secular Palestinian separatist group. Included in this chapter are vivid quotations from incarcerated Palestinian terrorists interviewed in Israeli and Palestinian prisons by a team I directed, emphasizing how early in life they entered the path of terrorism, for their dedication to fighting for the Palestinian cause was "bred in the bone."[1]

Two of the cases, the Tamil Tigers (LTTE) of Sri Lanka and the Kurdish separatist group, the Kurdistan Workers Party (PKK), were highly identified with their charismatic leaders; Vellupillai Prabhakaran was the articulator of—the very embodiment of—the cause of Tamil independence; it was Abdullah Ocalan who inspired his followers, who was the personification of the cause of Kurdish independence. Each of these men devoted significant attention and focus to eliminating rivals for power within their own movement, to ensure their sole controlling leadership. Each inspired a godlike reverence to the point where the LTTE and the PKK were leaders in utilizing the technique of suicide terrorism. For both the LTTE and the PKK, women played an important role, and were prominent among those giving their lives for the cause that defined their identity.

Two of the other nationalist-separatist organizations discussed, the Irish Republic Army (IRA) and Basque Homeland and Liberty (ETA), trace their origins more than 1,000 years, with a generational transmission of hatred. While there were heroic figures in each generation, they were not of charismatic stature, but were the bearers of the culture.

These champions of separate national identity had no legitimate voice in the political discourse, and advocated violence as communication to call international attention to their cause and to coerce the central government to respond to their needs. For all of these groups, the leaders and their followers were often imprisoned, which only intensified their commitment to the cause. Prison served as postgraduate education in terrorism, which was justified by the repressive system. When the dominant majority not only refused to recognize the rights of the minority, but even sought to deny their separate existence, a defensive intensification of identity occurred. This was true for both the LTTE and ETA. In both cases, the government banned the use of their language and of their very name. Mustafa Kemal Attaturk, in his zeal to establish a Turkic identity, sought to obliterate Kurdish identity and culture, just as Franco in his zeal to establish a homogeneous Spanish identity sought to obliterate Basque identity. The disregard of minority rights by the Sinhala majority in Sri Lanka and the Protestant majority in Northern Ireland, supported by Great Britain, similarly promoted a defensive intensification of identity by the aggrieved minorities. The Palestinian terrorists felt they had been expelled from their historical homeland and that the illegitimate Zionist entity occupied their land. These five groups experienced themselves to varying degrees as victims of "identicide."

Of these five examples, three—the PKK, the IRA, and ETA—and some of the Palestinian groups, couched their goals in Marxist-Leninist terms. Ocalan was in university when the wave of social revolutionary terrorism swept over Latin America and Europe, and the rhetoric of the elite capitalist dominating the proletariat fit their circumstances well. Unlike the social revolutionary terrorists of Latin America who sought to overthrow the dominating elite establishment, the goal for the PKK, the IRA, and ETA, was not to overthrow the central government, but rather to establish a separate state for their dominated minority. Some Palestinian terrorist groups, the "rejectionist front," maintained absolutist goals, to regain all of the "occupied territories," referring to all of the Holy Land, "from the river to the sea," whereas other groups sought a separate Palestinian state while acknowledging (reluctantly, to be sure) Israel's right to exist.

Latin American social revolutionary movements had wide-ranging influence on nationalist-separatist terrorism as well as European social revolutionary terrorism (the subject of section II). They had conceptualized a strategy for implementing their ideology, the strategy of urban guerrilla warfare. *The Mini-Manual of the Urban Guerrilla* by Carlos Marighella, a former member of the Brazilian Communist party, advocated a scorched earth policy, acts of sabotage designed to produce anarchy, which in turn would lead to undermining the authority of the government.[2] The mini-manual was widely used for indoctrination and training in Europe, not just for the European fighting communist cells, but also for nationalist-separatist terrorist organizations.

But while they deem violence to be necessary to call attention to the cause, some members tend to lose sight of its instrumental role in achieving their minority goals; for these people, being a fighter for the cause becomes the primary motivation. Compromise is not possible for the absolutists, and tensions develop within the movement. Absolutists often resist organizational agreement to or movement toward a cease-fire; many times they split from the majority of their movement that is willing to compromise. Terrorist acts by a minority of absolutists in turn frequently derail the fragile accords, accounting for the longevity of these movements. This has been true for Fatah, the IRA, ETA, the PKK, and the LTTE.

CHAPTER 2

SECULAR PALESTINIAN TERRORISM: "WHEN HATRED IS BRED IN THE BONE"

In the turbulent Middle East, the psychopolitics of hatred flourishes as violence begets counterviolence. The landscape is pockmarked with the craters of terrorist bombs. It is widely assumed that individuals and groups impelled to kill innocent women and children in pursuit of their cause must be crazed psychotics. Surely psychologically normal individuals could not commit such wanton violence.

As already discussed, individual terrorists are psychologically normal in the sense of not suffering from severe psychopathology. But this broad conclusion concerning terrorist psychology generally is drawn from sources other than the terrorists themselves. Belonging to closed clandestine groups, fleeing from the law, terrorists are not readily available for interview.

When the rare occasion to interview a terrorist presents itself, it offers a unique opportunity to gain insights into the mind of a terrorist. I had such an opportunity in the spring of 1996 in connection with the trial in federal district court of Omar Rezaq for the federal crime of skyjacking. It was Rezaq, a member of the Abu Nidal Organization, who played a central role in seizing the Egypt Air plane that was forced down in Malta in 1985. Rezaq shot five hostages—two Israeli women and three Americans—before the botched SWAT team attack by Egyptian forces, which led to 50-plus casualties. Convicted of murder in a Malta court, after seven years Rezaq was given amnesty and released because it was a political crime. But, relying on the new extraterritoriality doctrine, he was arrested in July 1993 by FBI agents for the crime of skyjacking.

Any trial is a contest of dueling frames of reference, of alternate explanations. The defense, in effect, put Israel on trial. They were aided in their endeavor by a remarkably one-sided portrayal of the Arab-Israeli struggle by a Middle East scholar, who depicted the Arab world in general, and the Palestinian people in particular, as victims of Israeli aggression, neglecting to mention the bloody history of aggression visited upon Israel by Palestinian terrorists and in the three Arab-Israeli wars. From the collective trauma of the Palestinian people, it was but a small further step to the specific traumatization of the defendant. With the assistance of a forensic psychologist, the defense elaborated a creative theory. They acknowledged Rezaq's direct and indirect role in the carnage that resulted, but claimed that as a consequence of the multiple traumas the Palestinian people had incurred at the hands of the Israelis, the defendant was suffering from post-traumatic stress disorder (PTSD). As a consequence he did not appreciate the wrongfulness of his act and accordingly should be judged not guilty by reason of insanity.

The diagnosis of PTSD provided by the defense was thoroughly discredited by Department of Justice forensic psychiatric experts. But the jury had not been provided with a sensible explanation to the question: How could a sane man wreak such carnage?

I had been asked by the Department of Justice to participate in the case as a psychiatrist expert in the psychology of terrorism. The other prosecution experts would demonstrate that Rezaq was legally sane, but it was my task to provide a sense-making explanation for the jury of how an individual who was sane could commit such a bloody atrocity. The story of Rezaq's life and progression on the path of terrorism that I developed through my interviews with the defendant provided that explanation.

The defendant epitomized the life and psychology of the nationalist-separatist terrorist. On the basis of some eight hours of interviews and the review of thousands of pages of documents, a coherent story emerged. The defendant assuredly did not believe that what he was doing was wrong, for from boyhood on Rezaq had been socialized to be a heroic revolutionary fighting for the Palestinian nation. Demonstrating the generational transmission of hatred, his case can be considered emblematic of many from the ranks of ethnic/nationalist terrorist groups, from Northern Ireland to Palestine, from Armenia to the Basque region of Spain.

OMAR REZAQ: A FAMILY SAGA OF DISPLACEMENT[1]

Rezaq's mother was from Jaffa, originally a Muslim suburb of Tel Aviv. When she was eight, she and her family were forced to leave their home during the

1948 War of Independence, fleeing to the West Bank, where she and her family lived in refugee camps. The mother's displacement from her ancestral home by Israel was an event of crucial importance that became a key element in the family legend.

The third child of a family of six, Omar Rezaq was born in 1958 in Jordan but as a young boy moved to a village on the West Bank where his grandfather was a farmer. Rezaq described his boyhood in the village as pleasant; they lived in their own home, with no economic problems, no worries about food or money. His father worked as a nurse for the Jordanian military. As a career military nurse, his father was often away from home.

But when Rezaq was eight, his relatively pleasant existence changed abruptly in the aftermath of the 1967 Arab-Israeli war. His father, with the Jordanian military, had already left in anticipation of the arrival of the Israeli army. After two months, his mother decided to follow his father. She bitterly announced, *"This is the second time I've been forced from my home."* Rezaq indicated: *"From this time, everything changed."*

Jordan was crowded with refugees. After staying in Amman, Jordan, for one year, they moved to the refugee camp Talibiya, some 25 to 35 kilometers outside of Amman. The living circumstances there were very difficult; the whole family was crowded into two rooms, with no bathroom or kitchen and little privacy. Food was supplied by the United Nations relief agency, UNESCO. There was little money.

The father was a strict, harsh man, who, when he was at home on leave from the military, would punish his son, beating him with a belt or stick for minor infractions. Rezaq felt closer to his mother, a quiet and gentle woman, who took responsibility for the family. She often discussed her life and how it had changed in 1948 when her family had to leave Jaffa.

Indoctrination in Palestinian Nationalism and Recruitment into the Movement

In 1968, the Battle of Karameh occurred. Yasser Arafat led a group of Palestinian guerrillas who fought a 12-hour battle against a superior Israeli force, galvanizing the previously dispirited Palestinian population. The spirit of the revolution was everywhere, especially in the camps, and the Palestine Liberation Organization (PLO) became a rallying point. In Rezaq's words, *"The revolution was the only hope."*

In the UN school, where Rezaq was an average student, he was rewarded for learning Palestinian songs. Palestinian teachers would propagandize the students, focusing their resentment for the difficult living circumstances on Israel and instilling Palestinian nationalism and feelings of hatred against Israel. As young teenagers, Rezaq (now 12) and his friends went to the youth camp two to three hours a day, where they received some political indoctrination and began military training, learning how to clean and handle guns, jump barriers, and the like. The father did not join the revolution and was opposed to Rezaq becoming involved. If he saw his son go to the camp, he beat him.

Rezaq was the only one in his family to join the revolution. His Palestinian teacher, who was in the PLO and was a member of al-Fatah (the military wing of the PLO co-founded by Yasser Arafat), was a role model for him. This juxta-position of the harsh father who was opposed to the revolution with the positive model of the Palestinian teacher who was a member of Fatah intensified young Rezaq's attraction to joining the revolution and to begin developing an identity as soldier for the Palestinian cause. His teacher told young Rezaq that *"the only way to become a man was to join the revolution and take back the land stolen from your parents and grandparents."*

Like many young men of his generation in the camps, Rezaq was psycho-logically lost, with no clear path before him. His teachers both focused his hatred against Israel as the cause of his people's problems and charted a valued identity, becoming a soldier in the revolution.

After finishing intermediate school, Rezaq went on to technical school under UN auspices. There were branches of the revolution in this school; each group tried to recruit the new students. Rezaq became more deeply involved in politics. He was taught that the only way to get back his country was if the PLO would fight against Israel. And he was increasingly determined to join that fight.

Two years of obligatory service in the Jordanian army were required. In 1977, at age 19, he was sent to a camp near Iraq for military training. There the Palestinians were treated as second-class citizens.

Joining the Revolution and Indoctrination in Anti-Zionist, Anti-U.S. Views

After only three months in the Jordanian army, Rezaq went absent without leave and joined Fatah. He went to a military camp where he was given a uni-form and was trained in the use of machine guns, pistols, and hand grenades. He also received intense political indoctrination. This was the first time he heard of Zionism.

Now he was energized, fully committed at last, in a fighting revolutionary organization. He *"wanted to work, wanted to fight. There was only one way to regain*

Palestine and that was to fight Israel in order to regain all of Palestine, from the sea to the river."

In 1978, fighting in Lebanon broke out between the PLO and Israel. The camp in which Rezaq was training sent 100 people to join the fight in South Lebanon against Israel. He was there for two months, close to the action. There was fighting every day, and he felt part of the revolution. After he returned to base camp, being away from the scene of action, he became restless and resigned from the Fatah branch. Asked why he was leaving, he replied that he was bored and had nothing to do, that he had joined Fatah to fight and was not fighting.

He moved from group to group, initially enthused and then disillusioned, each group more militant than the preceding one. When he was next involved in guerrilla action, he had pride in what he was doing as a soldier for the revolution. "*I started dreaming that one day we will have a country, have an identity, [and be] our own citizens.*" After attacking an Israeli patrol, his morale took a major boost. "*This was for my country.*" He felt this was the right way, the path for him to follow. He felt a sense of excitement in the danger.

Rezaq was still with the PLO in Lebanon in 1980, the year the "explosive war" occurred, with the Phalangists and Israel against Palestinians and other Lebanese. There were bombs and explosions everywhere, every day, bombs in cars, in supermarkets. In a close call, Rezaq almost lost his life in a car bomb explosion that destroyed a cafeteria he had just left. Had he remained, he realized, he would have died. He had never thought of his own death before. This near miss, apparently, was extremely traumatic for Rezaq, and in the aftermath he experienced symptoms of PTSD, symptoms that subsided over the years. He began to have dreams about his death, started getting suspicious, feeling on guard, while before he did not care.

The 1982 Israel Invasion of Lebanon and Disillusionment with the PLO

When Israel invaded Lebanon in 1982 and penetrated deeply into Lebanon, there was very little resistance by the PLO, and Rezaq found himself wondering about the revolution that had lost so easily. He had been ready to fight for two years, and when the opportunity came, the movement to which he had committed himself had not fought. It was a disillusioning experience.

As a result of U.S.-brokered negotiations, Arafat and the PLO were to leave Lebanon. Disillusioned with Arafat and the mainstream PLO, Rezaq decided to stay on in Lebanon to fight. He first joined the militant Fatah

Intifada group, but finding it insufficiently militant, he ultimately made his way to the most violent of the Palestinian terrorist groups, the Abu Nidal Organization (ANO).

After intense training, he was given an important mission: to hijack an airliner in order to obtain the release of antigovernment Egyptians imprisoned in Egypt. He felt good about the mission; he now had a purpose. This is what he had been preparing for since boyhood. On the night before the mission, he did not sleep well. He described himself as being on edge, keyed up. It was the feelings of the soldier on the eve of battle.

The Operation

In describing the operation, Rezaq related the entire episode in a cool, matter-of-fact manner—logical, detailed, calm, not emotionally overwrought: the professional military man reporting on a military action.

After the terrorists took over the plane, in accordance with the plan, they forced it down in Malta in order to refuel before the final leg. The control tower said it would not provide petrol until the hostages were released. Rezaq, the deputy commander of the team, who took over after the commander was shot in the takeover, informed the control tower they would not release the hostages until the plane was refueled. Malta control refused, insisting that the hijackers release all of the hostages or there would be no petrol.

Rezaq remembered the mission instructions concerning the Israelis and Americans. If there were Israelis in the plane, he was told he must kill them directly, for they were enemies of Palestine. Since America supported Israel, Americans should then be used as leverage, and should be killed if no petrol was provided. His negotiations with the control tower, which were captured on tape, were compelling. The absence of emotion was chilling as he described the bloody events that followed. Rezaq went through the passengers' passports and found those of two Israeli women and three American men.

He then gave an ultimatum to the control tower that he would begin killing hostages unless they refueled the plane. When they did not provide petrol, he told the flight attendant to bring him one of the Israeli women. *"I had to make them take me seriously,"* he explained. *"When the porter brought one of the Israeli women forward, I grabbed her hair in my left hand and placed the revolver to her temple* [graphically illustrating]. *I told the control tower that I had an Israeli woman passenger and I was going to blow her brains out unless they gave me fuel. And they, foolish people, said, 'We told you, we won't give you fuel until you release the passengers.' So I blew her brains out."*

He told the control tower that he had killed the Jew. Now that he had demonstrated that he meant business and that they should take him seriously, he gave a second ultimatum. He added, *"But by now I was getting hungry, so I asked the porter to get me some lunch and he brought me a very nice lunch."*

Rezaq went from describing blowing the woman's brains out to being hungry without changing his pitch. It was as if killing her was no more consequential than taking out the trash. When I asked him about his emotional state at the time of the killings and how he reacted to killing a person at close range, he looked at me with perplexity and responded, as if it should be self-evident, that it was what he had been instructed to do, it was the plan for the mission. He continued: *"I thought surely now they would give me the fuel. By now I had brought the second Israeli woman passenger forward. I said, 'OK, I have killed one Jew. I am ready to kill a second. Will you give me the fuel now?' And they, foolish people, said again that they would not give me fuel until I released the hostages."*

He then described, while demonstrating, *"So I grabbed her hair in my left hand, placed the revolver to her temple, and. . . ."* I interrupted him to ask, "How did it feel, killing a woman?" He responded that there was no difference: *"It was explained to me that in Israel, both men and women served in the army, so they both were the enemy and they both deserve to die."*

He continued to describe shooting the second Israeli woman in the head, *"blew her brains out."* The description was remarkable for his lack of empathy for the human beings he was killing. They were the enemy and enemies should be killed.

The Maltese authorities still had not provided petrol, so Rezaq then ordered the air crew to bring him the Americans. Rezaq shot the first American. Because there was still no petrol, he then had them bring the second American and shot him in the head. He then shot the third American passenger in the head. The storming of the plane followed.

Seeking Revenge for Damage Done to His Family

For Omar Rezaq and many of his generation, developmental experiences shaped their attraction to the path of terrorism, defined in their minds as "joining the revolution." The psychological soil had already been prepared by Rezaq's mother recounting the expulsion from Jaffa. This was in many ways a classic case of nationalist-separatist terrorism, carrying on the family cause, seeking revenge for damage done to parents and grandparents, the generational transmission of hatred.

Like his fellow terrorists, Rezaq believed that his actions were justified; they were not wrongful but were righteous acts in the service of the Palestinian revolution. He had been socialized to blame all of his and his people's difficulties on the enemy and to believe that violent actions against the enemy were justified.

This was the alternate sense-making explanation provided to the jury. Like thousands of his generation, Rezaq did indeed experience many traumas. The issue of rebutting his alleged mental illness was important. The government and its forensic psychiatrists had been quite effective in countering the defense assertions in support of not guilty by reason of insanity, demonstrating that the defendant was fully aware of the legal consequences of his act.

It was important to augment technical forensic testimony by emphasizing that serious psychiatric illness is incompatible with the role of the terrorist. Political terrorists are not seriously psychologically ill. Indeed, as observed in chapter 1, a psychologically disturbed, mentally unstable terrorist would pose a major security risk, just as a military unit cannot tolerate an emotionally unstable soldier because he would pose a danger to the unit.

Rezaq was in the Abu Nidal Organization (ANO) for two years, in training, being observed. ANO, more than other groups, was especially careful about its members, monitoring closely their performance in training. Terrorist experts doubted that a 1994 terrorist attack attributed to ANO was actually an ANO operation because it was so unprofessional. On the basis of Rezaq's extensive period in camp and in training, he was selected for this important mission and named the number-two man, which indicates that the organization believed in his stability and professionalism; he did not disappoint them.

It was important to convey to the jury that the ANO was, at the time, the bloodiest and most professional Palestinian terrorist organization, with operations in more than 20 countries and having killed or injured more than 900 people. Abu Nidal was the architect of the massacres at Rome and Vienna airports and was responsible for shooting the Israeli ambassador to Great Britain, which was the final trigger to the Israeli invasion of Lebanon after a long campaign against Israel by groups operating out of Lebanon. While Rezaq may not have known who the Abu Nidal group—the Fatah Revolutionary Council—was when he first joined the organization, by the time he rejoined ANO, he surely knew their reputation. He *chose* to join the bloodiest of all groups.

Individuals with post-traumatic stress disorder tend to avoid circumstances that resemble that which occasioned the original trauma. Not only did Rezaq not seek to avoid violent circumstances, he actually sought out ever more violent circumstances. Indeed, when a group was insufficiently violent, he left them for a more violent group, finally reaching the very acme of violence in the Abu Nidal

Organization. As he proudly declaimed, "*I live to fight, and only feel alive when I am fighting.*"

Did he believe that what he did was wrong? Assuredly not. He had rationalized, justified that what he was doing was in the service of Palestine. He believed it was the right thing to do. But this belief was not a consequence of mental illness. It was the consequence of his entire life experience, of being inspired and trained to be a soldier for the cause. His beliefs and activism were shared with thousands of his peers. Psychologically Rezaq was of the same mind-set of radical Palestinian terrorists, who were also socialized to the path of violent terrorism.

When Rezaq was selected for the hijacking mission, it was the culmination of a dream. Rezaq was taught to hate all Israelis and their American sponsors. He was taught to blame all of the difficulties in his life on the Israelis, whom he saw as enemies in the war in which he was a heroic soldier. When he carried out the hijacking, it was the very pinnacle of his life, a dream come true. But the dream turned into a nightmare, with tragic consequences. More than 50 people lost their lives in the hijacking and botched SWAT team attack. Rezaq is now serving a life sentence in federal prison.

LEILA KHALED: PALESTINIAN HEROINE

I made the ring from a bullet and the pin of a hand grenade.

—Leila Khaled in the *Guardian*, January 26, 2001

Just as the refugee camp experience was crucial in consolidating the identity of Omar Rezaq, so too the bitterness of Leila Khaled was steeped in the cauldron of the camps decades before Rezaq was born. Khaled occupies a heroic niche in the history of the Palestinian people. It was she, at the very onset of the modern era of terrorism, as a member of the Palestinian Front for the Liberation of Palestine (PFLP), who in 1969 commandeered a TWA jet en route from Rome to Israel, forcing it to land in Damascus. The following year, in the midst of the Black September conflict, she was again involved in an attempted hijacking, this time of an El Al airliner, one of five hijackings by the PFLP. Although the attempted hijacking was foiled, Khaled's stature as a Palestinian freedom fighter grew, capturing international notoriety and calling attention to the plight of her people.

In her autobiographical memoir, Khaled recounts the misery of existence in the camps: "*I was abused in all the meaning of abuse. I was deprived of my home, my family, children like me living in a miserable situation, no work for our fathers, our mothers did not work. We were just lost."*[2]

In an interview with the *Guardian* in 2001, Khaled addressed her pioneering role as a woman terrorist: *"In the beginning, all women had to prove that we could be equal to men in armed struggle. I no longer think it's necessary to prove ourselves as women by imitating men. . . . I have learned that a woman can be a fighter, a freedom fighter, a political activist, and that she can fall in love, and be loved, she can be married, have children, be a mother. . . . The question of women is part of our struggle but not the only part. Revolution must mean life also; every aspect of life."*[3]

Historic Mission Formed in Refugee Camp

Born in Haifa in 1944, Khaled and her family were forced from her home when she was four years old, at the time of the 1948 War of Independence. She would be raised and educated in a refugee camp in the West Bank. There, in her words:

> I discovered that I have historic roots, that my people have a history of struggle. . . . Above all I learned that my class, the working people, the unemployed, the refugees, the oppressed everywhere could liberate mankind from the shackles of superstition and backwardness.
>
> I knew that I had a role to play. I realized that my historic mission was as a warrior in the inevitable battle between oppressors and oppressed, exploiters and exploited. I decided to become a revolutionary in order to liberate my people and myself.

Mother and Teacher Shape Her Revolutionary Role

When in 1951, at age seven, she did not participate in a demonstration, her mother, who emerges from Khaled's autobiographic memoir as a powerful shaping force, angrily confronted her: *"As a Palestinian girl, you should have joined your sisters to protest against the Zionist occupation of Palestine."* Her mother then lectured her on *"the three historic days of betrayal that every Palestinian should remember,"* the Balfour Declaration (1917), the partition of Palestine (1947), and the proclamation of the state of Israel (1948). *"Ever since, these dates have become a vital and integral part of my life."*

Khaled dates her politicization to 1953 when, living near a camp, with tens of thousands of displaced Palestinians, she complained to her mother that she was cold, that she had no shoes, only sandals. Her mother explained that she was lucky to have sandals, and talked of the poverty of the Palestinian people.

Don't you know that the Zionists slaughtered our people, and those who escaped them died of thirst or starvation? I could tell you a million tales of woe, but I want you to understand this: you are an alien here in Lebanon, and your homeland is under foreign occupation. We fought and fought valiantly to save the land; we lost and were driven out. You Leila, and your brothers and sisters must never forget Palestine and you must do your utmost to recover her.

But it was only after a visit to the tent-camp with her teacher, after a fight with a little girl from the camps ("*the scum of the earth, or so I thought*"), that her life mission took form. Recounting her teacher's firm conviction that the inhabitants of the camp had been "*forced out*" of their homeland to "*make room for the Zionist intruders,*" Khaled describes in painful detail the misery and hunger she witnessed in the camp:

I saw the maimed, the diseased, the broken-hearted. I saw bare-footed children with swollen stomachs, fathers with heads bowed, pale mothers with sickly children, grandparents in despair. I saw the meaning of poverty and hunger and felt the despair of deprivation to my bones.

Undeterred by this harrowing spectacle, she returns home "*intoxicated by the wine of reality*" and describes how she was "*crucified and redeemed at the same time.*"

A Soldier for the Revolution by Age 13

By age 13, in 1958, Khaled described herself as a soldier, sharing sentinel duty and other military obligations, and had earned the right to candidate membership in the Arab Nationalist Movement (ANM). But now that the civil war was over, her mother felt that "*girls should stay at home and leave the politics to men*" and insisted that "*this child politician [Leila] must stay home.*" But Leila overcame her mother's objections and became actively involved in the movement. By May 1961, the thirteenth anniversary of the founding of Israel, she gave her first political speech on Palestine. Demonstrating her expertise in the history of the Palestinian people and their privations, the speech was very well received.

Political Activist at American University of Beirut

Leila applied and was accepted at the American University at Beirut, but while "*my nominal education was taking place at AUB, my real education was in the lecture hall of the Arab Cultural Club of Beirut and in the ranks of the ANM.*"

While political activity was banned on campus, she and her fellow Palestine activists became engaged in an underground movement and confrontation politics in 1963. When the Jordanian ambassador threatened to withdraw their passports, she *"told the ambassador in no uncertain terms that we would slash his throat if he withdrew the passports."* The ambassador assured them the passports would not be canceled: her violent threats were rewarded. When the dean of students called Leila in over a political tract she was distributing and asked her if she understood that she could be expelled for distributing political literature without permission, Leila went on the attack again. Her words are vivid as she declared that her advocacy of Palestinian rights was an expression of her core identity:

> *"Palestine is not politics to me," I declared. "It is a question of life and death, and no one, certainly no Yankee who can't even speak Arabic, can tell me how to act on this issue and how to fight for my country." The dean considered me a recalcitrant student, who needed discipline and she threatened to expel me. "I dare you to do so!" I screamed in English and declared war on her as a CIA agent and on AUB as the servant of the Pentagon and oil cartels. "Yankee dean, there will come a time when I will be sitting in your chair and I will expel all of your kind." I stormed out of her office shouting, "Long live Palestine, long live the ANM, long live the revolution!" The dean was shocked, and probably had to take a few tranquillizers before settling down to a day of bureaucratic business.*

A Lifetime as a Palestinian Revolutionary

It was the fall of 1963; Leila Khaled was 19, a committed Palestinian revolutionary. Six years later, in 1969, at the age of 25, she carried out the airline hijackings that catapulted her into the ranks of heroic Palestinian revolutionary fighters. From the moment her family was forced to flee Haifa, when she was four, her life course was a linear path to those dramatic events.

Khaled emphasized the requirement for intelligence and persistence in pursuit of the Palestinian people's goals. She spoke of grieving for the loss of her *"homeland, for the loss of a whole people, the pain of my entire nation. Pain truly affects my soul; so does the persecution of my people. It is from pain that I derive the power to resist and to defend the persecuted."*

Addressed to her people and her land, she committed herself to resisting in an eloquent poem that emphasizes the power of her words:

> *Palestine, my love, for you I shall fight . . .*
> *Today I am a volcano, a revolutionary volcano . . .*

TERRORISTS IN THEIR OWN WORDS: INTERVIEWS WITH INCARCERATED SECULAR PALESTINIAN TERRORISTS[4]

In a sample of incarcerated secular Palestinian terrorists from al-Fatah and the Palestinian Front for the Liberation of Palestine, General Command interviewed during the lull between the two intifadas, a major finding was that painful early background experiences shaped identity and steered Palestinian children and youth onto the path of terrorism. Over 80 percent of the secular group members reported growing up in communities that were radically involved.

Family Background and Early Life

As with most of the other Palestinian terrorist organizations, there was a dichotomy between how families felt in theory about their sons joining organizations and how they felt in reality. Publicly, families supported the organization and were proud of their sons for joining. Privately, they feared for their sons as well as for what the security forces might do to their families. Members were seen as heroes, but on the other hand, families who had paid their dues to the war effort by allowing the recruitment of a son tried to prevent other sons from enlisting too.

While most Fatah members reported their families had good social standing, their status and experience as refugees was paramount in their development of self-identity: "*I belong to the generation of occupation. My family are refugees from the 1967 war. The war and my refugee status were the seminal events that formed my political consciousness, and provided the incentive for doing all I could to help regain our legitimate rights in our occupied country.*"

For the secular Palestinian terrorists, enlistment was a natural step, a step that increased social status.

> *Enlistment was for me the natural and done thing . . . in a way, it can be compared to a young Israeli from a nationalist Zionist family who wants to fulfill himself through army service.*
>
> *My motivation in joining Fatah was both ideological and personal. It was a question of self-fulfillment, of honor and a feeling of independence . . . the goal of every young Palestinian was to be a fighter.*
>
> *After recruitment, my social status was greatly enhanced. I got a lot of respect from my acquaintances, and from the young people in the village.*

Decision Making and Military Hierarchy

Soldiers in the revolution exhibited a stark absence of critical thinking, with no questions concerning instructions and carrying out actions: *"There was no room for questioning. The commander got his orders from his superiors. You couldn't just take the initiative and carry out an armed attack without the commander's approval."*

View of Armed Attacks

In addition to being motivated to cause as many casualties as possible, it was our impression that armed action provided a sense of control or power for Palestinians in a society that had stripped them of it. Inflicting pain on the enemy was paramount in the early days of the Fatah movement.

> I regarded armed actions to be essential, it is the very basis of my organization and I am sure that was the case in the other Palestinian organizations. An armed action proclaims that **I am here, I exist, I am strong, I am in control, I am in the field, I am on the map**. An armed action against soldiers was the most admired. . . . The armed actions and their results were a major tool for penetrating the public consciousness.
>
> The various armed actions (stabbing, collaborators, martyrdom operations, attacks on Israeli soldiers) all had different ratings. An armed action that caused casualties was rated highly and seen to be of great importance. An armed action without casualties was not rated. No distinction was made between armed actions on soldiers or on civilians; the main thing was the amount of blood. The aim was to cause as much carnage as possible.

Attitudes toward Casualties and Weapons of Mass Destruction

There was no discrimination between military and civilian targets. They were all occupiers of their land.

> The organization did not impose any limits with regard to damage or scope or nature of the armed attacks. The aim was to kill as many Jews as possible and there was no moral distinction between potential victims, whether soldiers, civilians, women or children.
>
> As for the kind of weaponry we would like to have, mass destruction or conventional weapons, we have never given it any thought.

Another ex-prisoner stated similarly that

> As for non-conventional weapons and weapons of mass destruction, we never gave it any thought during the armed struggle, but morally I don't see any problem with using such

weapons, and had I been able to get them, I would have used them gladly precisely because the casualties would have been that many times greater. I would not have had any problem with 200,000 casualties.

But another Fatah prisoner observed,

As for weapons of mass destruction and unconventional weapons, as an underground organization, we never needed anything more than light automatic weapons and grenades.

The consistency of views expressed by the Palestinian terrorists we interviewed was striking. Much of this "unity of purpose" finds its roots in one person: Yasser Arafat. No discussion of Palestinian terrorism would be complete without a portrait of Arafat, who provided the "sense-making," unifying explanation for their difficulties and brought the Palestinian cause to international attention.

YASSER ARAFAT

Identities in Conflict[5]

Arafat's past is shrouded in mystery, a cloud that he maintained throughout his life, for his birth in Egypt marred his image of displaced Palestinian. Born in Cairo in 1929, Arafat's early years were apparently extremely difficult. His mother died when he was four, and he and a younger brother were sent to Jerusalem, where he was raised by his uncle, not returning to his father's household until he was ten years old, when his eldest sister, Anam, took over as surrogate mother. Thus during those crucial early years Arafat was without the emotional support and nurturance of both his parents, a wound that must have produced deep scars. The relationship with his father was a distant and strained one, characterized by resentment and bitterness that continued throughout Arafat's life, so that Arafat rarely mentioned his father's name; he did not attend his father's funeral and did not visit his father's grave in Gaza when signing the Oslo Accords. Arafat's single-minded pursuit of the goal of becoming the father of the Palestinian nation, this man who grew up without a father, may well have had its origins in that troubled relationship.

Being born in Egypt, not Palestine, and not being a refugee would assuredly diminish his appeal as champion of the Palestinian cause. Indeed, throughout his life he avoided speaking about his early years and claimed to have been born in Jerusalem and to have been a refugee. In a 1969 interview, in his well-practiced victim role, he stated, "*I am a refugee. Do you know what it means to be a refugee? I am a poor and helpless man. I have nothing, for I was expelled and dispossessed from my homeland."*

Very sad, a compelling story. But not true.

His sister recalled him as a ten-year-old acting like a military commander, marching children up and down the street. A childhood playmate recounted that "he always wanted to be the boss." This dominating aspect of his personality, which appeared so early, was to characterize his leadership.

In 1947, the United Nations partitioned Palestine into a Jewish and a Palestinian state—what the Arab League characterized as "the catastrophe." The Arab nations' rejection of the partition led to the 1948 Arab-Israeli War. Arafat's participation in the war was minimal. He described leaving Cairo for Gaza with two friends in the spring of 1948: *"Here we are, three men going to fight Jews . . . with only one weapon. We must be crazy."* As they neared the border, they were confronted by an Egyptian officer who confiscated their gun and sent them home. In their political biography of Arafat, Barry Rubin and Judith Colp Rubin observe: "It seems to have been Arafat's most direct experience in the 1948 war and must have been a traumatic one. In effect, Arafat was being told by a professional soldier in a well-pressed uniform to go home like good little boys and let the real men—and non-Palestinians too—get on with the real job of smashing the Jews. Such an event would have challenged his self esteem and taught him resentment and distrust of Arab regimes and disdain for the supposed expertise of career officers."[6]

At that time, Arafat's resentment against the West was targeted toward the British. They had authored the Balfour Declaration in 1917, which declared in response to the Zionist movement spearheaded by Theodore Herzl that Britain would "view with favor the establishment in Palestine of a national homeland for the Jews" and sponsored the UN partition of 1947. After the resounding defeat in what Israel came to call the War of Independence, Arafat applied for admission to a university in Texas. But in the postwar ferment Egypt was roiling with political activism and bitterness against the newly established Jewish state of Israel, and Arafat was swept up in this fervor.

He enrolled in the engineering school at King Fuad Cairo University in 1949, where, according to a good friend, "his only activity was politics. Very seldom would he come to the School of Engineering." In the mid-1950s, Arafat joined the Muslim Brotherhood, which was championing the Palestinian cause. With their support, he was elected head of the Palestinian Student Union at the University of Cairo, from which he graduated after seven years. In the late 1950s, Arafat moved to Kuwait where in 1959 he founded Fatah (Palestine National Liberation Movement—the acronym of which, reversed, means "conquest" or "death"). He observed at the time, *"People aren't attracted to speeches, but rather to bullets."* From the beginning, by virtue of his dominating personality, Arafat was the undisputed leader of Fatah. Arafat chose as his *nom de guerre* Abu Ammar, who, Arafat explained, had been *"captured, tortured to force him to give up his faith.* [He was] *the first martyr of Islam, whose name became the symbol of total fidelity to one's faith and beliefs in the Arab world."*

Due to Arafat's total commitment to the Palestinian cause, he was at the helm of the Palestinian resistance from the formation of Fatah in 1959 until his death in 2004.

Arafat was to apply himself assiduously to expanding his base and to broaden his support among the Palestinian people. He reached out to other Palestinian leaders, such as Hani al-Hassan, who had been working in Germany and developed a large political organization of Palestinian students studying there. But due to Arafat's domineering personality, he clashed with other Fatah leaders who sought a collective leadership, and emerged from this struggle in control.

Troubled by the unconstrained Palestinian commandos, which he believed threatened his authority in the Arab world, Egyptian president Gamal Abdul Nasser determined to create a Palestinian organization to serve as the official voice of the Palestinian people, with a military wing to be called the Palestinian Liberation Army, all to be under the control of Arab governments.[7] The founding conference of the Palestinian Liberation Organization (PLO) was held in East Jerusalem in 1964, and an Arab League firebrand, Ahmed Shukeiry, was appointed its leader. Its charter or covenant called for armed struggle against the Zionists and the destruction of the state of Israel:

Armed struggle is the only way to liberate Palestine. Thus it is the overall strategy, not merely a tactical phase. The Palestinian Arab people assert their absolute determination and firm resolution to continue their armed struggle and to work for an armed popular revolution for the liberation of their country and their return to it.

Commando action constitutes the nucleus of the Palestinian popular liberation war. This requires its escalation, comprehensiveness, and mobilization of all the Palestinian popular and educational efforts and their organization and involvement in the armed Palestinian revolution.

The liberation of Palestine from an Arab viewpoint is a national duty and it attempts to repel the Zionist and imperialist aggression against her Arab homeland, and aims at the elimination of Zionism in Palestine . . . the partition of Palestine in 1947 and the establishment of the State of Israel are entirely illegal, regardless of the passage of time, because they were contrary to the will of the Palestinian people and to their natural right in their *homeland, and inconsistent with the principles embodied in the Charter of the United Nations, particularly the right to self-determination.*

The Balfour Declaration, the Mandate for Palestine, and everything that is based upon them, are deemed null and void. Claims of historical or religious ties of Jews with Palestine are incompatible with the facts of history and the truer conception of what constitutes statehood. Judaism, being a religion, is not an independent nationality. Nor do Jews constitute a single nation with an identity of its own. They are citizens of the states to which they belong.[8]

While the PLO was popular throughout the Arab world and was positively received by Palestinian groups, it was seen as a creature of Nasser, and was resented by Arafat and his expanding Fatah base. The destruction of Israel was a goal of Fatah from its founding, and its members did not take exception to the extremity of the positions of the PLO Covenant. To the contrary. Rather the quarrel was over who was to be in charge. What right, Arafat asked, did an Egyptian leader have to speak for the Palestinian people? He determined to take it over. By February 1969, Fatah succeeded in wresting control of the PLO away from Nasser and the PLO Executive Committee, of which they gained control. Fatah named Yasser Arafat the new PLO chairman. Increasingly, Arafat came to personify PLO and from this base to be seen as the voice of the Palestinian people.

The struggle of Fatah then was not merely with Israel but with the Arab world. After the devastating defeat of the Arab nations under the leadership of Nasser in the 1967 Arab-Israeli War, when the Israelis won the West Bank, Gaza, Jerusalem, and the Golan Heights, Fatah's contempt for the feckless Arab nations grew. It was determined to mount its own guerrilla campaign against Israel from its base in Jordan, actions that in 1968 provoked Israel to mass its troops for a major retaliatory raid. According to Arafat, "*The Israelis were massing in an arrogant way.*" At his urging, the small group of irregulars bravely confronted the Israelis crossing the river into Jordan and, with the aid of Jordanian troops, destroyed a number of Israeli armored vehicles. After a 12-hour battle, the Israeli forces retreated, with 27 of their soldiers dead and 90 wounded. In the Arab world, having the courage to stand up to a superior enemy is a mark of heroic leadership. Arafat claimed an overwhelming victory, the first Arab victory over the hated Israeli enemy. The news of this triumph at what came to be known as the Battle of Karameh rocketed through the Palestinian camps, and Arafat's reputation soared. After the humiliation of the 1967 war, this was a restorative and Yasser Arafat was their recognized champion and hero. It was Arafat's heroic leadership in the battle of Karameh that inspired young Rezaq to enter the path of the revolution. And it was this triumph, and his growing fame as heroic revolutionary leader, that enabled Arafat to take over the Palestinian Liberation Organization in 1969 from Nasser's leadership. The PLO was now an umbrella organization of Palestinian revolutionary groups, with Fatah as its largest and dominant group.

Heady with success, in 1969 Arafat and the Fatah leadership determined to take over the leadership of Jordan, the Hashemite kingdom, from King Hussein, creating a state within a state. A two-year struggle known as Black September resulted, with King Hussein ultimately succeeding in expelling Palestinian forces in 1971. It was a humiliating defeat for Arafat, but, like the proverbial phoenix, he was to rise again. Arafat and his Fatah soldiers retreated to Lebanon, where they participated in the 11-year "war of the bombs" that tore the pluralistic Lebanese state asunder. Muslim factions battled against Christians in a ferocious civil war, which restored Arafat's reputation as heroic Palestinian revolutionary.

A pivotal moment in Arafat's career, in what was assuredly a diplomatic breakthrough, was his appearance in that palace of peace, the United Nations, on November 19, 1974.[9] Seeking to emphasize his revolutionary identity, he appeared in battle fatigues and sought to enter with a pistol, only being persuaded at the last moment to leave it behind. Reflecting his two conflicting identities, revolutionary leader of the unified Palestinian resistance and aspiring founding father of a Palestinian state, he addressed the UN General Assembly wearing an empty holster.

His language reflected no ambivalence, and made clear he was seizing the opportunity in the international spotlight to burnish his revolutionary credentials. He first declared that Zionism and Israel were too evil to be allowed to exist. He then declared that Palestinians were classic Third World victims of oppression, violence, western imperialism, and racial discrimination. He went on to deny charges of terrorism, explaining that anyone fighting "*for the freedom and liberation of his land from the invaders, the setters and the colonialists cannot possibly be called terrorists.*"

Over the next several years Arafat used his base in southern Lebanon to attack Israel. Threatened by the instability in its neighbor, Israel invaded Lebanon on June 6, 1982. These actions led to another humiliating defeat for the Palestinians under Arafat, as they were forced to leave Lebanon on August 30, 1982, with Arafat establishing his base in Tunisia. This defeat led many in the Palestinian movement to become disenchanted with Arafat's leadership and to form the so-called rejectionist front. Omar Rezaq was among them. A member of Fatah at the time, Rezaq was disillusioned by what he deemed to be Arafat's weak and cowardly leadership; his heroic idol had been toppled from the throne.

Arafat had unerring bad judgment, as reflected in Black September and Lebanon and again, dramatically, in 1990–1991, when he threw his support behind Saddam Hussein after Iraq's invasion of Kuwait, leading Arafat watchers to quote Israeli diplomat and politician Abba Eban's bon mot that "Arafat never missed an opportunity to miss an opportunity." Yet, aided in large part by his public relations flair, in which he embraced the victim's role, regularly winning sympathy for the Palestinian diaspora, he continued to maintain his leadership of the PLO and his international reputation as the embodiment of the Palestinian cause.

Facing His Mortality[10]

A consummate survivor, throughout his revolutionary career Palestinian leader Yasser Arafat led with his finger squarely in the wind, extremely sensitive to the tide of public opinion. While he consistently espoused the goal of an independent Palestinian state, an examination of his career suggests that his highest priority was always securing his reputation as leader of the unified Palestinian resistance. On any number of occasions, by recognizing Israel's right to exist, Arafat could have placed unbearable international pressure on Israel in the service of movement toward a Palestinian entity, but his wish to be the leader of the unified Palestinian resistance in effect gave a veto to the extremist wing of the Palestinian movement.

But this was to change in 1992. When Arafat's plane crashed in the Libyan desert on April 4, it was initially feared the PLO leader had been killed. He was found the next day, dazed, by the wreck of the private plane in which his pilot has been killed. In June, suffering from severe headaches, he was rushed to King Hussein Hospital in Amman, Jordan, for emergency neurosurgery to remove two blood clots pressing on his brain, a life-threatening result of the trauma he had sustained eight weeks earlier.

It was after this surgery that he entered into the secret negotiations that were to result in the Oslo Accords, beginning the peace process that culminated in the Wye River Accords. Having confronted his mortality and seeing that his time was limited, Arafat resolved to take an unprecedented step to achieve his goal of a Palestinian state, to ensure his place in history, to ensure that history books would record Yasser Arafat as the father of the Palestinian nation.[11] As a consequence of the Oslo Accords, Arafat won not only the Nobel Peace Prize, but also the lasting enmity of the absolutist extremist wing of the Palestinian movement for selling out the cause.

After their revolutions succeed, few revolutionary leaders are successful in leading their newborn nations, for the tasks and abilities of leading a group in opposition against the hated enemy are very different from those required by a nation-builder. To rouse a group against the hated establishment is very different from becoming the establishment. Only a few have made this transition. Fidel Castro is an exception to this general rule, but his success in fending off criticism of his internal leadership has been facilitated by the U.S. economic embargo, which has permitted the Cuban dictator to continue to externalize, blaming enemies in the North for his internal problems.

Arafat, in becoming president of the Palestinian Authority, was not an exception to the general rule and did not make this transition well. He continued to demonstrate an autocratic leadership style more congenial to a fighting revolutionary than to a nation-builder and was criticized by moderate Palestinian leaders for not developing a more participative democracy as he strove to develop the infrastructure of the newly established Palestinian Authority. Moreover, in dealing with the negotiations during the peace process negotiations, he continued to be absolutist in his demands, not offering any compromise in response to the extreme flexibility shown by Israeli Prime Minister Ehud Barak. Further, as Barak was preparing the Israeli public for the necessity of making painful concessions and compromises in order to achieve the long-desired peace, Arafat did not prepare the Palestinian public to compromise. To the contrary, he continued to maintain a public posture that total satisfaction of Palestinian demands for East Jerusalem as a capital, control over the holy sites, and the right of return—the most contentious of the issues—would be required.

At Camp David II, the summit convened by President Clinton between Arafat and Israeli Prime Minister Ehud Barak in 2000, a solution to the long standing impasse was tantalizingly close. But Arafat's refusal to offer any reciprocal response to Barak's major concessions ultimately doomed the talks. In the long run, however, putting into play the previously taboo issues of Jerusalem and the right of return was a major accomplishment.

With the failure of the talks due to Arafat's absolutist demands and unwillingness to compromise, the region was again thrown into violent conflict, a major step back from the accomplishments of recent years. Shelving his Nobel Peace Prize medal, Arafat once again exhorted Palestinian youth to "fight for Jerusalem" and praised the youthful "martyrs" who had lost their lives in the

conflict. It was as if the leader of the unified Palestinian resistance was his primary identity, his psychological default position, which had won out over his
more fragile identity as father of the Palestinian nation. Ominously, Arafat
released from Palestinian prisons radical members of Hamas and the Islamic
Jihad, militant Islamist terrorist groups, some of whom were responsible for the
wave of suicide terrorist attacks that claimed 57 lives in 1996. Arafat brought a
number of these leaders into a decision-making committee to plan and coordinate the violent protest, leading to fear in Israel of a new wave of terrorist
attacks. Despite repeated pleas to seek to constrain the violence, Arafat did not
do so. Rather he placed the entirety of the blame on Israel, justifying Palestinian
violence in terms of a legitimate response to the Israeli occupation and disproportionate violence by the Israeli military, with no acknowledgment of
Palestinian participation in the cycle of violence. Once again, in this competition of victimhoods, each side justified its violence as a required response to the
aggression of the other. It may be, however, that having again unleashed the
genie of violence, Arafat was afraid that calls for restraint would go unheeded
and betray the weakness of his leadership position.

Arafat was ill and nearing the end of his career. In November 1999, after a
conference celebrating the twentieth anniversary of the Camp David Accords at
the Ben Gurion University of the Negev, with original participants at the negotiations, the U.S. participants in the conference traveled under armed guard to
Arafat's headquarters in Ramallah in the Occupied Territories to have an audience with Arafat. Although I knew he had been ailing and was reported to be
suffering from Parkinson's disease, I was shocked by his appearance. His eyes
were sunk deeply in his head; he appeared exhausted and displayed a major
tremor around his mouth. (I believe this was not Parkinson's disease per se, but
a Parkinsonian tremor, secondary to the brain trauma and neurosurgery he
underwent in 1992.) Yet, when he spoke, his rhetoric was fiery, as he exclaimed,
"*I have kept my promises. The reason for the failure of the peace negotiations is him,
Netanyahu. He cannot be trusted and has broken his promises.*"

We then drove to Jerusalem, where, after lunch, we had an audience with
Israeli Prime Minister Binyamin "Bibi" Netanyahu. Apparently both men had
the same speechwriter, for Netanyahu stated, "*I have kept my promises. He* [refer-
ring to Arafat] *cannot be trusted and has broken his promises.*"

Thus, the ill-fitting garb of peacemaker had been replaced by the much
more familiar battle fatigues of the revolutionary fighter. Could Arafat return to
the path of peace? Each morning as Arafat looked into the mirror and was confronted with his aging, tremulous visage, he was reminded that his time was short
and that his goal of achieving a Palestinian state has not yet been accomplished.

For Arafat, two clocks were ticking. When illness claimed him in 2004, his wish to go down in history as the father of the Palestinian state had once again fallen casualty to the default position in his political psychology, leader of the unified Palestinian resistance.

When one has been nursed on the mother's milk of hatred and bitterness, the need for vengeance is bred in the bone. In ethnic/nationalist conflicts, hatred has been transmitted generationally, and the psychopolitics of hatred are deeply rooted. The generational transmission of Palestinian hatred exemplified by the lives of terrorists Omar Rezaq and Leila Khaled, the deep-seated hatred reflected in the interviews of secular Palestinian terrorists, all inspired by the model of Yasser Arafat, argue for continuation of Palestinian/Israeli hatred and perpetuation of the violent struggle. As was the case with the agreement of the now-failed Oslo Accords entered into by Arafat and Ehud Barak, the signatures of Mahmoud Abbas and Ariel Sharon or his successor, Ehud Olmert, on a new peace treaty would not signal the end of the fear and hatred that has been passed from generation to generation.

CHAPTER 3

IRISH REPUBLICAN ARMY (IRA)

This is one race of people for whom psychoanalysis is of no use whatsoever.

—Sigmund Freud on the Irish

Despite this warning concerning the psychological impenetrability of the Irish mind, found on the business card of an Irish pub in Washington, D.C., I will attempt, drawing on the lives and words of Irish activists and terrorists, to lead the reader into their minds. But to do so it is important first to characterize the political and historical context that shaped those minds.

While the historical origins of the troubles in Northern Ireland do not date back quite so far back as biblical times, the struggle is deeply rooted in history, with each generation absorbing the bitterness of the previous generation, each vowing to take on the struggle to redress their long-standing grievances. In Northern Ireland, for many Catholics and Protestants alike, hatred has indeed been bred in the bone.

The origins of this struggle can be traced back to 1169 when English mercenaries first invaded Ireland; the fight for control has been waged ever since. The geographic split came to pass in 1607, when the area now known as Northern Ireland was given to the English and Scottish colonists after the English had defeated the last of the Ulster kings. The religious split followed, with the arrival of the new Protestant settlers displacing the native Catholic inhabitants. The British, to justify their conquest, propagated a theory that the Irish were an inferior people. "Ireland," wrote the English essayist Thomas

Carlyle, "is like the half starved rat that crosses the path of the elephant. What must the elephant do? Squelch it—by heavens—squelch it!"[1]

And squelch them they did. Between the sixteenth and nineteenth centuries, a number of laws were passed that were intended to prevent the Irish from taking any part in the commercial or intellectual life of their country. Called the Penal Laws, they left the Irish with no right to vote or hold office, no right to purchase or lease land, no right to educate a child in any way at home or abroad, no right to engage in commerce. Priests were banned and hunted with bloodhounds.[2]

ORIGINS OF THE IRISH REPUBLICAN ARMY

In the Irish fight for independence from Britain, the demand for Home Rule was of central importance to the nationalists. The possibility of a united Ireland threatened the distinct minority of Protestants who feared the overall Catholic dominance (80 percent) in the new parliament. The Unionists founded the Ulster Volunteer Force (UVF) to combat the possibility of being excluded from the domain of Home Rule. This in turn led the Irish Republican Brotherhood (IRB)—formed after the Protestant Rebellion of 1850—to start organizing Catholic volunteers. A minority of the IRB, not satisfied by Home Rule alone, split off to work toward complete independence of Ireland from Great Britain; they called themselves the Irish Republican Army (IRA). The very name—Irish Republican *Army*—revealed its members' militancy and their belief that only violence could achieve their separatist goals.

The leadership of the IRA planned a rebellion for Easter Sunday 1916 and issued the Proclamation of the Republic, which is known as the founding document of the IRA.

POBLACHT NA H EIREANN

THE PROVISIONAL GOVERNMENT

of the

IRISH REPUBLIC

TO THE PEOPLE OF IRELAND

IRISHMEN AND IRISHWOMEN: In the name of God and of the dead generations from which she receives her old tradition of nationhood, Ireland, through us, summons her children to her flag and strikes for her freedom.

Having organized and trained her manhood through her secret revolutionary organization, the Irish Republican Brotherhood, . . . having resolutely waited for the right moment to reveal itself, she now seizes that moment, and . . . she strikes in full confidence of victory. We declare the right of the people of Ireland to the ownership of Ireland, and to the unfettered control of Irish destinies, to be sovereign and indefeasible. We hereby proclaim the Irish Republic as a Sovereign Independent State, and we pledge our lives and the lives of our comrades-in-arms to the cause of its freedom, of its welfare, and of its exaltation among the nations.

The Irish Republic is entitled to, and hereby claims, the allegiance of every Irishman and Irishwoman. . . . Until our arms have brought the opportune moment for the establishment of a permanent National Government, . . . the Provisional Government, . . . will administer the civil and military affairs of the Republic in trust for the people. We place the cause of the Irish Republic under the protection of the Most High God, Whose blessing we invoke upon our arms, and we pray that no one who serves that cause will dishonour it by cowardice, inhumanity, or rapine. In this supreme hour the Irish nation must, by its valour and discipline and by the readiness of its children to sacrifice themselves for the common good, prove itself worthy of the august destiny to which it is called.

JAMES CONNOLLY
The "Socialist Silver Tongue"[3]

A signatory and a principal drafter of the Proclamation of the Republic, James Connolly emerged from poverty—his father was a manure carter in "Little Ireland," an Irish slum in Edinburgh, Scotland—to become a champion of Irish rights. In 1882, at the tender age of 14, Connolly joined the British Army in which he was to remain for nearly seven years, all of it in Ireland. In the army, he witnessed firsthand the mistreatment of the Irish people by the British, which led to an intense hatred of the British Army. This hatred was of central importance in forming Connolly's identity as a fighter for the Irish cause.

Through his older brother, John, James came in contact with socialist agitators in Edinburgh, and eventually succeeded John as secretary of the Scottish Socialist Federation. The pattern of his life was set: "He spent the rest of his days as a wandering agitator, pamphleteer, and union organizer, a voracious reader of socialist theory, and a self-taught intellectual. Such work didn't pay well, and his growing family lived in extreme hardship and poverty. But through his journalism, he became a prominent voice in European socialism, one of the very few who had no university training."[4]

By the time of his death in 1916, he had published six books, including *Socialism Made Easy* (1909) and the *Re-Conquest of Ireland* (1915). He founded many organizations, including the Irish Socialist Republican Party (1896), became head of the Transport and General Workers Unions (1913), and co-founded the Irish Citizen's Army (1913), which later, during the Easter Rising, joined with the Irish Republican Brotherhood.

Connolly's verbal skills were legendary, earning him the sobriquet "Socialist Silver Tongue" for his ability to speak and write with great clarity and strength. The future Labour Member of Parliament Joseph O'Toole recorded that "Connolly was one of the most convincing speakers I ever heard in my life, a man with a great passion for the cause of the laboring classes, and probably a greater passion for the cause of Ireland."[5]

Connolly is one of the most quoted and influential of all Ireland's heroes. His passion for Ireland and its people can be seen in his many actions and writings. A vivid example: "*The man who is bubbling over with love and enthusiasm for 'Ireland' and yet can pass unmoved through our streets and witness all the wrong and the suffering, the shame and degradation, wrought upon the people of Ireland . . . without burning to end it, is, in my opinion, a fraud.*"[6]

With regard to the British crown, Connolly wrote: "*A Resurrection! . . . Our cards are on the table. If you strike at, imprison, or kill us, we will still evoke a spirit that will thwart you, and mayhap, raise a force that will destroy you. We defy you! Do your worst!*"[7]

Jailed for attending a public demonstration in support of labor strikes, Connolly went on a hunger strike in September 1913, becoming the first person to use the act of hunger strikes as a protest against the unjust treatment of Irish Republicans. Irish hunger strikers have become a symbol of the desire of the Irish people to be free of oppression.[8]

Leader and Martyr of the Easter Rising of 1916

It was the Easter Rising of 1916 that enshrined Connolly's name in the pantheon of Irish heroes. From the General Post Office in Dublin, the leaders of the Irish Republican Brotherhood proclaimed Irish independence from British rule. The British forces quickly controlled the uprising, captured the leaders, and executed them. The brutal suppression of the uprising and the execution of the leaders made them martyrs for Ireland, roused the previously uninterested Irish public, and turned them against British rule: "The insurgents fought with a typical Irish gallantry, attacked by soldiers using artillery and outnumbering them twenty to one. Cut off from all possible support from the country, or from reinforcements of any kind, they held out for almost a week, during which Dublin was badly damaged . . . the leaders knew their rising was bound to fail, but they were prepared to barter their lives against the possibilities of their various dreams coming true after their deaths."[9] Patrick Pearse, who put this philosophy into practice with the Easter Rising, wrote, *"Bloodshed is a cleansing and satisfactory thing, and the nation which regards it as the final horror has lost its manhood."*[10]

There are a number of reasons why James Connolly's execution had a powerful impact on the Irish population. Most important is the effect his writing and lectures had on people. He had the ability to *say* what others *felt* but could not express, and he did it in a way that would capture any audience. Moreover, the manner of his execution was particularly brutal. Connolly, who had been badly wounded during the fighting, was the last to die. His execution took place the day *after* the British House of Commons promised there would be no more executions. And even though it was British policy not to execute a wounded man, they tied Connolly to a chair to be shot since he was too weak to stand. These 16 executions had a striking effect. As one County Clare IRA man, Sean Clancey, later recalled: *"The papers carried the news, and you could see the change of heart in the people. Each day, the British shot two or three, dragging it out over a few weeks. When they shot McDermott [Mac Diarmada], who was basically a cripple, and then put James Connolly into a chair to shoot him because his leg was gangrenous and he couldn't stand, well, that was it for me. I was utterly appalled and just had to do something."*[11]

Ensuring that his words would outlive him, Connolly managed to slip his final statement to his daughter Nora as she visited him the night before his death. An excerpt follows:

> [We believe] that the British Government has no right in Ireland, never had any right in Ireland, and never can have any right in Ireland, the presence, in any one generation of Irishmen, of even a respectable minority, ready to die to affirm that truth, makes that Government for ever a usurpation and a crime against human progress.
>
> I personally thank God that I have lived to see the day when thousands of Irish men and boys, and hundreds of Irish women and girls, were ready to affirm that truth, and to attest it with their own lives if need be.
>
> —James Connolly, Commandant-General, Dublin Division,
> Army of the Irish Republic[12]

Connolly's role has been memorialized in a rousing ballad extolling rebel courage and cursing England as a *"cruel hearted monster"* whose *"deeds would shame all the devils in Hell."*

> A great crowd had gathered outside of Kilmainhem
> With their heads all uncovered they knelt on the ground
> For inside that grim prison lay a brave Irish soldier
> His life for his country about to lay down.[13]

In the five years that followed the Easter Rising, the growth of Republican activities, particularly under the direction of Michael Collins, led the British government to search for a reasonable solution to the problem. They first tried to create separate Home Rule for both the northern and southern parts of Ireland. Even though it was accepted by the Unionists, it was rejected by the Republicans, who continued their fight for independence. This disagreement led to the treaty of 1921, which created the 6-county Northern Ireland that remained part of the United Kingdom and the 26-county Irish Free State under British dominion in the South. Civil war ensued between pro- and anti-treaty forces in the Irish Free State.

In August 1923, Sinn Fein (literally "our selves" but commonly translated as "Ourselves Alone"), the political wing of the IRA, emerged as the second biggest party in the general elections held in the Irish Free State. But Sinn Fein members declined to occupy their seats in parliament indicating that they neither recognized the Irish Free State nor its parliament. They only took their seats to counter a law that was proposed to fight the IRA.

JOE CAHILL

Inspired by James Connolly[14]

Just before the civil war started, a man who would become a noteworthy figure in the IRA was born. Joe Cahill came into the world on May 19, 1920, "to the sound of gunfire and explosions, sounds which would echo in his ears for most of his life."[15] In the first 13 months of his life, 455 people died and over 2,000 were wounded. The violence heard was that of the struggle between the IRA and the Black and Tans.*

Joe was the first of 9 surviving children of the 11 born to Joseph and Josephine Cahill. Josephine Cahill, in particular, was always anxious "to instill in her family a sense of Irishness and a love of all things Irish,"[16] and told young Joe stories of the Easter Rising all through his childhood.

At age 16, around 1936, he joined the *Na Fianna Eireann*, which can be considered the Republican "cub scouts" for the IRA. The boys were taught Irish

---

* The Black and Tans were a "boost" effect of the British government to aid the policing of the increasingly anti-British Ireland in the wake of the Easter Rising of 1916. Known locally as the Tans or Auxies (Auxiliaries), they received their unique nickname when so many men joined up that Britain did not have enough uniforms. The new recruits were given khaki pants with a dark shirt, cap, and belt; hence, the Black and Tans.

history and used as lookouts for IRA meetings. By the time Joe turned 18 he decided to join the IRA. Each man and woman who was interested in joining the fight had to prove their loyalty to the cause: "*You had to go through these classes in history, political awareness and security. It was a long process, because you had to do examinations. You were told what lay before you, what you could expect—membership in the IRA could mean being on the run, imprisonment or death. They asked you to think about all these things. They actually painted a very black picture of what could happen to you.*"[17]

Within a few years of becoming an active member of the IRA, Cahill was arrested and sentenced to be hanged after an assignment to distract the Royal Ulster Constabulary (RUC) from an illegal Easter Rising anniversary march that went terribly wrong. All six men (18 to 22 years of age) were sentenced to death for the death of one, Constable Patrick Murphy. Cahill recalls the brutal violence of the RUC officers: "*We shouted down that we were going to surrender and had put down our arms. They flew up the stairs and battered the hell out of us. They gave us an awful lacing.*" Cahill received a "fractured skull, several broken ribs and extensive bruising."[18]

Tom Williams, the leader of the group, was hanged. After an enormous public outcry, the sentences of the rest of the group were commuted to life imprisonment only a few days before they were to be hanged.

In October 1949, the five men were surprised a second time when they were suddenly released. Joe himself never knew why they were released, but believed it might be linked to the announcement in September 1948 when the Irish government stated that it was dissolving all ties with Great Britain. Northern Ireland was determined to remain within the United Kingdom. The British government responded with the Ireland Act, which recognized that from August 1949, "Eire" ceased to be part of His Majesty's Dominion. In the future it would be known as the Republic of Ireland, but it was not to be regarded as a foreign country, nor were its citizens to be considered aliens. The Ireland Act also stated that no constitutional changes would take place in the North without the consent of parliament in Northern Ireland. Sir Basil Brooke, a parliamentary secretary in the Unionist administration, stated: "*What the Free State is after is the rape of Ulster; it is not marriage. It is the rape of Ulster they want, and when they have done that dreadful deed would throw the wretched girl on one side and rob her of her means.*"[19]

Cahill had his own interpretation of the events: "*There was no way you could work politically in the North then. There was an awful lot against us: the lack of opportunity to preach politics; Sinn Fein was banned, as were public meetings and processions. The laws were totally oppressive.*"[20]

A republican from Donegal reflects on the oppressive nature of the British government: *"Republican ideals to me came very, very natural because I resented British rule in Ireland. Totally resented it. And could see a grave injustice being done against our people. . . . Learning about the days as well when it was illegal to be a Catholic, illegal to speak the Irish language. This all give me, motivated me and give me, you know, inspiration and the aspiration of being a Republican."*[21]

DISCRIMINATION

Hundreds of thousands of Catholics in Protestant-dominated Northern Ireland were discriminated against in terms of jobs, education, and social services. But protests against any of these matters were confronted by "law and order dressed up in the uniform of oppression and bigotry."[22] While many deplored the necessity for armed struggle that resulted in deaths, at the same time, said Cathal Goulding, the IRA chief of staff: *"It is not within our power to dictate what action the forces of imperialism and exploitation will engage in to repress, coerce and deny ordinary people their God-given rights [making it necessary to speak] the language that would bring these vultures to their sense—the language of bomb and bullet."*[23]

A woman from Dungannon describes the changing nature of the civil rights activities: *"Initially, you didn't get the big crowds that you expected. And then it started to mushroom. The more violence there was, the more people wanted to stand up. And be counted. And that's what you will find. The more violence there is against another of their own, the more people will come out. If one man's knocked down, there's ten more to replace him."*[24]

A peaceful protest march was scheduled in 1952 by Nationalists to highlight the discriminatory housing policies in Northern Ireland. Protesters were soon met with police brutality: *"There was complete pandemonium—people screaming and cursing, the uninjured attempting to rescue those who were hurt, as jets of water continued to knock them off their feet. . . . This was the first time in the history of NI [Northern Ireland] that television film crews had been sent to cover a Nationalist march, and their film provided the world with stark evidence of RUC brutality towards peaceful protest."*[25]

This was in no way an isolated matter. Time after time, peaceful protesters trying to work within the nonviolent political realm were met with extreme police brutality. While Catholics were banned from having any kind of commemorative march, whether in remembrance of the Easter Rising or in hopes of civil liberties, Protestants were able to celebrate their domination of Ireland by marching through Catholic neighborhoods in the traditional Orange Day parades.* An IRA supporter recalls: *"As the date of the annual Apprentice Boys' Parade in Derry* [August 12, 1969] *drew near, there was a definite feeling of trouble brewing. For me the sound of those drums served as a flash-back to my childhood and I could feel tension and anger mounting within me."*[26]

The Derry violence began when Catholic and Protestant crowds exchanged insults, stones, and bottles as the Protestant Orange parade passed through the city center. Later, the pattern of Catholic versus police violence emerged: rioting, street clashes, and burning of buildings met with police baton charges and the use of tear gas in what became known as the Battle of the Bogside, in August 1969.[27]

After growing disorder, the three days of extreme violence culminated in British troops being put on the streets. Initially the troops were warmly welcomed by the Catholic minority as saviors against the brutal RUC; the IRA had never mobilized to offer protection. Joe Cahill also witnessed the Battle of Bogside and he distinctly remembered being intensely humiliated when Catholics welcomed the troops with tea and cake and dubbed the IRA "I Ran Away." *"The reception of the army brought tears to my eyes,"* he said later. *"People collaborated with the enemy because the IRA had betrayed them."*[28]

The IRA's earlier decision not to mobilize for the Catholics in the North proved costly.

SPLIT IN THE IRA

Founding of the Provisional Irish Republican Army

[The English] ruled Ireland with a mailed fist, literally. A grasp of iron and nobody stepped out of line. And it's only natural that a people are going to breed at some stage someone who says, "I am not going to take that." Now what does that make him? Does that make him a rabble rouser? Does it make him a trouble maker? It ought to. I mean, obviously if

---

* These parades dated back to 1795 when the Loyal Orange Institution was formed, named after the hero of the Northern Irish Protestants, the Protestant British king William of Orange, who on July 12, 1690, triumphed over the Catholic king, James II, confirming Protestant supremacy in Ireland. A year after its formation, the Loyal Orange Order held the first Orange parade. For more than 200 years since, marches have taken place in the period between Easter Monday and the end of September, with more than 3,500 parades held throughout Northern Ireland. Protestants parade throughout Catholic neighborhoods, triumphantly commemorating key historical events of their cultural heritage, often precipitating violent conflict.

he stands up and hits back it makes him a combatant. And it makes him, therefore, eventually, a rabble rouser and a murderer and a terrorist. And if that's what a terrorist is, I want to be a terrorist.

—Anonymous veteran of the Provisional Irish Republican Army (1984)[29]

Seeing the futility of the path of continued violence, in December 1969 the IRA decided it would not continue to support the path of violence but rather would employ political and negotiating remedies to gain the rights of the Nationalists in Northern Ireland. A significant minority, however, thought that the political arena was still too oppressive and would not accomplish their goals of a united Ireland and that violence was required to prove the seriousness of their desires. This caused a split in the group, and the Provisional Irish Republican Army (PIRA), also known as the Provos, was born. This was not the first time the movement split over doctrinal differences, nor would it be the last. Those in support of a political path became known as the Official Irish Republican Army (OIRA), which overall was a more ideologically driven leftist group committed to Marxist-Leninism.

Joe Cahill, after having played a crucial role in establishing the Provisional Irish Republican Army, became the official commander of the PIRA in Belfast. He stated: *"Thousands of young people were now attempting to join the Provisional IRA. Some were from old established republican families, while others admitted to being '1969 republicans'—young men and women radicalized by the experiences of the civil rights movement and the expulsion of nationalists from their homes. Veterans . . . never lost sight of the movement's primary objective—the establishment of a thirty-two-county Irish republic."*[30]

With the many new recruits, the PIRA launched a bombing campaign. As longtime PIRA observer J. Bowyer Bell observed, a crucial aspect of PIRA training was transmittal of the philosophy, indoctrination in the creed.[31] It is a creed palpably experienced when walking into any Irish bar and hearing ballads extolling the fallen martyrs. The theme is one of foreknowledge of death in pursuit of the cause, of doomed men who know they will die but have no choice. Consider, for example, the last stanza of this song:

Freedom Sons
At Easter time 1916
When flowers bloomed and leaves were green
There dawned a day when freedom's cry
Called on brave men come fight or die . . .[32]

In another example, reflected in the last stanza of "Irish Solider Boy," the lad wounded in battle seeks his mother's pride in his martyred death:

> Goodbye, God bless you mother dear
> I'm dying a death so grand.
> From wounds received in fighting
> Trying to free my native land.[33]

A song taught by parents to their children, along with lessons in the injustice of Irish history, was "A Rebel Heart," which emphasizes in the following verse the generational transmission of hatred:

> I was rocked to rest on a rebel breast
> I was nursed on a rebel knee
> Then there awoke and grew
> This rebel heart in me.[34]

The "rebel hearts" had been sensitized from childhood on, but had not yet become fighters for the cause. The triggering factor of Bloody Sunday led many to cross that line.

BLOODY SUNDAY

Support for the IRA was strong in the early 1970s, including significant financial contributions to the cause. The support increased dramatically after January 30, 1972, when a British parachute regiment, the Paras, opened fire on a crowd of unarmed anti-internment demonstrators in Derry, killing 14. The event came to be known as Bloody Sunday. An Italian journalist was present that day and later wrote: "I have never seen such cold-blooded murder, organized disciplined murder, planned murder. . . . There hadn't been one shot fired at them [the Paras]. . . . They just jumped out, and with unbelievable murderous fury, shot into a fleeing crowd. . . . It was unbelievable."[35]

This event radicalized many observers, as exemplified by the comments of an active young Republican the day after the funerals for those who had fallen: *"I have never taken the life of another person nor do I ever anticipate doing so, but if I had had a gun at that moment I would have had no hesitation in shooting British soldiers until my ammunition ran out."*[36]

Three days later, 30,000 people gathered in Dublin and burned down the British embassy. Thirty years later, Joe Cahill regretted what he saw as a lost opportunity to harness and direct the anger of the Irish people. *"We were not strong enough at that time to react politically. It had been said often that if we had been in a strong position politically, then we could have taken over the country. The feeling throughout the land was unbelievable. I have never seen such a wave of revulsion against British rule in Ireland. I have never witnessed the like of it before or since."*[37]

The lack of political strength led the Official IRA to declare a cease-fire in 1972, the worst year of the conflict, with 479 killed and 5,000 wounded.[38] With the departure of the OIRA from the political scene, people began calling the PIRA simply the IRA. Now and for many years to come it would be completely focused on violence, unlike the IRA at its origins, when it contained both political and militant elements.

THE IRA CAMPAIGN

Declaring 1974 the "Year of Victory," the IRA began a bombing campaign in Britain itself, hoping it would push the British to withdraw or to overreact and thereby intensify support for the Irish cause. Forty-three people were killed in the attacks on England's soil, 21 in the November 1974 Birmingham pub bombing.[39] The British Parliament passed the Prevention of Terrorism Act and the Northern Ireland Act, which together gave police sweeping powers such as arrest without a warrant and the ability to detain a suspect for a week without court proceedings. By allowing police such broad powers in the name of counterterrorism, the two "temporary" and "emergency" acts—which were renewed for 20 years—forfeited civil liberties in an effort to battle terrorism. Ultimately, it could be argued, they galvanized ever more support for the IRA.

HUNGER STRIKES

An important goal of the Thatcher government's increasingly hard-line posture toward the IRA was to delegitimize it politically. The British government retracted certain special privileges that political prisoners received as paramilitary convicts, such as their own special prison wing, and began to treat incarcerated IRA members as common criminals. Insisting they were political prisoners, the Republican prisoners refused to wear prison uniforms or empty chamber pots, thereby launching what came to be known as the Dirty Protest. Prime Minister Margaret Thatcher would not negotiate. After the failure of the Dirty Protest, prisoner Bobby Sands led a hunger strike in 1981. Joe Cahill remembers: *"There was a feeling amongst the leadership that Bobby believed his death was inevitable, and that Thatcher would be compelled to compromise before anyone else had died. But, as it turned out, she was such a cold ruthless person that her lust for Irish blood was not satisfied with the death of just one person."*[40]

BOBBY SANDS: HUNGER STRIKE MARTYR

To understand why Bobby Sands became involved in the movement and was willing to give his life for Ireland, one must look at his past. In his own words, *"I was only a working-class boy from a Nationalist ghetto, but it is repression that creates the revolutionary spirit of freedom. I shall not settle until I achieve liberation of my country, until Ireland becomes a sovereign, independent socialist republic."*[41]

Bobby Sands was born in a loyalist section of north Belfast in 1954. The sectarian realities of ghetto life became evident early in his life, when in 1962 his family was forced to move because of loyalist intimidation. In 1968, Sands had served two years of his apprenticeship as a coach maker when he was intimidated into leaving his job. A few years later, his entire family was again forced out of their home. Soon after, at the age of 18, Sands joined the Republican movement. Arrested within his first year of IRA membership for possession of guns, he was sentenced to five years in prison. Although Sands had stayed in school until he was 15, like many other young republicans, he received his true education during his first stint as a prisoner. Sands read about Irish and international revolutionaries, such as James Connolly and Che Guevara. He read widely, taught himself Gaelic, and began writing extensively.[42]

Sands was released in April 1976, and then arrested (for the second and final time) six months later in October, with three other young men. Each was sentenced to 14 years in prison because the police found one gun in the car they all occupied. In the four years between joining the IRA and his final arrest, Sands had spent only 16 months as a free man. Instead of deterring him, the prison experience hardened his resolve.

On March 1, 1981, Bobby Sands refused food while in prison, thus beginning a major hunger strike and making him one of the leading icons of IRA history. Almost two dozen more prisoners would join the hunger strike in the following days and weeks. The political background that led to the hunger strikes of 1981 centered on the republican prisoners' demands to have their political status recognized. Sands forcefully expressed these sentiments in the secret diary he kept through his first 17 days of the hunger strike: *"We wish to be treated 'not as ordinary prisoners' for we are not criminals. We admit no crime unless, that is, the love of one's people and country is a crime. I am a political prisoner because I am a casualty of a perennial war that is being fought between the oppressed Irish people and an alien, oppressive, unwanted regime that refuses to withdraw from our land."*[43]

On reading his diary, one can feel his depth of faith in the Irish people, the strength of his character, and what gave him courage while they emotionally abused him:

> *I always keep thinking of James Connolly, and the great calm and dignity that he showed right to his very end, his courage and resolve. Perhaps I am biased, because there have been thousands like him but Connolly has always been the man that I looked up to.*
>
> *Never give up. No matter how bad, how black, how painful, how heart-breaking. Never give up. Never despair. Never lose hope. Let them bastards laugh at you all they want, let them grin and gibe, allow them to persist in their humiliation, brutality, deprivations, vindictiveness, petty harassments, let them laugh now, because all of that is no longer important or worth a response.*[44]

Over 100,000 people attended Bobby Sands's funeral. His death provoked street protests in many cities around the world and riots in Northern Ireland, creating worldwide media attention and sympathy. Sands's death led him to be inscribed in the songs of Irish martyrs:

> *May God shine on you Bobby Sands for the courage you have shown*
> *May your glory and your fame be widely known.*[45]

In the words of Mickey Devine, Irish National Liberation Army (INLA) volunteer from Derry, who was the last of the 10 to die (August 20, 1981), going on a hunger strike was the last resort of those who felt that every other attempt to call attention to their plight had failed. Just before embarking on his hunger strike Mickey wrote: *"There is nothing that any human being values more than life. Every person clings to it with every ounce of strength of their being. To willingly surrender it is to acknowledge the greatest sacrifice anyone can make. Not only to die, but to choose death which is slow and agonizing, further serves to illustrate the depths of courage and sincerity among the men. . . . What it takes to willingly undergo this ordeal, willingly undergo suffering, none of us can possibly imagine . . . [but] all we have to give is our lives."*[46]

There are a number of reasons why Bobby Sands's voice is the one that stands out among the many voices who perished during the hunger strikes. First, he was the leader of the H-Block prisoners involved in the IRA. Second, he was the first prisoner to die. His suffering and selflessness prompted world attention. The hunger strike was never about him but the Irish Republicans: *"All men must have hope and never lose heart. But my hope lies in the ultimate victory for my poor people. Is there any hope greater than that?"*[47]

And, in April, he was elected to Parliament from prison. As Gerry Adams, President of Sinn Fein, was to argue of Sands' election: "His victory exposed the lie that the hunger strikers—and by extension the IRA and the whole republican movement—had no popular support."[48]

Thatcher claimed victory over the prisoners, but the international support shown for the hunger strikers demonstrated the impact of the hunger strikes and their power in calling to the attention of the international community the plight of the Catholic minority in Northern Ireland. The hunger strikers of 1981 gave republicans a sense of how elections could be used to the advantage of the struggle. It was those results that led Sinn Fein to review its electoral strategy.[49]

CEASE-FIRES AND PEACE TALKS

With many false starts, failed negotiations, and continued violence, peace negotiations resumed with positive results after the Labour Party's Tony Blair was elected prime minister in July 1997. Blair was unique among prime ministers in that he not only wanted peace, but also was willing to work for it and compromise with the Irish. The IRA and various other Protestant paramilitary groups declared a cease-fire, and Sinn Fein was readmitted into the peace talks. After Sinn Fein and the IRA had ensured they would have the support of their constituents, including Irish Americans, the talks led to the Good Friday Accords (the Belfast Agreement or, as it became subsequently known, the Good Friday Agreement) of April 12, 1998.

The Good Friday Agreement essentially paved the way for the establishment of a power-sharing government that would be formed with ministerial posts distributed according to party strength. The agreement was considered a historic breakthrough for its focus on "the achievement of reconciliation, tolerance, and mutual trust, and to the protection and vindication of the human rights of all."[50] The involvement of parties representing paramilitaries (primarily the Ulster Democratic Party, the Progressive Unionist Party, and Sinn Fein) depended on the maintenance of cease-fires and decommissioning of paramilitary weapons. A copy of the agreement was delivered to every household in Northern Ireland, and in May 1998 the accord was approved by an overwhelming majority.

Militant IRA members who disagreed with the Good Friday Agreement formed the Real IRA, led by Mickey McKevitt. On August 15, 1998, the Real IRA placed a 500-pound car bomb in the market square of Omagh, Northern Ireland. The attack, harming mainly women and children, was the most deadly single bombing in Northern Ireland (29 were killed, 200 injured) and could have put the peace accords into jeopardy. But, in fact, all sides were united in their abhorrence of what happened, and efforts both to dismantle the Real IRA and to renew the focus on moving forward with the peace process were galvanized. The Real IRA publicly apologized for the bombing, stating that civilians had not been the intentional target.

After the 9/11 terrorist attacks on the United States, increasing international revulsion against terrorist violence led the politically astute Gerry Adams to recognize that the climate had irrevocably changed. He accordingly announced on October 23, 2001, that the IRA would begin to destroy its arms. The IRA later ordered its volunteers not to engage in other paramilitary activities and in July 2005 ordered an end to the armed campaign. The IRA announced on September 28, 2005, that its decommissioning process was complete.[51] But the IRA's long-standing goal of a 32-county Irish Free State is not over, as Joe Cahill states: *"It is generally believed, and I believe this myself, that the changes that have taken place make it possible to work effectively politically now to achieve a united Ireland. You hear people shouting that republicans only want a united Ireland, and they are dead correct. That is republican policy. Our goal is a united Ireland, and the strategy we are using today is directed to taking us to a united Ireland by peaceful means."*[52]

On May 8, 2007, an event occurred that at one time seemed impossible, a power sharing agreement between "once implacable foes."[53] Witnessed by officials from Great Britain, the United States, and elsewhere, the fiery Reverend Ian Paisley, leader of the Democratic Unionist Party, the dominant party among Northern Ireland protestants, and Martin McGuiness, deputy head of Sinn Fein, whom Paisley had long accused of being an IRA terrorist, were sworn in as leader and deputy leader of the Northern Ireland executive government, vowing to resolve future differences through political reconciliation.

CHAPTER 4

BASQUE HOMELAND AND LIBERTY (ETA)

Like the historical roots of the struggle for Northern Irish separatism, the roots of the struggle for Basque nationalism can be traced back to the medieval period in European history. During the re-conquest of Spain in 1492 led by the Catholic monarchies, the Basque territory was incorporated into the kingdom of Navarre, which became part of what is today known as Spain.[1] Recognizing the unique aspects of Basque identity, the Catholic monarchies in France and Spain granted the Basques the *fueros* (statutory rights) designed to protect local culture and preserve political autonomy. But these rights came under attack in the Carlist Wars in Spain (1832–1839, 1872–1879) in which Basques played a prominent role fighting to preserve their special status. The defeat by the central government in Madrid led to the state regimes abolishing the *fueros* in 1876, ending the special status of the Basques.[2]

The erosion of these traditional Basque privileges and the perception that Basque identity and culture were being undermined contributed to the growth of Basque nationalism in the mid- to late 1800s, culminating in the founding in 1895 by Sabino Arana of the Basque Nationalist Party (PNV—Partido Nacionalista Vasco) to guarantee Basque rights and liberties.

SABINO ARANA: FATHER OF BASQUE NATIONALISM

My patriotism is not founded on human reasons, nor is it guided by material aims: my patriotism was founded and is every day further founded in my love for God, and for which purpose I pursue to lead my brethren to God: my great family the Basque people.

—Sabino Arana[3]

Sabino Arana is considered the father of Basque nationalism. He was born on January 26, 1865, in Abando, which in 1890 was annexed to the city of Bilbao. Raised in a Carlist family of Catholic faith, Arana developed a strong sentiment for Basque nationalism based on the elements of race, language, religion, Basque traditional customs, and sovereignty.[4]

At the age of 12, he was required to register and become part of the first generation of Basques to serve obligatory military service outside the Basque Country since the abolition of the *fueros*.[5] Influenced by the Basque nationalist views of his brother Luis, Arana decided at the age of 17 to dedicate himself to the study and preservation of the Basque people, their history, their language, and their rights.[6] Influenced by the Basque historical context, Arana published, from 1886 to 1893, several works of linguistic, historic and literary character. The publication of his work titled *Bizkaya por su Independencia* (Bizkaya for its Independence) in 1892 served to launch the Basque nationalist movement. His inflammatory rhetoric sought to purify the Basque race, an "ethnic cleansing" of Spanish contamination. His articles in the newspaper *Bizkaitarra* (1893–1895) and later in the *Baserritarra* (1897) focused on the uniqueness of the Basque identity and called for political and social actions against the Spanish state and Spaniards. On July 31, 1895, the Basque Nationalist Party was officially founded to guarantee Basque rights and liberties, transforming Basque nationalism into a political entity. In the words of Arana, the aim of PNV was to teach Bizkainos "*the history of their motherland*" and to awaken his compatriots "*who disgracefully ignored the language of their race.*"[7]

The Basques are indeed one of the few remaining truly distinct ethnic groups. Comparative linguists have been unable to determine a connection between the Basque language, Euskera, and any other language; rather guttural, it is quite distinct from the liquid Spanish tongue. Nor have physical anthropologists been able to relate the unique physical characteristics of the Basques to any other ethnic groups. In his writings in the *Bizkaitarra* newspaper, Arana emphasized these differences, idealizing the Basques and contemptuously denigrating the Spanish. A few noteworthy examples:

> The Biscayan walks confidently and in a manly fashion; the Spaniard does not know how to walk, or if he does, he is of feminine type.[8]
>
> The Biscayan is enterprising, . . . the Spaniard undertakes nothing, dares to do nothing, is utterly useless (examine the state of its colonies). The Biscayan is not worthy to serve, he has been born to be a gentleman; the Spaniard has not been born for more but to be a vassal and servant.[9]

A great number of them [Spaniards] seem to be undeniable testimony of Darwin's theory, since rather than men they resemble apes, rather less beastly than gorillas: do not search in their faces for the expression of human intelligence nor of any virtue; their eyes only reveal idiocy and brutishness.[10]

Arana emphasized the requirement for a separate Basque nation: "*There is perhaps no Biscayan of pure race that deep down does not sympathize with the separatist doctrine.*"[11]

Basque demands for autonomy increased after the collapse of the democratically elected Spanish Second Republic in the Spanish Civil War (1936–1939). The Basque response to the Franco civil war was by no means uniform. Demonstrating the heterogeneity within Basque society, in contrast to the northern provinces, the southern Basque provinces of Alava and Navarra supported the coup d'etat that brought Franco to power and were richly rewarded for doing so. The two northern Basque provinces, Gipuzkoa and Bizkaia, were singled out for having supported the republic in the hopes of having Basque claims for special status recognized; they were officially named "treacherous provinces" and subjected to repressive polices and martial law.[12] In retaliation, and in an attempt to create a homogeneous Spanish identity, the Franco regime prohibited the public use of the Basque vernacular language, forbade the christening of children with Euskera names, banned political parties throughout Spain, and infringed on the rights of freedom of association, assembly and expression.[13] This forcible attempt to totally eliminate Basque culture and identity had the opposite effect, galvanizing a heightened sense of Basque identity. This sentiment is apparent in the statement by Dodeca Salegi, the father of an ETA prisoner, who recalls Franco's repression of the Basque people: "*Franco made us nationalists by his persecution.*"[14] For the generation of Basques that grew up in the aftermath of the civil war, authorities labeled all things Basque as "traitorous" and acts of social transgression. This in turn revived Basque bitterness over the loss of their special status during the Carlist Wars of the nineteenth century, rekindling resentment toward the central authority in Madrid. A collective memory of repression became part of Basque social psychology. An era of both symbolic and physical violence against the Basque people by the central Spanish authority led to a culture of violence, the precondition for the formation of ETA.[15]

THE FOUNDING OF EUSKADI TA ASKATASUNA (ETA—BASQUE FATHERLAND AND LIBERTY)

ETA was founded on July 31, 1959, by a group of university students. Impatient with the lack of progress of the Basque Nationalist Party (PNV), which had a relatively moderate political approach, ETA's founders came from the party's youth wing, Eusko Gaztedi (EGI). They split off from the PNV to form ETA, seeking the unification and independence of the seven Basque provinces. Although ETA based itself on Sabino Arana's nationalist themes, its ideology, goals, and means differed on several levels. Based on Marxist principles, ETA rejected autonomy as an insufficient political goal and pledged itself to an armed resistance against Franco's dictatorship in order to establish an independent socialist state. For the most part, Basque nationalism and ETA initially were centered in towns and rural areas rather than in industrialized areas of the Basque region, so it can be argued that the movement was in part a consequence of modernization and secularism, the basis for ETA's later cloaking itself in Marxist-Leninist socialist ideology.[16]

MOTIVATIONS FOR JOINING

Noted Spanish terrorism expert Fernando Reinares found that the overwhelming majority (9 out of 10) of ETA members have been male, although more women have joined the organization in recent years. The following quotations, from interviews conducted by Reinares, exemplify the reasons and motivations why individuals joined ETA.[17]

A former ETA member who joined in the mid-1970s at the age of 16 emphasizes the romantic allure of joining for an adolescent Basque male:

> *Man, we all had this conspiratorial mindset, you know? This way of thinking that if we really hit them right where it hurts, or if we got a lucky break, well, we could change history. You know, this thing about believing that we could help bring a whole new world into existence overnight. It's one of those exciting things . . . there was a real over the top romanticism. But it's also this . . . really exciting thing, a really awesome feeling, that's for sure. And I couldn't help but being attracted to it. All the other stuff . . . whatever you think of it. There's also this sense of adventurous spirit, something of that sort is absolutely fundamental.*[18]

While men are lured to ETA for ideological reasons, women seem to join the organization based on social relations with other ETA members. The following accounts provide insight as to how sentimental relationships were the primary social factors for the recruitment of women into the terrorist organization. The casualness with which they became associated with this violent group is remarkable:

> *They just suggested it to me. There was this guy I was going out with. He joined and I did, too.*[19]

I went to the other side, well, because he went over. And I was out of work just then, and anyway, I wasn't feeling too good about myself in a lot of ways and I sort of said to myself: right now I haven't got too much going for me here so I might as well see what happens there, do your see? So I went to live with him.[20]

The next quotation is from a middle-class Vizcayan man, recruited into ETA in the early 1980s, at the age of 27. Referring to two infamous women members of ETA, *etarras*, he provides his observation of the disadvantages female militants face within the terrorist organization:

Women have always come into ETA under a disadvantage, with this slight handicap. They've always got to prove something. They themselves were the first ones to tell me so. Take . . . the one they call The Tigress. She used to say that a woman in ETA has to show twice as many balls as a man just to be accepted as a militant. And I'd say to her, don't worry, you just do your job and you'll be recognized for it. And in the case of [another female member], you heard the same thing from her, that they have got to show everyone they were twice as good as the next guy.[21]

Reinares has found that the majority of ETA members are single. Not being distracted by family responsibilities when actively involved in the terrorist organization aids in maintaining clandestine activity.

My love life in ETA before I got sent to jail was nonexistent. I suffered a lot emotionally because . . . well, I couldn't even think about. . . . I couldn't make any plans for having a family or a girlfriend, because they might get me from one day to the next. . . . It didn't look good to me having some of the comrades living a family life. I saw the family as an obstacle to ETA's struggle . . . within ETA, at least.[22]

According to the interview study conducted by Reinares, joining ETA is a viable alternative for many radical juveniles. In the next statement, an ETA member who joined the terrorist organization in the late 1980s, at the age of 19, explains the alternatives available to young individuals and his reasons for becoming a terrorist:

Young people . . . I mean those who went to school with me or who looked like they'd be going on to university . . . I guess they would have had their political ideas, just like anybody else. But in any rate, they pretty much kept them to themselves, they didn't go out of their way to get involved in things. Then you had the ones like me who had been working since they were 16. And then there were those who didn't want to finish their studies, only they didn't want to go out and get a job, either. So then, it was like this automatic thing. If you didn't get involved in something political, you turned into a druggie. It was as simple as that.[23]

This is reminiscent of the findings of Franco Ferracuti concerning Italian youth.[24] In terms of family background, Ferracuti was unable to distinguish among those who became political activists, those who became terrorists, those who joined a youth gang, and those who entered the drug culture. The main determinant was who one's friends were.

Robert Clark has made a provocative observation of the first generation of ETA members. Some 8 percent of marriages in the Basque region are inter-marriages, with children of these Basque-Spanish marriages looked on with contempt, seen as "half-breeds." After analyzing the origins of members of ETA by their names, Clark concluded that upward of 40 percent came from mixed Spanish-Basque marriages. It was as if they were trying to "out-Basque the Basques" to demonstrate their psychosocial authenticity.[25]

USE OF VIOLENCE

What began as a political movement evolved into an armed struggle in the 1960s. There were numerous assassinations during the late 1960s and early 1970s, but ETA's most spectacular success was the assassination with a car bomb, on December 20, 1973, of Admiral Luis Carerro Blanco, Spain's prime minister and the man who was widely expected to succeed Franco. Franco retaliated by executing two Basque political prisoners.

ETA's campaign of terror continued throughout the next decades, but with the Spanish political system's transition from an authoritarian regime to democracy, the terrorist organization *escalated* its violent attacks! Although the new constitution of 1978 had granted greater autonomy and political and economic power to Basque institutions, ETA refused to compromise its goal of establishing a socialist and independent Basque state. The significant autonomy granted in the late 1970s did not suffice for the radical faction that was absolutist in its insistence on independence; this is reminiscent of the Real IRA continuing the struggle and splitting off from the mainstream IRA, after its political wing, Sinn Fein, negotiated the Good Friday Agreement.

In a 1973 interview, two ETA leaders in their mid-20s expressed the following: *"We want a Basque country that is free, united and socialist."*[26] *"We will not lay down arms until we achieve it."*[27]

Of the more than 600 deaths attributable to ETA between 1968 and 1991, fully 93 percent occurred after Franco's death in November 1975, when recognition of Basque rights was at last occurring.[28] What is the basis for this apparent paradox? After all, if the suppression and attempted elimination of Basque rights was the basis for ETA violence, should not the beginnings of achieving those rights have led to a diminution of violence? Perhaps this increase in violence is a reflection of the brutality of the authoritarian control exerted by Franco. And after Franco, what was previously perceived to be impossible became possible. Or, as terrorism scholar Peter Merkl whimsically asks, "Are members of terrorist organizations, once assembled, like the sorcerer's apprentice, who, unwilling to be dismissed when the job is done, continues the violence?"[29] Rather, I would suggest that when an alienated, isolated individual has joined a group and has had the pulsating excitement of taking action for the group's cause, to succeed in accomplishing the cause may be threatening, for that would mean losing one's connection with the very group that made one feel alive and vital. Perhaps this explains why the nationalist-separatist causes are so persistent, the groups so absolutist in their dedication. In effect, being a fighter for the cause becomes more important than the cause itself; to achieve the cause would mean returning to the assembly line, losing what was perhaps the most exciting role one has pursued. Recall the Fatah terrorist who, when asked about the violence, explained: *"I regarded armed actions to be essential, it is the very basis of my organization and I am sure that was the case in the other Palestinian organizations. The aim was to cause as much carnage as possible. The main thing was the amount of blood. **An armed action proclaims that I am here, I exist, I am strong, I am in control, I am in the field, I am on the map.**"*[30]

Thus the cause is *not* the cause; the cause rather is the rationale, the body of ideas associated with recruitment. Once in the group, it is belonging to a group larger than oneself, dedicating oneself to that cause, that becomes the raison d'etre. This persistence despite many of the goals having been fulfilled is a pattern that has been seen in other terrorist groups. It suggests that being a fighter for the idealized absolute cause—in this case independence, total separatism—has become more important than accomplishing the goal of autonomy. It is not easy to return to a mundane job when one has been in the adrenaline-charged heroic environment of the group fighting for a noble cause.

As successive antiterrorist campaigns weakened the group's infrastructure, extremists tended to resort to an escalation of violence and terrorism to demonstrate that ETA was still alive. For example, a January 2005 letter from the leader of ETA's military front, Garikoitz Azpiazu Rubina, alias Txeroki, criticized two ETA militants for failing to carry out terrorist attacks that would be of *"great importance. Especially when the enemy is repeatedly rejoicing in the organization's weakness and when our people's confidence is in crisis."*[31] In the next letter, Txeroki called for violent action: *"I understand what you* [plural] *are saying to me and that because of it you haven't carried out any* ekintzas [Basque for "actions"], *but even though the atmosphere is "tense" THERE IS NOTHING and we have to put bodies on the table as soon as possible. . . . You'll have to bump off a uniformed enemy (it doesn't matter what uniform or where)."*[32] Again, it is violence that gives the group authenticity and wins it headlines.

GENERATIONAL CHANGES

Many former ETA members have been extremely critical of the increasing number of young recruits who engage in political violence without understanding the essence of Basque nationalism and the founding objectives of ETA's struggle:

> *They never had to live under repression; they never had to go through repression. It's these characters who have swallowed what they read in three or four books and heard in three or four speeches, and the ideas they've had poured into their heads through a funnel and that's it, as far as they're concerned. What I mean is they're full of Marx and Lenin. They haven't got the slightest idea of . . . what the Basque roots are and what this struggle is all about. They haven't got the slightest idea, none. They weren't living under Franco and they haven't lived through anything . . . they just aren't nationalists.*[33]
>
> *In those days, the underpinning of our movement was above all nationalistic. However, this has changed. . . . It used to be that a militant was a militant because he knew why he was a militant and knew what he was fighting for. Now this has trailed off into something that is borderline criminal, borderline social misfit. . . . But for a militant like us, above all nationalist, well, . . . nobody has to tell me which one is and where is my homeland. I already know it, and that I should love my homeland. I already know that. And either I love it or I don't love it, but at least I know all that.*[34]

DISILLUSIONMENT AND COUNTERTERRORISM TACTICS

Not all ETA militants and activists remain loyal and active supporters of the armed national-separatist movement. Well over 100 ETA militants have dissociated themselves from the group, participating in reinsertion programs (that is, reentering mainstream society and leaving ETA), or accepting individual pardons offered by the Spanish authorities.[35] ETA's first military chief, Xabier Zumalde, alias The Goat, was a candidate for punishment by ETA due to his public criticism of the terrorist organization in an exhibit in Museo del Terror. Zumalde does not deny being an ETA member, but he denies being a terrorist.

"I am an ETA member. I agreed with the armed struggle against the dictatorship [under Francisco Franco] and I fought. Later, when the ballot boxes opened, I thought that the weapons had to be buried." Zumalde is also quoted saying that he was *"disillusioned"* with the current ETA. *"I am still a patriot, but I do not destroy, but rather build."*[36]

ETA's political leader from 1989 until 1992 was José Luis Alvarez Santacristina, alias Txelis. After his arrest in 1992, Alvarez Santacristina wrote a six-page letter in Euskera, stressing that *"the message from the Basque people is clear: they want to see no more blood."* He called on ETA to engage in *"civil resistance or active unarmed resistance,"* as *"our people are loudly calling for an end to the armed conflict."*[37]

After the arrest of many of ETA's leaders in 1992,* Mikel "Antza" Albizu Ariarte, a member of the Executive Committee, assumed the leadership of Herri Batasuna, ETA's political wing, until he too was arrested in 2002. Under his leadership, ETA sustained one of the longer-lasting cease-fire agreements with the Spanish government, between September 1998 and November 1999. Despite both parties' attempts to achieve a peaceful solution to the conflict, the cease-fire agreement collapsed and ETA resumed its violent campaign.

In response, the Spanish government implemented antiterrorist policies in an attempt to limit the group's activities. Some of the government's actions included banning Herri Batasuna, increased police and military pressure, and diplomatic agreements with France to prevent safe haven for ETA members fleeing from the law.[38]

The political influence and operational effectiveness of the nationalist-separatist group has been weakened by the ban of its political party and the numerous arrests of its leaders and members beginning in the early 1980s. Splintering within ETA occurred, with rising sentiment within Euskadi against ETA violence becoming manifest in the late 1980s and early 1990s.[39] In light of international events and processes, civil society has become more assertive, more intolerant of terrorism and more sensitive to human right issues.[40] Basque nationalism has also evolved over time. The number of nationalists continuing to demand an independent Basque state seems to have diminished over the years; instead, most opt for greater autonomy and the right to determine their relationship to Spain and the European Union.[41]

---

* "Txelis," along with Francisco Mugica Garmendia, alias "Artapalo" (considered the leader of ETA) and Jose Maria Arregui Erostabe, alias "Fiti" (ETA's bomb expert), were arrested in the French town of Bidart in 1992.

In the mid-90s, because so many of their objectives had been gained, recruitment was falling, and within the Basque territories there was growing popular disapproval of ETA's terrorist activities; an increase in the number of mass demonstrations against ETA terrorism showed society's growing lack of tolerance for violence.

ENDING THE ARMED STRUGGLE

Justifying the struggle, but probably reflecting a debate within the leadership, on September 27, 2005, ETA delivered a communiqué in commemoration of the thirtieth anniversary of the *Gudari Eguna* (day of the Basque solider). In the communiqué, part of which was reproduced in the newspaper *Berria*, ETA says *"a real chance exists to bring about a truly democratic situation that will recognize the rights of the Basque Country"* while reminding supporters of ETA's commitment to the Basque people and the struggle: *"We have kept the flame of independence burning. Today, in the early years of the 21st century, if the Basque Country has an option of becoming a free country, it has been because we have kept up the struggle without ceasing."*[42]

ETA also offered these words of comfort and encouragement: *"The bitterness of struggle sometimes impedes our ability to perceive the true progress we have made. We have saved our people from the threat of imminent extinction, and we have brought them this far. . . . We have paid dearly for this, we continue to pay for it dearly, but we cannot deny that it is worth it to participate in this struggle, bitter yes, but also wonderful. Because the Basque Country deserves it!"*[43]

This statement set the stage six months later for the surprising ETA announcement of a permanent cease-fire to begin on March 24, 2006.

Issued in the Basque Country in March 2006:

ETA's Appeal

We issue an appeal to all players to act in a way that is both responsible and commensurate with the steps taken by ETA. . . . All of us players have to make a firm, responsible commitment aimed at building the democratic solution the Basque Country needs. This is the moment to take bold steps and far-reaching decisions, to move from words to deeds.

We call on the Spanish and French authorities to respond in a positive way to this new situation and to remove the obstacles or limitations in the way of the democratic process, by ceasing their repression and attitude of denial, and by displaying a willingness to resolve the conflict through negotiation.

We call out to the Basque public, and on the members of the Basque national-ist left in particular, to become fully involved in the process and to fight for our rights as a people.

ETA's Commitment

ETA's wish is that the process begun should be concluded satisfactorily and that a genuine democratic situation should be achieved in the Basque Country by overcoming the conflict that has been going on for many years, and by building peace based on justice. . . . The conflict can be resolved here and now. That is ETA's wish.

> *Long Live a Free Basque Country!*
> *Long Live a Socialist Basque Country!*
> *For independence and socialism!*[44]

The "permanent cessation of its armed activities" ended on December 30, 2006, when a powerful car bomb exploded at Spain's busiest airport, killing 2 and injuring 19. ETA claimed responsibility for the bombing but indicated that the aim had not been to kill and stated that the cease-fire would still be in effect. Not surprisingly, the Spanish government took this as a violation of the cease-fire, and the violent struggle continues.

Chapter 5

KURDISTAN WORKERS PARTY (PKK)

In this and the following chapter, we address two other nationalist-separatist terrorist groups, the Kurdistan Workers Party (PKK, Partiya Karkerên Kurdistan) and the Liberation Tigers of Tamil Eelam (LTTE). These groups differ from the IRA and ETA in that both had powerful charismatic leaders. So powerful was the hypnotic leadership of the charismatic leaders, Abdullah Ocalan of the PKK and Vellupillai Prabhakaran of the Tamil Tigers, that their followers would give their lives for the nationalist cause, which had the power of religious faith. Accordingly, both the PKK and the LTTE utilized suicide terrorism as a compelling tactic.

KURDISH IDENTICIDE

On the one hand, you say that the Kurds are as much owners of these lands as the Turks, that all their national and social rights will be recognized; on the other hand, even our name is denied. This is what led to the violence. We are surely the side that should be least responsible. We wanted our identity. We wanted our democracy. We wanted our culture. Can anybody live without culture? Can anybody live without democracy? What do you expect us to do after even our name has been denied?

—Abdullah Ocalan, founder of the PKK, in his 1998 cease-fire declaration[1]

The Kurdish population, numbering some 20 to 25 million, is the largest ethnic group without a nation. Issues concerning Kurdish identity are central to understanding the origins and development of the Kurdistan Workers Party and the rise of its charismatic leader. The so-called Kurdish question, concerned with Kurdish nationalism and the concept of self-determination among the Kurdish people, had long rankled within the region of Kurdistan. "Kurdistan" first appeared on maps in the eleventh century. One of the great Muslim leaders, Saladin, revered for his valor in repelling waves of crusaders in the twelfth century and preserving Jerusalem, was a Kurd, a fact that is often forgotten. For more than 400 years, Kurds within the Ottoman Empire enjoyed considerable autonomy in return for service in the military as well as payment of tribute.

This situation persisted until the end of World War I, when Kurdish nationalism was given new impetus following the fall of the Ottoman Empire and the founding of the Turkish Republic. After the empire's defeat in World War I, it accepted the 1920 Treaty of Sèvres, which provided for the dismantling of the empire and the formation of Arab nation-states along the lines of ethnic and cultural self-determination: British mandate states of Jordan and Iraq, the French mandate state of Syria, plus Armenia and the Turkish Republic. Although the prospect of a Kurdish state was established in the treaty, for complicated sociopolitical reasons—more than half of the Kurdish population lived in Turkey, mainly in the mountainous southeastern region, and the remaining balance split among Syria, Iran, and Iraq—a nation of Kurdistan was not formed.

Furthermore, after legitimating territorial integrity in the Lausanne Treaty of 1923, Mustafa Kemal (Ataturk), founder of the modern state of Turkey, spoke of a pluralistic nation of Turks and Kurds as equals, with a sentiment of brotherhood developing. But duplicity all too soon became apparent as Ataturk proceeded vigorously to establish the core ideology of the newborn state, through what later came to be called Kemalism: based on centralism, secularism, and nationalism, the goal was to create a homogeneous ethnic population of Turks and deny the existence of ethnic minorities in its territories. A decree based on the 1924 constitution banned all Kurdish schools, associations, publications, religious fraternities, and *madrassas* (religious schools).

After 1925, Turkey adopted a policy of uniformity, so that Turkish culture was the sole and exclusive culture of the new modern nation: "Whenever the Kurdish question was mentioned in Turkish state discourse, it was mentioned as an issue of political reaction, tribal resistance, or regional backwardness, but never an ethno-political question. In Turkish state discourse, the Kurdish resisters were not Kurds with an ethno-political cause, but simply Kurdish tribes, Kurdish bandits, Kurdish sheikhs . . . all the evils of Turkey's pre modern past. . . . The Kurdish movement represented the demand for traditional, religious, reactionary and irrational order of the past which had been abolished by the present—the present presenting progress and prosperity."[2]

In order to consolidate Turkish nationalism by creating a mono-ethnic nation, official history books were revised, asserting that all Turks originated from Central Asia and migrated to different parts of the world, spreading civilization. By 1936 Kurds were identified as a population of Turks, called "Mountain Turks." Rather than the equal partnership they had been promised, the Kurds were instead the object of a concerted policy of "identicide."

With the centralized control from Ankara, an increasingly authoritarian government restricted basic freedoms, social justice, and cultural diversity in the name of security. The Kurds clung to their tribal mores, and Kurdish unrest continued into the '30s. Every revolt during the period 1925 to 1938 was brutally suppressed, followed by massive deportations of Kurdish groups to resettle in the west. In contrast to the 1920s, when fully ninety percent of Kurds lived in the mountainous southeast, as a consequence of forced migration and economic hardships, by the 1990s, only fifty percent remained in the southeast. Moreover, economic neglect and lack of investment in the southeast continued to keep the Kurdish population there isolated and impoverished.

But this internal exile laid the foundations for a new wave of educated, urbanized and resentful Kurdish youth in the western region of Turkey and had the unintended effect of consolidating the ideal of Kurdishness, with Kurdistan as their homeland for these youth.

Just as Francisco Franco's attempt to consolidate a homogeneous Spanish identity and eliminate Basque cultural identity ultimately failed, so too Ataturk's drive to establish a homogeneous Turkish national identity by obliterating Kurdish identity and culture proved unsuccessful. Paradoxically it consolidated an intensification of Kurdish identity, another example of defensive identity strengthening when the primary identity is under assault. This attempt to suppress cultural differences in the service of consolidating Turkic identity is also reminiscent of Lenin's attempts to consolidate the identity of new Soviet man and inculcate loyalty to the new Soviet Union. In Lenin's judgment, this required, the suppression—indeed the destruction—of other loyalties, both nationalistic and religious. This ruthless attempt to stamp out what were viewed as competitive national and ethnic identities did not destroy them; rather, they went underground both in the Soviet Union and in Turkey.

The fires of nationalism were diminished during World War II, but the attempted obliteration of Kurdish identity was the foundation for a new wave of Kurdish nationalism in the 1950s, which intensified in the 1960s.

NEW WAVE OF KURDISH NATIONALISM

The Kurdish attention to culture was a response to a policy of forced systematic assimilation emanating from the Turkish center. Starting in the early 1960s, for example, Kurdish peasant children were sent to boarding schools in large villages in which Kurdish was forbidden.

—Chris Kutschera[3]

In the postwar era, in the 1950s, the central government's continuing denial of Kurdish cultural freedom in order to consolidate Turkish identity, with one culture in one nation, led to a resurgence of protests, now from a new generation of educated and urbanized Kurdish youth in the western region of Turkey. This was the postcolonial era, with widespread struggles for national liberation, often supported by the Soviet Union. Soon renewed Kurdish nationalism entered the political mainstream, in the form of Kurdish left-wing groups.

Reflecting the international wave of social-revolutionary groups in the late 1960s to early 1970s, both Turkish and Kurdish left-wing Marxist groups were vocal in their attacks on the central Turkish government. One such group was the Turkish Revolutionary Youth Federation (Dev Genc), through which Abdullah Ocalan entered the radical political scene, early becoming a powerful voice, and founding the Kurdistan Workers Party (PKK), from which base he would charismatically lead the struggle for Kurdish independence and recognition of Kurdish nationality and culture.

ABDULLAH OCALAN

Born around 1946, Abdullah Ocalan was the son of a Kurdish farmer and an ethnic Turkman mother, and one of seven children. At his 1999 trial, Ocalan described his background in a revealing manner, sharing his perceptions of his family and the Kurds traditions:

> My family was poor and had lost its tribal traditions, but it continued with strong feudal values. I studied in the Republic's elementary school, located in a different village, commuting barefoot. The villages surrounding us were half Turkish, half Kurdish. My family from my mother's side could be considered Turkman and was from a neighboring village. Turkish and Kurdish were spoken together. Relations between our villages were very friendly, as there was no national animosity at all. . . . At an early age, after a sizable disagreement with the family and with many tears and continuous sobbing, I left the village. In this, the share of reaction to family members who want to live

outside of a life of toil is great. . . . My conflicts with my mother were strong. My mother was an independent, headstrong woman. My rebellious side may have come from her. My father was helpless, bringing myself up independently became an important part of me.[4]

Revealing the duality of his nature, Ocalan observed that as a boy in his village, he was described by *"the villagers who knew me as someone who would not 'hurt a fly.' On the other hand, when they saw a snake, they would call me 'the snake-hunter.' I was also a hunter of birds. Roaming in the hills was a passion."*[5]

A number of points emerge from this self-portrait. That he considered his father weak, and both admired and resented his strong, dominating mother is notable. But the fact that his opposition was not to his family per se but to family feudal ties, to the constraints of the Kurdish tribal structure, is particularly important, for throughout his career as leader of the PKK, he targeted the traditional Kurdish feudal system mercilessly. His independent nature was not to yield but was to rebel against the constraints of Kurdish society. From its beginnings, the PKK sought to undo the tribal/feudal structure of traditional Kurdish society, and the majority of the PKK's victims were in fact Kurds. Ocalan's original revolutionary goal of eradicating the traditional tribal order proved too challenging however. Needing at least the neutrality of the feudal and tribal chieftains if not their support, he eventually reconciled with them, which led to a diminution of the PKK's original revolutionary zeal.

Ocalan hinted at positive religious influences in his life, quoting *"the imam in my village, who [said] if I kept on in the same way, one day I would fly like angels."*[6] Yet there was resentment of the constraints of religion as well, *"Until high school there were religious influences. This was a conservative defensive reaction to a modern society."*[7]

With an early strain toward independence, rebelling against both his family and the feudal Kurdish culture of his village, Ocalan was extremely receptive to the wave of social revolutionary movements that swept the globe in the 1960s and 1970s. He went off to Ankara to enter the university, where he was removed from his village yet estranged from the cosmopolitan society in which he found himself. With other alienated Kurdish students, he began to establish his new identity as a revolutionary. He studied political science and dedicated himself to the study of revolutionary thought. Although he did not complete the degree because of his growing involvement in student revolutionary activity, his exposure to revolutionary ideology had a lasting impact on him: *"In the seventies, I developed an interest in leftist ideology and became aware of my Kurdishness.... In time I dedicated myself completely to ideological work.*"[8]

At Ankara University, Ocalan found himself drawn to the growing number of student-based social and cultural organizations that drew attention to the economic hardships of southeastern Turkey and the cultural oppression inflicted on the Kurdish people. It was in these organizations that he found his new identity as an oppressed Kurd exploited by what he labeled the "colonial powers" of Turkey and the backward feudal nature of Kurdish tribal society. Reflecting on this issue, Ocalan observed, "*I did not create the Kurdish question. I found it in front of me in Ankara.*"[9]

Ocalan first joined Dev Genc (Revolutionary Youth), which was notorious for its violent activities.[10] Ocalan had also been a member of ADYOD (Ankara Association of Democratic Students of Higher Education) after the 1971 military coup when human rights violations were rampant. His involvement with these groups probably stemmed from his desire to belong to a group that was distinctive and opposed to the society from which he felt alienated. And it gave him the opportunity to dedicate himself to a higher cause and to achieve greatness as a leader. Early on he declared that what the Kurdish people needed was a Mustafa Kemal, clearly seeing himself as such a leader for the Kurdish independence movement, just as Ataturk was the embodiment of "Kemalism" and the strong Turkish state.[11]

The inability of the civil authorities to contain the youthful unrest that threatened the stability of the nation led to stringent measures, ultimately leading to the 1971 and 1980 series of military coups and repressive counterrevolutionary activities. These actions in turn heightened Ocalan's growing sense of Kurdish nationalism and solidified his relationship with the revolutionary cause. And it introduced him to the necessary role of violence to accomplish political goals, ultimately justifying for Ocalan the requirement for revolutionary violence to combat the oppressive forces of the Turkish state.

Following the 1971 military coup, Ocalan spent a few months in prison for his involvement in leftist groups. For many youthful adventurers swept up in the massive arrests, this prison experience led to a hardening, a consolidation, of revolutionary identity. The Kurdish groups that survived the military coups had been "socialized in a culture of conflict—infatuated with firearms but also influenced by the heavy-handedness of security forces against the expressions of Kurdishness."[12] The surviving groups' durability substantially reflected Kurdish traditional tribal culture, a conflictual society characterized by incessant infighting and armed conflict, the environment in which Ocalan had been socialized.[13]

The PKK

Ocalan, and several others, gave voice to the concept of a separate Kurdish state as best realizing their newfound nationalistic feelings. They founded the PKK on November 27, 1978, at Lice in southeast Turkey, adopting the philosophy that violence was necessary to achieve a just revolution against the oppressive state. The PKK began as an offshoot of a 20-man Marxist student group in Ankara called Revolutionaries of Kurdistan.

Forced to operate underground, Ocalan began to build a secure base at Lice, focusing on tribes that had not coexisted peacefully with the government. The leadership drafted a document "The Path of the Kurdish Revolution" which became their manifesto, arguing that *a radical revolution was needed to establish an independent Marxist-Leninist Kurdistan where the peasantry and proletariat could enjoy true independence.*[14]

In effect, Ocalan wed Marxist ideology with Kurdish nationalism by emphasizing the economic subordination of the Kurds, depicting it as a class struggle. Unlike earlier Kurdish movements that recruited among educated elite and intellectuals, the PKK recruited among lower-class Kurds, the peasants and tribes who formed the majority of the population of southeastern Turkey, where there is no industry and no working class. In addition to opposing the Turkish civilian and military leaders based in Ankara, the PKK opposed traditional Kurdish tribal leaders, accusing them of perpetuating the exploitation of the Kurds by "colonial powers." While the rhetoric is strikingly Marxist-Leninist revolutionary in nature, the cause is that of establishing a separate nation: Kurdistan. It should be noted that a number of the nationalist-separatist movements at this moment in history, including the IRA, the PLO, and ETA, had Marxist-Leninist revolutionary groups operating under their nationalist banner. Despite the Marxist-Leninist ideology of the organization, the main attraction for the new recruits was the appeal to Kurdish nationalism. In a 1993 speech, Ocalan himself stated that he was not a Communist or Marxist but believed in "democratic-socialism."[15] (This was, to be sure, after the implosion of the Soviet Union.)

The PKK program recognized that the geographical region called Kurdistan had been divided into four regions by four separate countries that Ocalan called "colonial powers": Turkey, Iran, Iraq, and Syria. The aim of the movement was to achieve freedom for the Kurdish people because they had been oppressed, were victims of colonialism, and were entitled to the right of self-determination. The goals then were not solely for a Kurdish state separate from Turkey, but more broadly for a Kurdistan incorporating Kurdish people from the four countries with significant Kurdish populations.

Turkish sociologist Dogu Ergil well describes the situation following a military coup in 1980 and an aggressive effort to crack down on revolutionary groups such as the PKK: "The PKK grew rapidly in size and popularity, thanks in part to the Turkish government's dismantling of rival democratic Kurdish organizations and its prohibition of all expressions of Kurdish identity. Trapped in a traditional society divided by tribalism and inequality, young Kurds found in the PKK an appealing and unifying cause. Young men and women saw the organization as a means to personal emancipation as much as a political movement."[16]

By escaping the coup d'etat of 1980 and relocating to Damascus, Syria, the PKK established itself as a powerful guerrilla force capable of challenging the Turkish state. From 1980 to 1984 it consolidated its organizational structure by recruiting and training guerrilla fighters, and establishing bases of operation, within Syria as well as in southeastern Turkey. Although the PKK had won little popular support by the early 1990s with its brutally violent actions, "[i]t gradually came to enjoy the grudging admiration of many Kurds, both for the prowess and recklessness of its guerrilla fighters and for the courage with which the arrested partisans stood up in court and in prison."[17]

Contributing to the support for the PKK was the continuing denial of Kurdish identity by the Turkish government. This policy, dating back to the 1930s, was exemplified by remarks in parliament in 1994 by the minister of the interior, Nahit Mentese: "I want to reiterate that we do not have an ethnic problem; we may have geographical problems, economic problems, but we categorically do not have an ethnic problem. In Turkey—I do not even want to pronounce it—there is no Kurdish issue."[18]

Ruthless, Controlling Leadership

During the early years of the PKK, Ocalan consolidated his role as the undisputed leader, creating his status as indispensable—the very personification and embodiment of the movement. He created a personality cult resembling that of Mao Zedong or Kim Il-Song. Seeming to model himself after Joseph Stalin and his show trials and ruthless purges of the late 1930s, Ocalan often used brutal methods to eliminate rivals, dissenters, and any threat to his power. Selahattin Celik, a PKK Central Committee member, commented on the extent of the violence: *"There were between 50 and 60 executions just after the 1986 elections. In the end there was no more room to bury them! Some of them were simple militants, Lebanese Kurds accused of being 'agents,' guilty of 'not implementing orders.' "*[19]

Compromise was not an arrow in Ocalan's leadership quiver. He insisted on his way as the only way, and those who disagreed with him were wrong. Not only were they in error, but they needed to be eliminated. Ocalan justified the manner in which he eliminated rivals. Despite *"comprehensive educational and organizational efforts against challengers or miscreants, the most deviated ones of them could only be neutralized by internal struggles."*[20]

Sensitive to potential threats to his authority, Ocalan acted to limit the possibility that anyone could oppose him. Few members of the PKK had university degrees, and those who did were posted outside of "Kurdistan" to Europe. Reflecting on the contrast between the personal emancipation she sought and the authoritarian control she experienced, a female member, who eventually became a military commander of 150 female PKK fighters, observed ruefully: *"I went to the mountains to liberate my country and for the independence of Kurdistan. [But] one man decides everything, nobody else can say what they think."*[21]

Even Ocalan's "loved ones" were not spared his wrath. Shortly before the 1986 PKK Congress that precipitated the violence just described, Ocalan's wife at the time, Kesire Yildirim, a member of the Central Committee, was arrested with two other committee members, Duran Kalkan and Selahattin Celik. In 1993, his brother Osman was removed from his position of authority on the Central Committee and arrested.[22]

It is ironic to observe that Ocalan's autocratic controlling leadership style closely resembled that of the tribal chieftains whose backwardness he decried and sought to escape.

Narcissistic Personality

At the core of Ocalan's leadership is an intensely narcissistic personality. He sees himself as the very model of behavior for all: *"Everyone should take note of the way I live, what I do and I don't do. The way I eat, the way I think, my orders and even my inactivity should be carefully studied. There will be lessons to be learned for several generations because Apo is a great teacher."*[23]

While this self-proclaimed greatness will strike many as arrogant, it has an appeal for the weak and threatened, translating into a strong confident leader on whom one can rely, the only true representative of the Kurdish people. Reflecting the same arrogance, Ocalan asserted, referring to the two principal Kurdish political leaders, *"Barzani and Talabani are like feet or arms, but I am the main head or mind."*[24]

Not surprisingly, in his view, successes of the organization were due to his leadership; any faults were due to history or to others.[25] *"These shortcomings were caused by faults in the Kurdish character: its individualism, its lack of foresight, its incapacity for collective action, its narrow-minded vision. So I want to transform this personality.*"[26]

The underlining insecurity and distrust of others regularly shines through in Ocalan's words, with the associated readiness to destroy any threats to his power. When things go wrong, the burden is (unfairly) upon him: "*In this revolution, I have felt the greatest amount of pain; all those faults of history, instead of being owned by others have fallen solely on my shoulders.*"[27] "*I establish a thousand relationships every day and destroy a thousand political, organizational, emotional and ideological relationships. No one is indispensable to me. Especially if there is anyone who eyes the chairmanship of the PKK, I will not hesitate to eradicate them. I will not hesitate in doing away with people.*"[28]

The narcissistic characteristic of over-optimism about his chances and devaluation of the adversary is a regular feature of his reflections. As the PKK suffered major reverses at the hands of the Turkish forces in the second half of the 1990s, Ocalan stated, "*The latest Turkish operations have been a disaster for them. Even though we are unable to obtain a militarily advantageous position, we are far from defeat.*"[29]

THE UNRAVELING OF THE PKK

Nevertheless, the Fifth Congress of the PKK, held January 8–27, 1995, marked the beginning of a new and massive restructuring of the organization and its policies in line with the changing world order. Beginning to distance itself from the notion of separatism, in the declaration emerging from the Congress, the PKK stated that the preferred approach to Kurdish issues was through a democratic solution within the existing borders of Turkey. At that same conference, PKK delegates voted to reject the concept of Soviet socialism and other dogmatic policies, emphasizing once again that it had to keep up with changes in world history. In accordance with these changes, the PKK Party Regulation program was also completely rewritten.

The Congress decisions included a major reference to the importance of political and diplomatic activities to be carried out alongside guerrilla warfare, emphasizing that armed struggle was only instrumental in the conflict, not a goal in itself. Diplomacy in this period was thus accepted as important as the Kurdish fight for freedom and self-determination.

Earlier in this conflict, the Turkish Security Forces were unprepared for the extent of the PKK's attacks and limited in their ability to combat the guerrilla fighters; however, from 1995 on, Turkish forces delivered major blows to the PKK in Turkey and in northern Iraq. Hundreds of PKK fighters were either killed or captured. The magnitude of the Turkish repression, including evacuation and punishment of local villagers, was so extreme that "the European Court of Human Rights . . . found Turkish security forces responsible for torturing, killing and 'disappearing' Kurdish villagers and burning them out of their homes."[30] But even after 1995, when the PKK started to absorb heavy losses from the Turkish security forces, Ocalan declared, *"Our guerillas are stronger than ever."*[31]

In December 1995, the PKK announced its second unilateral cease-fire. While it sought to reduce its violent activities, the PKK also began to consider for the first time the use of suicide bombings. By 1997 Turkey had dealt a major blow to the organization, effectively diminishing its ability to continue guerrilla warfare on the same scale it had a decade ago. Using Palestinian Hamas-style suicide bombings, the PKK organized suicide operations, waged mainly by women terrorists, in Tunceli, Adana, and Sivas in 1996 and 1999.

SUICIDE TERRORISM

Ocalan has publicly decried the practice of suicide terrorism, but given his unilateral control of the organization, there can be little question that he sponsored and directed the campaign. The suicide terrorism of militant Islamists has been explained in terms of the religious justification provided by radical religious clerics to their followers, including Islamic groups such as Hamas, Hezbollah, al-Qaeda, and the global Salafi jihad.

But as a secular leader, Ocalan was opposed to the traditional Muslim tribal leaders in Kurdistan. How then can we explain the number of suicide terrorist attacks by PKK members? The answer is to be found in the powerful charismatic leader-follower relationship between Ocalan and his followers. According to an audio transcript, before going to her death, 17-year-old Leyla Kaplan spoke of giving her body to the organization and its cause. She did not mention martyrdom. *"The organization and its cause have replaced the sanctity of religion."*[32]

For the dispirited Kurdish youth, there was no place else to go. Ocalan provided the elements of an expanded sense of self, a self that had been threatened by the Turkish campaign to eliminate Kurdish identity. A former member of the PKK stated, *"Many people stay in the organization because they have no alternative, they have nothing else to believe in."*[33]

Their primary identity was as members of the one group, the PKK, that was fighting to preserve their Kurdish identity, which was under threat. It was a cause of almost religious importance. Ocalan had a godlike stature for them, and their individuality was subsumed by their collective identity. Just as teenage followers of Ayatollah Khomeini would march unarmed into battle in human wave attacks, promised that their martyrdom would ensure their ascension to paradise, and the force of his leader personality quelled any doubts, so too, when Ocalan declared that an action would serve the cause of Kurdish nationalism, his followers uncritically accepted his words.

TERMINAL ODYSSEY: THE MAN WITHOUT A COUNTRY

By 1998 the PKK had suffered severe setbacks. The group was losing ground on the battlefield and through political and diplomatic channels. Ocalan began making frequent public statements on a Kurdish broadcasting station based in London, MED-TV, pleading with European powers to intervene in the conflict between the PKK and Turkey. As long as Ocalan had safe haven at his headquarters in Damascus, the conflict could continue indefinitely. In October 1998, as Turkey threatened military intervention and pressure on the Syrian government mounted, PKK bases in Syria were closed down and Ocalan was forced to leave the country.

After fleeing Syria, Ocalan embarked on a journey taking him to Greece, Russia, Italy, Belarus, Corfu, and finally Nairobi in search of political asylum. Fearful of the political consequences, no nation allowed him to remain. His arrest in Rome in November 1998 by Italian authorities, under pressure from Turkey, led to massive protests across Kurdish communities, especially in Europe, demanding his release and then that his life be spared. Hunger strikes, self-immolation, and instances of rioting in European cities filled the news. Turkey demanded that Italy extradite him, but Italy refused since Turkey still had the death penalty at the time. Ocalan in turn asked for political asylum.

In December 1998, the imprisoned Ocalan declared on Med-TV: "*I categorically reject self immolation. . . . If there is anything to burn it is not our sacred lives but individuals and institutions. . . [but] there will be hundreds of explosions. Turkey has to know this. . . . Now, I can hardly stop them . . . it is not my responsibility to do so anyway.*"[34] Having already refused to extradite him, concerned about the scale of the protests and the political consequences of retaining this explosive personality in their country, Italy refused Ocalan's asylum request as well and expelled him in January 1999.

ARREST, TRIAL, AND LIFE IMPRISONMENT

Ocalan eventually sought political asylum in the Greek embassy in Nairobi. Discovered there by U.S. intelligence on February 16, 1999, Ocalan was captured by Turkish intelligence agents and taken back to Turkey.

The immediate reaction to Ocalan's arrest was shock and intensified resolve and a call to preserve their beloved leader's life. In the words of the European spokeswoman for the PKK: *"He is the leader of a nation, not only the leader of the PKK. He is still a very important figure. But this by no means is the end of the struggle. The struggle will continue, because the Kurdish question remains. It is completely impossible that the Kurdish people will surrender. . . . The Kurds are prepared to continue the armed struggle."*[35]

Ocalan had created an image not solely as a heroic commander of Kurdish soldiers, but as a caretaker for the Kurdish people, referring to himself as "Apo" a nickname for Abdullah, which has an affectionate connotation, *"The name of Apo has been identified with the Kurdish people who have risen and are fighting for independence."*[36]

The following statement from Nizamettin Tas, member of the PKK Central Committee and General Command of the People's Liberation Army of Kurdistan (ARGK), was broadcast on MED-TV on February 16, 1999:

> *Chairman Apo is presently in the hands of the fascist Turkish state, a criminal state which knows no laws. The life of chairman Apo is in great danger. The Turkish state has been waging a genocidal war against the Kurdish people for years. It is unlikely that Turkey will allow the leading figure of the Kurdish people to remain alive. Europe played a role in the fact that chairman Apo is now in the hands of the Turkish state. . . . At the moment, the most important task is to protect the life of our chairman Apo. All forces of resistance must join in this, the struggle must be waged on this basis.*
>
> *We know that our people are extremely angry at the moment, but we call on them . . . not to act with rage, but in a manner which makes a lasting struggle possible. . . .*
>
> *The PKK has grown to millions through chairman Apo. It is an undying spirit which will never surrender to the enemy. The PKK has proven this in the past. We must now show this living spirit, determined for victory, by means of our struggle. Each one of us must become an Apo, and in this spirit of Apo we must explode in the brain of the enemy.*[37]

The PKK demanded Ocalan's release and initiated a second campaign of suicide terror in March 1999. After a brief trial, on June 29, 1999 Ocalan was sentenced to life imprisonment on Imrali Island. (While there was sentiment for the death penalty, in order to meet European Union conditions for membership, by then Turkey had annulled the death penalty.)

Even from prison, Ocalan persisted in his ruthless absolutist leadership. Mizgin Sen, the European spokeswoman for the PKK, became the first woman to publicly voice her disapproval and loss of faith in Ocalan as her reasons for resigning from the party in May 2004. On May 19, 2004, Ocalan reportedly gave a strict order insisting that high officials who run away from the party commit suicide. Sen disappeared shortly thereafter.[38]

Believing that without Ocalan's leadership the PKK was finished, in 2004 the Turkish government declared victory. Rather than enact polices to respond to Kurdish grievances, they sat on their laurels, which led some hard-line Kurdish leaders to conclude that without violence, there would be no redressing of their long-standing issues and, albeit in a weakened form, the struggle would continue. However, the loss of Ocalan's charismatic leadership struck a mortal blow to the PKK.

Still Charismatic for Some

But charismatic power does not easily yield to reality. Ocalan as a heroic figure and champion persists in the minds of many Kurds. An Iraqi Kurd, in his early 30s, who immigrated to London conveyed his disappointment and dismay when Jalal Talabani become the president of Iraq in 2005, indicating that he would have preferred Ocalan in the position to fervently champion the Kurdish struggle.[39]

After Ocalan's arrest in Kenya, a 14-year-old Kurdish girl living in England set herself on fire. She declared: *"Ocalan is very special to me. He has done a lot for the Kurdish people. If something happens to Ocalan, if anything happens to my leader, I will do it again, I will set fire to myself again."*[40] The heroic aura surrounding Ocalan helps explain how so many Kurdish youth, especially teenage girls, participated in suicide attacks, including the wave precipitated by his arrest.

A statement made by Ocalan on MED-TV in 1998 well captures his charismatic appeal: *"The faith and voice of millions is making my heart grow stronger every day. You millions of Kurds, I kept in my heart for many years. I tried to protect you against dangers. Actualize your own strength and unite!"*[41]

In response to a comment that he was a kind of Kurdish Jesus, Ocalan modestly stated: *"That might be. . . . Often I compare my deeds with those of the prophets. . . . I often liken my colleagues to Jesus' disciples. And tell them that they should emulate them. . . . They have no homes and families, own nothing for themselves, and believe they are living to serve mankind."*[42]

But Seen as Traitor by Others

The image of the totally committed heroic Ocalan was severely tarnished by remarks made during his trial: he apologized to the Turkish people and said he was responsible for their pain and loss, that the violent methods he and the PKK had employed were wrong, and offered his services to the Turkish state to democratize the regime.[43] He was seen as selling out—a traitor to his people. Three senior members of the PKK condemned Ocalan, whom they accused of having given up the historical goal of his party—the independence of Kurdistan—in order to save his life. One angry member, Nizamettin Tas, angrily denounced Ocalan: *"Abdullah Ocalan now says the Kurds are members of the Turkish nation. He openly claims he is a Kemalist, and that the Turkish state can rely on him,"* and another senior official bitterly complained, *"Ocalan, the man who used to call people 'traitor' has himself betrayed us."*[44]

That those who once uncritically revered Ocalan and accorded him godlike respect were now accusing him of treason reflects the fragility of charismatic appeal. Although leaders are idealized in charismatic leader-follower relationships, when their gloss is tarnished, the magnitude of the disillusion and the rapidity of the fall from grace can be precipitous, as it was for Ocalan.[45]

PERSISTENCE OF THE PKK AND THE KURDISH CAUSE

Almost a decade has passed since Abdullah Ocalan was arrested, tried, and imprisoned on Imrali Island for life. The charismatic leader has been isolated from the world, and his control and influence over the PKK and the Kurdish nationalist movement has been brought to an end—or so it was thought. However, in hindsight, Ocalan and the PKK were more than a militant group or a terrorist organization. They were and continue to be symbols of an ideal that struck a resonant chord throughout the region and animates the neglected and chagrined Kurds of Turkey, Iraq, Iran, and Syria. Ideals, unlike an organization, cannot be contained so easily. While the Kurdish people want peace and normalization of relationships, insofar as the Turkish state has not yet come to terms with the Kurdish people and their needs, the forces that originally gave rise to the PKK persist and the PKK pursues violence in the name of the Kurdish people. In recent years, government, business, and police targets have been the primary focus of these attacks, indicating that the PKK is willing and still capable of fighting for the Kurdish cause.[46] Currently, Turkish authorities estimate that the PKK still has 4,000 to 5,000 fighters in the mountainous borders of northern Iraq.

The fall of Saddam Hussein and the growth of the Kurdish Regional Government in Iraq have revived decades-old grievances against the Turkish government's neglect of Kurdish issues. Yearnings for a separate Kurdish nation in the region have been revived, and the PKK has been emboldened. Iraq has become a more stable staging ground for the PKK from which to launch attacks and escape with impunity.[47]

An important and highly symbolic event was the establishment of the Ocalan Culture Center in Baghdad in July 2006, 500 yards away from the Turkish embassy. The culture center has become a PKK contact bureau, to coordinate political activities, maintain international contacts with PKK members (and probably other interested Kurdish groups), and monitor the treatment of injured PKK fighters. Turkish officials fear and suspect that the center may also be used to facilitate terrorist activities in Turkey.[48]

The opening of the cultural center suggests a continuing and strengthening sentiment concerning Kurdish rights and autonomy within the region. Even more it signifies that Ocalan, despite his defeat, remains a symbol of the cause, a source of inspiration. He continues to be admired by the people who once addressed him as Apo. But because Ocalan managed to fuse his personality with the cause of Kurdish independence, and so dominated the movement, his capture and incarceration severely—some would say fatally—wounded the once-dominant Kurdish separatist organization he founded and led from its inception. But the implications of developments in Iraq for the Kurdish nation may portend a revival of the wounded and weakened PKK. Whether another figure like Ocalan will emerge that can summon the same passion for a movement that has haunted the Turkish Republic for nearly 20 years remains to be seen.

In many ways, Abdullah Ocalan served as a role model for a large community of rural Kurds troubled by their lack of economic opportunity, their government's negligence, and their own tribal society's obsolete traditions. He brought together elements of the Kurdish community, cutting across tribal lines and socioeconomic status through inspirational rhetoric, a promise of hope, and, most of all, ruthless aggression. This is what defined him as a leader, and these were necessary elements in the PKK's 15-year campaign of terror. The next few years will determine if beheading the organization will ultimately spell its demise.

CHAPTER 6

LIBERATION TIGERS OF TAMIL EELAM (LTTE)

Sri Lanka's historical past weaves an intricate web of religious and ethnic diversity. Its past, present, and future are represented by the symbols of its two competing peoples, the Sinhala (lion) and the Tamil (tiger). Unlike other conflicts deeply rooted in ancient historical claims, the ethnic tension between the Sinhalese majority and Tamil minority did not emerge until the nineteenth century.[1] Situated in the northern and eastern regions of the country of Ceylon, the Tamil people effectively governed themselves until the British arrival in 1833, with the Portuguese as the first colonizers in 1505 and the Dutch in 1658.[2] The British decision in 1818 to unite the nation of Ceylon under one administration and eliminate the separate nationalist entities is arguably one of the main factors that sparked the notion of a Tamil homeland, and the formation of the Liberation Tigers of Tamil Eelam (LTTE) movement over a century later. When Ceylon gained independence in 1948, the Sinhalese nationalist wave took root with an elected Sinhalese prime minister. Sinhala chauvinism set in with an officially instituted language, culture, and body of politics.[3] The dominance of the Sinhala majority over all aspects of civil life led in turn to an intensification of Tamil nationalism by the threatened Tamil minority, who made up less than 20 percent of the population. The Tamil base was loath to depart from the democratic system, but the state's failure to protect them inevitably pushed them defensively to the path of nationalism.[4] And this movement toward Tamil nationalism was given powerful voice by the founding leader of the LTTE, Vellupillai Prabhakaran.

VELLUPILLAI PRABHAKARAN
Profile of a Leader

If it [the peace process] were to fail, for whatever reason, the destiny of Sri Lanka with its 20 million people would still be in the hands of one man: Vellupillai Prabhakaran.[5]

M. R. Naryan Swamy, *Inside an Elusive Mind*

Without the consent of one shadowy man, there will never be peace in Sri Lanka. Vellupillai Prabhakaran, the leader of the Liberation Tigers of Tamil Eelam, is an enigma, surrounded by questions of legitimacy and shrouded by myths. Yet he is believed to be the sole dominant force in the ethnic conflict between the Sinhalese majority and the Tamil minority.

The "evolution of the ice cream loving small boy . . . to the most ruthless guerrilla leader in the world" began with a childhood surrounded by poverty, violence, and oppression.[6] Born in 1954 in the Jaffa Peninsula, Prabhakaran experienced early the Sinhalese subjugation and the discrimination and oppression felt by fellow Tamils. In one of the rare interviews given to journalists, in March 1986, Prabhakaran laid out his rationalization of the LTTE armed struggle, stemming from his early experiences as a witness to the Sinhalese atrocities: *"It is the plight of the Tamil people that compelled me to take up arms. I felt outraged at the inhuman atrocities perpetrated against an innocent people. The ruthless manner in which our people were murdered, massacred, maimed and the colossal damage done to their property made me realize that we are subjected to a calculated program of genocide. I felt that armed struggle is the only way to protect and liberate our people from a totalitarian Fascist State bent on destroying an entire race of people."*[7]

The poorly educated young man did not appear to have a good relationship with his *"very ordinary family,"* as Prabhakaran himself labeled it.[8] Instead, he was drawn from an early age into revolutionary politics.

The swelling thirst for freedom led me, when I was a fourteen year school boy and seven like minded youngsters in our school, to form a movement with no name. Our aim was to struggle for freedom and to attack the army. I was the leader of the movement. At the time the idea that dominated our minds was somehow to buy a weapon and to make a bomb.

This is how I spent my youth, filled with thoughts about struggle, freedom and the urge to do something for our people [who had] such a life of struggle; they should bear *witness to the deep scars born of this life of struggle and convey the various currents of emotion generated in the course of the struggle.[9]*

Prabhakaran was fascinated by power, admiring the commanding military leadership of Alexander the Great and Napoleon, as well as Indian leaders involved in the armed struggle for independence against the British.[10] He also reveled in comic books, especially the dynamic character of the Phantom, who "fought evil doers single-handedly."[11] His pursuit of violence began during his adolescent years, evident by his interest in martial arts as a teenager, brutal experiments on insects, and the transformation of his favorite hobby, kite flying, into a vicious pastime. "When he did not have a kite, he would catch a dragon-fly, tie a thin thread to it and see it fly."[12] The torture of animals and insects by children is one of the indicators of an emerging psychopathic personality, with a defect in conscience and scruples, what has been called "moral insanity."[13] The anger and frustration rooted in his childhood experiences formed the basis for his political activism and gave him the justification to embrace violence. Leaving home at age 19 never to return, he lost contact with his parents.[14] To Prabhakaran, the situation was very clear: major discrimination and the ultimate destruction of the Tamil people justified the act of armed struggle for rightful recognition of the Tamil homeland.

Formation of Tamil Nationalist Identity

Without representation in the larger political system, ethnic Tamils embraced revolutionary means and entered the political mainstream by creating numerous political groups. The Tamil uprising coalesced in the mid-1970s with the emergence of the Tamil United Front (TUF), which became the Tamil United Liberation Front (TULF), an organization favoring nonviolent civil advocacy, and the Tamil New Tigers (TNT), which Prabhakaran created and which, from the beginning, advocated violence in pursuit of Tamil liberation.[15] The TNT and other radical groups provided the foundation for a national separatist movement—proclaiming an independent, autonomous Tamil homeland and declaring the necessity of violence against government, security, and military officials. In the early days of the Tamil Tigers, Prabhakaran was especially enthralled by the model of Che Guevara, seeing "guerrilla action" as the key to mobilizing followers.[16]

Marxist-Leninist ideology strongly colored the revolutionary rhetoric of these groups, which regularly engaged in lengthy political indoctrination sessions. Following his capture in 1986, an LTTE guerilla described these sessions: *"The leaders always spoke about Marxism. They wanted a Marxist Eelam. That was their main idea."* Another captive observed: *"We were hoping to establish a Tamil socialist state in the north and east."*[17] The ideology of Marxist-Leninism admirably fit the political landscape of Sri Lanka (changed from Ceylon in 1972) and was utilized effectively by Prabhakaran but probably did not reflect his core ideas; in fact, he perceived it as tedious. Indeed, he considered ideology of little value, but nevertheless incorporated Marxist-Leninist rhetoric in the group discussions with new recruits.[18] In contrast, A. S. Balasingham, who became second in command in the LTTE hierarchy, was its leading theoretician. A decade older than Prabhakaran, Balasingham was a committed Marxist and is considered in many ways to be a mentor to Prabhakaran. His analysis of the conflict in Sri Lanka was couched in a Marxist framework.[19] For example, consider the following ideologically couched statement, reminiscent of the turgid prose in the Red Brigade's communiqués: *"The political objective of our movement is to advance the national struggle along with the class struggle, or rather, our fundamental objective is national emancipation and socialist transformation of our social formation. . . . Our total strategy integrates both nationalism and socialism into a revolutionary project aimed at liberating our people both from national oppression and from the exploitation of man by man."*[20]

The emphasis of the academic Balasingham, who died in December 2006, on Marxist rhetoric infuriated Prabhakaran, the man of action. Author and journalist M. R. Narayan Swamy cites a telling exchange, where after Balasingham declaimed on the requirement of first politicizing the people, the impatient Prabhakaran interrupted, *"We have to do some action first. People will follow us."* When Balasingham persisted, Prabhakaran contemptuously retorted, *"You [armchair] intellectuals are afraid of blood. No struggle takes place without killing. What do you want me to do? You people live in comfort and try to prove me wrong. So what should I do? Take cyanide and die?"*[21]

Just as the zeal of the Turkish government under Ataturk to establish a pure Turkic identity contributed to the rise of Kurdish nationalism, so too did the attempts of the Sinhalese government to marginalize the Tamil ethnic minority contribute to the formation of Tamil nationalistic fervor by consolidating the people's identity. Throughout the 1970s and into the early 1980s, violence and ethnic tension throughout the country led ethnic Tamils who had lived among the Sinhalese to migrate north and east. A strong sense of identity formed as the Tamil population became geographically concentrated in the north, increasing LTTE membership exponentially. This collective identity provided a need for a nationalistic leader to emerge and champion the movement for an independent Tamil homeland.

Charismatic Leadership at a Young Age

Arguably, Prabhakaran happened to be the *right* leader in the *right* place at the *right* time, connecting with the Tamil people and inspiring them to embrace the very struggle that had personally shaped his life. Only 18 years old when he created the TNT, later renamed the Liberation Tigers of Tamil Eelam, Prabhakaran had a powerful vision, clear foresight, and a charismatic leadership style. "*I wanted to achieve something through action rather than waste time in idle fancies,*" he said.[22] He emerged on the scene during a time of declining Tamil political ideals and a new generation of "*Tamil youth chafing under Sinhalese chauvinism and state repression.*"[23]

The murder of the Sinhalese mayor of the city of Jaffna in 1975—an assassination of which Prabhakaran, then 21, was quickly accused—inspired a slew of "hotheaded" youth to join Prabhakaran's cause.[24] This marked a key point in his early development as a leader, bringing Prabhakaran out from the shadows of the underground world to bask in the national limelight. Prabhakaran would go on to orchestrate the wave of assassinations and human bombs that killed many more government officials, policemen, and innocent civilians, including masterminding the plot to kill Indian Prime Minister Rajiv Gandhi in 1991.

Prabhakaran claimed that the LTTE killed only with a justified reason and in the fight for Tamil freedom. Not only did the assassination of Jaffna's mayor demonstrate Prabhakaran's view of the necessity of violence for an uprising, but it sent a powerful message to the LTTE that he was truly the undisputed leader of the group.[25] The assassination not only "established him as a cold-blooded man who could kill," but it brought to the attention of the Sri Lankan people the sobering realization of the deep-seated enmity and injustice felt by the Tamil people. "Until that day most Sri Lankans had thought that the sense of injustice felt by Tamils . . . was exaggerated"[26] and continued to believe that a political solution could be found for the ethnic tensions. This assassination and other acts of violence by the Tamil rebels led, in the late 1970s, to the passage of the Proscription of Liberation Tigers of Tamil Eelam and Other Similar Organizations and the Prevention of Terrorism Act. For the next 15 years Sri Lanka was, in effect, under a state of emergency.[27] But without redressing the disparate social status and legitimate grievances of the Tamil people, repressive security actions were doomed to fail, and in fact they produced further sectarian violence. Author Thomas Marks notes the parallel between the "population-as-enemy" philosophy of both the Sri Lankan and Israeli strategies, with an overreliance on concomitant harsh reprisals and the failure to achieve political solutions.[28]

Evading Capture

The early assassination of the Jaffna mayor shaped Prabhakaran's elusive character and signaled the beginning of a life of evasion from the many enemies he would make. Prabhakaran's multiple brushes with death and capture evoke the powerful image of an almost sacred, godlike figure shielded from danger, immortal. Accounts of his behaviors in hiding indicate a strong sense of paranoia. Seldom seen in public and constantly moving between hideouts with the strictest of secrecy, he is wary of his most trusted commanders, reportedly murdering those suspected of treason.[29] His so-called secret pistol group carries out the targeted assassinations of traitors and enemies.[30]

Throughout the 1980s, the "devilishly compelling figure" earned a cult-like status and a fanatical followership to go with it.[31] But his success as LTTE leader was not without failures. Internal differences emerged in 1980, as former TULF member Uma Maheshwaran rose up to compete for respect and power over leadership rights of the LTTE. When Prabhakaran requested "overriding powers in the group [he] was turned down. He did not hide his disgust."[32] This was a blow to his image, undermining his legitimacy as LTTE leader. With tears in his eyes, Prabhakaran stated: "*I have done so much for the movement, but no one recognizes it.*"[33] Instead he called it quits and then adamantly refused to change his mind, as if he were in control of the decision. Publicly insulted, Prabhakaran demonstrated an overwhelming sense of wounded pride deriving from his exaggerated self-importance. Instead of relinquishing some of his powers, he refused to compromise. This was reminiscent of Ocalan of the PKK, who would let no one else share the limelight of leadership. An intensely narcissistic man, Prabhakaran views compromising as futile unless it strengthens one's cause. This traumatic experience solidified his determination to secure a homeland for his people under his leadership, no matter what the cost.[34]

Forging a New Path for LTTE

Taking haven in southern India's Tamil Nadu region and working with Tamil Eelam Liberation Organization (TELO), Prabhakaran was able to move forward and rebuild the LTTE foundation, despite his fugitive status. He faced arrest in May 1982, with a bounty of 300,000 rupees on his head, and possible extradition back to Sri Lanka.[35] As Swamy has observed: "A man wanted for several murders and bank robberies would normally have faced the wrath of justice systems of both India and Sri Lanka. Prabhakaran, however, had a powerful combination of luck, local Tamil sympathies . . . and a seemingly obliging Indian government on his side."[36]

Three months later, with the help of P. Nedumaran, a senior politician in India, Prabhakaran was released on bail and ordered to stay in Tamil Nadu. While Prabhakaran denounced Tamil politicians, he had an intense respect for Nedumaran, and a close relationship developed. Nedumaran opened the young man's eyes to a network of contacts, which would inevitably help expand the LTTE army through financial support and procurement of weapons.[37]

Prabhakaran's time spent in Tamil Nadu, which would later serve as a foothold for the LTTE's cause outside Sri Lanka, marked a significant period in his leadership development. He is quoted as saying *"The years of struggle have strengthened my determination and sharpened my vision."*[38] As he became engrossed in Tamil literature, Indian history, and the lives of Che Guevara and Fidel Castro, his imagination ran wild as his dream for an independent Tamil homeland crystallized. *"How I wish . . . that I too would be able to see at least 100 LTTE armed members walk in a marching column one day,"* he said, referring to a march to the national anthem.[39] In 1982, eager to return home to his LTTE cadre and fight for the Tamil cause, Prabhakaran demonstrated his elusiveness once again, escaping from Tamil Nadu.

Gaining International Recognition

An 1983 LTTE ambush of an army patrol sparked a retaliatory anti-Tamil uprising by bloodthirsty Sinahelese gangs—*"the July Holocaust,"* as Prabhakaran called it.[40]

"A Norwegian woman tourist recalled with horror how a mob halted a mini bus in Colombo, splashed petrol over it and set it on fire. Even as its 20 odd Tamil occupants begged to be spared, the doors were pushed back into the burning vehicle. All the passengers were burnt to death, as screams and cries rent the air."[41] This violent event, which resulted in a massive emigration of Tamil people to Tamil Nadu, became the turning point for obtaining recognition from the international community.[42]

The Indian government's involvement in the ethnic conflict over the next few years yielded safe havens, weapons, and financial support for the Tamil fighters. By playing both sides of the fence, Prabhakaran convinced the Indian government that the LTTE was focused on targeting the local adversary in the ethnic conflict, not an outside party, such as India.[43] Yet Prabhakaran was strategically employing both sides as targets of LTTE attacks. The assassination of Prime Minister Indira Gandhi in 1984 by Sikh bodyguards in response to the

Indian siege against Sikh terrorists in the Sikh Golden Temple brought her son Rajiv Gandhi to power and a change in Indian policy toward the Tamil insurgents. Perhaps in reaction to his mother's death at the hands of terrorists, Rajiv made it clear to Tamil authorities that an autonomous Tamil state was not an acceptable solution, and India's previous covert support of the Tamil insurgency was significantly reduced.[44] The year 1987 brought a sweeping change in India's policy toward the conflict, with the signing of the Indo-Sri Lanka Peace Accord by the Sinhala president of Sri Lanka, J. R. Jayawardene, and Indian Prime Minister Rajiv Gandhi. The Tamil Tigers refused to honor the treaty as it failed to acknowledge Tamil independence and brought the Indian Peace Keeping Force (IPKF) into Tamil territory.[45] In the LTTE's view, India, an outside actor that had provided substantial support to LTTE independence, had now created major obstacles to achieving this goal. However, increasing demands by the Sri Lankan government ultimately forced the IPKF out in 1990. What remained in the minds of LTTE members was a collective redefinition of the Indian government, which not long before had supported the Tamil Tigers, as the external enemy.

Defining Moment for the Tamil Movement

The killing of former Indian Prime Minister Rajiv Gandhi by a female suicide bomber in 1991 marked the dramatic onset of the LTTE's violent terrorist tactics against India. This suicide bombing would be a defining moment for the Tamil movement—a compelling response to the 180-degree turn in India's support to the LTTE, justified previously by Gandhi himself, who had stated: "I know things did not work out the way they should have but the blame rests entirely on the LTTE and its leader. It would be delusional for the LTTE to think that they defeated the Indian army. If we wanted, we could have finished the whole business."[46]

Prabhakaran had converted the looming fear of an IPKF return into a threat to the Tamil cause, effectively providing justification for Rajiv Gandhi's murder. However, it was not until June 29, 2006—15 years after the assassination—that the LTTE admitted to the assassination, publicly apologizing for what it described as a *monumental historical tragedy*."[47] A major shift in policy, the LTTE confession was likely a last-ditch effort to interfere with the increasing Sri Lankan–Indian government relations, which, acting in unison, could severely damage the rebel Tamil Tigers.[48]

SINHALESE NATIONALISM: SETTING THE WAVE IN MOTION

A pattern of suicide bombings ensued over the next couple of years as LTTE projected its fears and insecurities back onto its original nemesis, the Sri Lankan government. A number of key political leaders were killed: the Sri Lankan defense minister in 1991, President Premadasa in 1993, and in 1999 President Kumaratunga was wounded in an assassination attempt at an election rally. LTTE has been involved in a substantial number of killings of government and military officials, which provides an overwhelming sense that the Tamil nationalist cause is born out of revenge for the wave of Sinhalese nationalism that emerged during Sri Lankan independence in 1948. One can attribute this historical animosity to the ruling Sinhalese family, the Bandaranalikes. The first Prime Minister, Solomon Bandaranalike, set in motion the wave of discrimination that led to the marginalization of the ethnic Tamil people. His family, which ruled for over 60 years in his footsteps, likely serves as the enemy in the eyes of the LTTE.

Escalation of Violence

Violence in Sri Lanka has continued and escalated in recent years. In rapid succession, explosion after explosion coordinated by LTTE rebels and subsequent offensives waged by the government have killed over 65,000 people. In 2002, peace negotiations, under the direction of Norwegian facilitators, temporarily halted the bloodshed.[49] With financial and human resources drying up, the climate was ripe for LTTE to convene at the negotiating table. Negotiations bought the LTTE time to reconstitute itself. Over the next year, three rounds of negotiations occurred concerning Tamil autonomous rule and self-determination; however, due to the LTTE's profound feelings of marginalization, the talks broke down in April 2003. Further damage to the already fragile peace process occurred with a resurgence of violence in July 2004, when a suicide bomber detonated a bomb in Colombo, the seat of Sri Lankan government. Ironically, relative calm came with the devastating tsunami in December 2004, which killed 30,000, but the assassination of the Sri Lankan foreign minister, Lakshman Kadirgamar—allegedly by the Tamil Tigers—only nine months later led to the unraveling of the cease-fire agreement, as waves of violence continue.

Leader-Follower Dynamics

Followers speak of Prabhakaran as a hero, and even go so far as to worship him as a god. Prabhakaran knows how to appeal to followers, and backed by strong nationalistic ties to the Tamil homeland, he is easily elevated to a heroic position. In a Newsweek interview in 1986, he spoke about the LTTE armed struggle and "genocide" that the Tamil people face, never once admitting to the brutality of his movement and killing of innocent civilians. His language is inspirational and visionary, capturing a sense of nationalistic pride that is quite appealing. In an interview earlier that year, Prabhakaran attributed his heroic stature to the choice made by the Tamil people: *"I cannot help this kind of projection and characterization. I am only concerned with the political liberation and social emancipation of oppressed people. My people are aware of my commitment and trust me to lead them on the right path. That is why they show great affection. These projections may be expressions of people's love."*[50]

There is certainly a powerful relationship between Prabhakaran and his followers, which those followers mark by taking an oath of loyalty to his every word. Evident also are sacred acts worshipping the godlike Prabhakaran, referring to him strictly as "Leader," because his true name *"inspires such awe,"* and the central role he plays in the lives of the LTTE, shown by the photograph of Prabhakaran displayed in a Tiger's home.[51]

As a young cadre declares: *"The Leader can do no wrong. I could fill a thousand books with all the wonderful memories of him,"* a high-ranking LTTE commander praises: *"They love him and adore him as mother, father, brother or god."*[52]

A Jaffna psychiatrist describes the sheer impact of Prabhakaran's divine presence: "Many of my patients regard Prabhakaran as higher than their own god." Flocks of LTTE would make "pilgrimages to Prabhakaran's former home in nearby Valveddithurai to fill little boxes of soil 'like a holy ritual, as though they are collecting water from the Ganges.'"[53]

A Catholic bishop in Jaffa observes that the LTTE are the sole source of inspiration for the demoralized Tamil people: "They are the Tamil people's only true champion. . . . No one else has had the courage to stand up for their freedom."[54]

A common thread of revenge weaves through a June 2006 interview with four Tamil Tigers fighters dressed in tiger-stripe camouflage. Each describes how they were motivated to join the LTTE cause.

MALE, 28, TIGER FOR EIGHT YEARS: *In the late '90s when I was in school, the Sri Lanka military bombed my village. An elderly woman lost both legs, one person died and two students were injured. I was angry with the [military] and joined the Tigers one year later.*

MALE, 34, TIGER FOR FOUR YEARS: *The army shelled the village Nedunkerni, which was next to mine. My family fled our village but we had to travel through Nedunkerni.*

And when we did, I saw the dead bodies scattered all over the ground. I was 17. I remember seeing four bodies, but they were too mutilated to tell whether they were men or women.

FEMALE, 28, TIGER FOR 11 YEARS: *I was nine and the Indian peacekeeping forces came to my village and started to round people up. Then they brought out a masked man who started identifying certain people who were removed from the others. Shortly after we heard gunshots and crying. Among those taken away were my aunt, who was nine months pregnant. Seventeen were killed altogether that night; 14 were related to me. The bodies were in the morgue the next day. It was said on the news that these people that had been killed were terrorists, so they were even denied a decent burial. We don't even know what happened to those bodies. I know they weren't terrorists.*

FEMALE, 28, TIGER FOR SEVEN YEARS: *The army bombarded Jaffna where I lived in 1995. Our house was destroyed and my family had to leave our home. I wasn't even able to finish school.*[55]

THE ELITE BLACK TIGER FORCES

The LTTE has a differentiated special operations capability, with attack units including the Sea Tigers, Air Tigers, Baby Brigade, Leopold Brigade (orphaned children), Freedom Birds (female unit), Internet Black Tigers (the first cyberterrorist group), and the most elite force of all, the Black Tigers. Known for its suicide squads and cultlike fanaticism, the Black Tigers could not be portrayed in a more noble and glorified light than during one of Prabhakaran's rare public speeches at the Black Tigers celebration day in July 1993:

> *I have groomed my weak brethren into a strong weapon called Black Tigers . . . [they] constitute the armor of self-defense for our ethnic group, and also serve to remove the barriers coming in the way of our struggle. They are the balls of fire smashing the military prowess of the enemy with sheer domination. The Black Tigers are different and are also unique human beings. They possess an iron will, yet their hearts are so very soft. They have deep human characteristics of perceiving the advancement of the interest of the people through their own annihilation. The Black Tigers have cast aside fear from its very roots. Death has surrendered to them. They keep eagerly waiting for the day they would die. They just don't bother about death. This is the era of Black Tigers. No force on earth today can suppress the fierce uprising of the Tamils who seek freedom.*[56]

Prabhakaran has instilled a profound sense of being freedom fighters in the Black Tigers; they believe in the struggle for Eelam and do not accept the terrorist label.

The use of the cyanide pill, worn as a symbol of pride by all Tamil Tigers, conveys divine allegiance to the Tamil movement. The cyanide pill was first introduced to Prabhakaran by a Tamil fighter named Sivakumaran, who, at a young age, instead of surrendering to the police, swallowed a cyanide pill, thereby avoiding interrogations. This experience left a stark impression on the young Prabhakaran of a genuine hero, one who rose up to evade capture.[57] Two Tigers comment on the pride with which they wear the cyanide pill:

> MALE, 28, TIGER FOR EIGHT YEARS: *That's what it's for. Not to be captured alive is a tradition of our movement. It's also a necessity at this period of time in our nation. Why? First, because information can't be given to the enemy. Second, we must not be humiliated in front of the enemy. Third, we don't want to be tortured. The past has taught us that. Everything we do is dedicated to the nation.*
>
> FEMALE, 28, TIGER FOR 11 YEARS: *In earlier fighting experiences we see our cadres' bodies; they are almost always mutilated. I've seen it with my own eyes. It's far better to die than be taken alive.*[58]

DISSENSION WITHIN THE GROUP

A highly controlling and authoritarian leader, Prabhakaran has established an infrastructure within LTTE that limits the emergence of potential competition within the group. "According to scores of accounts from defectors and others who have escaped Tiger tyranny, many of his own lieutenants have been murdered; Tamils who have criticized him, even mildly or in jest, have been picked up for years in dungeons, half starved, hauled out periodically for battering by their guards."[59] Prabhakaran's extreme sensitivity to criticism and his controlling leadership style reflect his narcissistic and authoritarian personality. Nevertheless, there has been some dissension within the group. A senior leader who did not automatically acquiesce to Prabhakaran's wishes and expressed contrary views was seen as a traitor. *"The most frustrating aspect has been the betrayal of some of my trusted friends."*[60] The most profound instance of this betrayal was the March 2004 armed revolt from within the ranks of LTTE by Vinayagamoorthy Muralitharan, former Prabhakaran bodyguard turned prominent LTTE commander of the Eastern Province. Under the nom de guerre Colonel Karuna, he led a revolt to create a separate nationalist Tamil party. According to the LTTE, long-standing differences between the two men erupted when Karuna refused to send additional troops to the north per Prabhakaran's order. Karuna's revolt appears to be in response to a series of leadership decisions discriminating against his forces and ordering unnecessary recruitment and deployment of more fighters during peacetime. In an interview on March 3, 2004, with the Associated Press, Karuna explained the reason for the split. "*In the past it did not seem a big issue. Now it's peace time, people and parents are trying to analyze why they have to give [up] soldiers during peace time.*"[61] Karuna felt personally discredited and his sense of legitimacy as a commander undermined.

Prior to Karuna's uprising, he addressed a letter to Prabhakaran "complaining of discrimination against LTTE cadres from the East by the leadership. . . . Pointing out 4,550 fighters . . . had so far sacrificed their lives in the struggle for Tamil Eelam . . . and 2,248 were serving in the North." Karuna appeared to be extremely piqued by the continued isolation of the Eastern Command and the careless, extravagant behaviors of leadership in other Tamil divisions. His struggle to choose between his devotion to Commander Prabhakaran and a strong moral conscience is clearly depicted in the letter: "*We do not want to desert you. We look to you as our god. Sometimes this decision of ours can anger you. The reason is that I do not like to commit the historical mistake of not disclosing to you the hopes of the people and the fighters here and not respecting their feelings. If you believe in the people here and the fighters here, allow us to work independently under your leadership.*"[62]

The March 2004 revolt was a major blow to Prabhakaran's legitimacy as a ruler, and subsequently the integrity of the LTTE. Not only did it damage Prabhakaran's leadership, but it also depleted LTTE's manpower. Of the 15,000 LTTE fighters, 6,000 joined Karuna's cause.[63] Breakaway factions of this nature could pose a serious threat to the LTTE movement as well as Prabhakaran's leadership.

EMBRACING SUICIDE TERRORISM

The notion of self-sacrifice, elevated above all other virtues, has a mesmeric, mystic hold over Tiger territory. Like Christian saints, famous suicide bombers and hunger strikers have their own days of remembrance. Tiger villages are often dominated by martyrs' graveyards with thousands of headstones, sometimes near purpose-built viewing halls where villagers can gaze at the bodies of dead battlefield heroes.[64]

Alex Perry, "Tiger Country"

Until 2003, the LTTE reigned as the most prolific group conducting suicide tactics. Between 1980 and 2000 the Tamil Tigers carried out 168 of 271 globally known suicide attacks.[65] While traditionally most suicide missions are religiously motivated—killing in the name of God—the secular nationalist goal of obtaining Eelam does not preclude the LTTE from martyrdom. Rather it demonstrates the absolute sacrifice of body and soul for Tamil Eelam and total devotion to the divine Prabhakaran, which in turn escalates the martyr's status in death. With Prabhakaran's godlike stature came the high-minded religious devotion of Tamil Tiger believers willing to carry out any mission, even self-sacrifice. This tactic became a major emblematic and terrifying component of LTTE's repertoire. Martyrs' deaths became memorialized on the LTTE calendar. A suicidal attack on July 5, 1987 using a "land torpedo" demolished the main Jaffna telecommunication center. The driver, Millah, won an honored place in LTTE lore, and this date is memorialized as the "Day of the Black Tiger."[66]

As Marks observes, the Sri Lankan military was all too aware of the power and efficacy of this tactic. In a prescient anonymous memo assessing "Troops/Terrorist Capabilities in the Jaffa Peninsula" sent in February 1986 by a "senior infantry major," it was opined that

> the terrorists will use a vehicle bomb which will be driven into a camp at high speed by a suicidal terrorist and set off in the middle of the camp. TO DESTROY THE ENTIRE ARMY, NAVY AND AIR FORCE IN THE OPERATINAL AREAS, THEY ONLY NEED 40 SUCH VOLUNTEERS. At the rate the Armed Forces are antagonizing the Tamil Public by their frequent atrocities, we are probably creating persons who will be willing to undertake such tasks.[67]

In February 1996 a suicide truck bomb destroyed the financial center of Colombo, killing 91 and wounding 1,400.[68] Recognizing the propaganda and recruitment value of these attacks, the LTTE filmed the suicide operations, including human wave attacks clearing minefields, a technique used with such great effectiveness by Khomeini in the Iran-Iraq war.[69]

The group's full embrace of martyrdom reflects the charismatic leader-follower relationship between Prabhakaran and his followers. The Black Tigers, before embarking on their honorable missions, were treated to dinner with the leader himself.[70] Female Tamil Tigers, who had conducted 30 to 40 percent of LTTE suicide missions in 2003, by nature are more attractive candidates for they can discreetly wear a suicide belt and penetrate farther through security perimeters without provoking suspicion. Like men, women are drawn to martyrdom for a sense of belonging and revenge against personal grievances, but for many, the path of martyrdom holds striking appeal. "According to Hindu faith, once a woman is raped she cannot get married nor have children. Fighting for Tamil freedom may be the only way for such a woman to redeem herself. This idea of sacrifice is ingrained in Tamil culture."[71]

RECRUITMENT OF CHILD SOLDIERS

In addition to embracing the phenomenon of suicide terrorism, the LTTE has mastered the use of child soldiers for combat operations. According to a February 2005 United Nations report, more than 4,700 children have been recruited into the ranks of LTTE since 2001.[72] A number of these children were seized by force while walking to school or taken from parents who were threatened if resisted; many were drawn to the glamour that embodied a Tamil Tiger fighter. As mentioned, the organization offers a sense of belonging and means to unleash revenge against perceived grievances festering in these young minds.[73]

An aspiring young doctor turned LTTE child soldier proudly tells her story of "*trad[ing] in her school uniform for the Tiger's striped fatigues and a cyanide capsule on a neck string.*" After having witnessed the bloodshed on her Tamil homeland at the hands of the Sri Lankan military for years, it was the traumatic experience at age 12 of seeing her neighbor's head blown off right in front of her eyes that led her down the path of revenge. She says, "*I remember the hatred building up in me. . . . I remember thinking, 'I should go and kill the person that did this.'* "[74]

At age 14, she joined the LTTE without her parents' consent. "*It was the happiest day of my life. The Tigers became my family.*" Rising to the challenge as a comrade lay dead, she grabbed his AK-56 and fired back, killing 15 soldiers in her first all-out fire exchange with enemy forces. "*In training, we use birds for target practice. . . . Soldiers are so much easier to hit.*"[75]

When asked in a 1985 interview about the young generation's commitment to Eelam, Prabhakaran responded: "*The incidents in Eelam show that an Eelam, a separate state, is the only solution. After facing so many genocidal attacks, the Tamils realize there is no solution other than Eelam for them if they are to live in peace and security.*"[76]

Like other nationalist-separatist groups, hatred has been "bred in the bone," and Prabhakaran has demonstrated an outstanding ability to draw in frustrated youth, hungry and restless for revenge, as he himself once was.[77] In a coldly calculated manner, a goal of some of his most extreme and bloody attacks is to promote overreaction against the Tamil population by military and civilians, which in turn will lead to increased recruitment of youth seeking revenge. A dramatic example occurred in 1985, when LTTE terrorists disguised as soldiers attacked first a bus station and then Buddhist pilgrims at a sacred shrine in Anaradapura. This in turn led to the goal of the operation, precipitating mob violence against Tamil civilians by enraged mobs of Sinhalese civilians.[78]

LONG ROAD TO PEACE

Despite Prabhakaran's loyal followership, the LTTE's erratic path—from peace talks to violence back to peace and then to brutal violence again—is discouraging support. As suicide attacks continue, each bombing damages the hope of reactivating the peace process any time soon. The frequent use of suicide bombers as well as the recruitment of child soldiers has caused a firestorm in the international community, which has branded LTTE as terrorists.[79] But Prabhakaran brushes aside this pejorative label: "*We are not terrorists. . . . We are not mentally demented to commit blind acts of violence impelled by racist and religious fanaticism. . . . Misguided by the false malicious propaganda of the Sri Lankan state, some of the world governments have included our liberation movement in their list of international terrorist organizations.*"[80]

While LTTE support has been marginalized in recent years, its brutal yet powerful tactics command an audience in Sri Lanka, and it is a main player at the peace table. The LTTE has approached the negotiating table asserting that Tamil self-determination already exists, thereby disagreeing fundamentally with the international vision for a peace negotiation to settle the ethnic conflict. In Prabhakaran's view, the liberation of the Tamil people and autonomous rule can be won only by violent struggle: "*our history shows that nothing can be solved through talks. . . . There should be peace as a prelude to talks [with the Sri Lankan government]. Every day they are killing us.*"[81]

THE POWER OF ONE CHARISMATIC LEADER

Prabhakaran, the "plump, baby-faced, small-time smuggler turned guerrilla," maintains mesmerizing power over an estimated 10,000 fighters demanding Tamil independence; he essentially holds hostage the entire nation's future.[82] With the power to manipulate and the masses waiting to be empowered, Prabhakaran has even convinced the adversary—the Sinhalese government—that he is the one who must provide consent in order for there to be peace in Sri Lanka.[83] "After nearly three decades, Sri Lanka had no alternative but to talk to the man [in order to] end a civil war that has claimed several thousands of lives, left many more homeless and as refugees around the world, and virtually torn apart the country's economy and social fabric."[84]

Amid the backdrop of peace negotiations is the reality of an ongoing bloody, violent ethnic conflict with over 65,000 killed on both sides since it began in 1983.[85] As long as the LTTE continues to recruit and train young soldiers and buy arms and weapon caches under the negotiating tables, peace will remain as elusive as Prabhakaran himself. He is the only one who can embrace the path toward a greater Sri Lankan peace, but he is too far down the path toward an independent Tamil homeland.[86] Prabhakaran and his followers have created a powerful collective identity that rests singularly on the leadership of Prabhakaran. It may be that the force of the movement will be diminished only when the leader is killed or captured, as happened with Ocalan of the Kurdish separatist group the PKK. There have been rifts within the LTTE's organizational structure, such as the rebellion led by Karuna in the eastern provinces in March 2004, and supporting dissenters can continue to weaken the internal cohesion of the group. But given the godlike status of this accomplished guerrilla leader, reducing his powerful charismatic grip on the LTTE will not be an easy task.

SOCIAL REVOLUTIONARY TERRORISM: REBELLING AGAINST THE GENERATION OF THEIR PARENTS[1]

The nationalist-separatist terrorists of the 1960s–1970s often employed Marxist-Leninist rhetoric, for it admirably fit their economically disadvantaged minority status. But their primary goal was to establish a separate state and obtain social and economic justice. The ideological trappings were thin. In contrast, the social revolutionary terrorism of that period emerged from the so-called New Left. The core issues, now cloaked in Marxist-Leninist rhetoric, were not new, but were stimulated anew in the rapidly expanding industrial era, in which economic disparities were magnified. Youth, always idealistic, sought social justice. Frantz Fanon's *The Wretched of the Earth* (1961), which spoke of "the liberating influence of violence," became the bible of the New Left.

The origins of their revolutionary ideology and practice can be traced back to the anarchist era of the late nineteenth century, and in particular the concept of "propaganda by the deed." Initially introduced by an Italian, Carlo Piscane, it was developed and incorporated into anarchist ideology by the Russian revolutionary Pyotr Kropotkin, who argued that a demonstration to awaken the consciousness of the masses was necessary, including the gun and the bomb: *"By actions which compel general attention, the new idea seeps into people's minds and wins converts. One such act may, in a few days, make more propaganda than thousands of pamphlets."*[2]

John Most, publisher of *Freieit*, the leading German newspaper advocating terrorism, in his *Advice for Terrorists*, emphasized "Action as Propaganda": *"We have said a hundred times or more that when modern revolutionaries carry out actions, what is important is not solely these actions themselves, but also the propagandistic effect they are able to achieve. Hence we preach not only action in and for itself, but also action as propaganda.*"[3] Thus revolutionary violence is violence as communication.

Youth were simultaneously at the barricades in Paris and Berlin, at Columbia University and Berkeley, allied in their struggle against social injustice, stimulated in the age of television by the courageous acts of their brothers and sisters across the ocean. Especially in the United States, aroused by the war in Vietnam, there was a strong and growing antimilitarism. The New Left's sit-ins, protests, and marches on Washington led the increasingly besieged President Lyndon Johnson, an architect of the Vietnam War, to not seek a second term. It was a time of widespread social protest, of youth decrying the corrupt exploitation of the Third World and the disadvantaged in their midst by corrupt capitalist leaders.

Initially, the student movement mounted legitimate political protest. But as it was perceived by many in the ranks to be "sound and fury, signifying nothing" and not accomplishing its idealistic goals, splits developed within the leadership's ranks, with some factions arguing that only violence could "sensitize the masses," that legitimate protest was ineffective and insufficient.

When those militant factions split off to form their own groups, they became the foundation of violent revolutionary groups. This was the case with the Red Army Faction, whom the press dubbed the Baader-Meinhof Gang, in West Germany as they split from the Socialist Union of German Students, the legitimate student protest movement; and this was the case in Japan when the Japanese Red Army emerged from the student group Zenga Kuren. At about the same time, the Red Brigades emerged in Italy, Direct Action in France, the Combatant Communist Cells in Belgium, Dev Sol in Turkey, First of October Anti-Fascist Resistance Groups in Spain, Popular Forces 25 April in Portugal, and Revolutionary Organization of 17 November in Greece.

These groups, which terrorist scholar Dennis Pluchinsky has called the fighting communist organizations (FCOs), found their ideological guide in Marxism-Leninism. He has identified 13 principles as forming the core of their ideology.[4]

1. The world is viewed through "dialectical materialism," the Marxist-Leninist approach to the analysis of history.
2. Capitalism is the root cause of all the problems of the proletariat.
3. Capitalism can only be displaced by force.
4. The proletariat does not currently possess the necessary revolutionary consciousness to carry out the violent overthrow of the capitalist system.

5. The traditional communist parties have forfeited their right to represent the proletariat.

6. The fighting communist organizations are forced to fill the revolutionary void left by the traditional communist parties.

7. In order to survive its present crisis, capitalism must resort to industrial "restructuring."

8. Imperialism is also in crisis.

9. Western Europe serves as the "imperialist center" that is composed of a "chain of imperial states," manufactured by the United States.

10. The latent fascist tendencies of the capitalist, imperialist state must be exposed to the proletariat.

11. The revolutionary war against imperialism will be a long, protracted armed struggle.

12. The revolutionary armed struggle consists of two phases. The first phase would be the armed propaganda phase, with three components: a revolutionary strategy, a fighting communist organization, and initiation of armed combat. The second and final phase is the revolutionary civil war. The "armed propaganda" phase reflects the anarchist "propaganda by the deed" concept.

13. The next revolutionary stage for an FCO is the "fighting Communist party."

These social revolutionary terrorist organizations, the fighting communist organizations, shared the following features: secrecy; willingness to carry out lethal attacks; adherence to Marxist-Leninist ideology; an urban operating environment; a cellular, compartmentalized organizational structure; and democratic centralism in decision making. For the European fighting communist organizations, which were highly ideological at the onset, there was a decline in the intellectual ideological justification, and increasing recruitment of working-class members and criminals over the generations.

Just as splits within the protest movement in Europe led to the development of several fighting communist organizations, so too in the United States a militant faction of the Students for a Democratic Society (SDS) split off to form the Weather Underground. The Weathermen took their name from a line in the popular 1963 Bob Dylan song *Subterranean Homesick Blues*, "you don't need a weatherman to know which way the wind blows." In their manifesto, in Marxist-Leninist language, they declared their principal goal to be "*the destruction of U.S. imperialism and the achievement of a classless world: world communism. . . . Someone not for revolution is not actually for defeating imperialism either. . . . Long live the Victory of People's War!*"[5]

Particularly animated by the Vietnam War, at the Days of Rage rally in Chicago, which was designed to "Bring the War Home," the protestors were led by Bernadine Dohrn as they memorably chanted "HO, HO, HO CHI MINH, THE NLF IS GOING TO WIN!" In 1970, she issued "A Declaration of a State of War": "*All over the world people fighting American imperialism look to America's youth to use our strategic position behind enemy lines to join forces in the destruction of the empire. . . . Tens of thousands have learned that protests and marches don't do it. Revolutionary violence is the only way.*"[6]

The Weather Underground then published a 150-page creed, justifying their actions and spelling out their goals, titled *Prairie Fire: The Politics of Revolutionary Anti-Imperialism.*[7] In it they stated:

> We are a guerrilla organization. We are communist women and men, underground in the United States for more than four years. We are deeply affected by the historic events of our time in the struggle against US imperialism. . . . Our intention is to disrupt the empire, to incapacitate it, to put pressure on the cracks, to make it hard to carry out its bloody functioning against the people of the world, to join the world struggle, to attack from the inside. . . . Our intention is to engage the enemy, to wear away at him, to isolate him, to expose every weakness. . . .
>
> > Without mass struggle there can be no revolution
> > Without armed struggle there can be no victory.

The Weather Underground claimed credit for 25 bombings, targeting corporations and high-profile targets of the American government, including the State Department building, the Capitol building, and the Pentagon. The Vietnam War was the main animating force, and with its end, the Weather Underground faded away. But their violent actions and radical rhetoric stimulated the fighting communist organizations in Europe, just as they were stimulated by their fellow revolutionaries in Europe.

In some ways the European and North American social revolutionary terrorist groups were stimulated and inspired by the success of the social revolutionary terrorist organizations in Latin America in the late 1960s–early 1970s. There the major economic disparity between the elite class and the peasant class provided a natural home for Marxist-Leninist ideology. Initially the main arenas of operations were Uraguay (the Tupamaros), Argentina (the People's Revolutionary Army and the Monteneros), and Brazil, which had several small groups.

A major ideologue of not only Latin American urban guerrilla movements but of the international movement was a former Brazilian communist, Carlos Marighella, whose *Handbook of Urban Guerrilla Warfare* (which became popularly known as *The Mini Manual of the Urban Guerrilla*) was translated into many languages and was widely read in social revolutionary circles. Not an ideological tract, the mini-manual was predominantly concerned with urban guerrilla tactics. It emphasized, for example, that "*the urban guerilla must know how to live among the people and must be careful not to appear strange and separated from city life."*

Peru and Colombia were both to become the foci of social revolutionary terrorist campaigns. In Peru, three groups were especially prominent, the National Liberation Army, the Tupac Amaru Revolutionary Movement, and Sendero Luminoso (Shining Path). Tupac Amaru was a Marxist-Leninist social revolutionary terrorist organization, whose most notorious action was the December 1996 occupation of the residence of the Japanese ambassador in Peru, holding more than 100 international hostages for more than four months. Sendero Luminoso was a Maoist insurgency under the leadership of a philosophy professor at the university in Ayacucho, Abimael Guzman, who achieved near godlike stature among his *mestizo* Indian followers in a powerful charismatic movement. In Colombia, there were a number of groups, including the April 19 Movement, which subsequently went on to enter the political process; the National Liberation Army; the Popular Liberation Army; and the oldest and largest guerrilla group in Latin America, the Revolutionary Armed Forces of Colombia (FARC), which has an estimated 12,000 to 18,000 men under arms and has proclaimed itself a politico-military Marxist-Leninist organization of Bolivarian inspiration.

This section on social revolutionary terrorism considers two of the European fighting communist groups—the Red Brigades of Italy and the Red Army Faction of West Germany—and two Latin American social revolutionary groups—Sendero Luminoso of Peru and FARC of Columbia.

CHAPTER 7

RED BRIGADES (BR)

The end of World War II brought about dramatic change in Italy. After Mussolini's fascist government had fallen, a democratic shift occurred in the country. In 1946 the monarchy was replaced by a republic, and two years later Italy had a new constitution. In the years immediately following the war Italy thrived, evolving both structurally and economically in what was referred to as an "economic miracle."[1] Production was on the rise and jobs were created everywhere. Italy, which formerly had an agriculture-based economy, was rapidly transformed into an industrialized nation, with massive industrial build-up and population growth around the major cities.

Along with Italy's rapid recovery came many problems often experienced by other rebuilding nations with shifting economic focus. Among the chief concerns were overcrowding in the major metropolitan areas, poor housing, lack of adequate water and sewage systems, and disease. These problems were intensified in Italy by the speed with which they occurred. Other industrialized nations had advanced gradually over a longer period of time, allowing their infrastructure and social programs to make adjustments. The newly formed Italian government had not anticipated or prepared for this rapid degree of change and the massive influx of people that clogged the urban areas.[2]

In the years following World War II, a baby boom occurred all over the world. The Italian children born in these first postwar years would be the origin of the student and worker protest movement, from which the Red Brigades terrorist organization emerged.

In many of the major cities, the educational system was stagnant. Previously only children of wealthy families had the means or abilities to attend the universities, but the laws were changed to allow for anyone to attend, effectively clogging the system with more students than it could handle. Just as migration to the major cities had not been anticipated, the university system had not prepared for such massive overcrowding, with insufficient professors, lecture halls, desks, and even books.

Concurrently with student protests in the United States in the tumultuous 1960s, the universities in Italy became the scene of student activism and protest. In the spring of 1967, during the so-called Week of Vietnam, students occupied the universities of Pisa, Naples, Turin, Milan, Venice, Trento, Bari, and elsewhere. In an article entitled "New Political Objectives" in the left-wing journal *Lavoro Politico* (Political Thought), the author asserted that it is not possible to have a democratic university in a capitalist society. The leader of the student protest in Turin wrote: *"The university functions as an instrument of ideological and political manipulation geared to instill a spirit of subordination in respect to power."* "In 1968 the Italian scene was set ablaze by a Marxist-inspired cultural revolution propelled by the youth in the universities and subsequently in the secondary schools. . . . The demands of the students included group exams, choice of texts and examination questions, guaranteed passing grades, diplomas, and degrees, and the establishment of political collectives in the schools. To show their strength, these students would seize school premises and perpetrate various forms of vandalism and violence."[3]

If students were able to successfully navigate the treacherous university system and actually graduate, the only jobs waiting for them were well below the level for which their university education had prepared them, mainly unskilled factory work. "The university became a social ghetto for young people who the economic system could not absorb, and with the growth of this intellectual proletariat, students began to feel a kinship with the traditional proletariat of Marxist analysis."[4]

As the students learned of the perils that awaited them, the university system became a breeding ground for Marxist intellectual thought. These feelings were further enhanced in the Red Belt of Italy, the areas of Italy with strong communist, socialist, and leftist influence. These regions also had more industrial facilities than some of the other regions of Italy. Former students working in the factories spread Marxist rhetoric to the less educated factory workers, converting many to hard-line leftist ideology.

Another major issue concerning postwar Italy was the fact that many people who were openly fascist during Mussolini's reign retained their place in society long after fascism had fallen. On the opposite side of the spectrum was a large contingent of communists and socialists, committed to Marxist-Leninist doctrine, who existed secretly during the war and gained prominence after fascism fell. The two extremes served as counterweights to each other.

The fascists of Italy were primarily represented by the Italian Social Movement (MSI—Movimento Sociale Italiano), made up of hard-liners who held onto their views and social positions following World War II.[5] There had been a strong leftist movement in Italy since the time of the Russian Revolution, but the fascists suppressed the communists and socialists and outlawed them as political parties. The end of World War II gave leftists more credibility as the Soviets were a symbol of triumph over fascist forces.

RENATO CURCIO: "FATHER" OF THE RED BRIGADES

Renato Curcio was born in September 1941 in a province of Rome. His birth was the result of an affair between a housemaid, Yolanda Curcio, and a married man, Renato Zampa. As a young boy, Renato saw his father only rarely, but grew very attached to his uncle Armando, a Fiat auto worker who was murdered by fascists in 1945.

This event contributed to Curcio's development of leftist ideologies and hatred of fascists. Curcio later wrote in a letter to his mother: *"There come to my mind memories from long ago. Uncle Armando, who carried me piggyback on his shoulders. His clear eyes, always smiling, which looked far ahead towards a society of free and equal men. And I loved him like a father. And I have picked up the rifle that only death at the hands of the Nazi-Fascist assassins had ripped from him."*[6]

It is doubtful that Curcio, only three years old when his uncle died, could recall very much about the man, especially his "generous vision of a better society." Likely he modified the memory of this loss to support his struggle against fascist oppressors and justify his revolutionary actions. Curcio's organization was based on the idea of the resistance and an "us" versus "them" mentality.

Curcio's father began to see the boy somewhat frequently in the late 1950s and even offered to give him his surname, Zampa. After Curcio refused this gesture, neither he nor his mother saw Zampa again. In 1964, Curcio won a scholarship to study at the university at Trento. He accepted without telling his mother and disappeared. Heartbroken, his mother took a job in England. At the university Curcio studied Marx, Lenin, and Mao in great depth, joining the student movements but focusing on strategy and theory instead of joining the front lines of instigators. In the fall of 1967 at Trento, Curcio would create the "negative" or "counter-university"; the idea was to offer courses completely opposite from what was being taught, including courses on anti-capitalism, revolution, and Maoist thought.[7]

The time for revolution was at hand as across the country student protests and takeovers brought the Italian university system to a grinding halt. It was at Trento that Renato Curcio would meet Margherita Cagol, who would become his wife and the "mother" of the Red Brigades.

MARGHERITA CAGOL, "MOTHER" OF THE RED BRIGADES

Margherita "Mara" Cagol was born near Trento in 1945. Her family life was unremarkable: conservative, religious, economically comfortable, and apolitical. Cagol was a bright, determined girl who pursued her interests with full force and passion. She was also very compassionate and giving, and cared deeply about helping others. Traits such as these would be vital to a social revolutionary. Cagol decided to study sociology at the university at Trento, but had not prepared for the political firestorm that she was about to enter. Here she met and fell in love with the introverted Renato Curcio for his intellect and highly articulate nature.[8] Margherita's sister talks about her and her relationship with Renato: "Renato was very important for Margherita. He was her only man. She loved him profoundly and he loved her with equal intensity. However, it is not possible to say that it was only Renato who changed Margherita, not even politically. When they met, neither of the two had a precise political orientation. They matured together. Many now say, she went along behind him, followed his ideas. It is not true. Margherita was an intelligent girl, perfectly aware of what she did. . . . It was a choice."[9]

In the fall of 1967 Curcio, Cagol, and several other comrades began publishing a small revolutionary journal called *Political Work*. Maoist in nature, the journal dealt with issues concerning the Third World revolutionary movement. Though not widely successful, the ideas set forth in *Political Work* provided an ideological foundation for future groups including the Metropolitan Political Collective (CPM), which Curcio, Cagol, and others from various factory and industrial collectives formed in September 1969.[10] In an early document that reflects their sense of unity with their revolutionary comrades in the United States and that laid the foundation for the urban guerrilla, the CPM declared: "*The objective conditions for the transition to communism exist already in the metropolitan areas of North America and Europe. . . . The city today is the heart of the system, the organizational center of the politico-economic exploitation. . . . It is here, in its heart, that the system must be struck.*"[11]

This emphasis on the city was to be found in a number of the leftist groups, such as the tract from the Proletarian Left "Let's seize the city!" The collective focused on improving problems in housing, factories, and the educational system.[12] In July 1969, after Margherita Cagol earned her degree from Trento, she and Renato Curcio were married and moved to Milan.

CREATION OF THE RED BRIGADES

A militant faction within the CPM led by Curcio and Cagol splintered off to form the Brigate Rosse (BR), or Red Brigades, in 1969. In its infancy, the Red Brigades attempted to engage in political activity as well as clandestine militant operations in what is known as double militancy. Increased police attention and arrests led the BR to abandon this idea as ineffective and go underground in May 1972.[13] It then established a system of regulars and irregulars. Regulars went underground, abandoning their previous lives to devote their full time to the cause. They were paid out of organizational funds acquired by bank robberies and other financial appropriations. Irregulars served part time, performing smaller, less dangerous roles while maintaining jobs in factories or other places of political influence where they could attract supporters and new members. In its early years, the organization had many sympathizers who contributed financially, logistically, and otherwise. Sustaining their dedication to the cause was the romantic concept of the revolutionary given form by Francesco Alberoni, which can be traced back to Sergey Nechaev's *Catechism of the Revolutionary* (1869).[14] Alberoni wrote: "*Their moral being consists in being revolutionaries, in acting for that single aim, sacrificing all else to it: their personal life, their individual tastes and preferences their own gentleness, their sympathy for the individual man and woman, their own maternity and their own children. . . . Leninism is a political asceticism in which there are no rights because everything is subordinated to an objective.*"[15]

Life as an underground revolutionary terrorist was usually difficult and boring. Actions often required months of tedious planning. Large-scale actions, such as kidnappings for extended periods, presented difficulties of properly caring for a hostage. Terrorists living clandestinely faced the same daily problems as anybody else with concerns for money, food, and clothing. Red Brigades regulars who lived clandestinely were completely supported by the organization and received a minimal salary equal to that of an Italian metal worker.[16] Poor living conditions combined with little excitement often led members to become disillusioned with the revolutionary terrorist lifestyle.

Structure and Early Actions

The Red Brigades were set up like a corporation in a pyramid design. The pinnacle consisted of the executive committee and strategic directorate, who were responsible for primary decisions and direction of the group. The second tier contained the various fronts that dealt with functional specifics, such as logistics, but also specific areas of focus, such as factories, political parties, and the prisons. The third tier consisted of the five operational divisions, or columns, set up in Milan, Turin, Genoa, Rome, and Venice. In each city multiple four- to five-person cells (brigades) operated independently of each other, but often worked together on larger operations.[17] For recruitment purposes, the BR looked to militant members of other leftist organizations, as well as other disaffected university students, who shared their mind-set.[18]

During its first two years in operation, the BR engaged only in property damage, primarily setting automobiles on fire. These actions were more of an annoyance, and the acts were relatively simple and did not harm anyone. Eventually the BR expanded operations by firebombing vehicles at factories or places where the damage would aggravate corporations. Nevertheless, their actions received only minor attention due to the unstable political environment in which many revolutionary groups were performing many actions. It was not until 1972 that the BR adopted kidnapping as a tactic in order to gather attention.

The BR primarily targeted "fascist" factory bosses for kidnapping. Through these kidnappings, the group intended to influence factory bosses to change their ways, often making victims undergo a humiliating political trial for the crimes they had committed against the workers. Kidnapped victims were generally treated well and released a short time later. Idalgo Macchiarini was kidnapped by three Red Brigadists on March 3, 1972 while leaving his office in Milan. Only held for 20 minutes, he was questioned as part of a political show trial after being put in a van and handcuffed. The BR left a sign around his neck that said: *"Red Brigades—bite and flee!— nothing will go unpunished—strike one to educate one hundred—all power to the armed people!"*[19]

After the BR became more adept at maintaining safe houses, it began to hold prisoners for longer periods of time; these longer incarcerations also served to increase publicity.

Tactical Shift

In 1974, the Red Brigades underwent a strategic shift in focus and targets. The Italian government had become more oppressive and was shifting power in order to create a stronger executive branch while weakening the parliament. Previously the BR had attacked only factory managers and property. Now it directed its attacks to the Italian government in an attempt to "carry the attack to the heart of the state."[20]

On April 18, 1974, the Red Brigades kidnapped Mario Sossi, assistant attorney general of Genoa. Sossi was a hard-line fascist judge who handed down extremely harsh prison sentences to leftists. The Italian judiciary system was not impartial, and many judges were openly fascist. During Sossi's captivity, the BR publicly humiliated him using a political trial in which he admitted wrongdoing in previous judicial decisions and extreme prison sentences. The texts of these political trials were distributed in leaflets around the country.

The BR sought the freedom of eight political prisoners in exchange for Sossi's release. After negotiating an agreement, the Italian government, under the authority of General Prosecutor Francesco Coco, reneged, causing delays in Sossi's release. He was finally released unharmed after 35 days in captivity. The political prisoners were not released.[21]

ESCALATION

In June 1974, a BR commando group raided the fascist MSI party office in Padua, near Venice. Although the BR had expected to find the office empty, to their surprise, they found two MSI officials whom they reflexively killed. Though the killings were not planned, they represented an escalation of what the BR would do if necessary. News of this act partially tarnished the public image of the Red Brigades.[22]

In September 1974, BR leaders Renato Curcio and Alberto Franceschini met with a prospective member named Silvano Girotto. Girotto, an ex-Franciscan priest, had earned the nickname Father Machine Gun because of his leftist teachings and dealings with guerrilla fighters in Bolivia and Chile. The BR intended to convince Girotto to work with it by setting up an anti-infiltration unit. Unbeknownst to Curcio and Franceschini, Girotto had been recruited earlier by General Dalla Chiesa's Carabinieri, a military antiterrorist force, to trap the Red Brigades. The trap worked, and the carabinieri arrested Curcio and Franceschini. Poor planning and lack of counterintelligence security measures contributed to this arrest.[23]

Renato Curcio was not to remain imprisoned for long, though, as the Italian prison system had its own share of security problems. In February 1975, his wife and a BR commando team broke Curcio out of a poorly secured prison under the guise of delivering a package. Cagol pulled out a hidden machine gun, made her way into the prison cells, and found her husband. Right before his release, Curcio had been reading a book on making explosives that was available in the prison library. The group escaped without incident.[24]

At his 1976 trial, Curcio was tried and convicted in absentia. Codefendant Alberto Franceschini wrote to the judge explaining why he was a "combatant communist." *"Since every act of this trial has been predetermined and you are simply carrying out the orders that your masters have imparted to you, . . . the trial is a farce and I consider myself too serous a person to take part in it. What you call justice is nothing else but a relationship of force."*[25]

Kneecapping

May 1975 signaled another escalation in tactics and violence. The Red Brigades wounded a conservative member of the Christian Democrats of the Milan city council by deliberately shooting him in the knees, "a tactic that was to be repeated so often as to give rise to a new verb—*gambizzare*, to kneecap."[26] Prior to this new tactic, the BR had not intentionally harmed victims. Kneecapping was a quick and effective method to convey a threatening message without killing, and it was a highly efficient tactic that required minimal planning. Kneecappings also served as a constant reminder to victims and those around them, as they usually walked with a limp for the rest of their lives. Renato Curcio observed: *"The city must become a treacherous terrain for the enemy, for the men who exercise an ever increasing hostile power extraneous to the interest of the masses. All their gestures must be observed, all abuses must be uncovered."*[27]

Elimination of Key Figures Leads to Membership Change: Less Ideological, More Criminal

In June 1975, the organization suffered a major blow. Carabinieri forces searching for a kidnapped businessman came across the house where the Red Brigades were holding him. In the ensuing shootout, Margherita Cagol was shot twice, once in the shoulder and once in the neck, killing her. After his wife's death, Renato Curcio became severely depressed.[28] In January 1976, Curcio was recaptured in Milan by carabinieri forces and placed back in a secure prison, this time for an extended stay. Imprisonment may have ended Curcio's physical presence in the organization, but he was still able to make decisions and communicate with the outside world.

Nonetheless, over time the organization changed. In contrast to the first generation when the group was composed primarily of disaffected university students with some factory workers, in the next generation membership became heavily composed of working class individuals and high school students. The newer members, much younger than the original members had been, were increasingly militant. Eventually, criminals were recruited for their particular speciality. Although they possessed the necessary criminal skills, they lacked the strong ideological underpinnings of the original members.

Assassinations

In June 1976, the Red Brigades further escalated the violence by assassinating Prosecutor General Francesco Coco in retaliation for his key role in opposing the release of the eight political prisoners in exchange for the release of Mario Sossi.[29] Coco, his bodyguard, and his driver were killed in a hail of bullets under the command of leader Mario Moretti. The highly militant, quick-to-violence Moretti was one of the last remaining original members of the BR. Coco's assassination can be viewed as a revenge killing, but it also fit the Red Brigades goal of attacking the heart of the state. This was the first planned assassination by the BR, and more were to follow. The group's most recognized accomplishment as a terrorist organization would also be the prelude to their downfall.

Each assassination was the occasion of a lengthy communiqué explaining the ideological justification for their act. When for example, the BR assassinated Leamon Hunt, director general of the Multinational Observer Force (MOF) in the Sinai in February 1984, the communiqué spoke of their sympathy with the Palestinian people but also of:

> the absolute and grotesque impotence of the United Nations. An extremely eloquent indication of the deterioration of international relations, . . . how the imperialist powers calmly ignore the UN when their interests are at stake and when it is a matter of dealing a decisive blow to the national and popular liberation movements, which struggle against oppression and exploitation.

The long communiqué ends with the ringing declaration:

> UNITY OF THE PROLETARIAT WITH THE PROGRESSIVE PEOPLES IN THE STRUGGLE AGAINST IMPERIALISM.
>
> LET US STEP UP AND ORGANIZE THE STRUGGLE AGAINST THE GOVERNMENT'S WARMONGERING AND ANTI-PROLETARIAN POLICY.

LET US EXTEND THE MOBILIZATION OF THE MASSESS AND THE
VANGUARD TO THESE WATCHWORDS.
IMMEDIATE WITHDRAWAL OF ITALIAN TROOPS FROM THE MIDDLE
EAST.
NO TO THE MISSILES AT COMISO AND REARMAMENT
GET ITALY OUT OF NATO![30]

Assassination of Prime Minister Moro

Aldo Moro had been the Italian prime minister five times; his career was dedicated to politics. He served as president of the Christian Democrat party and was well respected, though not well liked. He was a leading figure in the "historic compromise," an agreement in which the Christian Democrats and the Italian Communists (PCI) were working together to unify Italy.

On March 16, 1978, the Red Brigades ambushed and kidnapped Moro in a highly organized, meticulously planned attack that left his five-man security detail dead. Moro, not injured during the exchange of gunfire, was grabbed by commandos and taken to a secret location.[31] The BR subjected Moro to a political trial in which he was accused of crimes against the Italian people and found guilty. The sentence was death.

When a photograph of Moro was sent to the government and displayed on television, it showed him with a long communiqué from the BR around his neck.

The BR released multiple communiqués and letters written by Moro to the public over the course of the kidnapping. In his letters, Moro pleaded for the Italian government to secure his release. But the government refused to negotiate with the BR on the principle of not giving in to terrorist demands. On May 9, 1978, after all attempts at negotiations had repeatedly failed, the Red Brigades executed Aldo Moro. They put his body in the trunk of a car which they parked on a street in central Rome. The headquarters of the PCI were at one end of the street, the Christian Democrats on the other: a symbolic location given Moro's role in the "historic compromise," which the BR opposed.

Mario Moretti, who organized the attack later said, *"We did not kidnap and kill Moro the man, but his function. We reject the accusation of political homicide."*[32]

Although it was true that Moro was a symbol and a political figure, the public did not view Moro's death and that of his five bodyguards in the same light. The Red Brigades not only killed Moro, but they also killed whatever public support they still retained. Police powers involving search and seizure and preventive detention were increased. Prison sentences for terrorist actions were also increased to deter acts. The most productive new measure introduced was the *pentiti* (repentant) law that reduced prison sentences for captured terrorists who cooperated with the authorities.[33]

PATRIZIO PECI

Patrizio Peci had been the commander of the Turin column of the Red Brigades at the time of his capture in February 1980. A member of the BR since 1974, Peci had participated in several murders, but never killed anyone himself. Over time Peci had become disillusioned with the revolutionary terrorist struggle and highly opposed the idea of spending the rest of his life in prison.

Whenever people asked Peci of his past involvement with the BR, he became very defensive:

> Almost everyone who approaches me, attorneys, officers, magistrates or newspapermen, sooner or later, try to find in my childhood psychological reasons, some warning sign and who knows what aberration. But everyone in San Benedetto could testify that I was what is known as a nice boy and that mine was a normal family, actually a very normal one.[34]

> It is evident that had I been born in Australia instead of the Marches I would not have ended up being a brigadist. On the other hand, it could be argued that, had I been born in 1903 instead of 1953 I would have, like so many others, perhaps been a fascist, a shock trooper and then a partisan. Everyone is a product of his times.[35]

According to Peci, he joined the Red Brigades because, at the time, there had been no real killings (except for the first two deaths of MSI fascists, an unintended accident, not the objective), only kidnappings and kneecappings. Peci also reasoned that there would be little risk of jail for lengthy terms because the government had not yet organized itself to deal with the terrorist groups. However, his early experiences within the group did little to encourage his depth of faith in the cause. In fact, his disillusionment started when he had dinner with the leader of the Turin column, Raffaele Fiore.

> I was already sad when Fiore, who wolfed down his food, finished before I did. I kept on eating. He settled down to watch television. I kept on eating. He put his feet, those enormous feet, on the table and then, suddenly he took off his shoes, without even undoing the

*laces. There was a horrible stench. But the worst was yet to come. He took off his socks as
well; he grabbed the bread knife, one of those long, serrated knives and began to pry off the
filth from between his toes with the point of the knife. Zap! And off came the filth from
between two toes. He was very adept. Zap! Zap! Zap! Zap! What kind of manners are
these? I said nothing and I tried to minimize things in my mind. "They are just little things,
nothing," I thought, but I was worried. "If everybody behaves like this, how will I be able
to live among them?"*[36]

Peci later told himself: *"I will try. . . . Let's see how it goes and then perhaps I
can get out."*[37]

He approached joining the Red Brigades like a trial offer, which shows he
was not fully committed from the start. He reasoned that other people leave
similar groups; at the time he joined, the BR was not yet violent as it would
become. However, after he had joined, Coco and Moro had been kidnapped and
murdered, catapulting the Red Brigades into a realm unforeseen by Peci. As he
became more disillusioned, he realized, *"to profess to dislocate that giant of a State
with some pistol shots is like trying to kill an elephant with a B.B. gun. We only managed to be a pain in its ass."*[38]

Cooperative Terrorists

Around the time of Peci's arrest, the Italian government was in the process of
creating laws that provided reduced prison sentences to terrorists who dissociated themselves from the group, cooperated with authorities, and provided
useful information. This was known as *pentiti*, the repentant law. In truth,
terrorists did not necessarily have to show remorse for their actions; the willingness to give up information on others was of higher importance. Sensing
his chance for freedom, Peci agreed to cooperate with authorities by telling
them all he knew about the organization, including hideouts, weapons
caches, but most of all, names of fellow members. Information from Peci led
to the arrest of at least 85 members of the Red Brigades. This was a devastating blow to the organization. Peci's rationalization for turning informer was
embedded in his desire to "save" his comrades: *"you figure that, sooner or later,
they'll end up in jail anyway, if they are lucky and are not killed in a fire fight. It
seems to you that you are doing them a favor. And you know that by having them
arrested you save the lives of those they want to kill, it seems to redeem those you
killed, to repay part of your debt to humanity. . . . Therefore, I talked."*[39] Yet Peci
recognized the guilt that is intertwined with the role of informer: *"The bottom
line is that I am a traitor."*[40]

The *pentiti* law was later followed by the *dissociati* (dissociation) law, which enabled captured terrorists to confess their crimes but not inform on former comrades. Both laws proved to be highly successful against the Red Brigades in the subsequent years.[41]

Since Patrizio Peci was in protective custody and the Red Brigades could not get to him to retaliate, they instead killed his brother Roberto. Similar killings of repentant terrorists led to turmoil and fractures within the group. Logistical networks and former alliances began to disappear, and individual brigadists began to focus on their own individual goals. The group began to cannibalize itself as arguments and heated accusations against members for destroying the BR structure led to rapid deterioration. The increasing number of assassinations of high-ranking law enforcement and members of the judiciary led authorities to focus their efforts on destroying the group.[42]

THE LAST HURRAH: KIDNAPPING GENERAL DOZIER

As the group was fragmenting, there was an organizational decision to carry out a terrorist spectacular. I observed in an essay on the threat of nuclear terrorism that one of the motivations for terrorist spectaculars is to resuscitate terrorist "losers"; as a group is on the way out, it may be motivated to create a "big bang" in order to once again attract attention and recruit new members.[43] This may well have been an underlying motivation for the BR decision to kidnap a NATO official in December 1981. In order to divert the attention of Italian law enforcement resources from Rome so that the Rome column could carry out major attacks as part of the Red Brigades' "Winter of Fire" campaign, the BR Executive Committee decided to kidnap a senior NATO official. On December 17, 1981, they kidnapped Brigadier General James Dozier, one of the highest-ranking American officers in Italy.[44] Carabinieri forces questioning individuals connected to the militarist group were able to produce solid leads and eventually located where Dozier was being held. On January 28, 1982 a specially trained assault team rescued the general and subdued the four terrorists without firing a shot.[45] The BR's targeting of Dozier demonstrated that social revolutionary terrorists operating in Europe were not only an internal threat, but a worldwide threat. This event forcibly brought home to U.S. leadership the fact that the United States was not merely an interested observer of the violent terrorism affecting allies, but were squarely in the terrorists' gun-sights. This led to active U.S. involvement in a cooperative international effort to counter terrorism. In many ways, however, the Dozier kidnapping spectacular was the last hurrah of the Red Brigades.

In time, the remaining factions and offshoots of the Red Brigades dwindled or were apprehended by authorities, although the group never officially disbanded. Socioeconomic conditions were beginning to improve in Italy, and the importance of social revolutionary terrorist groups had faded. Splinter cells using the BR name and ideology continued to engage in sporadic actions in the following years, but they were a far cry from what Renato Curcio and a group of disaffected students and factory workers so long ago had envisioned for a leftist social revolutionary movement.

CHAPTER 8

RED ARMY FACTION (RAF)

STUDENT MOVEMENT

World War II led to the fall of the fascist German government and the beginning of the baby boom generation, which would later flood the unprepared university system. If students were able to obtain a diploma, employment as unskilled laborers became their most viable option. Disillusionment with the university system and the government led many students to political activism when they then witnessed an even more inadequate government in action.

Consistent with the New Left movement that emerged in the late 1960s, believing that the government was fascist, corrupt, and desperately needed to be replaced with Marxist-Leninist communism, there was a generational effect unique to the character of the German student movement concerning "[t]he revulsion felt by many young Germans toward the sins of Nazism. . . . The older generation [had] failed to realize even those limited ideals that it set as standards to guide German youth. It [had] failed, for example, to eradicate the Nazi past."[1]

Jillian Becker, co-founder of the Institute for the Study of Terrorism, suggests in the title of her book *Hitler's Children* the generational dynamics associated with the radical left in Germany.[2] In the wake of World War I, when their own fathers were either absent or unable to provide for their families in the hyperinflation that wracked the German economy, the youth was attracted to the promised strength of Hitler's leadership and became the Hitler youth cadre.[3] Becker suggests that a generation later, their children were repelled by their fathers who were leaders of the Nazi movement. They were, as reflected in the generational matrix in chapter 1, rebelling against the generation of their parents that was loyal to the regime. One of the Red Army Faction leaders was later to remark: "***This is the generation of corrupt old men who gave us Auschwitz and Hiroshima.***"[4]

"At the center of the students' protest was, first of all, the emergency law imposed and enforced exclusively by the Great Coalition,* the still unassimilated Nazi past, the abuses arising from life in a consumer society, the concentration of the press, the hierarchical-authoritarian structure of the universities and, last but not least, the American involvement in Vietnam."[5]

PRECIPITATING RADICALIZING EVENT: THE DEATH OF BENNO OHNESORG

Throughout the 1960s there were many peaceful demonstrations against the atom bomb, Germany's rearmament, the perils of the university system, and the Vietnam War. This tone changed dramatically on June 2, 1967, when the Shah of Iran visited West Berlin on a state-sponsored trip. Many protests against the Shah's visit took place, culminating with a riot that evening at the Berlin Opera House. It is unclear how the riot started, whether it was students throwing stones or if police charged first. "But the police did charge, stones and other things were hurled, staves were wielded, batons were swung, arrests were made. Many tried to escape, but there were the police blocking them off, using a prepared and rehearsed 'liver-sausage' tactic—seal both ends and attack them as they burst out of the center."[6]

One of the many caught in this tactic was Benno Ohnesorg, a 26-year-old student, married, with a child on the way, who was participating in his first political demonstration. He was unarmed, running away from the police, when he was shot in the back of the head. That the plainclothes sergeant, Karl-Heinz Kurras, was later found not guilty of the charges, further enraged the already reeling student culture. Ohnesorg became a martyr and the victim of the "first political murder in the Federal Republic"[7] of Germany. His murder, the blatant police brutality, along with the failure of the state to protect its citizens or bring the sergeant to justice, radicalized a generation and led them to believe that the only way to fight violence was with violence. Bommi Baumann, a later RAF member, recalls the feeling at the time, "*You have to see that people can be driven only so far, that they can only free themselves by irrational aggressive actions.*"[8]

---

* In 1966 and 1967 the Social Democrats and Christian Democrats merged to form the "Great Coalition." This made the citizens feel improperly represented in parliament as the authoritarian coalition had very little parliamentary opposition, so the people took their opposition to the streets.

Another way the people could "free" themselves was to not look at the enemy as human beings. Peter Merkl, a leading U.S. expert on West German politics and terrorism, states that the "sociopathic streak that dehumanizes all law-enforcement and military personnel as well as targeted politicians and bureaucrats, perceiving them as creatures that deserve to be killed, is also common to the sympathizer literature."[9] According to Ulrike Meinhof: *"We say the guy in uniform is a pig, he is not a human being, and we have to tackle him from his point of view. . . . It is wrong to talk to these people at all and of course the use of guns is allowed."*[10]

It is easier to kill a pig than a person.

BAADER-MEINHOF GANG

The "Baader-Meinhof Gang," a title bestowed by the media, grew out of the left-wing student movement, just as the Red Brigades emerged from the student movement in Italy. They can be considered the first generation of the Red Army Faction (RAF—Rote Armee Facktion) and provided the ideological foundation for the RAF.

It was deeply felt by a group within the student movement, the SDS (Sozialistischer Deutscher Studentenbund, the Socialist Union of German Students), that one could no longer work within the system; the system was the enemy, it had failed them, and the only way to destroy the system was with violence. On April 2, 1968, two Frankfort department stores were set ablaze by firebombs. Two days later Gudrun Ensslin, Andreas Baader, Thorwald Proll, and Horst Sohnlein were arrested and charged with the crime.

The executive committee of the SDS disowned any connection with the arson and issued this statement: "The SDS is deeply dismayed to think there are people in the Federal Republic of Germany who believe they can express their opposition to the political system and social state of the nation by acts of terror which cannot be justified."[11]

Many others, however, supported the action, as succinctly expressed by Fritz Teufel (later an RAF member): *"It's better to set fire to a department store than to own one."*[12]

Bommi Baumann, who also soon would be a member of RAF, stated: *"It made no difference to me at the time whether they'd set fire to a store or not, what mattered was just that people had broken out of the system for once and done a thing like that, even if the way they did it meant they'd been caught. Arson is competitive, of course. The one who hits hardest points the way to go."*[13]

Ulrike Meinhof published numerous articles in *konkret*, a popular left-wing student newspaper, in support of the action. She later pledged her life as a free woman to the cause by participating in the breakout of Baader from jail, thereby, committing herself to an underground life. (Ensslin had escaped recapture after she and Baader jumped bail for their role in the fires.)

After Baader's breakout, Meinhof wrote a communiqué "The Concept Urban Guerrilla" that was the first to use the term "Red Army Faction."[14] The revolutionary tone is revealed in this excerpt: *"If we are correct in saying that American imperialism is a paper tiger, i.e., that it can ultimately be defeated, and if the Chinese Communists are correct in their thesis that victory over American imperialism has become possible because the struggle against it is now being waged in all four corners of the earth . . . —if this is correct, then there is no reason to exclude or disqualify any particular country or any particular region from taking part in the anti-imperialist struggle because the forces of revolution are especially weak there and the forces of reaction are especially strong."*[15]

To understand the subsequent events, one must look at the backgrounds and personalities of the principal leaders. Gudrun Ensslin, Andreas Baader, Ulrike Meinhof, and Jan-Carl Raspe were the founding members of the Baader-Meinhof Gang, which spawned the next 30 years of terrorist activity in Germany.

Gudrun Ensslin[16]

Gudrun Ensslin, born in 1940, was indoctrinated to political awareness at a very early age. Her father, Helmut Ensslin, a pastor in the Evangelical Church of Germany, led a congregation in which he promoted an overall education in social, political, and international affairs. He was against unquestioned obedience to authority, against German rearmament, and for reunification with East Germany. Politics were always discussed in the household, so Ensslin grew up with a keen awareness of world issues. When she was 18, she studied abroad in the United States under the International Christian Youth Exchange where she was *"horrified by the political naiveté of Americans."* She found much fault with America—its social injustice, its material inequality.

After she returned to Germany, she attended the university on scholarship for her excellent grades. There she met an intellectual and idealistic young man, Bernward Vesper, a left-wing German, who led her into greater political involvement. He himself entered politics in rebellion against his father, William Vesper, a writer known for pro-Nazi nationalist literature. Together they started a small publishing house called *Studie neue Literatur* and became involved in antinuclear demonstrations. They married and in 1967 had a child, Felix Robert, who was introduced to political protest, attending demonstrations against nuclear weapons and Vietnam while in his baby carriage with signs attached to the handle stating: "When I am big I will carry my machine gun with me always. Use your head!"

Shortly thereafter, the Benno Ohnesorg incident occurred, which profoundly upset Gudrun. She was said to have wept uncontrollably for days, and his death fundamentally altered her perspective on the world. *"Now that I have experienced reality, I cannot be a pacifist any longer."* She made many speeches after Ohnesorg's death in which she said: *"They'll kill us all—you know what kind of pigs we're up against—that is the generation of Auschwitz. They have weapons and we haven't. We must arm ourselves."*

As she became increasingly involved in the trendy left-wing culture and the need for violence, motherhood "felt like a trap." She decided to leave her husband and child behind in January 1968 and dedicate herself to organizing and protesting against the fascist government with Andreas Baader, whom she had met the summer before.

Andreas Baader

He was a bully who liked to use his fists. He wanted to be a gang leader, and if a boy did not wish to follow Andy, he could expect a bloody nose.

—Jillian Becker, *Hitler's Children*[17]

Born in May 1943, Andreas Baader was raised entirely by women, his father having died in 1945 serving on the Russian front. Andreas did poorly in school, yet his mother and other female relatives doted on him. His mother firmly decided that he was quite intelligent; it was the "ordinary schools having failed to develop her son's latent intellectual gifts" that were to blame.

Andreas seemingly had no ambition or drive. He was lazy, given to sulking, and never completed high school, which made him one of the few RAF members who did not attend university. "Having nothing to do and no money, he became more and more sure that the way society was run was profoundly wrong. Here he was, penniless, while others *less worthy* were driving around in big, fast, expensive cars (which he too would later do). It sickened him; the rat race, the consumer society, the social injustice."

One thing Baader did have in excess was allure and charm. He was quite successful with women and was never at a loss for female companionship. This charm and propensity to violence drew Ensslin to his side and kept her there until the end of their days. Baader, in turn, enjoyed the respect Ensslin received within the left-wing community for her intellect. He rode her coattails by keeping silent during fervent discussions, letting everyone assume he was as intelligent as she. "Yet just by being by her side he was transformed into that difficult intellectual thing, an idealist; and, even grander, that ideological thing, a revolutionary."

Ulrike Meinhof

Ulrike Meinhof, who was born in 1934, came from a well-to-do family. Her father, Werner Meinhof, was born in 1901 to a bourgeois, religious family and later earned a doctorate. He died of cancer when Ulrike was only 6 years old. Her mother, Ingebord Guthardt, was born in 1909 to a mildly socialist, nonreligious family and also earned a doctorate later in life. She too died of cancer, leaving Ulrike, then 14, and her older sister, Wienke, orphans.

Fortunately, Renate Riemeck, a close family friend of her mother, took the girls into her care. Renate and Ingebord had become fast friends at university, sharing a mutual dislike of Hitler, a dislike that, at the time, was dangerous to think, let alone verbalize. Renate had become a co-parent, a female stand-in for their father, to the girls in the eight years between their father's and mother's deaths. After her mother died, Ulrike said to Renate numerous times, "*Now we've got only you.*" Insecure from these early losses, Ulrike needed and was to seek in the years to come "family" groups to which she could belong and be important.

Ulrike was considered an intelligent and kind-hearted person who "consciously emulated Renate," setting a pattern for her life. She typically adopted the views of adults (and later peers) on whom she was emotionally dependent, and never truly learned the art of independent critical thinking. She was strong-willed and opinionated, but very rarely were the opinions originally hers, even when, years later, she was considered one of the best female journalists in Germany. Renate commented on Ulrike's confidence: "She always needed someone stronger than herself to back her up. She was an intelligent child, and her character was good, but she always reflected her environment."

While attending university, she was not involved in politics, in which she had scant interest. Her opinions were "general acceptance of vague leftist sympathies, tinged with sentimental preference for Eastern Europe with its austerity, idealism, and suffering, and a particular opposition to the atom bomb." Yet, in 1957, when she met Klaus Rohl, editor of the student paper *konkret*, her political interest solidified. "'Her love affair with communism and her love affair with him [Rohl] were 'the same thing.' " They married three years later. The marriage lasted only seven years, producing twin daughters, Bettina and Regine, born in 1962.

Earlier in 1962, Ulrike continued to demonstrate against both the atom bomb and Germany's rearmament. "*One does not change the world by shooting,*" she wrote. "*One destroys it. One accomplishes more by negotiating, avoiding destruction.*" However, by the time she left Rohl in 1967, her tone had changed dramatically as she was spending much more time with the more radical left. She "*candidly praised lawbreaking for the sake of lawbreaking*" and saw the answer to society's troubles in "*rebellion, resistance, overthrow, breakup, and violence.*"

Jan-Carl Raspe

Like Baader, Jan-Carl Raspe was raised by women after his father, a chemical factory worker, died of heart disease mere months before his son's birth in July 1944. Raspe was said to be a gentle child who found it difficult to communicate, loved animals, and abhorred violence. As a youth, he attended school in the western sector of Germany and lived in the eastern sector. On the night of August 12, 1961, he was spending the night at an uncle's house in the western sector. The next day the Berlin Wall was raised. He wrote to his mother informing her of his decision to stay on the western side thereby becoming one of the many would-be members of the RAF who were refugees from East Berlin. "He became increasingly involved emotionally in the student actions of the later 1960s. When Benno Ohnesorg was shot, 'he saw it as plain murder.' It was then that he became politically engaged."

RADICALIZING EVENTS

The Shooting of Rudi Dutschke

A second event that further radicalized the youth population was the assassination attempt on Rudi Dutschke, student leader of the SDS, who was shot and wounded on April 11, 1968, by a young unskilled worker, Josef Bachmann. "News of the attempted assassination had spread through Berlin like wildfire. Rudi Dutschke's shoes still lay inside the chalk circle in front of the SDS Centre, where students gathered. It was deathly still. No loud discussion, no inflammatory speeches, only the silence of rage and despair."[18]

Soon the silence turned into action, as expressed by Ulrike Meinhof: "*If you throw a stone, it's a crime. If a thousand stones are thrown, that's political. If you set fire to a car it's a crime; if a hundred cars are set on fire that's political.*"[19]

Positioning themselves in the mainstream of revolutionary thought, in the early 1970s the RAF declared, *"The armed campaign is the highest form of class struggle."*[20] In their publication *Build Up the Red Army*, emphasizing the importance of the student movement, they stated: *"It is not the organizations of the industrial working class, but the revolutionary sections of the student bodies that are today the bearers of the contemporary conscience."*[21]

Hunger Strike Death of Holger Meins

The third significant event that triggered even more sympathizers for the Red Army Faction was the hunger strike death on November 9, 1974 of Holger Meins, who had become one of the principal leaders of the RAF, who was protesting mistreatment in prison. He joined the RAF in 1971 after growing tired of police harassment for his leftist political views as a filmmaker in Berlin. Hans-Joachim Klein, would-be OPEC assassin, spoke of the effect of Meins's death on him: *"If all I needed not only to propagate armed struggle but also to take it up myself was the right 'kick,' then Holger Meins was this 'kick.' His death made my misery and my powerlessness in the face of this political system reach such a pitch that it became too much for me. I had had enough of legal policy and I was prepared to fight. Definitely."*[22]

In revenge for Meins's death, members of the 2nd of June Movement, a leftist group loosely linked with RAF, murdered the president of Germany's Superior Court, Gunter von Drenkmann, who had never tried any of the Baader-Meinhof Gang. The assassination polarized Germany's population. "Many people interpret Meins' death as a murder, pure and simple, and join the growing number of 'sympathizers' who support the terrorists' cause. Others are stricken by the murder of von Drenkmann and look for the government to stop the terrorists by any means necessary."[23]

INTERNATIONAL CONNECTIONS

In June 1970, members of the Baader-Meinhof group decided to travel to Jordan to get paramilitary training from the PFLP (Popular Front for the Liberation of Palestine), a Palestinian secular nationalist-separatist group with Marxist ideology, but they did not stay long. Their hosts asked them to leave in August after many arguments about discipline, arrogance, and women's roles took place. Baader was seen as *"a coward who is performing the whole revolt to cover up his cowardice. We wouldn't even take him on a patrol."*[24]

Subsequent generations of the RAF achieved much more success with their international terrorism connections. The RAF and PFLP hijacked an Air

France flight from Tel Aviv to Paris in June 1976, each group demanding that certain members in prison be released. Other groups the RAF worked with included the Red Brigades, the Palestine Liberation Organization (PLO), Ramirez Sanchez (better known as Carlos the Jackal), and Black September (al-Fatah's terror squad), whom the RAF assisted in the logistics and planning for the iconic event for the modern era of terrorism, the seizure of the Israeli Olympic village at the 1972 Munich Olympics, in which 11 Israeli athletes were killed.[25]

GENERATIONAL CHANGES

Since 1972, after the first and original generation was captured, an ever-widening gulf, with few exceptions began to open up between the goals of the original leadership and those of their successors.[26]

The Baader-Meinhof generation ended in 1977, after the Lufthansa jet hijacking failed to secure the leaders' release from prison. With the failure of the operation and loss of hope, Andreas Baader, Gudrun Ensslin, and Jan-Carl Raspe all committed suicide in prison on October 17, 1977.* Some believed their "suicides" were really covered-up government assassinations.

Individual and Group Psychology of the First Generations of the RAF

An investigation in 1979, as part of a research project backed by the Federal Ministry for Domestic Affairs, published in four volumes, analyzed 227 life histories of leftist terrorists (RAF and 2nd of June Movement).[27] The terrorists came from mainly upper-middle-class backgrounds, their educational level was above average, yet, at the time they joined the group, only 35 percent had full-time jobs. Many terrorists came from broken homes; those who didn't showed strained, unloving relationships with their fathers. A breakup of personal ties preceded joining the group.[28]

The study's conclusion was reminiscent of the findings of Franco Ferracuti's research on Italian left-wing terrorists.[29] No demographic circumstances differentiated youth who became terrorists from those who ended up in the drug culture or youth gangs. Rather the main determinant was who their friends were.[30]

---

* Ulrike Meinhof had earlier committed suicide on Mother's Day 1976, after being ostracized from the group and growing feelings of depression.

The solidarity and security that so many of the German terrorists seemed to be looking for in their families were later found in the group:

> My first political group made as many demands on me as I made demands on it. I . . . was treated there like a comrade among comrades and I felt like that. Every time I was addressed as comrade I was mighty proud of that. . . . It was the pride of being acknowledged and accepted as one of many. Of equal value. . . . solidarity, of sticking together, love and respect without competition and its anxieties. Help. . . even for the weakest member of the group. . . . That really was a fantastic experience for me.[31]

While many enthusiastically embraced the camaraderie found within the group, it came at a very high price. Performing the required illegal activities—bank robberies, kidnappings, bombing, murders—and the constant threat of being caught/sentenced to prison for a very long time were not the only pitfalls. There was also the problem of pressure from *within* the group; a member from one of the later generations explained:

> *Of course, the pressure of permanent persecution influences the group. All the relationships of the people in the group are eclipsed by this pressure which finally becomes the only connecting link that holds the group together. They call it the 'dialectics of persecution' and believe that it strengthens the unity of the group. . . . But in reality an extreme tension develops, which erupts in quarrels, the forming of cliques, and sneering remarks to one another.*[32]

Bommi Baumann agrees: *"We've never managed to retain the sensitiveness within the group because the pressure from outside is so strong that it catches up with you."*[33]

Being underground and participating in terrorist activities leads to massive isolation from the world. "The loss of their own identity is compensated for by the demonstration of the collective strength. [This was the o]nly way to mask their own ego-weakness. The political socialization of terrorists—as a process of permanent self-indoctrination by the group—finally leads to a total loss of reality and a complete miscalculation of the political and social environment."[34]

Even though the RAF's ideology declared the group to be opposed to authority, the leadership of the RAF cells was remarkably authoritarian, as reflected in the following anecdote. A new member of the Heidelberg cell of the RAF had been very impressed by the actions the organization had taken against industrialists and senior government officials. He was stunned when he went to his first meeting and learned that the group planned to set off firebombs in the local KaDeWe department store (a particularly opulent department store chain in Germany.) "*Gótt in himmel,*" he blurted out. "*There will be all these innocent victims.*" A chill fell over the room, and he realized he had questioned the group consensus. He might be deprived of his membership at the very onset. Worse, he might be killed, for it was said that "the only way out of a terrorist group was feet first, by way of the graveyard." "*Hans,*" asked the leader, in an icy tone, "*have you been to a KaDeWe store? If you have been, you will know that the people who shop there are not innocent victims, they are capitalist consumers. They deserve to die.*"[35] This comment reflects a polarized thinking. There are only two classes of people: those who support us and those who don't. Those who don't are the enemy and deserve to die.

Less Ideological in Subsequent Generations

Although they claimed that their actions were in harmony with the goals of the founding generation, the second, third, and succeeding generations increasingly formed their own largely autonomous groups and carried out independent actions, with less ideological coherence.[36]

The 2nd of June Movement, which took its name from the date of Benno Ohnesorg's murder at the Shah of Iran protest, acted as another generation and as an example of the growing autonomy. Former member Gerald Klopper discussed the difference between the RAF and the 2nd of June Movement:

> The RAF, with its intellectual origins, saw itself globally as the extended arm of the anti-imperialist liberation movement. We, however, did not need such derivative reasons. We wanted to free ourselves and did not require the bombing of the Vietnamese people as a reason for resistance. If you have to show up at 7:00 A.M. in your factory and put up day after day with the despotism of factory life (as old Marx called it), with repression and denial of your rights, then that is your reason.[37]

But at the end of the 1970s, the 2nd of June Movement officially abandoned the armed struggle. The RAF remained active throughout the 1980s and into the 1990s, but its membership had changed significantly. The university-educated ideologically motivated founding generation had been succeed in subsequent generations by ideologically less inspired individuals who had been recruited from the criminal class. The RAF, dominated by violent criminals, increasingly carried out violent crime for personal gain, with scant ideological justification.

EFFECT OF REUNIFICATION WITH EAST

The Berlin Wall, which was constructed by the German Democratic Republic on August 13, 1961—"to keep its citizens from voting against communism with their feet"[38]—had become a rallying point for the student movement and radical left wing, a concept and idea that validated their claims of the greatness of communism. The absence of personal contact with those living with communism led to idealization of their lives according to Marxist-Leninist tenets. The collapse of the Berlin Wall and subsequent German unification seemed to stun German left-wing terrorists and drastically shrunk their small base of sympathizers, as the failings of communist rule in East Germany, including Stasi (the secret police of East Germany) repression, clandestine support for the RAF, and the total failure of the economic utopia of communism became manifest.

OFFICIAL END

The RAF's activities in the 1990s consisted of a few sporadic bombings, the arrest or surrender of the few remaining leaders, and a long-overdue communiqué, in 1998, which stated the Red Army Faction had officially disbanded. In part it reads:

> We stand by our history. The RAF was the revolutionary attempt by a minority of people to resist the tendencies in this society and contribute to the overthrow of capitalist conditions. We are proud to have been part of this attempt. . . . The end of this project shows that we were not able to succeed on this path. But this does not speak against the necessity and legitimacy of revolt. The RAF was our decision to stand on the side of those people struggling against domination and for liberation all across the world. For us, this was the right decision to make.
>
> **The revolution says**:
>
> > *I was*
> > *I am*
> > *I will be again*
>
> > —Red Army Faction
> > March 1998[39]

CHAPTER 9

SHINING PATH (SL)

Just as the Kurdish separatist group PKK is highly identified with its charismatic founder, Abdullah Ocalan, and the Tamil Tigers is the virtual embodiment of its charismatic leader, Vellupillai Prabhakaran, so too is the Peruvian social revolutionary group Shining Path (SL—Sendero Luminoso) is highly identified with its founder, Abimael Guzman.[1]

Guzman was born on December 3, 1934, in the village of Tambo near the port of Mollendo, Peru. The illegitimate son of a wealthy merchant, Guzman spent the first five years of his life with his mother until her death. He then lived with his mother's family until he was 13, when he moved in with his father. They settled in the southern town of Arequipa, where he received a private Catholic school education. It is interesting to observe that, like Fidel Castro, the illegitimate Abimael grew up without a father and then went on in his autocratic charismatic leadership to be the strict and controlling father to his movement and, in his messianic dreams, to his nation. But underneath his over-compensatory grandiose facade, there rests at the core of his personality a wounded self.

At the age of 19, Guzman enrolled in the National University of San Agustin, in Arequipa, where he studied philosophy and law and developed a special interest in communism. Former classmates later described Guzman as "shy, disciplined, obsessive, and ascetic," but his academic achievements served to gain him the respect of his peers and elders.[2] His path to revolutionary philosophy was strongly influenced by several key figures. Guzman was introduced by his philosophy professor, Miguel Angel Rodriguez Rivas, to the writings of Immanuel Kant, who opposed direct democracy because it limited individual liberty.[3] It was the painter Carlos de la Riva who first inspired in Guzman an admiration for communist heroism.[4] The writings of José Carlos Mariategui, founder of Peru's Communist party, were also an inspiration to Guzman, as were those of other communist figures, especially Karl Marx, Vladimir Lenin, Joseph Stalin, and Mao Zedong. The following quotes from an extended interview with Guzman reveal the extent to which his political thinking was influenced by contextual events and communist theory, which ultimately led to him to join the Communist party of Peru:

> In the mid-1950s, when I was a university student [in Arequipa], I slowly approached Marxism and I matured through witnessing struggles. I was very impressed by the Arequipa uprising in 1950. Much blood was shed. The uprising was prompted by a strike by students.
>
> All this and other things have marked me. During this forging class struggle, my mind was opening, controlled by my reading which was gradually drawing me closer. . . . At that time, we were formed by studying the books on Stalin . . . Questions About Leninism . . . is an extremely important work. . . . I admired Stalin. . . . He was a great Marxist-Leninist, a great man.
>
> At that time, there was a trend in the University of Arequipa that allegedly championed the workers by propounding the odd tenet that only the children of workers could become Communist Party members. . . . This situation prevented me from joining the party for a long time, maybe years, due to my social status as I was not the son of a worker. Nevertheless, I insisted on becoming a party member, and finally became one.[5]

Guzman's commitment to the revolutionary change began to take shape when he witnessed the plight of the poor while conducting a census after an earthquake devastated Arequipa. It later intensified upon seeing the social condition of peasants in Ayacucho:

> My greatest and deepest need was to meet and discover the peasants in Ayacucho. Their reality shook my eyes and my mind. I saw the peasant's struggles and the strong repressions. I could sense the plight of the poor Peruvian peasants who have struggled and worked in the communities for centuries. But the centuries have not managed to exterminate them. They are vigorous and fight against all odds. . . . I saw that the peasants are the cornerstone of Peru.[6]

Upon his graduation in 1962, Guzman was appointed professor of philosophy at the Universidad Nacional de San Cristobal de Huamanga in Ayacucho, which had reopened only four years earlier, after being closed since 1886. Ayacucho's remote location in the Peruvian highlands and the free rein and encouragement given to the faculty in terms of social engagement permitted the organizational and conceptual framework of the Shining Path to develop relatively unnoticed by the central Peruvian government over a 17-year period before the declaration of "People's War."[7] At the university Guzman taught Maoist doctrine and subsequently became the dean of the Faculty of Letters. His influential position and charismatic personality allowed him to organize and recruit university students and poor young Peruvians into the Communist party. In February 1964 Guzman, then 29, married 18-year-old Augusta La Torre, the daughter of the local communist leader, Carlos La Torre.[8]

A growing division between Russia and China in the mid-1960s influenced Peru's Communist party to split into two factions in 1964: one that supported the Soviet (Russian) worker-based revolutionary approach of Karl Marx and Vladimir Lenin, and the other the Chinese peasant-based revolutionary approach of Mao Zedong, which Guzman chose as being much more applicable to Peru's situation. Fidel Castro's successful revolution in Cuba inspired several uprisings across Peru, primarily aided by the pro-Soviet faction. Although Guzman was a member of the pro-China faction and disagreed with the Soviet-Cuban influenced insurgencies, he was nevertheless a communist and perceived as a threat by Peruvian authorities.[9] To evade possible arrest, he was sent by the party to cadre school in China in 1966 where he had the opportunity to experience the country's Cultural Revolution (1966–1976) on three extended visits and learn the theory of the People's War. Guzman describes the degree to which Chinese communism influenced him: "*I visited China—the best political school on earth. This represents pride for a communist, pride at managing to receive such an extremely solid theory. This represents an indelible mark for me. I learned a lot. I have often said that the party is deeply indebted to the Chinese Communist Party. It has deeply marked us forever.*"[10]

Guzman also recalled his Chinese class on explosives and demolition: "*When we were finishing the course, they told us anything could be used for an explosion, and then, in the final part, we picked up our pens, and they blew up, and we sat down and our seats blew up. It was like fireworks everywhere, perfectly measured to show us that anything could be blown up if one had the ingenuity. I believe that school was essential in my formation and my beginning to value Chairman Mao Zedong.*"[11]

Guzman returned to Peru to find the pro-Chinese faction in a disorganized state. Some had left to join the insurgency in Cuba, against the counsel of Mao. As a consequence of the political climate abroad, in particular the controversy over the Cultural Revolution in China, the pro-Chinese Communist faction splintered into separate groups in 1967, with one faction leaving the party, and Guzman remaining in the faction following the lead of Mao under the party leader Saturino Paredes.[12] Threatened by the increase in insurgent uprisings, the Peruvian military forces overthrew the country's democratically elected civilian president, Fernando Belaunde Terry (1963–1968). Dismayed by General Juan Velasco's launch of a leftist reformist course, which included nationalizations and extreme agrarian reform, the pro-Chinese Communists and Guzman led the fight against the military government.[13]

THE FOUNDING OF SENDERO LUMINOSO

After a brief incarceration for leading antigovernment demonstrations, Guzman broke away from Paredes and, in 1970, founded Sendero Luminoso (SL, the Shining Path). Abimael Guzman came to be called Chairman Gonzalo by his followers.

Prior to the initiation of Sendero Luminoso's terrorist campaign in the 1980s, Guzman dedicated himself to the group's reorganization and preparation for armed and violent action. It was during the 1970s that its charismatic founder developed the SL's ideological framework, which served as the "guiding thought" of the organization's reign of terror.

Ideology

Sendero Luminoso incorporated the revolutionary thought and actions of Marxism, Leninism, and Maoism to create its unique ideological framework that came to be known as Gonzalo Thought (an augmentation of Mao Zedong thought tailored for the Peruvian environment). Calling his adaptation Gonzalo Thought and thus putting himself on the level of Marx, Lenin, and Mao indicates Guzman's messianic narcissism. The following quote emphasizes the unique (in his judgment) nature of Gonzalo Thought.

> It is the application of Marxism-Leninism-Maoism to the Peruvian revolution that has produced Gonzalo Thought. Gonzalo Thought has been forged in the class struggle of our people, mainly the proletariat, in the incessant struggles of the peasantry, and in the larger framework of the world revolution, in the midst of these earthshaking battles, applying as faithfully as possible the universal truths to the concrete conditions of our country. In sum, Gonzalo Thought is none other than the application of Marxism-Leninism-Maoism to our concrete reality. This means that it is principal specifically for our Party, for the people's war and for the revolution in our country.[14]

Abimael Guzman was the generator of the SL's social revolution and his importance to the cause was stressed in one of the organization's slogans,

"Uphold, defend and apply Marxism-Leninism-Maoism, Gonzalo Thought, Mainly Gonzalo Thought!"[15]

In order to emphasize the theory of revolution, Guzman never wore a uniform or sported a weapon; instead he opted to lead his followers with a book.[16] As stated in a Shining Path pamphlet: *"To wage war it is necessary to be a philosopher. Comrade Gonzalo's battle plans are political, not technical."*[17] Indigenous followers oftentimes referred to Guzman as Dr. Puka Inti (Quechua for "Red Sun"), while others simply called him Shampoo *"because he brainwashes you."*[18]

SL members suspected of not unreservedly following Gonzalo Thought engaged in the process of criticism and self-criticism, which the Peruvian journalist Gustavo Gorriti defines as "the admission of error, describing their mistakes in the harshest terms, implacably lashing themselves, thanking others for having attacked them, declaring that their subjugation to the party, its guiding thought and general line, slogans, plans, and programs, was complete, absolute."[19] Such a process had a dual purpose: to reaffirm Guzman's authority and maintain the organization's unity. Guzman was often heard saying: *"I don't have friends. I only have comrades."*[20] An example of criticisms and self-criticisms of Shining Path cadres cited by Gorriti follows:

> FELIPE: *I accept my mistake of failing to direct myself to C. Gonzalo as the party leader, of being irresolute, I condemn my black attitude; I support with fervor the furthering of what C. Gonzalo has said; I am for sweeping away with this, ready to deliver over my life.*[21]

Discipline was crucial to the organization's survival: *"We must impose discipline with rigor no matter what the cost; the slightest weakness means death and hunger. To act with implacable severity, whosoever does not act in this way is a traitor."*[22]

Guzman was described as a "highly disciplined person who didn't smoke, was never seen drunk, and had no known vices; in sum, a highly disciplined individual."[23] He demanded that his followers and supporters adopt and display such discipline in character. Militants and communities under SL control were prohibited from consuming alcohol, using illicit drugs, and engaging in other vices such as gambling and prostitution.

LEADERSHIP AND ORGANIZATION

At the very top of Sendero's pyramidal organizational structure was Abimael Guzman, serving as the president. The highly centralized leadership was tightly controlled by its founding leader, who was principal "ideologist, strategist, and internal contradiction synthesizer, and [who] explicitly fostered a cult of personality." All power flowed from Guzman.[24]

The next level of authority consisted of the Central Committee and the Political Bureau, responsible for the execution of political and military policies. Below this upper echelon was the Central Apparatus, which carried out political, social, and psychological operations and provided overall logistic support.[25] The next level comprised regional Intermediary Organizations and Party Committees, followed by a hierarchy of local cells composed of five to nine members.

According to an SL document, the main objectives of the group were the *"demolition of the Peruvian State, . . . to sweep away all imperialist oppression, mainly Yankee, and that of Soviet social-imperialism, . . . to destroy bureaucratic capitalism, . . . the liquidation of semi-feudal property, . . . to respect the property rights of the national bourgeoisie, or middle bourgeoisie, in the country as well as the city, . . . develop the People's War, . . . through revolutionary army of a new type under the absolute control of the Party, . . . and to complete the formation of the Peruvian nation."*[26]

SUPPORT BASE

Sendero Luminoso had 23,430 armed members and the support of 50,000 to 100,000 Peruvian sympathizers at the height of its power in 1990.[27] Members and supporters were from various socioeconomic backgrounds, including peasants, the proletariat, and professionals. Within the organization, students made up its largest social group. Gorriti provides a concise description of typical Shining Path cadres: "young people, thin, serious introverted; in general, from poor families, some of which had made efforts to give them a college education; without behavior problems—to the contrary, they were frequently obedient children and siblings, neat, quiet, hard-working, not charismatic enough to awaken strong devotion, but rather a silent appreciation."[28]

Sendero Luminoso principally targeted the young due to their vulnerability to indoctrination and the allure of excitement. This quotation from Guzman shows his admiration for the young: *"Youths are rebellious. If they were not this way they would not be youths. It is not bad for youths to rebel. It is right. It is right for their age, as a part of their maturity cycle. A youth who is not rebellious becomes aged. He is kicking cans. A youth has to be vigorous, strong, dynamic. He has to be a rebel for the sake of the future, and has to be a direct participant."*[29]

The next quotes are from two university students who, in offering their reasons for joining the revolutionary movement, show how they have fully accepted Guzman's worldview. One said: *"I could not tolerate the injustice, the* poverty, and the corruption in the state. I had to act in order to change the system. There is no place for those who comply with the exploiters who cause hunger and misery for the people. . . . President Gonzalo is a highly prepared brain; he will always be the light that guides us and the guarantee of triumph."[30] Another said: "To liberate the country from oppression, misery, and poverty, there had to be borne someone and it's our President Gonzalo, the guide who created the armed struggle to defend our people. He is the great world leader of our era."[31]

Demonstrating the manner in which Gonzalo Thought incorporated elements of Marxist-Leninism as well as Maoism, Guzman emphasized that both the peasants and the proletariat were important participants in Sendero's armed revolution, "The peasantry, especially the poor peasants, are the main participants, as fighters and commanders at different levels in the People's Guerrilla Army. The workers participate in the same ways, although the percentage of workers at this time is insufficient."[32]

Professionals were also sympathetic to the revolutionary struggle and could be found among the ranks of SL. One architect offers these reasons for joining: "I entered Sendero Luminoso because of the need to change our country, which for centuries has been the estate and the property of the rich. The injustices and the abuses committed always against the poor pushed me to enter the ranks of the Communist Party of Peru, the only true director of the popular war, aiming at the conquest of power in order to install the dictatorship of the proletariat."[33]

Women also played an important role in the predominately male terrorist organization. Although Sendero did not sexually discriminate in its recruitment of cadres, there was a selective preference for certain women, as one leader indicated: "Not just any woman can be involved in the revolution. They have to be young, because as long as women remain unmarried and have no children, they are much more insensitive and colder than men and are thus willing to do anything."[34]

Women of all ages were, nevertheless, found among the various echelons of SL. Rosa, a 42-year-old sociologist, served as a political leader for the group. In the following quotation, she explains her reasons for joining Sendero: "I entered Sendero Luminoso because I could no longer bear seeing on one side so much hunger and misery, and on the other side wealth and extravagance. The exploitation has to stop. There has been enough injustice and abuses, humiliation and contempt. The discussion has finished. It's the hour for action."[35] She also describes her admiration for Sendero Luminoso and Guzman extolling "the clarity and firmness with which they develop the war. Their valor and courage to achieve the installation of the dictatorship of the poor. A communist does not fear death, because the communist's life is surrendered to the party. . . . He is the man who awoke the political consciousness of the *poor people to use violence.... As philosopher and as a valiant man ... he equals Marx, Lenin, and Mao; he taught us to apply the law of contradictions.*"[36]

RECRUITMENT AND INDOCTRINATION

Although SL appeared to have a massive base of support, not all of its members were willing participants. Sendero's use of selective, targeted, and focused violence intimidated many to join the group, while threats against members' families prevented them from defecting. Children as young as eight years old were also indoctrinated into SL and trained to engage in brutal acts of violence and terrorism.[37]

The indoctrination of cadres into Sendero's ideological framework was the central element in preparation for the group's armed social revolution. The future leaders and cadres of SL were groomed and trained for the armed movement through its military school, established in April 1980. Guzman delivered his famous speech, "We Are the Initiators," at the closing ceremony of the ideological training that marked the beginning of the armed struggle.[38] The struggle that they began in Peru would be international in scope, transforming all of society. In dramatic and inspiring rhetoric, Guzman declared:

> *Comrades: Our work with hands unarmed has concluded.... A period has ended. Here we seal what had been done; let us open the future, actions are the key, power the objective. This we will accomplish ourselves, history demands it, class exhorts it, the people have prepared for it and want it; we must do our duty and we shall. We are the initiators.*
>
> *Revolution will find its nest in our homeland; we will make sure of it.... The people's war will grow every day until the old order is pulled down, the world is entering a new era: the strategic offensive of world revolution.*
>
> *The people rear up, arm themselves, and rise in revolution to put the noose around the neck of imperialism and the reactionaries, seizing them by the throat and garroting them....*
> *The flesh of the reactionaries will rot away, converted into ragged threads, and this black filth will sink into the mud; that which remains will be burned and the ashes scattered by the earth's winds so that only the sinister memory will remain of that which will never return, because it neither can nor should return.*
>
> *The trumpets begin to sound, the roar of the masses grows, and will continue to grow, it will deafen us, it will take us into a powerful vortex.... There will be a great rupture and we will be the makers of a definitive dawn. We will convert the black fire into red and the red into light. This we shall do, this is the rebirth. Comrades, we are reborn!*

We are the initiators. . . . Comrades, the hour has come, there is nothing further to discuss, debate has ended. It is time to act, it is the moment of rupture, and we will not carry it out with the slow meditation that comes too late, or in halls or silent rooms. We will make it in the heat of battle.

DEMOCRACY IN PERU

A second coup d'état in 1975 put General Morales Bermudez in power. Despite the transfer in leadership, Peru's social and economic problems mounted. Increasing opposition eventually led to the reelection of President Belaunde in 1980. Although democracy resumed in Peru, 12 years of socioeconomic suffering had prepared the stage for Sendero Luminoso to emerge and take action in the most virulent form of armed revolution.

In May 1980, in the election that resulted in President Belaunde's reelection, SL launched its political terrorist campaign with the burning of ballot boxes in the village of Chuschi. Despite the return of a civilian government, Guzman expressed disappointment in the electoral process of democracy and explained why the armed struggle must continue: *"What do elections imply? Is it in the people's interest to vote? Looking at Peru's experience, what revolutionary transformation has the people achieved through voting or in parliamentary activity? Every triumph has originated in the acts of popular struggle, and it is on the basis of its results that laws have been promulgated that recognize the masses."*[39]

TACTICS OF SENDERO LUMINOSO

Sendero's campaign employed these tactics: "dynamiting and fire-bombing of police stations, department stores, petrol stations, embassies, restaurants, banks, hotels, offices and factories."[40] Guzman emphasizes the principles behind people and the use of weapons:

Chairman Mao Zedong has told us that the main thing is mankind. Weapons are useful. So our task is to aim especially at people, at strengthening them ideologically and politically, at building the army ideologically and politically in this case, as well as building it militarily. This is our point of departure.

With regard to weapons, the Chairman says that the enemy has them and so the problem is to seize them from him, and this is principal. Modern weapons are necessary, but their performance depends on the ideology of the man who wields them. Lenin taught us that.[41]

Guzman decided to launch what he called the Gold-Sealed Finishing Stroke of the Great Leap, and in June 1986 SL guerrillas rioted in Lima's prisons, resulting in the death of least 210 prisoners.[42] According to Guzman, the death of fellow comrades was an act of heroism: *"The prisoners of war . . . carry on winning battles beyond the grave, they live and fight in us gaining new victories; we feel their robust and indelible presence, throbbing and luminous, teaching us today, tomorrow and for ever to give our lives to the party and the revolution. Glory to the Day of Heroism!"*[43] The following poem commemorating the death of Sendero militants in the prison massacre is graphic in its glorification of violence:

> *Glory to the fallen heroes,*
> *long live the revolution!*
> *Blood does not drown the revolution,*
> *but irrigates it!*[44]

During Sendero's next phase, *To Develop the Support Bases* (1987 to mid 1989), the organization managed to infiltrate judiciary and educational systems and erode the state's economic and political infrastructures.[45] In Guzman's words: *"We are developing the New Power only in the countryside. In the cities it will be developed in the final stage of the revolution. It is a question of the process of people's war."*[46] Guzman launched Sendero's fifth and final military phase, *Developing Bases in Order to Conquer Power*, in August 1989. The stated goal was to overtake the cities and defeat remaining enemies, with the ultimate purpose of installing *"throughout Peru the Popular Republic of the New Democracy as the first stage of the proletariat dictatorship."*[47]

REVOLUTIONARY VIOLENCE AND THE QUOTA

Sendero Luminoso relied on violence and terrorism to achieve the political goals of the social revolution. The extent of the violence SL perpetrated during the 1980s was remarkable. David Scott Palmer, a distinguished expert on Latin America and Sendero Luminoso, estimates that "more than twenty thousand Peruvians were killed, $10 billion worth of infrastructure damaged or destroyed, some five hundred thousand internal refugees were generated along with an almost equal number of emigrants."[48] The gross national product declined by 30 percent with a staggering hyperinflation of more than 2 million percent. The Peruvian nation was on the verge of collapse.

According to SL documents, violence was not only part of the historical process but also a necessary means for a successful revolutionary struggle:

> [T]he party cannot be developed more but through the use of arms, through armed struggle. That is the hard lesson that we have learned in 50 years, a great lesson we should never forget: We have no power because we have no guns. Like Chairman Mao has written, whoever has more guns has more power.[49]
>
> There is no construction without destruction, these are two sides of the same contradiction.[50]

Guzman often said: *"You either use power or they will use it against you."*[51]

The Quote of Blood

For Guzman, the loss of life was part of the armed struggle. Thus, he expected Sendero militants to sacrifice their lives for the revolution. As Gorriti explains: "the willingness, indeed expectation, of offering one's life when the party asked for it" is known as "the quota."[52] Guzman emphasized that the concept of the quota applied not only to Peru, but to the world revolution as well.

> About the quota: the stamp of commitment to our revolution, to world revolution, with the blood of the people that runs in our country. . . . The quota is a small part of the Peruvian revolution and of world revolution. . . . Most [of the deaths] are caused by the reaction [of the state] and fewer by us. They fill lakes while we only soak our handkerchiefs.[53]
>
> Marx, Lenin, and principally Mao Zedong have armed us. They have taught us about the quota and what it means to annihilate in order to preserve. . . . If one is persistent, maintains politics in command, maintains the political strategy, maintains the military strategy, if one has a clear, defined plan, then one is able to meet any bloodbath. . . . We began planning for the bloodbath in 1980 because we knew it had to come.[54]
>
> Blood makes us stronger and if it's this 'bath' that the armed forces have made for us, the blood is flowing, it's not harming us but making us stronger.[55]

According to a manuscript captured from an SL prisoner in Lurigancho Prison in 1985, Guzman is critical of those unwilling to give up their lives for the revolution: *"others are careful, afraid to make mistakes, therefore are not sincere, they make excuses, they try to save their skin, what are they protecting? If you have nothing, if you've given everything to the P[arty], your life is not your own, it belongs to the Party."*[56]

In December 1982, *Military Thought of the Party*, believed to be written by Guzman and senior SL leaders, mentions the cost of the armed struggle for the Shining Path: *"This is nothing but a good start, a fruitful beginning watered with good blood; . . . this [is] nothing but a preview. . . . This blood steels us . . . it makes us . . . more willing to ford any river, to cross hell, and to assault the heavens. . . . The cost, in the end is small.*"[57] The theme of "*good blood,*" and that "*blood steels us*" is striking.

During one of Gorriti's visits to a prison, he witnessed captured Senderistas shouting, in an organized and precise fashion, SL slogans and songs that glorified Gonzalo. A portion of one of the songs that Gorriti recorded is notable for its adoration of Gonzalo.

> *Except for power, all is illusion.*
> *Assault the heavens with the force of a gun! . . .*
> *It is Gonzalo! the fire sings,*
> *Gonzalo is armed struggle. . . .*
> *Gonzalo! the masses roar*
> *And the Andes shake,*
> *They express the burning passion,*
> *A steeled and sure faith.*[58]

Endowing sacrificing your life for the cause with heroic status strengthened the militants' resolve. The virtue of filling the quota of blood is extolled in the next ballad written by an anonymous Shining Path militant:

> *On the way out of Aucayacu*
> *there's a body, who could it be*
> *surely it's a peasant who gave his life for the struggle. . . .*
> *Today the quota must be filled*
> *If we have to give our blood for revolution, how good it will be.*[59]

Some 70,000 people were killed in the armed revolution of Sendero Luminoso and the counterterrorism campaigns of the Peruvian government.[60] Sendero's violent attacks drew several criticisms from human rights groups, but to that Guzman responded, "*We reject and condemn human rights because they are bourgeois rights, reactionary, counterrevolutionary.*"[61]

THE LOSS OF SENDERO'S SUPPORT AND SOCIETY'S REACTIONS

One of the objectives of SL's campaign was to instill fear among the population, regardless of affiliation. Real and perceived enemies of the armed revolution became victims to the group's use of violence. The majority of SL's victims were leaders of local communities, labor unions, and peasant organizations, including innocent citizens. Numerous individuals were executed under Sendero's "people's trials," while others were mutilated, beaten, and humiliated in public.

The following account is from a girl who witnessed a people's trial conducted by Sendero militants in her village: "They stood the boy in the plaza, calling him a traitor and a coward. Then, in front of everyone, they cut off his head with a knife. There was nothing we could do to save him. Five minutes later one of them yelled, 'Whoever does the same thing will receive the same punishment.' Then they left shouting allegiance to Comrade Gonzalo."[62]

As the violence (which earlier had been rigorously targeted and focused) expanded and targeted innocents, the organization, which earlier had great support from its constituency, began to inspire terror among the very populace from which it had drawn support and recruits.

In an interview conducted by Billie Jean Isbell, an anthropologist specializing in Andean studies, in Ayacucho in 1986, one community leader from the province of San Miguel commented on SL's extreme violence: "We are more afraid of Sendero than we are of the army or of the police. Let me tell you [about] something [that] happened. . . . In a meeting of the five communities there which [a friend] attended, they told about one thousand Sendero militants who entered the region and killed the young and old. They carved off the flesh with knives and carried it off in sacks. They left behind only bones and skeletons."[63]

INCREASINGLY AUTHORITARIAN GOVERNMENT RESPONSES

As the violence intensified in the 1980s, a series of counterterrorism efforts were employed by the Peruvian government to counter the threat of Sendero Luminoso. Such measures included the mobilization of *rondas campesinas*, or peasant patrols, police forces, and the Peruvian military. The effectiveness of the counterinsurgency measures were not immediately felt and sometimes seemed only to aggravate the plight of the Peruvian population. Peasant patrols formed to defend villages from Sendero raids sometimes took advantage to attack neighboring rival villages. Some police forces were infamous for their use of force and brutality.

Faced with an ineffective police force, President Belaunde turned to the Peruvian military as part of the government's antiterrorist campaign. Trained in conventional warfare, the military found itself unable to fully counter Sendero's terrorist tactics.[64] A confidential memo from an Ayacucho district attorney to the attorney general describes the problems in confronting the Shining Path threat: "This proselytizing work of the Shining Path is now operating . . . in all of the schools. . . . In many incursions made in schools, always noted has been the presence of fifteen- and sixteen-year old youths . . . without any student or teacher confronting them with a discussion to clarify matters at least, since it is understood that there is fear that they will be executed on the spot. . . . In the 'Mariscal Caceres' National High School . . . two months ago . . . once all of the students had begun to sing our National Anthem, they changed the note and began to sing out loudly the guerrilla songs and hymns."[65]

Military Criticizes Government

Some officers of the military were cognizant of the underlying conditions that led to the emergence of Sendero's armed revolution and criticized the government's policies to remedy the threat: "We can and are beating Sendero militarily, but there is another aspect in which we are not winning: the political and psychological one. We are not getting the resources we need to correct the causes of the war. It is going to take very radical means to win this war, a greater political cost than this government is willing to pay."[66]

Election of Fujimori and Declaration of Martial Law

In response to Sendero's escalating violence, in July 1990, Alberto Fujimori was elected president of Peru. Upon election, he immediately invoked martial law. The drastic measures taken to contend with Sendero Luminoso resulted in numerous human right abuses.[67] In spite of the external and internal challenges, counterinsurgent forces were able to conduct successful operations against Sendero Luminoso. Improvement in intelligence gathering and unit coordination allowed the counterinsurgent forces to raid Sendero safe houses, confiscate vital documents and computer files, arrest several SL leaders and militants at regional and local levels, and restore government control in certain areas.[68] The crowning achievement for the state's counterinsurgent forces came with the arrest of Abimael Guzman in 1992.

Narcissistic Hubris Precedes Downfall

The very personality qualities of Abimael Guzman that contributed to his powerful and autocratic leadership were to become the seeds of his downfall. The consummate narcissist, with dreams of glory, has a tendency to overvalue his morality and prospects for success while underestimating the adversary.[69] Seeing himself as invincible, Guzman and Sendero became increasingly careless, both in terms of the targeted violence becoming ever more indiscriminate, causing the loss of support of Sendero's constituency, but also becoming less concerned with security and protection for its indispensable leader.

SENDERO LUMINOSO DECAPITATED: HOW THE MIGHTY HAS FALLEN

Abimael Guzman was arrested in Lima on September 12, 1992. During the arrest, General Antonio Vidal, head of the National Directorate Against Terrorism (DINCOTE), supposedly said to Guzman: "In life, one had to know how to win and lose. As a man of the dialectic, you should know that you have lost." Guzman, while pointing a finger to his head, replied: "*You can take anything away from a man, except what he had here. And even if he is killed, his followers will remain.*"[70]

After his capture, Guzman stated: "*We are the sons and daughters of the people and we are fighting in these trenches, this is also part of the combat, and we do this because we are communists!*"[71] Part of Guzman's mystique and charismatic appeal was that he was never seen in public. The ultimate survivor, always eluding capture, he had an almost mystical, larger-than-life presence. Prior to his trial, Guzman was confined to an open cage in the public square, showing the world an unshaven, obese man, with his potbelly drooping over his striped prison uniform belt, urinating in public. In what was to be his last public speech, September 1992, he defiantly proclaimed, "*Some think this is a great defeat. They are dreaming and we tell them to keep on dreaming! It is simply a bend, nothing more, a bend in the road. The road is long and we shall arrive. We shall triumph. You shall see it. You shall see it.*"[72] His capture and public humiliation gravely damaged the image of this charismatic figure, a mortal blow to the organization he founded, just as the PKK never recovered from the capture of its charismatic leader, Abdullah Ocalan. Nevertheless, Guzman retained the loyalty of many under the continuing sway of his charismatic power. One primary school teacher expressed her continuing adulation for Guzman: "*President Gonzalo [Guzman] is the red sun who will illuminate the path towards the conquest of power and the elimination of this decrepit and rotten state. . . . President Gonzalo has shown that he is an intellectual of the highest level, a philosopher and strategist. He fell for tactical reasons; he will be freed and the reconstruction of the party will be made.*"[73]

Guzman was tried by a court of hooded military judges and sentenced to life in prison. The former Shining Path leader was transferred to maximum security prison at a naval base in Callao. His appeal for a peace agreement in 1993 elicited different responses from Sendero militants and supporters; some dismissed it entirely, others perceived it as a sign of defeat, and some felt that it was a forgery or a coerced declaration.[74] Thereafter, the SL fragmented in a manner reminiscent of the PKK after Ocalan's trial and his subsequent recanting.

Guzman, a charismatic narcissist with totalitarian control over his movement, considered his "Gonzalo Thought" to be the "Fourth Sword of Communism," along with Marxism, Leninism, and Maoism. While the military and Fujimori learned from the government's mistakes, as the SL gained strength, Guzman became increasingly convinced of the inevitability of his fulfilling his dreams of glory and no longer paid the attention to detail that had led to his success, in particular being careless concerning counterintelligence and personal security.[75] A careful strategist, he had planned meticulously and prepared thoroughly, turning an unfavorable objective reality into a favorable one. And then, overconfident and complacent, seeing himself as invulnerable and his success inevitable, he grew careless and inaccurately assessed his situation, which resulted in his capture, a mortal blow to his movement. Like Icarus, heedless of his father's anguished warnings to fly the middle course, Guzman soared too close to the sun. In contrast to the flat organizational structure and dispersed leadership of al-Qaeda under Osama bin Laden, which has contributed to its organizational resilience, the highly centralized leadership of Guzman made Sendero Luminoso especially vulnerable to effective counterterrorism. His capture as a consequence of highly effective counterterrorist police work was a fatal blow, decapitating this once-powerful revolutionary terrorist movement.

CHAPTER 10

REVOLUTIONARY ARMED FORCES OF COLOMBIA (FARC)

FARC does not engage in war for the sake of war, but . . . engages in war in search of peace.

—Commander Raúl Reyes[1]

War isn't just about shooting a gun. War is a fight against hunger and a struggle so that you don't die. War is a fight so that you have clothes. War is a fight to have a roof and to not get rained on. War is a fight to be able to read and not be illiterate. What I mean is that war is a fight so that you don't die.

—Fabian Ramirez[2]

INTRODUCTION

The Revolutionary Armed Forces of Colombia (FARC—Fuerzas Armadas Revolucionarias de Colombia) was founded in 1964 as a social revolutionary organization with Marxist-Leninist ideological foundations with the declared intent to overthrow the democratic Colombian government. FARC is Latin America's oldest, largest, most capable, and best-equipped insurgency with perhaps 12,000 fighters, located mostly in rural areas of Colombia, South America's oldest democracy.[3] While FARC no longer retains the strictest adherence to this original ideology, the group's senior members still consider themselves Marxist-Leninist, and much of the documentary material obtained in recent years still employs strong Marxist-Leninist rhetoric.[4] In addition to its attacks on Colombian military, political, and economic targets, FARC has been heavily involved in narcotics trafficking, kidnapping for ransom, extortion, murder, and other criminal acts, to the point where the group is better known for its major role in the illicit narcotics industry than for its insurgent activities. Yet its leadership is still committed to its social revolutionary goals and employs terrorist tactics to intimidate its political adversaries.

HISTORY: ORIGINS OF MAJOR PLAYERS AND MAJOR ISSUES

The history of Colombia is bathed in blood. The current internal crises there are but the latest phase of a civil war that started over a century ago. The culmination of the civil war between the Liberals and the Conservatives was the "national bloodletting," referred to as the La Violencia, from about 1948 to 1958, which resulted in an estimated 200,000 deaths. The basic catalyst for violence was the refusal of government officials to comply with the people's demands for socioeconomic reform. At the beginning of La Violencia, Manuel Marulanda described the fear, desperation, and sense of marginalization that led to the formation of FARC: "*I started to look for a solution. Already you heard people saying, 'Who do we get? Who will join us? Guns? Where are the guns, and how do we get them? If we stay quiet, they're going to kill us all. We couldn't take any more punishment.'* "[5]

Such statements reflect the initial general attitudes, considerations, and motivating forces of Latin American social revolutionary groups seeking to overthrow the capitalist economic and social order that, in the case of Colombia, led to corrupt and violent practices inflicted by the landed elite on the peasant settlers. Besides FARC, a number of other social revolutionary terrorist groups were formed and became active during the same period, including the April 19 Movement (M-19—Movimiento 19 de Abril) and The National Liberation Army (ELN—Ejército de Liberacion Nacional of Columbia, and the Shining Path (SL—Sendero Luminoso) and Túpac Amaru of Peru.

A military coup ended La Violencia and a power-sharing arrangement led to the liberals and conservatives forming the National Front (Frente Nacional, 1958–1974). However, during this violent period, landless locals banded together in self-defense communities, forming *autodefensas* under the leadership of Marulanda, who was on the left wing of the Liberal party. The families, who described themselves as a movement of rural workers, had cleared land for farming, with the support of the Colombian Communist party, and had asked the government to build roads and schools and grant them access to loans to expand their agricultural efforts. In the absence of government support, the peasant communities declared themselves Marxist-Leninist agrarian "independent republics."[6] The largest cooperative, Marquetalia, which had 1,000 members, was located in the remote mountainous regions in the Andean plains. In the late 1950s, after the civil war, the Colombian government, with the assistance of a U.S. assessment team, put together a pacification strategy, Plan Lazo, and struggled to reassert its control over the state and reduce the number of subversive groups, including the communist republics in southern and central Colombia.[7]

In the early 1960s the government attempted unsuccessfully to occupy Marquetalia, which increasingly was perceived as "the epicentre of the revolution."[8] On May 18, 1964, approximately 2,000 soldiers surrounded the peasant enclave and blocked the entrance of food and medicine. This Operation Marquetalia lasted three months and formed part of Plan Lazo, which was supported by the U.S. military. The survivors of this siege, who were able to escape along secret paths on the night of June 14, declared war against the government of Colombia and founded the Southern Bloc.

THE FOUNDING OF FARC

Two years later, in 1966, at an annual conference of guerrilla leaders, the Southern Bloc expanded its military efforts into a nationwide group, the Revolutionary Armed Forces of Colombia (FARC—Fuerzas Armadas Revolucionarias de Colombia). Since its inception, has been led by former peasant farmer Pedro Antonio Marín, who is generally referred to as Manuel Marulanda-Vélez and whose enemies refer to as *Tirofijo*, Spanish for "Sureshot." Referring to the siege, Marulanda stated, *"The self-organized and self-led resistance of the potential victims, the peasants, emerged [due to] reactionary violence."*[9]

The Founding Generation

Pedro Antonio Marín, or Marulanda, was born between 1928 and 1930 into a peasant family in a coffee-growing region of west-central Colombia. He had only four years of formal education. His family supported the Liberal party, and when a civil war began in 1948 following the assassination of a Liberal president, Marulanda and a few cousins moved to the mountains and became guerrillas.[10] Marulanda is considered to be a professional survivor and a determined commander.

Only five feet tall, he is a charismatic chieftain who has been personally involved in combat and inspired unrivaled confidence in his followers. Marulanda's peasant origins and his sense of military strategy have earned him nationwide recognition as a leader in leftist political and guerrilla circles. According to one of his top commanders, Raúl Reyes: "*Commander Manuel Marulanda, who lives in the mountains with the rest of the guerillas, occupies himself with teaching . . . forms of battle to the masses of the villages. [Marulanda] is the teacher and guide who is most clear and experimental in the political, military, and organizational [aspects] of the formation of the new combatant staff. [Marulanda spends] a good part of [his] time in designing and controlling the practice of the political-military plans of all FARC groups.*"[11]

Jacobo Arenas, Marulanda's close friend, second-in-command, and FARC's political founder, aspired to establish an agrarian communist state, with small-size industries. Arenas integrated a political agenda with FARC's military strategy of overthrowing a government it perceived to be plagued by elitism and corruption.

As conceptualized by the founding generation, there are two primary goals for FARC: to overthrow the state and to establish a communist-agrarian state in its place.[12] Such aims will be accomplished to the extent that solidarity is achieved among the entire Latin American Communist revolutionary movement.

For decades following La Violencia, the insurgent groups, including FARC, remained largely outside the focus of the government, patiently creating an alternative society.[13] During the 1970s and 1980s, like Hamas in its formative stage in Gaza, FARC established its own schools, judicial system, health care, and agrarian economy, thereby creating its own *de facto* state in remote regions of southern Colombia and building significant social capital. Eventually, there were in effect two Colombias: the remote area east of the mountains, which is the domain of key insurgent groups, characterized by harsh mountain and forest regions with undeveloped, dirt roads, and scattered villages, and the more developed regions west of the mountains, where the landed elite live. The internecine conflicts in Colombia have always been about power, and in this country, power stems from control of the land. As long as the guerrilla groups confined their activities to their section of Colombia, the government would leave them alone, acting only when the insurgents' actions demanded a response. However, FARC became more ambitious.

Creating a Revolutionary Army Funded by Narcotics

In a pivotal meeting at a party conference held in May 1982, FARC decided that the priority task was to create a revolutionary army that would be able to take on the security forces. In order to fund this effort, FARC decided to exploit the narcotics trade. By taxing all aspects of the drug trade, it could reap profits; by protecting and controlling production areas, it would not only secure its income but would also be able to recruit from the marginalized peoples living in these regions.

As the crops became more lucrative, FARC began levying a 10 percent tax on fields of coca and opium poppies, the raw material for cocaine and heroin, and collecting fees for every narcotics flight leaving controlled regions. Indeed, the ability to employ tactics that may have at once seemed counter to FARC's original Marxist-Leninist ideology signifies what Commander Reyes rationalizes as FARC's ability and obligation to adapt to changing times: *"FARC is characterized as a political force that is nurtured by the Marxist-Leninist principles . . . under the assumption that Marxist-Leninism is not a dogma but has to be a guide for revolutionary action. For this reason, we consider that on today's stage, it is necessary that each time we are able to innovate more and learn from various experiences in the revolutionary battle, so as not to fall into using obsolete schemes that would distance us from reality."*[14]

In examining motivations for Colombians' involvement in FARC and FARC's involvement in drugs, it is clear that the concepts of narco-terrorism and political terrorism are not mutually exclusive. Indeed, FARC is involved in the narcotics trade as a way of "funding the revolution." While the group did consider the negative aspects of links to the drug trade, the benefits with regard to financial resources and popular support were too great. The money and the manpower led to FARC's remarkable resurgence. In 1982, FARC was a small organization of 15 fronts with approximately 2,000 guerrilla fighters, worried about attracting followers. By 1990, as a consequence of the large infusion of drug-related funds, it had expanded its forces to 43 fronts with about 5,000 fighters. The practical benefits of such a size increase include the ability to move to mobile warfare and to use large units capable of directly confronting military units of equal size and of overrunning military instillations and smaller units.[15] FARC's views on the legitimacy of drug trafficking are interesting: *"We tax everything under our control. Everybody else lives on this money. Why shouldn't we? We regulate drug areas, defending the rights of campesinos who have little other opportunities."*[16]

A number of commentators have asserted that FARC camouflages its illegal activities under the cover of political ideology, that hiding behind a political screen has allowed it to maintain the appearance of a semi-legitimate political force in Colombia while continuing to engage in criminal activities and fill its coffers with illegal profits. As FARC defector Carlos Ploter notes, drug money is creating *"false needs"* among guerrilla fighters and distracting them from their initial objective of fighting for social justice. FARC members have succumbed to consumerism and long for luxuries, such as expensive cars and watches. Moreover, as *Washington Post*'s Marcela Sanchez notes, those FARC members caught in the middle of a conflict that began 40 years ago and that is now part of both the war on drugs and war on terrorism have "achieved little else other than a twisted sense of upward mobility."[17]

One FARC defector, "José," describes the link between FARC and the drug trade: "*To end the war you have to end the guerrillas. As long as there are guerrillas there are drugs. They exist together.*"[18]

However, there is a consensus among those who have followed FARC since its inception that the Marxist-Leninist ideology of the founding fathers remains a powerful, indeed the core, motivating force. Thomas Marks, professor of insurgency, terrorism, and counterterrorism at the National Defense University and a noted expert on revolutionary warfare and FARC, observes that "in all of its basics—from vocabulary to analytical categories to societal analysis to combat doctrine, FARC remains Marxist-Leninist."[19] The members' mind-set is communist; the communist watchword "God is party" still pertains. FARC's ideological rigidity is almost akin to evangelical belief. Its national strategy is of a prolonged people's war and occupation of territory. FARC plans a gradual encirclement of Colombia's principal cities and a final assault on Bogotá.[20]

GROUP PROFILE AND MEMBERSHIP

An analysis of the group makeup provides further insights into motivations for joining FARC and involvement in its activities. Sociologist James Peters states that 80 percent of FARC's members are peasants. Most are young, poorly educated people from rural areas, some of whom indicate that they are more attracted to FARC for its "*relatively good salary and revolutionary adventurism than for its ideology.*"[21] In contrast to most other Latin American guerrilla and terrorist groups, FARC leaders also generally are poorly educated peasants. For example, Manuel Marulanda, FARC's chief leader, had only four years of grammar school education. His predecessor, Jacobo Arenas, had only two years of school.

Many new recruits do not seem to have a choice about whether to join FARC. Although FARC has stipulated that 15 was the minimum age for recruitment, this standard has not been respected.[22] According to Colombian authorities, a 10-year-old used by FARC to deliver a bomb was killed on April 17, 2002, after the bicycle he rode up to a military checkpoint exploded. Members also reportedly pressure indigenous people to become involved in the conflict, and media reports indicate that FARC had recruited adolescents from native Amazonian tribes in Brazil. FARC has been accused of forcibly conscribing Colombian youth in areas where it has difficulties recruiting or in instances in which landowners are unable to meet FARC demands for "war taxes."[23] A 19-year-old pleading for refugee status before a U.S. court of appeals stated that he was working on his family's farm when he was approached by a group of men who identified themselves as members of FARC. The youth testified that the guerrillas asked him to join the group and stated that *"life could be rough"* if he refused. He refused and later received two phone calls demanding that he join. After he again refused, the guerrillas told him that *"[he] should be careful because the offense [he] had made against them was unforgivable."*[24]

While for some, there does still seem to be ideological motivation for joining FARC, poor farmers and teenagers join out of boredom or simply because it pays them about $350 a month, which is $100 more than a Colombian army conscript. Considering the financial benefits, forced conscription, and lack of alternatives, FARC would seem to have a weaker ideological base than it professes to have, but some new recruits do subscribe to FARC's original Marxist-Leninist social revolutionary ideological platform. Ramón, a 17-year-old guerrilla, told a *Washington Post* reporter, *"I don't know the word 'Marxism,' but I joined FARC for the cause of the country . . . for the cause of the poor."*[25]

For the leadership echelon, Marxist-Leninist doctrine continues to reign supreme. While there are a few members of the younger generation in the secretariat, they are careful not to overstep their bounds, must be careful about being "pure," and do not have much influence. This is not likely to change in the near term unless Marulanda dies, which emphasizes the importance of the health status of this aging leader.[26]

Aging Leader

Marulanda has been pronounced dead several times in army communiqués, but reports of his demise were premature, as he has always reappeared in guerrilla actions. He is approximately 80 years old and his health is a point of concern for the group. His age is significantly affecting his leadership and vitality, probably accounting for the paralysis in FARC leadership and decision making in recent years. While he is still at the helm, few changes can occur, and new ventures or policy shifts are not anticipated.

However, the power of Marulanda, the leader of the moderate faction, who favors a political solution, is limited to some extent by FARC's main decision-making body, the seven-member secretariat.[27] As there is no clear successor, when Marulanda dies, there will probably be a power struggle. Jorge Briceño ("Mono Jojoy") represents FARC hard-liners, who favor military solutions and oppose the peace process. Marulanda's death will likely lead to domination of FARC by Jojoy and his fellow hard-liners. Mono Jojoy reportedly has been the primary cause for a division and contention between FARC's political and military branches.

Regardless of generational differences FARC, as noted by Commander Reyes, old members and new, strongly assert that their violent actions are simply a response to the government's military actions: "*there is no force directed to make policy through arms. However, if the enemy . . . insists on war, FARC has a responsibility of responding to that challenge each time [with greater force] and for that reason FARC requires the support and the solidarity of everyone.*"[28]

FARC recognizes the harm that its actions impose on the Colombian citizenry but states that despite such harm (and the resulting harm to FARC's public image), the violence will continue: "*Never are we going to renounce peaceful means, but if we are obliged to take part in armed battle, then we will also continue with such battle, with the pain that is implied for many people; in the field of combat there are many dead and destruction and pain for many people, and we hope to avoid all that.*"[29]

Such statements create the impression that FARC members are the victims of violence. In calling for solidarity among the masses, FARC perpetuates the impression that the masses should consider themselves victims of the government and should bear arms against "the enemy," alongside FARC.

SELF-DEFENSE FORCES OF COLOMBIA

In Colombia, there are several paramilitary self-defense organizations, the majority of which are grouped under the umbrella organization called the Self-Defense Forces of Colombia (AUC—Autodefensas Unidas de Colombia). Its founding leader, Carlos Castaño, who was assassinated several years ago, trained a generation of paramilitary militia. The atrocities committed during La Violencia by the semi-official armed groups referred to as "chulavitas" are carried out today by paramilitary groups. These are not government-sponsored "death squads" but rather appear to be more akin to vigilante groups.[30] Today's paramilitary militias were formed in the 1980s, with assistance from the landed elites, the Colombian army, and the drug traffickers who owned large plots of the country's best land. The peace talks with the AUC, which had begun in 2003, involved a hasty *de facto* pardoning of murders and drug trafficking charges.[31]

TRANSFORMATION OF COLOMBIA
UNDER PRESIDENT URIBE

When President Alvaro Uribe came to power in 2002, Colombia was mired in armed conflict and its economy was struggling out of its first recession in seven decades. Many Colombians assert that Uribe has helped transform the country since he came to office.[32] The economy has grown at an annual rate of 4.4 percent, rising to 5 percent in 2005, helped by high prices for oil and metal exports. Under his "democratic security" strategy (which has received strong support from the White House), life in the main cities is more secure, and it is becoming increasingly possible to drive between these cities with little likelihood of being kidnapped by FARC and other insurgent groups. Murders and kidnappings are at their lowest rates in two decades, according to government figures. Uribe, who came to office promising to bring a new, heightened level of security to Colombia, has made remarkable progress in achieving this goal. The number of murders has been cut in half, from 32,000 per year at its peak. Polls demonstrate that support for Uribe's program, which earlier was mainly confined to the urban middle and upper classes, now extends throughout the country.[33]

With some 12,000 members, FARC has continued to be active throughout Colombia and governs a region the size of Switzerland. It has waged its revolutionary struggle for more than 40 years, and its doctrine has emphasized patience and persistence in what inevitably will be a long struggle. FARC has, however, never really had mass support, and functions more like a *foco*,* with the combatants being the movement. This fact in turn has permitted the government to focus its security efforts on the FARC paramilitary adversary without being concerned with a broader population supporting FARC, in contrast to Hamas, where there is broad community support for the Hamas militants.

FARC members claim that they do not want to be thought of simply as terrorists who work outside the law: *"[I]t is so very important that we can also count on the support of many friends on the level of the distinguished members of parliament, on the level of distinguished social, intellectual, democratic, communist, and revolutionary organizations and of friends of peace for Colombia, in order to achieve the recognition of force for FARC that would permit FARC to compete for the favor of the popular masses in the public place, without the stigma of being an organization that is not recognized by international laws. This is an urgent necessity that exists."*[34]

---

* Inspired by Ernest "Che" Guevara in the 1959 Cuban Revolution, and formalized as revolutionary doctrine by Regis Debray, the *foco* theory of urban guerrilla warfare is that a small cadre of mobile guerrillas can serve as a focus (*foco* in Spanish) and mobilize popular discontent against the regime and lead to a general insurrection.

There is evidence linking FARC and other terrorist organizations, such as the IRA in Northern Ireland and ETA in the Basque region of Spain, to provide weapons, training, and safe havens. Links between the IRA and FARC reportedly go back several years and were established through the current relationship between FARC and ETA. These relationships demonstrate the extent of FARC business networking and operations, including extensive arms trading and technology exchanges.

Speaking to other communist groups in the Latin American region, Commander Reyes notes the solidarity FARC members are hoping to bridge with such marginalized sectors: *"[These groups] know that in FARC they have friends . . . confronted with the politicians of the imperialism of the United States of America and the Colombian oligarchy, who are determined to perpetuate their power at the costs of the pain, the exploitation, the misery, and the state repression of the dispossessed and marginalized individuals of our homeland."*[35] Although now in a period of strategic retreat, FARC does not believe it is losing. Rather, it has had to drop back to a different phase of Maoist struggle, planning to return to a more active struggle once Uribe is out of office.[36]

Joaquin Villalobo, former commander of the Farabundo Marti National Liberation Front (FMLN) of El Salvador, has observed that FARC has been on the decline during the Uribe years, having had difficulty responding to the Colombian army's reorganization. While FARC has existed for 40 years, it was more than 10 years ago that the group seriously challenged the state and less than five years ago that the state decided to confront the group. Colombia, in Villalobo's opinion, has *"achieved the most national and international legitimacy in its struggle against the insurgency, and FARC is the most illegitimate guerilla organization the region has known."*[37]

FARC is increasingly isolated internationally and will have difficulties overcoming its political incapacity and military weakness *"unless it received direct support from a neighboring government, which would mean covert logistics operations on a grand scale and a nearby rearguard."*[38] And that is exactly what the populist socialist leadership of Hugo Chavez in neighboring Venezuela has been providing.

Since Chavez came to power in Venezuela, he has provided financial support as well as weapons to his fellow social revolutionaries in FARC. The purchase of 100,000 AK-103s from Russia and the revised Venezuelan military doctrine, which emphasizes the "war of the fleas," that is, a campaign of terrorism and insurgency, suggests this trend will increase.[39]

RELIGIOUS EXTREMIST TERRORISM: KILLING IN THE NAME OF GOD

The wave of suicide bombing in Israel and Iraq, the suicidal skyjackings of September 11, 2001, in the United States, and the London transit bombings of July 7, 2005, are not a new phenomenon. Their provenance can be traced back to the early days of the Christian era. As the noted terrorism scholar David Rapoport observes, three English words—zealot, thug, and assassin—trace their origins to religious terrorist groups, the Zealots, the Thugs, and the Assassins.[1]

In the name of their faith, these groups took violent actions to change the political system; they were the first terrorists. They came from three different religions—Judaism, Hinduism, and Islam. The Zealots, a Jewish terrorist organization, induced a massive revolt against Rome in 66–70 CE, a conflict that ended in the spectacular mass suicide at Masada.[2] The movement lasted only 70 years, but in the space of a century two more Jewish terrorist uprisings were inspired by the Zealots. The Thugs were a seventh-century cult that terrorized India until the mid-nineteenth century. Serving the Hindu god Kali, the Goddess of Destruction, they considered themselves progeny of Kali. The Assassins were prominent actors from 1090 to 1215. A Muslim Shi'a Islamic sect, they fought to repel the Christian crusaders. The violent acts of the Assassins were sacramental, a divine duty, commanded by their interpretation of religious text. Their self-sacrifice would secure them a higher place in paradise. These were the historical forbearers of today's radical Islamist terrorists.

The early 1980s gave birth to two militant Islamist groups active today: Hezbollah and Hamas. The rise of Hezbollah was inspired by the Islamic revolution of the Ayatollah Khomeini in 1979, which introduced the concept of merging politics and radical Islam. Khomeini drew on themes in the historical experience of Shi'a Islam that justified violence and actions against non-Muslim states in the pursuit of the Islamic revolution. The legacy of Shi'ism, more than 1,400 years old, is one of martyrdom, persecution, torment, suffering, power-lessness, and insecurity.[3] According to Shi'ite doctrine, the meek are the right-eous and the strong are evil. Therefore, Khomeini argued, the strongest nations—the superpowers—are the most evil and *"responsible for all the world's corruption."* Khomeini early spoke of the universality of Islam, carving out an Islamic leadership role beyond the boundaries of Iran:

> Islam, while respecting one's homeland, which is one's place of birth does not place it before Islam. . . . The notion that we are Iranian and they are Lebanese or are from some other place is not propounded in Islam. . . . There are no separate accounts. . . .
>
> Islam has come to unite all the peoples of the world, whether Arab or non-Arab, Turk or Persian, with each other into a great umma called the umma of Islam, and to establish it in the world so that those who want to gain control of those Islamic governments and Islamic centers will be unable to do so.[4]

While we are currently preoccupied with Islamist militant terrorism, in fact, in the texts of each of the Abrahamic monotheistic faiths—Judaism, Christianity, and Islam—there is language that has been interpreted not only to permit killing, but where killing in the name of God becomes a sacred obliga-tion. In this section, we first consider the variant of religious extremist terror-ism that is currently posing a major threat to international security—Islamist militant terrorists killing in the name of Allah—with discussions of Hezbollah, Hamas, and al-Qaeda. But as observed, historically all fundamentalist religions have righteously killed in the name of their faiths. We then consider religious extremist terrorists killing in the name of other Gods, Jewish and Christian fun-damentalist terrorism, and the millennial religious terrorism of Aum Shinrikyo.

CHAPTER 11

HEZBOLLAH: THE PARTY OF GOD

PRECURSOR TO HEZBOLLAH

In 1978, while visiting Libya, Musa al-Sadr, a charismatic Lebanese Shi'ite Imam, mysteriously disappeared. The psychological and ideological foundations of Hezbollah can be traced back to this imam who arrived in Tyre, Lebanon in 1960 and began to organize Lebanese Shi'ites, who had been excluded from political and economic power since the Lebanese civil war of 1958. Attempting to form a Shi'ite mass movement, the charismatic al-Sadr established the Movement of the Deprived (Harakat al-Mahrumin) in 1974. Emphasizing themes of victimization and humiliation, al-Sadr spoke eloquently of transforming the social movement into a military organization, the Battalions of the Lebanese Resistance, also known as Amal:

> Today we shout out loud the wrongs against us, that cloud of injustice that has followed us since the beginning of our history. Starting from today, we will no longer complain or cry. Our name is not mitwali (a derogatory name for the Shia). Our name is "men of refusal," "men of vengeance," "men who revolt against all tyranny," even though this costs us our blood and our lives. Hussein faced the enemy with seventy men. The enemy was very numerous. Today we are more than seventy, and our enemy is not the quarter of the whole world.[1]

In Baalbeck, a month later, al-Sadr further emphasized this theme, which became the theological sanction for Shi'a youth entering the path of warfare: "*Arms are man's beauty. What does the government expect? What does it expect against rage except revolution?*"[2]

This theme of Shi'a discontent was further magnified by Lebanon's 1975 civil war.

In addition to the disappearance of Musa al-Sadr in 1978, the 1979 Islamic revolution in Iran and the Israeli invasion of Lebanon in 1982 served as further catalysts for the formation of Hezbollah. Israel's 1982 invasion of Lebanon, which caused Shi'ites to feel particularly threatened, led Amal to split over policy differences, with Amal's leader Nabih Berri preferring the political path.

In August 1982, Iran's Supreme Leader Ayatollah Khomeini convened the first Conference for the Downtrodden in Tehran, during which he met with a number of Lebanese clerics, including Ayatollah Fadlallah, Sheikh Abbas Musawi, and Sheikh Hasan Nasrallah. Khomeini urged them to return home to Lebanon and organize the community of observant Muslims to form a resistance to Israel's invasion. Upon returning home from this meeting, Sheikh Musawi stated, *"We are ready to fight Israel, we are martyrdom seeking (shahadah), and we will fight them even from the graves."*[3]

In 1982, Musawi, with a group of Lebanese Shi'ite Muslims, formed a party dedicated to establishing an Islamic state in Lebanon. Drawing on the Qur'anic injunction, "Verily the party of God shall be victorious!", they called themselves Hezbollah (the Party of God).

GROWING ANTI-ISRAELI SENTIMENT

Initially formed as a militant faction within the Shi'a religious group in Lebanon, Hezbollah dedicated itself to violent resistance against Israel, particularly in opposition to Israel's incursions into and occupation of Southern Lebanon. The group's statements have focused their attacks on Israel and on the United States for its support of Israel. Furthermore, Hezbollah has tapped into the larger anti-Israeli sentiments by condemning Israel's occupation of Palestine. Hezbollah officials have even compared Israel with a malicious disease, a common psychological warfare technique for dehumanizing an opponent. In language reminiscent of Adolf Hitler's medical anti-Jewish rhetoric,[4] one Hezbollah leader stated, *"I wish to draw your attention to the threat posed by this entity which has robbed Palestine; this cancerous tumor, this vile microbe, an entity that knows no limits that spreads out wherever Israelis are, wherever Israelis are, wherever there is a remnant from the Talmud or where a Jewish rabbi once sat. . . . Hope is rising for the fulfillment of the divine promise to eradicate this cancerous plague."*[5]

SHI'A ECONOMIC INEQUALITY IN LEBANON

In addition to anti-Israeli sentiment, economic inequality and the marginalization of Lebanon's Shi'a minority have formed the foundation of Hezbollah's popular support base. Prior to the 1982 formation of Hezbollah, the Shi'ites were essentially second-class citizens within Lebanon. Drawing on Imam al-Sadr's Movement of the Deprived, Hezbollah statements have intentionally appealed to the poor and downtrodden, calling themselves *"[t]he first party to oppose deprivation . . . champion of the peasants and the farmers, the laborers and the poor, the oppressed and the deprived, the workers and the homeless."*[6]

The crisis created by Shi'ite economic inequality in the 1970s played a pivotal role in fostering growing support for Hezbollah. Southern Lebanon and the Biqa' Valley were both economically neglected rural regions, and migrating Shi'ites found themselves equally marginalized in the suburbs of Beirut. Far from improving their lives, migration created a growing urban poor, who would serve as a pool of potential recruits for Hezbollah and other violent militias. As slum-dwellers in what were known as the "belts of misery," the Shi'ites formed the most disadvantaged segment of Lebanese society. Magnifying this Shi'a resentment, Hezbollah leaders ridiculed Lebanon's elite, noting that the wealthy Lebanese of American University, Beirut identified with the West, not with the country's poor.[7] This economic gap created a predictable and widespread sense of victimization among the Shi'ites, a resentment that would create a fertile environment for radicalism.

During the 1980s, Israel's actions in Southern Lebanon—particularly the mass detention of sizable portions of the male population—further exacerbated Shi'ite bitterness and hatred. One author notes that "by 1983, 10,000 Lebanese and Palestinians were held captive in Israeli-controlled jails. The Ansar prison camp alone is reported to have detained half the South's male population at one time or another between 1982 and 1985."[8] While the magnitude reported may have been exaggerated, it is clear that such actions compounded anti-Israeli sentiment within Lebanon. Resentment and anger toward Israel was further intensified by Shi'ite migrations away from conflict-stricken Southern Lebanon. The Israeli action, affecting an estimated 80 percent of Southern Lebanese villages and with claims that fatalities reached 19,000, prompted a mass migration of Southern Shi'ites, who subsequently relocated, expanding into the suburbs of Beirut where they formed hostile militant camps.

Hamza akl Hamieh, an Amal militia man, spoke of his feelings about recruitment and life in Hezbollah:

> I live in the town of Ba'albek, which has a population of about 150,000. I cannot recall a single friend of mine who wasn't a member of Hezbollah. Everyone I know is, including all the members of my family.
>
> From a very early age, I used to go to pray in the mosques. I later volunteered for the Amal youth movement, where I underwent early training, which helped me mature and reach the state of mind in which I eventually joined the Hezbollah.
>
> In those lessons we understood the unique nature of our religion and that the Ashura distinguishes us from the other streams of Islam. . . . In the lessons on religion and customs, I began to feel the revolutionary atmosphere. . . .
>
> After I enlisted, I felt a sense of pride and satisfaction. I was only part of a group when I went out on reconnaissance expeditions or participated in attacks on enemy positions. In all such cases, the atmosphere among the group members was good.
>
> As for using ideology to justify armed action, in the one serious military operation in which I participated, a sheik holding a Koran in his hand blessed us as we set off for the attack.
>
> I have no regrets for what I have done. The only thing I am sorry about is that I didn't study more. . . . The Jews who are Zionists want to live with racism. The moment you don't consider me a human being, you become criminals. And you are criminals because you don't treat Moslems as human beings.[9]

IRANIAN SUPPORT

In 1982, an estimated 1,500–2,000 Iranian Revolutionary Guards were deployed with a mission to train and support Hezbollah in the Beqa' Valley, signifying the beginning of Iran's sponsorship, support, and powerful influence of Hezbollah. Abbas al-Musawi observed that Iranian Revolutionary Guards *"were not perceived by the party as a normal part of the Islamic body, but as the head* [i.e. the mind of the group]."[10] With Iranian Revolutionary Guard training, Hezbollah expanded its military capabilities and received growing support from the domestic Shi'ite population. Amal, traditionally the larger and more powerful Shi'ite militia in Lebanon, began losing large numbers of radical Shi'ite recruits to Hezbollah. These recruits continued to increase in numbers in response to successive Israeli military actions, expanding popular support for Hezbollah.

Iran's backing of Hezbollah extends beyond training by the Revolutionary Guards. By the late 1980s, for example, the commanding officers of Hezbollah training groups reported to Mohammad Hassan Akhtari, the Iranian Ambassador in Damascus. When Ambassador Akhtari's power declined within Iran, support and guidance for Hezbollah was continued by both the Iranian secret service and various Iranian organizations, designed with the express goal of spreading the beliefs of the Iranian Revolution. Financial support from Iran has been no less critical in the development of Hezbollah. It is estimated that of Hezbollah's total annual budget of approximately $50–60 million, $30–40 million was supplied to by Iran. These figures are reported to have grown at one time to reach $150 million in Iranian contributions, but were later cut back as a consequence of Iran's difficult economic situation.[11] As a result of this involvement, Iran gained considerable control over radical groups within Lebanon, Hezbollah being the most notable example. At times, Iranian control appeared quite direct, as evidenced by Iran's ability to negotiate with the West during hostage situations in Lebanon in the late 1980s.[12]

SOCIAL SERVICE/POLITICS

Originally created to deal with an influx of refugees from Southern Lebanon, Hezbollah augmented its social services to include charities, humanitarian efforts, and social work. Emphasizing the Iranian connection, the social service network is known as the Relief Committee of Khomeini. The extensive financial support has built hospitals, medical clinics, schools, orphanages, and centers for the physically handicapped (estimates of funding have ranged up to tens of millions annually). Its effective delivery of medical and social services has won widespread support from the Shi'a community in Lebanon, which is amongst the nations' poorest, and makes up almost 40 percent of Lebanon's three million people. Hezbollah has a financial department that issues educational loans, as well as loans for business manufacturing and agricultural ventures. Furthermore, borrowers are only required to pay back loans as they are able, and without any interest payments, which would violate Islamic law.[13]

The ideological impact of Hezbollah's social services is magnified by the treatment of the largely poor Shi'a minority by the Lebanese Government. Shi'a regions and neighborhoods have historically been neglected by the central Lebanese Government, making Hezbollah's supplies and infrastructure the only source of aid for many impoverished regions.

Moreover, Hezbollah's political wing is deeply involved in Lebanon's political system. After a two-decade period without elections, Lebanon held parliamentary elections in 1992, resulting in Hezbollah wining 12 parliamentary seats. It currently has 23 seats in Lebanon's 128-member parliament and two Cabinet ministers.

THE ORIGINAL LEADERSHIP

Ayatollah Fadlallah

Ayatollah Sayyid Muhammad Husayn Fadlallah, the spiritual mentor of Hezbollah, has an ambiguous relationship with the group. While there is no formal organizational interaction or affiliation between Hezbollah and Fadlallah, it is clear that from an ideological perspective, Fadlallah has had a significant impact upon the group. As Martin Kramer, the director of the Moshe Dayan Center for Middle Eastern Studies at Tel Aviv University noted, "[b]orne aloft on a wind of words, he [Fadlallah] made himself the voice of Hezbollah's conscience and its spokesman to the world."[14]

Born in Najaf, Iraq, in 1935, Fadlallah was immersed in religious training from an early age. A gifted religious scholar with a unique ability to develop religious justification of action (later applied particularly in justifying violent acts of resistance), Fadlallah was characterized by his extensive training in traditional Islamic thought, combined with a flare for innovative interpretations. Fadlallah became known for the "originality of his intellect, and above all his ability to stretch convention without breaking it."[15] Fadlallah had a unique revisionist interpretation of the Koran, a "moral logic" by which he justified kidnapping, assassination, and suicide.[16] Fadlallah equated death as a suicide bomber with soldiers entering battle knowing that they would die, arguing that there was no moral distinction, and that the only difference was the time of death. Fadlallah used this moral logic to justify suicide bombings by Shi'a forces, classifying such bombings as actions justified by oppression and the militarily asymmetric nature of the war against Israel. *"If an oppressed people does not have the means to confront the United States and Israel with the weapons in which they are superior, then they possess unfamiliar weapons. . . . Oppression makes the oppressed discover new weapons and new strengths everyday."*[17]

Fadlallah's statements aimed to legitimize suicide attacks. He noted that while Islam only permitted such martyrdom under extreme circumstances, the Israeli occupation of Lebanon was just such a circumstance, and concluded, *"The self-martyring operation is not permitted unless it can convulse the enemy. . . . The believer cannot blow himself up unless the results will equal or exceed the [loss of the] soul of the believer. Self-martyring operations are not fatal accidents but legal obligations governed by rules, and the believers cannot transgress the rules of God."*[18]

Fadlallah regularly observed in his sermons that *"there is evil in everything good and something good in every evil."*[19] The practices of suicide, assassination, and hostage taking were extremes and should only be carried out in exceptional times. But these were exceptional times. This also became the justification for the practice of kidnapping, even though the Koran specifically calls for hospitality towards strangers. Concerning the kidnapping of thirty-seven American and Western hostages in 1982, Fadlallah's followers used the exceptional circumstances of the times to justify violating the strict Koranic proscription: *"Just as freedom is demanded for a handful of Europeans, it is also demanded for the millions of Muslims."*[20]

While Fadlallah was a religious leader by training, he demonstrated considerable command of political strategy. Realizing that efforts must be concentrated against a limited number of enemies, Fadlallah stressed the priority of combating Israel, with which he felt no compromise was acceptable. As a strategist, Fadlallah recognized the difficulties involved in a multi-front confrontation against both Israel and the United States, and thus attempted to focus on combating Israel, which he viewed as the greater evil.

Imad Mughniyah

Imad Mughniyah began working as a bodyguard for Fadlallah, but after developing close relations with the spiritual leader, rose to become Director of Special Operations Command, which is its security section. Mughniyah has been implicated in many of Hezbollah's attacks on American and Israeli targets, and is said to report directly to Iran. His first major task was planning the bombing of the Israeli Embassy in Buenos Aires in 1982, in which 22 were killed. (He was indicated by Argentina for this in 1999.) In 1983, he was the architect of an unprecedented escalation in mass casualty terrorism—Hezbollah's suicide truck bombings, first of the American embassy in March in which 63 were killed, and then of the Marine barracks the following October, in which 241 Marines on a peacekeeping mission were killed, leading to the decision by the Reagan administration to withdraw from Lebanon. Mughniyah has been indicted in the United States for his role in the 1985 skyjacking of TWA Flight 847 in Beirut and was considered responsible for the kidnapping, torture, and execution of CIA station chief, William Buckley, the kidnapping and subsequent hanging of Lt. Colonel William Higgins, commander of a UN truce monitoring detachment, and the kidnapping of British envoy Terry Waite. Mughniyah is said to have inspired Osama bin Laden to pursue the path of dramatic large-scale terrorism, culminating in the mass casualty terrorism of September 11, 2001. Prior to the Hezbollah-initiated conflict with Israel, Mughniyah reportedly met with President Mahmoud Ahmadinejad of Iran and President Bashar Assad of Syria.[21]

Abbas al-Musawi

Together with Fadlallah, Abbas al-Musawi, the Secretary General of Hezbollah from 1991 until his assassination by the Israelis in 1992, was one of the original moral/ideological leaders of Hezbollah who justified, and indeed in many cases required, the practice of kidnapping, assassination, suicide bombing, and related acts of terrorism. Al-Musawi made the strategy that flowed from this absolutist belief crystal clear when he declared, *"We are not fighting so that the enemy recognizes us and offers us something. We are fighting to wipe out the enemy."*[22] The absolutism concerning Israel was and is identical for Hezbollah and Hamas. A particularly uncompromising Biqa' valley leader, al-Musawi argued that attacks on the U.S. forces in Beirut were defensive acts against outside occupation. When al-Musawi was killed in 1992, Sheikh Hassan Nasrallah succeeded as the Secretary General.

Hassan Nasrallah

Images of Hassan Nasrallah, covered in a black-turban, his round face behind large glasses, appear everywhere in Southern Lebanon, and are as common as the destroyed buildings and scars from explosions that litter the ground. Known in every village and every town, Nasrallah has become a symbol and an icon.

The protégé of al-Musawi, Nasrallah became Secretary General of Hezbollah at the age of thirty-one. Nasrallah wears the black turban, signifying that he traces his lineage back to the prophet. He has won particular acclaim for not being merely a philosopher, but for being a man of action as well, so he is concomitantly the supreme political leader as well as the military commander-in-chief. "The perception of Nasrallah is that he is in the war room, making the decisions," says Bashshar Haydar, professor of philosophy at the American University in Beirut.[23] Nasrallah has won the distinction of being the only Arab leader to have evicted Israel from Arab land without having to sign a peace treaty.

Nasrallah's leadership is enhanced by his striking charismatic appeal. In September 1997 when his eighteen-year-old son, Hadi Nasrallah, was killed in a battle with the Israeli army, all expected him to cancel a speech scheduled for that evening, but he gave the speech, commemorating the anniversary of the September 13, 1993 massacre of Hezbollah fighters by the Lebanese army. After his prepared remarks, he broke off to observe that the country had given many martyrs the night before, reading each of their names, including that of his son. He then thanked God for electing his son to be martyr, and stated that his son's death was a victory not for Israel but for Hezbollah: *"We are now fighting together and falling as martyrs together. This is a great victory for us, of which we are proud."*[24] Nasrallah gained widespread publicity across religious denominations in 1997 when he refused to negotiate with the Israelis for the return of his son's remains. This refusal to negotiate magnified Nasrallah's stature among many Lebanese, including Christians and Sunnis not traditionally affiliated with Hezbollah.[25]

Nizarh Hamzeh, a Hezbollah expert from the American University of Kuwait, has observed Nasrallah's heroic stature within the Arab world, which was further magnified by the May 2000 Israeli withdrawal from Lebanon after eighteen years of occupation. It was widely portrayed that it was Hezbollah's unrelenting terrorism and rocket campaign that forced Israel to withdraw. The ability of this relatively small guerrilla, terrorist group to gain such a visible victory over the Israeli army gained Hezbollah significant respect within the Islamic and Arab world. Notably, Nasrallah has bridged the religious divide—gaining approval from both Shi'ite and Sunni groups. Yet at the same time, he has been outspoken in his criticism of the actions of other militant movements. Nasrallah told *Washington Post* reporter Robin Wright that the Taliban was *"the worst, the most dangerous thing that the Islamic revival has encountered"* and criticized the beheading of American contractor Nicholas Berg, saying, *"It is unacceptable, it is forbidden, to harm the innocent."*[26] But when Wright asked Nasrallah about suicide bombings in Israel, he explained, *"There [are] no other means for the Palestinians to defend themselves."* So what other Islamic groups do is to be criticized, but what he and his allies do is required.

EMPLOYING THE MEDIA

Hezbollah has proven highly effective at mobilizing modern-day technologies to suit their terrorist agenda and Nasrallah's image is regularly featured on Middle Eastern media. The organization employs computer and information technology experts to disseminate Hezbollah's agenda, using internet websites, and even computer games.[27] Likewise, Hezbollah uses television to broadcast its message and propaganda to its supporters, at first locally, and later to a broader regional audience that includes millions of Muslims. Al-Manar TV (the beacon) switched to satellite broadcasts in 2000, disseminating an anti-Israeli and anti-American message to a large Muslim audience. A typical Al-Manar broadcast televises a statement in favor of suicide martyrdom as a method of anti-Israeli resistance: "*In the culture of resistance the culmination of humanity and human dignity is the decision to perform istishhad [martyrdom] in order to grant life to one's people and dignity to one's nation and homeland.*"[28]

SUMMER 2006 CAMPAIGN

Nasrallah faced criticism from the Arab world—particularly Saudi Arabia, Egypt, and Jordan—and within Lebanon itself for causing the 2006 war between Israel and Lebanon—known in Lebanon as the July War—specifically because he drastically miscalculated the Israeli response to Hezbollah's kidnapping of two Israeli soldiers, which plunged the two countries into war. The conflict began when Hezbollah fired Katyusha rockets and mortars at Israeli military positions in an attempt to divert attention from an armed Hezbollah unit crossing the border which kidnapped the two Israeli soldiers and killed three others. Israel responded with massive air strikes, more than 12,000 combat missions, and artillery fire on Lebanese targets, including the Rafik Hariri International Airport, and established an air and naval blockade. Nasrallah admitted that he was caught off guard by the intense Israeli offensive, but made no apology for Hezbollah's initial attack. The conflict killed over 1,200 people, most of whom were Lebanese, severely damaged the Lebanese infrastructure, and displaced 975,000 Lebanese citizens. Despite the punishing Israeli air campaign, in an unrelenting manner throughout the conflict, Hezbollah fired more than 4,000 rockets, hitting Haifa, Hadera, Nazareth, Tiberias, Nahariya, Safed, Afula, and other cities and villages, and engaged in guerilla warfare with the Israeli Defense Forces from well-fortified positions.

A UN-brokered ceasefire went into effect on August 11, 2006. In an attempt to shift the blame away from Hezbollah and to the Israelis, Nasrallah claimed that Israel had previous plans for a war against Lebanon and Hezbollah and that Hezbollah simply "accelerated" the war and deprived the Israeli military of full preparation.[29] Moreover, he claimed victory because of Hezbollah's ability to withstand the ferocious Israeli attack while continuing to attack Israel.

Israel, in contrast, was subjected to harsh international criticism for its disproportionate response, and Israeli Prime Minister Ehud Ohlmert's government was severely weakened by its failure to stem Hezbollah's attack and end the rain of rockets on Israel, thus tarnishing its "invincible" regional image.

Some of Nasrallah's speeches during and after the 2006 summer campaign were notable. One of the more remarkable moments of terrorist showmanship occurred on the evening of Friday, July 14, when Nasrallah called in to Al-Manar, Hezbollah's television station. Not given to understatement, he first extolled the heroism of the martyrs who had given their lives *"in the noblest con-frontation and battle the modern age has known, or rather that all history has known."* He then reminded the audience that he had promised surprises, and announced they would begin momentarily, and went on, *"Now, in the middle of the sea, facing Beirut, the Israeli warship that has attacked the infrastructure, people's homes and civilians—look at it burning."*[30] As he spoke, an Iranian-made C802 missile crashed into the warship, producing an orange glow, with flares shooting up from the sea to the sky.

In an interview broadcast on al-Jazeera on July 22, 2006, Nasrallah spoke of the *"steadfastness"* of Hezbollah fighters and their *"full absorption of the Israeli strike."*[31] It is important to emphasize that the courage to stand up to a superior enemy in battle is strongly valued in Arab culture, and by courageously defying the powerful state of Israel in the conflict, Nasrallah's iconic stature had been magnified throughout the Islamic world.

With apparent disregard for the superiority of the Israeli military, Nasrallah demeaned the efficacy of the Israeli air attacks by saying that *"any army that has aircraft can do that,"* and further asserting that *"they failed in the face of the military infrastructure of the resistance. They succeeded in killing the children, women and the elderly."*

Employing his sophisticated media outlets during the 2006 conflict, Nasrallah used the widespread devastation produced by the Israeli bombings as a media blitz in order to blame Israel while bolstering Hezbollah support. His statements were strengthened by the remarkably lopsided casualties, which included large numbers of civilian deaths on the Lebanese side, reflected in an extended public broadcast by Nasrallah on August 9. *"I address you anew as we approach the end of the first month of this barbaric and aggressive war which the Zionists imposed on Lebanon and on every human being, stone, location, and symbol in Lebanon."*

Nasrallah's capacity to deflect critical questions and change the subject to enhance his charismatic appeal is striking. Questioned about popular support, Nasrallah asserted, *"I am not talking about some political forces. I am talking abut the people, the good people, those who in hard times reveal their chivalry, honor and patriotism."* Pressed on the criticism from Arab leaders—presumably referring to Egypt, Saudi Arabia, and Jordan—of the Hezbollah-initiated conflict, Nasrallah was contemptuous: *"They want to destroy any spirit of resistance in Lebanon. . . . They want to push the country to the point where words such as resist-ance would become unacceptable, and where words such as martyr, jihad, wounded, steadfastness, confrontation, liberation, freedom, glory, dignity, pride, and honor are unacceptable. . . . All these words should be erased from the Lebanese people's dictionary, from the press, from the popular literature, from the political mind, from the people's mind."*

Asked about Hezbollah's support from Iran and Syria, Nasrallah emphasized that his decisions were made independently, that Hezbollah was a resistance organization, and that this conflict was an act of defense. *"Today, Hezbollah is not fighting for the sake of Syria or for the sake of Iran. It is fighting for the sake of Lebanon."* In an interesting rhetorical reframing, when asked what he would consider was victory, Nasrallah replied that *"to succeed in defense is victory."* Identifying Hezbollah with Lebanon, he concluded, *"[b]eing forces that have zeal for Lebanon, its dignity and pride, I faithfully say that this is Lebanon's true battle of independence. If we win this battle, this means that we, the Lebanese people, will tell the whole world that we will be the decision-makers."*[32]

THE MANY FACES OF NASRALLAH AND HEZBOLLAH

Once the August 2006 ceasefire was implemented, Hezbollah once again gained a political and psychological boost. After over a month of fighting with a technologically and militarily superior Israeli military, many Lebanese, particularly Shi'a, claimed Hezbollah to be the victor once again—reminiscent of the 2000 Israeli withdrawal, which immortalized Hezbollah in the eyes of the Arab street. Given the group's martyrdom-driven philosophy, this drawn-out resistance only serves to reinforce Hezbollah's self-identity. Nasrallah and other Hezbollah leaders have taken every opportunity to emphasize their victory and confirmation of their anti-Israeli resistance. As Nasrallah has stressed: *"You will not be able to stay on our land. If you enter it, we will drive you out by force. We will turn the land of our precious south into a graveyard for the Zionist invaders."*[33]

Nasrallah's image as heroic military leader for Hezbollah's popular status is partially defined by the provision of basic needs and services for the marginalized and poor. Nasrallah emerged from the conflict in Lebanon as a heroic warrior, but he swiftly segued to champion of the poor and victims of the Israeli air campaign by providing with remarkable efficiency food, water, shelter, and financial support, aided by Iran.

Lebanon's post-ceasefire concerns were quickly focused on immediate humanitarian aid and reconstruction. Within a short time, Hezbollah mobilized, creating a combination propaganda machine and legitimate social service provider, both geared toward solidifying anti-Israeli and anti-American sentiment, all while simultaneously helping the most devastated regions of Lebanon, largely, although not exclusively, inhabited by Hezbollah supporters. Nasrallah and other Hezbollah leaders took every opportunity to accentuate the social and infrastructural costs of the Israeli bombing and Hezbollah's role in repairing this damage. "*Does anyone believe that all these bridges, roads, and infrastructure were destroyed only to cut off the resistance's supply lines? . . . or is the goal to destroy the infrastructure to exercise pressure on the Lebanese? The killing of civilians aims to put pressure on the Lebanese so as to surrender, yield to, and accept the Israeli conditions. . . .*"[34]

Examples of Hezbollah propaganda are widely visible; for example, in the southern Beirut suburb of Harat Hreik, Hezbollah covered destroyed buildings and rubble with bright signs and banners with such slogans as "Made in the US," "Smart Bombs for Stupid Minds," and "Extremely Precise Target." These messages were clearly designed to focus the blame on the United States and Israel while demonstrating the civilian nature of the areas that were bombed. Likewise, Hezbollah has distributed red baseball caps bearing the phrase "*Ja'a Nasr Allah,*" a play on words that combines "God's victory" with Nasrallah's name. For many of his followers, Nasrallah has adroitly managed to convert the massive damage his acts precipitated into a claim of victory that has enhanced his prestige. The supervisor of these PR efforts, Ghassan Darwish, stated, "*Hezbollah is not just about rockets and fighting, otherwise people would have left us long ago. We will be victorious in the reconstruction, just as we have been victorious against Israel's army.*"[35]

CHAPTER 12

HAMAS: THE ISLAMIC RESISTANCE MOVEMENT[1]

Established during the first *intifada*—the Palestinian civil revolt against Israeli occupation, which began in December 1987—Hamas, the Islamic Resistance Movement, traces its origins to the Muslim Brotherhood, founded in Egypt in 1928. The Brotherhood sought to revitalize Islam and to establish an Islamic state, with no distinction between religion and the state. Its members considered Palestine, permanently and exclusively, a Muslim land so designated by Allah. In their view, it is the duty of Muslims to liberate the entirety of the Holy Land from non-Muslim authority. "*Israel will be established and will stay established until Islam nullifies it as it nullifies what was before it,*" stated the martyred Imam Hassan al-Banna, founder and Supreme Guide of the Muslim Brotherhood. He went on to state: "*It is the nature of Islam to dominate, not to be dominated, to impose its law on all nations and to extend its power to the entire planet.*"

Despite these totalistic goals, which would clearly require *jihad* at some time in the future, Hamas initially took root as a social and religious movement, building hundreds of mosques in impoverished Gaza, and only declaring *jihad* after years of developing social support. This stands in contrast to Hezbollah, which began as a violent militia, later combining fighting forces with a network of social services and subsequent electoral success. Sheikh Ahmad Yassin and his colleagues, who were members of the Muslim Brotherhood, began developing extensive social services in Palestine from 1973 to 1987 through a network of mosques and religious and educational institutions. And only after 14 years of patiently establishing their base did they move into political violence. Growth and evolution have been trademarks of Hamas—a process that is gradual and incremental, but ever moving forward. Noted terrorism expert Bruce Hoffman, the author of *Inside Terrorism*, noted: "The terrorist campaign is like a shark: it must keep moving forward—no matter how slowly or incrementally—or die."[2]

When the first *intifada* erupted in 1987, Sheikh Ahmad Yassin convened a group of Muslim Brotherhood leaders. They decided to establish a nominally separate organization to participate in the *intifada*. This would shield them from blame should the revolt fail, but would allow them to claim credit if it succeeded. They called the new organization Hamas, which means "zeal," "force," and "bravery" in Arabic, but is also the acronym for *Harakat al-Muqawama al-Islamiyya* (the Islamic Resistance Movement). Formed during 1987 and 1988, Hamas prioritized both short-term goals—removing Israeli forces from the occupied territories—and its long-term agenda—the creation of an Islamic state in all of historic Palestine. When Hamas talks about historic Palestine and liberating occupied territories, they are referring to all of contemporary Israel; there is no "two-state" solution in this absolutist ideology.

Hamas issued the group's charter in 1988, entitled *The Charter of Allah: The Platform of the Islamic Resistance Movement*. The Charter unambiguously identifies Palestine as Islamic in nature, indicating Hamas's goal to create an Islamic State: "*Palestine is an Islamic Land which has the first of the two Qiblas [the direction to which Muslims turn in prayer], the third of the holy Islamic sanctuaries, and the point of departure for Mohammed's midnight journey to the seven heavens [i.e., Jerusalem].*"[3]

Hamas's Charter is fundamental in understanding the group's mentality, particularly in relation to Islam, historic Palestine, and resistance to the Israeli presence in Palestine.[4] Article 13 draws this direct comparison between the land and Islam: "*Giving up any part of the homeland is like giving up part of the religious faith itself.*" In a systematic paranoid exposition, the Charter develops a clear sense of the Jews and the Zionist entity as the enemy, blaming them for virtually every evil that has befallen Muslims and indeed the world as a whole:

> The enemy planned long ago and perfected their plan so that they can achieve what they want to achieve. . . . They worked on gathering huge and effective amounts of wealth to achieve their goal. With wealth they controlled the international mass media-news services, newspapers, printing presses, broadcast stations and more. . . . With money they ignited revolutions in all parts of the world to realize their benefits and reap the fruits of them. They are behind the French Revolution, the Communist Revolution. . . . With wealth they formed secret organizations throughout the world to destroy societies and promote the Zionist cause. . . . With wealth they controlled imperialistic nations and pushed

them to occupy many nations and exhaust their natural resources and spread mischief in them. . . .

They are behind the First World War in which they destroyed the Islamic Caliph and gained material profit, monopolized raw wealth, and got the Balfour Declaration [which laid the groundwork for the creation of Israel]. *They created the League of Nations so they could control the world through that organization. They are behind the Second World War. . . and set down the foundations to establish their nation by forming the United Nations and Security Council instead of the League of Nations in order to rule the world through that organization. . . . There is not a war that goes on here or there in which their finger are not playing behind it.*

Article 32 cites as the authoritative source for this international Jewish conspiracy the anti-Semitic counterfeit text *Protocols of the Learned Elders of Zion*, proclaiming: *"Today it's Palestine and tomorrow it will be another country, and then another. The Zionist plan has no bounds and after Palestine they wish to expand from the Nile River to the Euphrates. When they totally occupy it they will look towards another, and such is their plan in the 'Protocols of the Learned Elders of Zion.'* "[5]

A pivotal moment in the *intifada* occurred in October 1990 following the killing of seventeen Palestinians by Israeli security forces, within the Haram al-Sharif, or Temple Mount. Seizing on this opportunity, Hamas called for *jihad "against the Zionist enemy everywhere, on all fronts and with every means."*[6] This led to a dramatic increase in Hamas attacks. As Sheikh Yassin noted, *"[t]he Israeli occupation demonstrated that words were not enough to bring it to an end. Only armed resistance can achieve liberation."*[7] Hamas's move from social services to violence was probably also a reflection of the success of the Fatah political movement, and the recognition by Hamas leadership that without aggressive action, their existing system was insufficient to compete politically with Arafat and Fatah.

A second key turning point occurred in 1992 when Israel deported over 400 members of Hamas, including Sheikh Yassin and other key leaders. These deportations proved an essential catalyst for Hamas' strategic and political growth since, now isolated, the Hamas leadership was allowed time to carefully develop and plan their long-range strategy. The deportation also created interaction between Hezbollah and Hamas, and some members of Hamas even received Hezbollah training in Southern Lebanon.

Hamas became increasingly radical as Palestinians became frustrated with Fatah, angry with Israel, and willing to accept more hostile tactics. During the Oslo negotiations (1993–1994), Hamas initiated its campaign of suicide bombing and kidnapping to undermine the Oslo process and ensure that the Palestinian Authority would not be able to deliver peace. Those Palestinians unwilling to accept negotiations or compromise with Israel and those disappointed by Arafat and the PLO, increasingly turned to Hamas. Contributing to the rise in Hamas's popularity was the bitter resentment among Palestinian youth in the territories toward the takeover of the leadership and administrative positions by Arafat's men, who came out of exile. The Palestinian youngsters, who conducted the *intifada* and paid so dearly for their struggle, felt that they, rather than Arafat's cronies, should have been given the power positions in the newly established Palestinian Authority. In an attempt to gain political capital among Palestinians angered with the PLO's movement toward governance and the mainstream, Hamas stepped up terrorist acts in 1995 and 1996.[8] As with Oslo, Hamas made strong statements against the Camp David II peace efforts: *"The Palestinian people accuses all who seek this [solution] of weaving a plot against its rights and its sacred national cause. Liberation will not be completed without sacrifice, blood and jihad that continues until victory."*[9]

There was a growing perception among the Palestinians that Arafat and his government were corrupt. Particularly during the *intifada*, splintering, fragmentation, and paralysis of the PLO led to increase public and political support for Hamas. Hamas intentionally moved to distance itself from Fatah and Arafat. During the Gulf War, in a calculated attempt to distance itself from Fatah's rhetoric supporting Saddam Hussein, Hamas made public statements criticizing Saddam Hussein and the invasion of Kuwait. By creating a distinction between itself and Fatah, Hamas was able to gain funding and infrastructure development from several Arab Gulf states as a result.[10] With growing militarization, the military wing of Hamas, the Izz al-din al-Qassam Brigades, continued to grow. These military forces armed themselves with weaponry that included light automatic weapons, grenades, rockets, bombs, and explosives.

Leadership from prison has played a vital role in Hamas's strategic decision-making process. Incarcerated Hamas members enjoyed heroic status and legitimacy, based on their imprisonment for their acts for the Palestinian cause. As the most radical and committed group within the leadership, they were able to forward their radical agenda, pushing issues on the boundaries of policy. Their influence has been so extensive that some experts argue that none of Hamas's political actions would prove successful without the support of prison leadership. Sheikh Ahmad Yassin has been the most prominent example, as he directed Hamas activities during years of incarceration.

SHEIKH AHMAD YASSIN

Sheikh Ahmad Yassin was the principal leader of the militant faction within the Muslim Brotherhood (MB) in Gaza who founded Hamas as the military wing of the MB in 1987. A charismatic force, he remained as its spiritual leader until his death by assassination in 2004. Born near Askalon in 1936, Yassin and his family fled to the Gaza strip due to the 1948 Arab-Israeli War. As the result of a childhood injury, Yassin was severely disabled; he was nearly blind, paraplegic, and confined to a wheelchair. In 1957, he became a teacher in Gaza and then went on to study at the Ayn Shamas University in Egypt (1964–65) where he became involved with the Muslim Brotherhood. Yassin's activities led Egyptian authorities to expel him from the country and return him to Gaza. By the 1980s, Yassin had become the leading Islamic militant in the occupied territories.[11]

Yassin and his Muslim Brotherhood colleagues spent thirteen years, from 1973 to 1987, developing social services in Gaza. Yassin also led the Gaza Strip Steering Committee, a key leadership element within the Hamas organization. Because of resistance activities, he was imprisoned by Israeli authorities in 1984, but released as part of a prisoner exchange a year later. The leader of Hamas when the first *intifada* broke out in 1987, he was imprisoned again by the Israelis two years later. Ailing and aging, Shaykh Yassin was released in 1997 and flown to Jordan for medical treatment as part of a deal whereby Jordan released two captured Israeli intelligence officers who had been detained for a botched attempt to assassinate a Hamas leader several days earlier. After his release from medical treatment, Yassin returned to Gaza where he received a tumultuous hero's welcome. Until his assassination by the Israelis on March 22, 2004, the wheelchair-bound Yassin provided powerful charismatic leadership to Hamas.

Demonstrating the power of his charismatic leadership and his ability to inspire his young recruits, Yassin conveyed the goals of martyrdom to Nasra Hassan, a Muslim expert with the United Nations: "*Love of martyrdom is something deep inside the heart. But these rewards are not in themselves the goal of the martyr. The only aim is to win Allah's satisfaction. That can be done . . . in the speediest manner by dying in the cause of Allah. And it is Allah who selects martyrs.*"[12]

While Yassin's radical anti-Israeli statements reflect the extremity of language in the Hamas Charter, his more "moderate" rhetoric reveals strategic thinking. Particularly in his later years, Yassin made occasional use of less inflammatory statements. He carefully drafted his statements to allow culpability to be placed upon Israel for the continued violence while ensuring that Israel would be unwilling to accept Hamas's terms. His language also carefully avoided end-game solutions, claiming that issues such as 1967 borders and the return of Palestinian refugees were interim agreements, thereby leaving the creation of an Islamic Palestine as a topic for future discussion.

Just prior to his assassination, Yassin made a statement that on the surface seemed to reflect a move away from a strict rhetoric of violence, "Yassin asserted that the movement would agree to a temporary peace with Israel in exchange for the establishment of a Palestinian state, *'on the basis of the 1967 borders and the return of Palestinian refugees to Israel; the rest of the land, within Israel, we will leave to history,'* "[13] preconditions that Yassin knew full well were unacceptable to Israel. Yassin had made similar comments in the past, both in 1987 and 1989: "*I do not want to destroy Israel. . . . We want to negotiate with Israel so the Palestinian people inside and outside Palestine can live in Palestine. Then the problem will cease to exist.*"[14]

NEGOTIATION DOES NOT MEAN RENOUNCING ABSOLUTIST GOALS

Hamas's mention of negotiating with Israel apparently runs counter to the Hamas Charter, but such statements are not unique or unheard of. Abu Marzuq, the leader of the Political Bureau of Hamas, issued a similar political statement in 1994. Likewise, Abd-al Aziz Rantisi, a radical member of Hamas noted: "*The intifada is about forcing Israel's withdrawal to the 1967 boundaries . . . [this] doesn't mean the Arab-Israeli conflict will be over, but rather that its armed character would end.*"[15]

This point was emphasized in a remarkably candid statement by Mahmoud Zahhar, a pediatrician from Gaza and prominent Hamas leader: "*We must calculate the benefit and cost of continued armed operations. If we can fulfill our goals without violence, we will do so. Violence is a means, not a goal. Hamas's decision to adopt self-restraint does not contradict our aims, including the establishment of an Islamic state instead of Israel. . . . We will never recognize Israel, but it is possible that a truce [muhadana] could prevail between us for days, months, or years.*"[16]

But in fact, according to Farhat Asa'd, a prominent member of the Hamas political leadership on the West Bank, to enter into negotiations with Israel is to recognize Israel's right to exist and is to recognize the legitimacy of the occupation. This they will not do.

As noted by Shaul Mishal and Avraham Sela in their important study of Hamas, *The Palestinian Hamas*, the principle of "not ceding one inch" is quite consistent in its leaflets.[17] In leaflet no. 28, "Islamic Palestine from the [Mediterranean] Sea to the [Jordan] River," they assert: "*The Muslims have had a full—not a partial—right to Palestine for generations, in the past, present, and future. . . . No Palestinian generation has the right to concede the land, steeped in martyrs' blood. . . . You must continue the uprising and stand up against the usurpers whoever they may be, and until the complete liberation of every grain of the soil of . . . Palestine, all Palestine, with God's help."*

In a March 13, 1988 leaflet, they assert: *"Let any hand be cut off that signs [away] a grain of sand in Palestine in favor of the enemies of God . . . who have seized . . . the blessed land."* They are also adamant that there can be no negotiations with Israel, for *"[e]very negotiation with the enemy is a regression from the [Palestinian] cause, concession of a principle, and recognition of the usurping murderers' false claim to a land in which they were not born"* (August 18, 1988).

STATEMENTS AND IDEOLOGY

Hamas has proven a prolific public affairs machine, demonstrated during the *intifada* when the organization produced and distributed leaflets to the masses directing and coordinating demonstrations, boycotts, protests, and other political activities. Excerpts from these leaflets provide insight into Hamas, and particularly focus on Islam and the anti-Israeli *jihad*.[18]

> *We have no way to defend ourselves. We can only put pressure on Israel, and make clear that 'if you do not withdraw, then we will be able to cause death and destruction on your side'. The Palestinians turned from a cat into a tiger, because they put us in a cage with no chance to move.*
>
> —2000 statement by Hamas leader Abu Shanab, assassinated in 2003

> *The Jews—brothers of the apes, assassins of the prophets, bloodsuckers, warmongers— are murdering you, depriving you of life after having plundered your homeland and your homes. Only Islam can break the Jews and destroy their dream. Therefore, proclaim to them: Allah is great, Allah is greater than their army, Allah is greater than their airplanes and their weapons.*[19]

> *The blood of our martyrs shall not be forgotten. Every drop of blood shall become a Molotov cocktail, a time bomb, and a roadside charge that will rip out the intestines of the Jews.*[20]

SUICIDE BOMBING[21]

On January 14, 2004, a young mother of two carried out a suicide bombing at a Gaza security checkpoint.[22] To a western audience, it seems inconceivable that a mother would willingly commit such an act. Yet Hamas has carried out numerous such acts of violence, justifying them through public statements, and systematically instilling the acceptability of what they term "martyrdom operations": "*If [revenge] alone motivates the candidates, his martyrdom will not be acceptable to Allah. It is a military response, not an individual's bitterness, that drives an operation. Honor and dignity are very important in our culture. And when we are humiliated we respond with wrath.*"[23]

The wave of suicide bombings has been characterized as a required response to the provocation by Israeli settler Baruch Goldstein, who killed (or wounded) 130 Palestinian Muslims who were praying in the Tomb of the Patriarchs in the West bank town of Hebron on February 25, 1994. In fact, plans for the campaign had been well laid, and Hamas leadership was awaiting a propitious moment. Indeed, the first suicide operation by Hamas occurred on April 16, 1993, nearly a year before the massacre at the Tomb of the Patriarchs. By that time, Hamas and the Palestinian Islamic Jihad had already carried out seven suicide attacks, although to be sure, the suicide bombing campaign was accelerated after the Hebron massacre.

The decision to adopt the tactic of suicide bombings was made at the highest level of Hamas' leadership, as they had determined that anger within the Palestinian community had reached the tipping point. In reponse to the massacre at the mosque, Hamas escalated the conflict through a sustained, intense suicide bomb campaign against Israeli civilians. To implement the organizational decision, it required only a supply of willing recruits socialized to the glory of martyrdom. Ariel Merari, a noted Israeli terrorism expert, has been a pioneer in emphasizing the key role of social psychology, not individual psychopathology, in producing suicide terrorists. He has pithily described the "suicide terrorist assembly line," which has three key junctures.[24] First the volunteer or recruit is identified, usually by friends or relatives in the organization, and commits himself to becoming a *shahid*. Then he is publicly identified as a "living martyr," a member of "the walking dead." This brings great prestige both to the prospective martyr and to his or her family. Finally, just before the mission, he is videotaped reading his last will and testament, in which he explains his motivations and his goals. This cements his commitment, and makes it nearly impossible for him to back out, for it would bring unbearable shame and humiliation. These videos then are disseminated on Hamas websites, where they glorify the martyrs and contribute to further recruitment.

During the period between 1999 and 2004, Hamas faced new pressures. Salah Shehade, commander of the military wing al-Qassam Brigades, published a communiqué supporting and justifying the group's use of martyrdom operations. This communiqué attempted to counter the accusation that Hamas manipulated young recruits to become suicide bombers; instead, Shehade argued that Hamas applies strict requirements in considering potential suicide bombers: recruits had to be Muslims, with a level of education, and could not be the only provider for their family.[25] Hamas has made a conscious effort to publicize and celebrate its martyrs. In many Palestinian neighborhoods, "[t]he suicide bombers' green birds appear on posters, and in graffiti—the language of the street. Calendars are illustrated with the 'martyr of the month.' Paintings glorify the dead bombers in Paradise, triumphant beneath a flock of green birds. This symbol is based on a saying of the Prophet Mohammed that the soul of a martyr is carried to Allah in the bosom of the green birds of Paradise."[26]

The campaign of martyrdom attacks provided important political benefits for Hamas. In September 2000, with the eruption of the new *intifada*, Hamas gained significant popularity among the Palestinian population, particularly due to the group's military wing, which conducted the suicide bombing campaign.

Despite the glorification of martyrdom, there have been certain periods during which Hamas concealed its involvement in suicide bombing, placing the blame on a mysterious group known as "Islamic Jihad." For example, Hamas's reluctance to claim responsibility for suicide attacks—and its unsuccessful attempts to hide the identity of the bombers—in 1997 was not the result of criticism of the religious legitimacy of suicide. Rather, it was an attempt to avoid conflict with the Palestinian Authority which, at that time, was under extreme Israeli and American pressure to take measures against Hamas. Hamas leaders, and many Islamic authorities, have always maintained that martyrdom attacks are different from ordinary suicide and are not only religiously legitimate but are praiseworthy. "The Koran does not permit suicide in principle; on the other hand, it is a religious duty to fight and die for Allah and Islam. In theory, the martyr is supposed to submit to the will of Allah, and it is to be his own personal decision to do so. In practice, the candidates for martyrdom are heavily indoctrinated, chosen by the leadership, and assured that after their death their families will be taken care of."[27]

Clearly, economic difficulties in Palestinian territories have boosted the popularity of Hamas, made martyrdom more acceptable, and legitimized acts of violence in the minds of many Hamas supporters. The Palestinian economy is collapsing, and business activities are handicapped by Israeli checkpoints and barriers, preventing travel and commerce in the occupied territories. Hamas leaders incorporate these visible "symbols of oppression" into their inspiring externalizing rhetoric as they appeal to Palestinian youth to resist the occupation and enter the path of martyrdom. The impoverished occupied territories provide a psychologically bleak environment in which the majority of the population shares a sense of loss or injury, therefore creating a sizable pool of ready recruits, particularly among the young.

Twenty-three year old Mona Yousef is one such example. An unemployed translator, Yousef expressed support for Hamas's principles based largely on her own personal loss: *"Hamas must not give up the principles on which it was elected. They must still argue and fight for the prisoners, for the borders and for the Palestinian state. Hamas should not recognize Israel. I strongly believe this. . . . My grandfather died in the 1948 war. My brother was killed in the first intifada. He was 12, and the IDF shot him on his way to school. People have been sacrificing their lives to fight for their rights. Every house in Gaza has a story like this, a prisoner or someone killed by Israel."*[28]

Yousef's story is emblematic of sentiments in the West Bank, and particularly Gaza. Unemployed youth without future prospects, having already lost friends and/or family in violence they view as "Israeli hostilities," are easy targets for manipulation by terrorist recruiters.

Terrorists, both leaders and rank-and-file members, frequently display a number of similarities in their backgrounds and histories. Consider the leaders of Hamas as mentioned previously, Ahmad Yassin, Ismail Haniya, and Mahmoud Zahhar. All were influenced by the Muslim Brotherhood, lived in refugee camps or regions, were educated and involved in Islamic institutions of higher education, were part of the exiled group of Hamas leaders sent to Lebanon in the early nineties, and finally all gained legitimacy through imprisonment and the loss of family members.

The transition between ideological support for terrorist or resistance groups and the significant step of actually engaging in an act of violence or terrorism is incremental. Barber's surveys of 900 Palestinian male adolescent Muslims revealed that in the time period of the first *intifada*, 1987–1993, "participation in violence was high, with stone throwing in particular high for males (81 percent), while over two-thirds experienced both physical assault and were shot at. Over 80 percent of those interviewed by Barber admitted to supplying deliveries to activists, while a similar amount went to visit the families of dead martyrs. Yet from all of these youths, very few are likely to become operational activists for one of the main terrorist groups."[29]

The soil has been tilled, but it may require the loss of a relative or friend, as with Mona Yousef, to move the bitter youth seeking vengeance into the path of terrorism.

On the basis of extensive interviews with incarcerated members of Islamist Palestinian groups, we noted commonalities in the terrorist's personal histories. "The boyhood heroes for the Islamist terrorists were religious figures, such as the Prophet, or the radical Wahabi Islamist, Abdullah Azzam, [who was Osama bin Laden's professor]. Most had some high school, and some had education beyond high school. The majority of the subjects reported that their families were respected in the community. The families were experienced as being uniformly supportive of their commitment to the cause."[30]

This identification with religious and revolutionary figures provides justification or legitimacy for acts of violence by the powerless against the powerful oppressor—in this case, Israel. A member of the military wing of Hamas, who was arrested at age 19 and is now serving three life sentences, related his gradual path to violent action and indicated that Dr. Abdel Aziz Rantisi was his childhood hero, a source of inspiration.[31]

> I owe my start in the organization to the Moslem Center [established by Rantisi] which was active in the camp and helped residents in every sphere. I attended religious lessons and symposia in the mosque conducted by Muslim Center people and I was active on a voluntary basis in helping needy residents. During the intifada I joined Hamas and my political views grew stronger. . . . The intifada caused many of our young people to join the organization. In fact, Hamas was established with the eruption of the intifada and it spread throughout the territories, growing stronger all the time. The intifada, despite the oppression and difficulties it caused, created a positive dynamic for the organization. After carrying out an action, I felt enormous satisfaction and pride and knew that our success would eventually lead to the realization of our dream of independence and the establishment of a Palestinian state on the soil of Moslem Palestine. . . . I have not the slightest twinge of regret over my chosen path.

Islamic terrorist organizations appear to single out likely candidates for terrorist and particularly martyrdom operations, as noted by John Horgan in *The Psychology of Terrorism:* "Hamas and Islamic Jihad do not apparently favor married young men as potential martyrs, but rather appear more open to selecting and 'preparing' unmarried men, with no families to support—it is likely that the group is aware of the emotional responsiveness of people at a younger age and the increased susceptibility towards greater involvement this might bring."[32]

Hamas tended to select individuals whose lack of personal or social connections made martyrdom a more acceptable option. Recruits became easy targets because they already felt marginalized and yearned for social acceptance. Membership in Hamas carries significant social prestige, as the following interview quote reveals: *"Recruits were treated with great respect. A youngster who belonged to Hamas or Fatah was regarded more highly than one who didn't belong to a group, and got better treatment than unaffiliated kids."*[33]

HASSAN SALAME: SUICIDE BOMB COMMANDER

Hassan Salame, now serving forty-six consecutive life sentences, is considered the most prolific suicide bomb commander in the history of Palestinian terrorism in Israel, and was responsible for the wave of suicide bombings throughout Israel in the run-up to the 1996 election. Salame was born in 1971 in the Khan Yunis refuge camp, considered one of the more radical pockets of resistance to the occupation. The dominant organization there is the Islamic Center, led by Abdel Aziz Rantisi, Hamas founder Sheikh Ahmad Yassin's right-hand man. The Center has played a major role in recruiting new members and systematically converting them into suicide bombers. Salame can be considered an exemplar of Hamas terrorism and his compelling interview, previously unpublished, is quoted extensively.[34]

> We were a normal, well-established and respected refugee camp family. All the children went to school, and were considered quiet and well behaved. No-one in the family was involved in criminal activities; most used to pray in the mosque. Within the family we never discussed politics and our social standing was good.
>
> My childhood hero, like many of the kids in the camp, was Che Guevara, whom we saw as a leading revolutionary figure. . . . When I grew up, my hero became Dr Abdullah Azzam.
>
> From my childhood I leaned towards Islam. Most of my social activity was focused around the mosque. I attended lessons in religion organized by the Islamic center and that formed the basis for my ideology. . . . As far as people in the camp were concerned, they believed every young Palestinian should enlist. Recruitment was the order of the day and seen as a necessity. Every young person was obliged first and foremost to do what he could for the liberation of the people and the land. . . .
>
> At the start of the intifada, I joined Hamas. I was recruited by Jamil, a friend from the camp. . . . The intifada mobilized the entire Palestinian nation for the struggle, and took the Islamic movement another stage towards achieving its goal. . . . My joining up was the normal thing to do, as all the young people were enlisting.
>
> I felt great satisfaction at having been recruited to Hamas and was proud of my record. . . . I felt very good about what I had chosen to do, and I felt I was fulfilling my duty towards Allah, the Arab and Palestinian peoples, and to myself.
>
> Within the group, there is a feeling of solidarity and common cause. We share a common aim and destiny. There is an atmosphere of brotherhood. . . .
>
> Of course, my family supports me and my organization. . . . Most of the general population supports the recruits.
>
> In general, any organization that fights for the liberation of Palestine is a good thing. But we need to distinguish between religious and secular organizations. Religious

organizations understand that we also have to fight for Islam and not only for the nation and the land.

Fatah is a good positive organization, but mistaken in its ideology and deeds. Fatah, in its concessions to Israel, its recognition of the state of Israel, and its joining the peace process, is totally unacceptable to me.

Every young Moslem understood the importance of our armed actions and we never needed ideology to justify them. . . . A martyrdom operation bombing is the highest level of Jihad and highlights the depth of our faith. The bombers are holy fighters who carry out one of the more important articles of Islam.

The armed attacks are an inseparable part of the organization's activities. They are the goal of the military wing, and the reason it was set up. Jihad is conducted in different ways, and the military aspect is the most important. Without the military element, without the armed attacks, the organization will not be able to achieve its goals.

As for the peace process, I personally am against it. It runs counter to our views. It entails recognition of the State of Israel and that runs counter to Islam and the Hamas . . . Even if there ultimately is agreement between Israel and the Palestinian Authority, it will only be a stage in the long history of Islam. The Hezbollah too doesn't say what will happen after you leave Lebanon. . . . Of one thing, I am convinced: in the end Islam will triumph.

In response to Israeli counterterrorist actions, designed to inhibit the carrying out of terrorist activities by destroying the homes of the perpetrators' families, Hamas extolled the acts of the martyrs and supported their families:

Perpetrators of armed attacks were seen as heroes, their families got a great deal of material assistance including the construction of new homes to replace those destroyed by the Israeli authorities as punishment for terrorist acts.

Jessica Stern, author of *Terror in the Name of God*, observed that "hopelessness, deprivation, envy, and humiliation make death, and paradise, seem more appealing."[35] The manner in which hopelessness can be exploited is eloquently conveyed by an elderly resident of Jenin that Stern interviewed: "*Look how we live here, then maybe you'll understand why there are always volunteers for martyrdom. Every good Muslim understands that it's better to die fighting than to live without hope.*"[36]

THE INTERNET AND PUBLIC RELATIONS

Hamas has proven particularly effective at mobilizing the new media to support recruitment, information sharing, and coordination of logistics. The internet site for the al-Qassam Brigades maintains websites that allow communication between Hamas members and other sympathizers who may wish to engage in acts of violence as well as to move non-members sympathetic to the cause along the path of violence. A 2005 posting discussed the following internet exchange between two non-Hamas members, Palestinians who used the Hamas internet site to exchange terrorism information:

> *My dear brothers in Jihad. . . . I have a kilo of acetone peroxide. I want to know how to make a bomb from it in order to blow up an army jeep, I await your quick response.*

A response came approximately one hour later:

> *My dear brother. . . . I understand that you have 1,000 grams of Om El Abad. Well done! There are several ways to change it into a bomb.* [He proceeded to explain the specific details for making an explosive for a roadside bomb].[37]

Hamas has created an internet site providing instructions for building and producing a number of terrorist weapons, including rockets and explosives. Furthermore, the military wing of Hamas created a "Military Academy," which runs online courses for bomb-making, featuring a fourteen-lesson course as part of a program to expand the pool of terrorist bomb-makers. Additional topics include how to manufacture plastic explosives and the selection of terrorist targets. In 1996, the Hamas website posted *The Mujahideen Poisons Handbook*, a detailed, twenty-three page handbook on preparing poisons and deadly gasses intended for terrorist attacks.[38]

2006 ELECTIONS

Hamas agreed to an informal truce with Israel in February 2005 in return for Hamas being able to participate in the Palestinian elections. In 2006, Hamas won the elections based on its *"promises to provide effective, honest governance."* Hamas had long-voiced its acceptance of elections, provided that Palestinian elections were legitimate. Many of Hamas's supporters and members have stressed the point that Hamas will recognize the will of the Palestinian people. In the Palestinian town of Nablus, a Hamas student leader stated: *"In elections, Hamas will always accept the will of the people. There will be an Islamic state at the end, but only if the majority of the people opts for it. Hamas will never enforce its agenda on anyone."*[39] And Yassin stated prior to his assassination: *"In elections, it is always the people who decide. We will accept their decision as we have accepted their decision in all elections we have participated in."*[40]

The issue of corruption played a major role in the 2006 elections. Hamas attacked Fatah on the grounds of practicing corruption and cronyism while neglecting the plight of the Palestinians. Notably, Hamas was able to distribute around 95 percent of its funds to the needy Palestinian poor.[41] This helped to create a legitimate, fair, and just Hamas in the eyes of the public—compared with the corruption of the Palestinian Authority.

In the ensuing elections, Hamas won 76 out of 132 seats on the Palestinian Legislative Council. Despite this majority, only 45 percent of Palestinians voted for Hamas in the January elections. Widespread perceptions of Fatah as corrupt enhanced Hamas's electoral numbers, as some Palestinians voted for Hamas as a vote against Fatah. Overall, the voting results reflected a strong, but not universal support for Hamas's anti-Israeli platform.[42]

HAMAS IN POWER

Hamas leader and current Palestinian Prime Minister Ismail Haniya was elected in the 2006 legislative elections that brought Hamas to power, a result that shocked the West but confirmed the predictions of the Arab street. Haniya has a long history of close affiliation with the late spiritual leader Sheikh Ahmad Yassin. Haniya was born in the Shati refugee camp, west of Gaza City, in 1962 after his family fled from their original home during the 1948 Arab-Israeli war. Haniya was imprisoned several times, and with Yassin, formed part of the Hamas prison leadership that was fundamental in guiding the group. Haniya was one of over 400 Palestinian fighters and leaders expelled to southern Lebanon in 1992. He spent over a year at Marj al-Zahour refugee camp, where he became part of the exiled movement leadership, developing ideology and strategy for Hamas, and gaining worldwide media exposure.

Stressing the oppression of Palestinians by the Israelis, even after his election, Haniya stated, *"Our government will spare no effort to reach a just peace in the region, putting an end to the occupation and restoring our rights."*[43]

Continuing to oppose a two-state solution, consistent with the absolute principles in their founding charter, Hamas still refuses to recognize Israel's right to exist. The United States, the European Union, and Israel have withheld financial support from the Hamas-led Palestinian government, making it clear that the resumption of economic support is contingent upon Hamas foreswearing terrorism, recognizing Israel's right to exist, and reentering the so-called "road map" negotiations that will lead to a two-state solution. These sanctions have destroyed the already-weakened Palestinian economy—funds to the PA have been cut, and civil servants have gone as long as six months with essentially no pay. Many middle-class Palestinians, particularly those working for the Palestinian Authority, have been plunged into poverty, leading to public protests and rioting. The UN estimates the poverty rate in Gaza at 80 percent.[44] This poverty has contributed to harsh anti-Israeli opinion in the West Bank and particularly in Gaza, leading to a public largely sympathetic to Hamas. The following statements reveal the sentiments of various Gaza residents, and explain why Hamas's anti-Israeli program resonates widely with Gaza's poor.

Majeda al-Saqqa, 37-year-old NGO worker from Khan Younis:

> The situation now is just so bad: socially, educationally, economically. Israel has been destroying Palestinian society. . . . The issue is not should Hamas recognize Israel. The issue is that we are under occupation. We don't have a state yet, Israel does. They have embassies, offices, passports. We are the people who are neglected by Israel and the West. The basis for any solution is for Israel to recognize us.[45]

Fathi Tobail, aged 50, an employee of the Palestinian Authority:

> We are the ones who are oppressed, who need recognition, not Israel. It's for the occupier to recognize the oppressed, not for the oppressed to recognize the occupier. They have their own country, but we are still suffering to get our own state.[46]

Despite the profound economic hardship wrought by the economic boycotts by the European Union, the United States, and Israel, there is no indication of Hamas moving away from its founding principles. They persist in blaming Israel and the United States for the difficulties within Gaza without ever indicating that the economic policies are in response to Hamas's continued support of terrorist violence to obtain their totalistic goals.

As early as 2005, there have been indications of Hamas's increasing radicalization. Following Israel's August 2005 withdrawal from Gaza, Hamas, particularly its military branch, attempted to show the benefits of violence (as opposed to Fatah's diplomacy). Statements emphasized the benefits of *"four years of resistance, against ten years of negotiations."*[47] Likewise, the political branch produced tens of thousands of flyers titled *The Dawn of Victory*, which displayed masked photos of Hamas commanders, emphasizing their military success.

Since the victory of Hamas in the spring 2006 elections, the Palestinian territories have been disrupted by international sanctions and escalating cycles of Palestinian and Israeli violence. Hamas initiated talks with Fatah, proposing a national government designed to unify the Palestinian factions, but there are no indications that Hamas has changed its ultimate goals. Rather, it probably represented another "strategic" move consistent with Hamas's long-time goal of destroying the Israeli state. The gap between Hamas and the western-supported Palestinian Authority is increasing, and what has been characterized as a burgeoning civil war between Hamas and the Palestinian Authority militias is escalating. While it seems that the very future of the peace process, the Palestinian people, and Hamas (as both a terrorist group and as a political party), as well as Israeli security, currently hang in the balance, these crises have regularly plagued the region since the establishment of Israel in 1948.

CHAPTER 13

OSAMA BIN LADEN AND AL-QAEDA VERSION 1.0

What manner of men are these, living in American society, for years in some cases, aiming to kill thousands while dying in the process? Surely, one would think, no normal person could do such a thing, they must be crazed psychotics. But in fact, the al-Qaeda 9/11/2001 terrorists were psychologically "normal." By no means were they psychologically disturbed.

As I have come to understand them, the al-Qaeda suicidal sky-jackers differ strikingly from the youthful Palestinian suicide bombers in Israel. Older, they were in their late 20s to early 30s; Mohammad Atta, the ringleader was 33. A number of them had higher education. Atta and two of his colleagues were in graduate training at the Technological Institute in Hamburg. And, for the most part, they came from comfortable middle class families in Saudi Arabia and Egypt (15 of the 19 were Saudis). As fully formed adults, they had internalized their values. They were "true believers" who had subordinated their individuality to the group. They had uncritically accepted the directions of the destructive charismatic leader of the organization, Osama bin Laden, and what he declared to be moral was moral and indeed was a sacred obligation.

OSAMA BIN LADEN: A POLITICAL PERSONALITY PROFILE

What kind of leader could inspire such acts? How could the son of a multibillionaire construction magnate in Saudi Arabia become the leader of this powerful radical Islamic terrorist organization?

Osama bin Laden was born in Jeddah, Saudi Arabia, in 1957, the seventeenth of 20 or 25 sons of Mohammed bin Laden, who had 52 or 54 children in total.[1] Originally an immigrant from Yemen, Mohammed bin Laden, who befriended the royal family, had established a major construction company and had amassed a fortune of some $2 to $3 billion by the time of his death in 1967 in a plane crash. Although estimates range from $18 million to as high as $200 million, it is most commonly agreed that bin Laden inherited approximately $57 million dollars at age 16 from his father's estate.[2]

Osama was the only child of Mohammed and Hamida, the least favorite of Mohammed's 10 wives. Hamida, a Syrian woman of Palestinian descent, was reportedly a beautiful woman with a free and independent spirit who, as a result, often found herself in conflict with her husband.[3] Reportedly by the time Osama was born, Hamida had been ostracized by the family and had been nicknamed "Al Abeda" (the slave). As her only child with Mohammed, Osama was referred to as "Ibn Al Abeda" (son of the slave). Unlike the other bin Laden children, who had natural allies in their immediate circle of siblings, Osama had no natural allies in the family. As a consequence, there may have been a defensive alliance between Osama and his mother against the larger family, which treated the so-called slave and son of the slave with contempt. This familial exclusion may have set the stage for Osama bin Laden's later estrangement from his family. Reports are inconsistent as to how much of a presence Hamida was in her son's life during his early developmental years, but it is clear that Mohammed bin Laden divorced Hamida prior to his death in 1967, when Osama was 10 years old.[4]

Osama bin Laden attended King Abdul Aziz University in Jeddah. He is a certified civil engineer, and was working toward a degree in business management (although it is not clear whether he completed his course work) preparing him to play a leadership role in the family's far-flung business interests.[5] These two skill areas would serve him in good stead in Afghanistan.

An important influence on Osama bin Laden's political ideology was Abdullah Azzam, a radical Islamist professor at the university in Jeddah. Azzam obtained his doctorate in Islamic Jurisprudence at al-Azhar University in Cairo, where he was exposed to and absorbed the ideology of Sayyed Qtub, an influential leader of the Egyptian Muslim Brotherhood. During his time at university Azzam met both Ayman al-Zawahiri, later to become bin Laden's deputy, and Sheikh Omar Abdel-Rahman, "the blind sheikh," considered to be the architect of the first World Trade Center bombing in 1993.

Azzam became a central intellectual mentor for bin Laden. He issued a fatwah, *Defense of the Muslim Lands, the First Obligation after Faith*, in 1979 after the invasion of Afghanistan by the Soviet Union. It was Azzam who provided to bin Laden the vision of what should be done in response to the Soviet invasion of the Muslim state of Afghanistan, and what role bin Laden could play. In particular, he conveyed to bin Laden the importance of bringing together Muslims from around the world to defend Afghanistan against the godless Soviet Union. Demonstrating his already blossoming management skills, bin Laden assisted Azzam, who had founded the international recruitment network Maktab al-Khidamat (MAK—Services Office) in Peshawar, Pakistan, and advertised all over the Arab world for young Muslims to fight the Afghanistan *jihad*. In addition to the Arab and Muslim world, recruitment efforts were mounted in the United States and Europe. This massive international recruitment effort brought in Muslims from around the world—5,000 were recruited from Saudi Arabia, 3,000 from Algeria, and 2,000 from Egypt—who became known as the Afghan Arabs, the nucleus of bin Laden's loyal followership.

A leader is not formed until he encounters his followers. Bin Laden came to Afghanistan inexperienced and naïve, and his experiences during the struggle against the Soviet invasion was transformational for him as a leader. Using his own funds, he built clinics and hospitals, generously contributing to the *mujahideen* movement. Eschewing an opulent life style, he lived an ascetic life in caves with his followers. Inspirational in his rhetoric, bin Laden regularly preached about their holy mission and inspired his followers who came to adulate him. That they were able—with substantial American aid, to be sure—to triumph over the Soviet Union in what was to become its Vietnam, surely confirmed for bin Laden and his followers the correctness of his vision. In the Koran it is said that Allah favors the weak and the underdog. Surely they could not have triumphed over the godless Soviets unless God was on their side. This was the template for the destructive charismatic relationship between bin Laden and his religiously-inspired Islamic warriors, the *mujahideen*.

Bin Laden, following the lead of Abdullah Azzam, was taking on one of the three major enemies identified by Abd al-Salam Faraj, a noted Islamist intellectual in the tradition of Qtub. Faraj, referring to the obligation of *jihad*, wrote *The Neglected Duty: The Existing Arab State, the Western-Zionist Nexus, and the Communists*. Throughout the 1960s and 1970s, the critical enemy among this triad was the "enemy who was near"—the Arab state, according to leading Islamic fundamentalists. In Faraj's manifesto, he argued, "*We must begin with our Islamic country by establishing the rule of God in our nation . . . the first battle for jihad is the uprooting of these infidel leaders and replacing them with an Islamic system from which we can build.*"[6]

But attacking the Soviet superpower, which Azzam and bin Laden had come to see as a paper tiger that could be defeated, represented a fundamental departure from the strategy of Faraj, replacing "the enemy that is near" with "the enemy that is afar."

With the victory in Afghanistan, bin Laden the warrior king and his loyal Afghan Arab fighters were eager to continue to pursue the *jihad*. Bin Laden broadened his vision and determined to pursue the *jihad* on a worldwide basis, seeking to reconstruct the nation of Islam throughout the world and assist Muslims who were in conflict, including Algeria, Angola, Bosnia, Chechnya, Eritrea, Somalia, and Sudan.

While bin Laden was committed to the international struggle, Abdullah Azzam believed in focusing all efforts on building Afghanistan into a model Islamic state, which led to increasing tension between Osama and his mentor and an eventual split with Azzam in 1988. With the nucleus of his loyal followers, bin Laden and Ayman al-Zawahiri, a founding father of the Islamic Jihad of Egypt, established al-Qaeda (The Base) as a direct outgrowth of MAK. The following year Abdullah Azzam died in a mysterious car bomb explosion. Bin Laden was left as the undisputed leader of the movement. Between the dismissal of U.S. help and the removal of Azzam from his leadership role, bin Laden became solely responsible for the victory over the Soviet superpower and the expansion of the *jihadist* movement, both in his followers' eyes and in his own increasingly grandiose psychology.

BIN LADEN TRANSFERS ENMITY TO THE "ENEMY THAT IS AFAR"—THE UNITED STATES

With the defeat of the Soviet Union, bin Laden and his loyal warriors had lost their enemy. As Eric Hoffer has observed, the power of a charismatic leader derives from his capacity to focus hatred against a single enemy, as Hitler did in the 1930s, unifying the German people in their hatred of the Jews.[7] In 1993, bin Laden became incensed that his previous ally, the United States, had a military base on Saudi soil in the wake of the crisis in the Gulf. Decrying this desecration of holy Saudi soil by the "infidel Americans," bin Laden criticized the Saudi government for selling out to the United States. He was placed under house arrest but escaped and fled to Sudan, where he continued his anti-Saudi, anti-U.S. diatribes. He had seamlessly transferred his enmity from the first defeated superpower, the Soviet Union, to the remaining superpower, the United States.

As if to reinforce bin Laden's messianic vision to his followers, over the next decade al-Qaeda had a series of triumphs against this new enemy: the first World Trade Center bombing in 1993; the bombing of the U.S. military domicile, the Khobar Towers, in Dhahran, Saudi Arabia in 1996; the coordinated twin city bombings of the U.S. embassies in Kenya and Tanzania and the forced withdrawal of the U.S. from Somalia in 1998; the attack on the *U.S.S. Cole* in Yemen in 2000; and of course the most spectacular terrorist act in history, the events of September 11, 2001, an act of mass casualty super-terrorism. Each of these triumphs further confirmed for his followers that bin Laden had a special pipeline to Allah, and confirmed for bin Laden his own messianic role.

When bin Laden actively criticized the Saudi royal family for their apostasy by decrying their defiling their stewardship of "the land of the two cities," Mecca and Medina, by providing host to infidel U.S. military bases, the vigor of his criticism led Saudi Arabia to revoke his citizenship in 1994, and bin Laden's family, which depended upon the Saudi leadership for their wealth, turned against him as well. (It should be noted that in criticizing the Saudi royal family he was turning against the generation of his family that was loyal to and enriched by the Saudis. So, to be sure, he was an Islamic religious fundamentalist, but in criticizing the Saudi leadership, he was demonstrating the generational dynamics of the social revolutionary terrorist leader, a role he actively cherishes.)

Now bin Laden was righteously attacking the other two enemies in the triad of enemies—the Western-Israeli nexus, and one of the newly designated apostate Arab nations, Saudi Arabia. But he maintained the primary focus on the external enemy, the United States. Yes, the leadership of the apostate nations had to be replaced, but it was the United States that was the prime enemy, for America was responsible for propping up the corrupt governments of these countries. Thus he continued the strategy born in Afghanistan of focusing on the enemy who is afar, the Zionist-Crusaders, rather than the enemy who is near, the *targhut* (oppressive domestic rulers).

In the October 1996 Declaration of War, bin Laden justified his aggression as defensive aggression, asserting that the Islamic nation was under attack:

> . . . *The people of Islam had suffered from aggression, inequality and injustice imposed on them by the Zionist-Crusader alliance and their collaborators to the extent that Muslims' blood became the cheapest and their wealth looted in the hands of enemies. Their blood has spilled in Palestine and Iraq. The horrifying pictures of the massacre of Qana, in Lebanon are still fresh in our memory. Massacres in Tajikistan, Burma, Kashmir, Philippines, Somalia, Chechnya and in Bosnia-Herzegovina took place, massacres that send shivers in the body and shake the conscience.*[8]

With this, bin Laden and Zawahiri, who is widely believed to be bin Laden's pen, justified defensive jihad while blaming the Zionist-Crusader alliance for every fight against Muslims. But the fourth jihad, the jihad of the sword, is a defensive jihad only, which requires pious Muslims to take up the sword against those who take up arms against Muslims.[9] In 1996, the target was limited to the American military in Saudi Arabia, with the stated goal of expelling the U.S. military and their bases from Arabian soil. To bin Laden's stated dismay, the enemy "that is afar," the United States, in fact was near, indeed—within the holy "land of the two cities," Saudi Arabia.

In a major departure from the 1996 Declaration of War, in 1998, a major expansion of the mission occurred with the *Declaration of the World Islamic Front for Jihad against the Jews and Crusaders*, in which all Americans, civilian *and* military, were declared to be the enemy. The civilians became targets because they supported anti-Muslim U.S. policy, and they were to be killed wherever they were.

> From: Jihad Against Jews and Crusaders World Islamic Front Statement (February 1998 Fatwa)
>
> *In compliance with God's order, we issue the following fatwa to all Muslims:*
>
> *The ruling to kill the Americans and their allies—civilians and military—is an individual duty for every Muslim who can do it in any country in which it is possible to do it, in order to liberate the al-Aqsa Mosque and the holy mosque [Mecca] from their grip, and in order for their armies to move out of all the lands of Islam, defeated and unable to threaten any Muslim. This is in accordance with the words of Almighty God, "and fight the pagans all together as they fight you all together," and "fight them until there is no more tumult or oppression, and there prevail justice and faith in God."*
>
> *We—with God's help—call on every Muslim who believes in God and wishes to be rewarded to comply with God's order to kill the Americans and plunder their money wherever and whenever they find it.*

It should be observed that it is not bin Laden but God who has ordered religious Muslims to kill all the Americans; it is God for whom bin Laden speaks with authority. There is not an action that bin Laden orders that is not couched and justified in language from the Koran.

AL-QAEDA: IDEOLOGY AND PHILOSOPHY

The ideological and philosophical underpinnings of al-Qaeda can be found in several important documents. During my service as expert witness in the spring

2001 trial of al-Qaeda terrorists convicted for the bombings of the U.S. embassies in Kenya and Tanzania, I was provided with a copy of the al-Qaeda operations manual. This document, introduced into evidence by the U.S. Department of Justice, was seized in Manchester, England, in the home of Anas al-Liby, a fugitive charged in the al-Qaeda terrorism conspiracy. Ayman al-Zawahiri, Osama bin Laden's personal physician and designated successor, probably played a central role in developing the al-Qaeda terrorism manual.

This is an altogether remarkable document. On the one hand, it resembles nothing more than a basic tradecraft-training manual, concerned with how to operate in a hostile environment. There are detailed instructions on everything from ciphers to how to resist interrogation. It is also a manual of terror, with no less than three of the eighteen lessons (chapters) devoted to techniques for assassination.[10]

But it is not merely a list of instructions, for it is also written to inspire the undercover operator as he carries on his dangerous work—the language at times is quite eloquent. The document reflects a sophisticated approach on the part of al-Qaeda operational officials, for there is a continuing emphasis on lessons learned. Many of the chapters cite previous mistakes, which provide the basis for the points emphasized in the lesson. And they do not learn lessons only from their past mistakes, but from adversaries as well. In one section, they cite the astute observational skill of an Israeli Mossad counter-espionage agent who foiled a terrorist plot, and cite Soviet KGB sources in others. Thus the manual reflects the adaptive learning of the organization, and the care with which al-Qaeda prepares its operatives. No detail is too small, as exemplified by the instruction in lesson eight, which is concerned with Member Safety: "*Do not park in no parking zones.*"

Many of the instructions are accompanied by elaborate justification, citing *suras* (verses) from the Koran, augmented by scholarly commentary, as well as *hadiths* (words or deeds of the prophet Mohammed). These elaborate justifications are offered especially when the instructions recommended seem to contradict Islamic teaching. In this text, the *suras* are not numbered, and while some are fairly well known, others are more obscure. The authenticity of many of the *suras* and *hadiths* are questionable, and several of the *suras* are taken out of context. For the Islamic youth taught to respect without questioning religious scholars, these can provide apparently persuasive religious authority in justifying acts of violence. As Daniel Brumberg sagely notes, in evaluating the authenticity of the sources, the following *sura* 3, 78, which speaks to Christians and Muslims, seems most aptly to apply to the writers of this manual.

There are among them (People of the Book)

A section who distort

The Book with their tongues

(As they read the Book) you would think

It is part of the Book

But it is not part

Of the Book: and they say

"That is from Allah,"

But it is not from Allah:

It is they who tell

A lie against Allah

And (well) they know it.

As an example of an incorrectly cited authority, the assertion that the Prophet says, "Islam is supreme and there is nothing above it" cannot be found in the Koran. The singular in the statement is discordant with many *suras* in the Koran, which while advancing the truth of Islam, do not imply that Islam is superior, nor are they meant to suggest that previous religions were intrinsically untrue. Indeed there are many *suras* that speak of the people of the book, referring to the three monotheistic religions—Judaism, Christianity, and Islam.

The manual goes a long way toward explaining how the September 11 hijackers were able to maintain their cover in the United States, "the land of the enemies." Lesson Eight, "Measures That Should Be Taken By The Undercover Member," instructs the members to:

1. *Have a general appearance that does not indicate Islamic orientation (beard, toothpick, book, long shirt, small Koran)*
2. *Be careful not to mention the brother's common expressions or show their behaviors (special praying appearance, "may Allah reward you", "peace be on you", while arriving and departing, etc.)*
3. *Avoid visiting famous Islamic places (mosques, libraries, Islamic fairs, etc.)*

The explanation offered to "An Important Question: How can a Muslim spy live among enemies if he maintains his Islamic characteristics? How can he perform his duties to Allah and not want to appear Muslim?" in Lesson Eleven is compelling.

Concerning the issue of clothing and appearance (of true religion), Ibn Taimia—may Allah have mercy on him—said, "If a Muslim is in a combat or godless area, he is not obligated to have a different appearance from (those around him). The (Muslim) man may prefer or even be obligated to look like them, provided his actions brings a religious benefit." . . . Resembling the polytheist in religious appearance is a kind of "necessity permits the forbidden" even though they (forbidden acts) are basically prohibited.

Citing verses from the Koran, the justification says in effect that Allah will forgive you for not living the life of a good Muslim, for it is in the service of Allah, in the service of *jihad*.

The training manual specifies the "Characteristics of Members that Specialize in the Special Tactical Operations." Among the various characteristics listed is:

Tranquility and calm personality [that allows coping with psychological trauma such as those of the operation of bloodshed, mass murder]. Likewise, [the ability to withstand] reverse psychological traumas, such as killing one or all members of his group. [He should be able] to proceed with the work with calmness and equanimity.

That the special operations member should not only be calm in the face of mass murder but also able to kill "one or all members of his group," with calmness and equanimity is surely a description of person unburdened by conscience.

The training manual's dedication provides perhaps one of the best insights into the al-Qaeda leadership's view of their struggle:

In the name of Allah, the merciful and compassionate

To those champions who avowed the truth day and night . . .
And wrote with their blood and sufferings these phrases . . .

> *The confrontation that we are calling for with the apostate regimes does not know Socratic debates . . . , Platonic ideals . . . , nor Aristotelian diplomacy. But it knows the dialogue of bullets, the ideals of assassination, bombing, and destruction, and the diplomacy of the cannon and machine-gun.*

> *Islamic governments have never and will never be established through peaceful solutions and cooperative councils. They are established as they [always] have been*
> *by pen and gun*
> *by word and bullet*
> *by tongue and teeth*

The literary quality and rhetorical force of this dedication is striking. Socratic debates, Platonic ideals, Aristotelian diplomacy—characteristics of a democracy—are dramatically contrasted with the absolutist, uncompromising nature of the confrontation with apostate regimes, referring to the moderate modernizing Islamic nations who have strayed from the Islamist path, who will know only *"the dialogue of the bullet, the ideals of assassination, bombing and destruction, and the diplomacy of the cannon and machine gun."*

The three dangling last lines, in their pairing of qualities responsible for the establishment of Islamic governments pair words connoting violence (gun, bullet, teeth) with words reflecting persuasive rhetoric (pen, word, tongue). Powerful rhetoric is highly valued in Arab leaders, and a notable aspect of Osama bin Laden's leadership is his capacity to use words to justify and to inspire.

AL-QAEDA VERSION 1.0: LEADERSHIP, STRUCTURE, AND ORGANIZATION

The organizational structure that follows is that which characterized al-Qaeda before 9/11, and what, with apologies to Bill Gates and Microsoft, has been characterized as al-Qaeda Version 1.0. Al-Qaeda is unique among terrorist groups and organizations in its non-hierarchical structure and organization. Perhaps reflecting his training in business management, bin Laden in effect serves as chairman of the board of a holding company, which can be termed "Radical Islam, Inc.," a loose umbrella organization of semi-autonomous terrorist groups and organizations with bin Laden providing guidance, coordination, and financial and logistical facilitation.

Unlike other charismatically-led organizations, such as Guzman's Sendero Luminoso (Shinning Path) of Peru, or Ocalan's PKK (Kurdistan's Workers Party) of Turkey, both of which were mortally wounded when their charismatic and controlling leaders were captured, bin Laden established a flat and dispersed organizational structure in which subordinates were entrusted with clearly designated responsibilities, and their successors were seamlessly promoted into open positions.

Ayman al-Zawahiri has been designated as bin Laden's successor and his second in command. A leading Islamic militant, Zawahiri is a physician who founded the Egyptian Islamic Jihad and its new faction, Talaa'al al Fateh (Vanguard of Conquerors). It was Zawahiri's group that was responsible for the attempted assassination of President Hosni Mubarak of Egypt and is considered responsible for the assassination of President Sadat. Zawahiri, who is responsible for more day-to-day decisions, can be seen as serving as CEO to bin Laden as chairman of the board. Chairman of the Islamic Committee and responsible for many of the *fatwas* and other official writings of al-Qaeda, Zawahiri indeed is reputed to be even more apocalyptic and extreme in his views than bin Laden. There has been speculation about the amount of influence Zawahiri has over bin Laden, with some believing that Zawahiri is the "behind the scenes" driving force of al-Qaeda.

The number three, Mohammed Atef, also of the Islamic Jihad of Egypt, was chairman of the military committee and training before his death in Afghanistan in the fall of 2001, during U.S. raids following the September 11 attacks in the United States. In another example of the redundant organizational structure and the successor system, following Atef's death, Abu Zubaydah, formerly head of personnel and recruiting, became head of the military committee until his capture by U.S. and Pakistani forces in Pakistan in the spring of 2001. He was in turn succeeded by Khalid Sheikh Mohammad, the alleged mastermind of the 2001 attacks, who has also been captured. No doubt another successor has moved into the vacant position. Despite the fact that bin Laden has not been seen in public since the fall 2001 U.S. attacks in Afghanistan, the fact that al-Qaeda's global network continues to operate is testimony to the effective leadership structure of the organization.

Conceptually, al-Qaeda differed significantly from other terrorist groups and organizations in its structural composition. Unprecedented in its transnational nature, al-Qaeda has proved a challenge to law enforcement officials—its organizational structure, diffuse nature, broad-based ethnic composition, emphasis on training, expansive financial network, and its technological and military capabilities makes it not only a formidable force but one difficult to detect.

Al-Qaeda's global network consisted of permanent or independently-operating semi-permanent cells of al-Qaeda-trained militants, established in over seventy-six countries worldwide, as well as allied Islamist military and political groups globally.[11] The strict adherence to a cell structure has allowed al-Qaeda to maintain an impressively high degree of secrecy and security. Moreover, as was the case with the al-Qaeda bombings in Kenya and Tanzania, locals who have been trained by but are not official members of al-Qaeda may be activated to support outside operatives as needed to carry out attacks, for example establishing safe houses, procuring cars and local resources.

Al-Qaeda was reorganized in 1998 to enable the organization to more effectively manage its assets and pursue its goals. The revamped al-Qaeda structure had four distinct but interconnected elements: a pyramidal structure to facilitate strategic and tactical direction, a global terrorist network, a base force of guerrilla warfare inside Afghanistan, and a loose coalition of transnational terrorist and guerrilla groups.[12] Strategic and tactical direction comes from al-Qaeda's Consultation Council (Majlis al-Shura), which consists of five committees—Military, Business, Communications, Islamic Studies, and Media, each headed by a senior leader in the organization—which oversee the operations of the organization.

Al-Qaeda also maintained its own guerrilla army, known as the 55th Brigade, an elite body trained in small unit tactics. This group, comprised of approximately 2,000 fighters, was reportedly the "shock troops" of the Taliban, having been integrated into their army from 1997–2001.[13]

While bin Laden had developed this elaborate organizational structure and delegated responsibility and authority, he nevertheless watched closely over major operational planning, as exemplified by the following anecdote, which emerged from testimony offered at the 2001 trial of the al-Qaeda terrorists responsible for coordinated bombing attacks on the U.S. embassies in Dar es Salaam, Tanzania and Nairobi, Kenya.

> The embassies had been painstakingly surveyed for more than eighteen months. When photographs of the embassy in Dar es Salaan were brought back to al-Qaeda head-quarters in Afghanistan and shown to bin Laden, he reportedly pointed to a location by the embassy and indicated that that was where the explosive laden truck bomb should go.

Al-Qaeda's approach of allying itself with various existing terrorist groups around the world enhances the organization's transnational reach. Al-Qaeda has worked to establish relationships with diverse groups, not only geographically but ideologically as well—they have developed working relationships with organizations as diverse as Hezbollah and the Liberation Tigers of Tamil Eelam (LTTE), which do not follow the strict Wahabi al-Qaeda version of Salafi/Sunni Islam. Al-Qaeda established relationships with at least 30 Islamist terrorist groups, including such well-known groups as the Egyptian Islamic Jihad, Al Gama`a al-Islamiyya (GAI—Egypt), Harakat ul-Ansar (Pakistan); Al-Ittihad al-Islami (AIAI—Somalia); and the Palestinian Islamic Jihad and Hamas. In addition to its primary logistical base in Afghanistan, al-Qaeda maintained a direct presence in Sudan, Yemen, Chechnya, Tajikistan, Somalia, Indonesia, Malaysia, and the Philippines through relationships with Islamist organizations that already existed in these countries.[14]

In essence, bin Laden and his senior leaders have "grown" the al-Qaeda "corporation" through mergers and acquisitions. Bin Laden has worked to min-imize differences between the groups within the organization, emphasizing their similarities and uniting them with the vision of a common enemy—the West.

Having maintained bases in Pakistan, Sudan, Afghanistan, and elsewhere, as well as an ideological doctrine that rings true to much of the Islamic com-munity, al-Qaeda's membership base reached every corner of the world, encom-passing several dozen constituent nationalities and ethnic groups.[15] Its ideology has allowed al-Qaeda to unite the previously unorganized global community of radical Islam, providing leadership and inspiration. Beyond the actual al-Qaeda cells maintained in over 60 countries worldwide, al-Qaeda sympathizers exist in virtually every country on earth. The sympathizers are not only the disenfran-chised youth of impoverished communities; but also include wealthy and suc-cessful businessmen in such countries as Saudi Arabia and Egypt.

Like many terrorist organizations, al-Qaeda does not have a formal recruit-ment strategy; rather, it relies on familial ties and relationships, spotters in mosques who identify potential recruits, and the many new members/recruits vol-unteering, actively pursuing joining this revered organization. Al-Qaeda members recruit from their own family and social groups, and once trained, these new mem-bers are often reintegrated into their own communities. Very similar to the Muslim Brotherhood, the concept of "brotherhood" draws on the concept that familial ties in the Islamic world are binding. Al-Qaeda members refer to each other as "brother" and tend to view the organization as their extended family.

Al-Qaeda training camps trained both formal al-Qaeda members as well as members of Islamist organizations allied with al-Qaeda. According to reports, al-Qaeda training is broken into essentially three separate courses: Basic Training—training specific to guerrilla war and Islamic Law; Advanced Training—training in the use of explosives, how to carry out assassinations, and heavy weapons; and Specialized Training—training in surveillance and counter-surveillance techniques, forging and adapting identity documents, and conducting maritime- or vehicle-based suicide attacks.[16]

Al-Qaeda developed extensive training materials used in their camps and other training situations. In addition to paramilitary training, great emphasis is placed on Islamic studies—Islamic law, history, and current politics. These training materials produced by al-Qaeda, exemplified by the Al-Qaeda Training Manual discussed earlier, clearly demonstrate al-Qaeda's twin train-ing goals—the indoctrination of recruits in both military and religious studies.

But all of this centralized management structure was to change in the wake of the 9/11 attacks and the subsequent war against the Taliban regime in Afghanistan that had hosted bin Laden and his organization. Al-Qaeda Version 1.0 was no more. In contrast to hierarchical terrorist organizations with author-itarian control, which would have been devastated by such an attack on their command structure, al-Qaeda was an adaptive learning organization, and swiftly and effectively reacted to this assault, morphing into al-Qaeda Version 2.0 and the global Salafi *jihad*. This new organizational network will be described in Section IV, the Changing Face of Terrorism.

CHAPTER 14

KILLING IN THE NAME OF OTHER GODS

KILLING IN THE NAME OF JEHOVAH: JEWISH EXTREMIST TERRORISM

The Radicals of Gush Emunim, The Movement of the Faithful

The Israeli triumph in the 1967 Six Day War restored the old city of Jerusalem and the Western Wall to Israel. The seizure of the West Bank restored the boundaries of Judea and Samaria, so that the boundaries of Israel were essentially those of biblical Israel. To many religious Jews it seemed like a miracle.

Three weeks before the war, Rabbi Zvi Yehuda Kook had delivered a forceful sermon, "They Divided Up My Land," in which he decried the lost lands of Israel and declared, *"Every single inch, every square foot . . . belongs to the Land of Israel."*[1] The war endowed this sermon with prophetic force and led Rabbi Kook to declare that the regaining of the land of Israel signaled the imminent arrival of the Messiah.

In vivid contrast, the Yom Kippur war of 1973, which Israel nearly lost, shattered the myth of Jewish invulnerability and led to domestic pressure to trade land for peace. To the followers of Rabbi Kook, such a move would be a reproach to God and could delay the arrival of the Messiah for 1,000 years. This belief led them in 1974 to form Gush Emunim, the Movement of the Faithful, dedicated to fulfilling the biblical prophecy of Eretz Israel, the land of Israel, and not yielding "a single inch" of the God-given land of Israel.

Part of the ethos of religious belligerents is that an act of faith can hasten the arrival of the Messiah. To this end, a group of ardent Zionist militants within Gush began to plan to dynamite one of the most sacred sites in Islam, the al-Aksah Mosque and the Dome of the Rock on the Temple Mount, to demonstrate their religious fidelity. The Temple Mount is the holiest Jewish site; it is not only the location of the First and Second Temples, but when the Messiah arrives, according to legend, it will be the site of the Third Temple. This violent act, they believed, would transform the secular state of Israel into the Kingdom of Israel.[2] However, when they brought their plan to Rabbi Kook for his blessing, he was horrified. Recognizing that such an act would precipitate major conflict between Israel and the Arab world, he would not sanction the plan, which accordingly was aborted.

Following Talmudic Logic

While the Gush Emunim Temple Mount plot was aborted, there were numerous other attempts by Jewish extremists to destroy the Muslim shrines on the Temple Mount in order to prepare for the Third Temple. In 1988, with the facilitation of my colleague Ehud Sprinzak, I had the opportunity of interviewing Yoel Lerner, a member of a fringe group, the Temple Mount Faithful, several months after he was released from prison after completing his six-year sentence for his participation in a plot to destroy the Dome of the Rock and lay the cornerstone for the Third Temple, an action which was only discovered and prevented at the last moment by Israeli security forces. I spent a day with Lerner, who was a genial host. A portly man with a barbed tongue, he was born and educated in the United States. He boasted of getting 800 on his math SAT and attending MIT, where he majored in mathematical logic. He was inspired by Kahane's concept of "the fighting Jew," which drew on the Talmudic commentary, "If one comes to slay you—slay him first." After graduating from MIT he emigrated to Israel, where he became principal of a high school. The first political offense for which he was jailed was leading a group of his students and trashing the offices of a Christian missionary proselytizing in Jerusalem.

As I attempted to understand how Lerner justified his actions, he used a Socratic style that I could imagine had been highly effective in inspiring his student followers. Referring to his background in mathematical logic, he systematically led me into his own psycho-logic: *"As you know, Professor, in logic, there is a premise, you apply the engine of the syllogism, and a conclusion emerges. And I am sure you would agree that to have a conclusion without acting upon it is to render meaningless the chain of reason."*

Explaining how he decided to trash the missionary's facilities, he went on, "*Now, if you accept the premise of Israel as a Jewish state, does it make any sense to have a Christian missionary operating there? Of course not. Completely illogical. What other choice did we have?*"

We then went on to explore the Temple Mount plot. Had this plan succeeded, it surely would have led to a worldwide *jihad*. Lerner described his reasoning that led him ineluctably to his conclusion in identical language to that which he applied to the decision to trash the premises of the Christian missionary: "*Now, as to the decision to destroy the Abomination* [which is how Jewish extremists referred to the Islamic holy sites on the Temple Mount], *if you accept the premise of Israel as a Jewish state, does it make any sense to have Muslim holy sites on the holiest site in Judaism, the Temple Mount, the site of the third temple? Makes no sense whatsoever. Totally illogical. What other choice did we have?*"

For Lerner, the effect on the Muslim world was not in his calculus. Rather the planned destruction was a kind of urban renewal, preparing for the Third Temple. He was in no way emotionally disturbed. Lerner demonstrated throughout our day together wide-ranging knowledge and a nuanced flexible intellect, except in the area of his core beliefs about Judaism. In that bounded area there was a rock-hard rigidity. He knew the Truth, and his ideas were unchallengeable.

The Massacre at the Tomb of the Patriarchs

When Dr. Baruch Goldstein, a physician in a West Bank settlement, opened fire on worshipping Muslims in the mosque atop the Tomb of the Patriarchs in Hebron on February 25, 1994, killing or wounding at least 130, Israeli prime minister Yizhak Rabin was quick to characterize the act as a mental aberration, the act of an emotionally disturbed man. Like Lerner, Goldstein was a follower of Rabbi Kahane and believed in the concept of "the fighting Jew." Like his fellow settlers in the West Bank, he had become increasingly disturbed by Palestinian terrorist attacks on the Jewish settlements in Gaza and the West Bank, and on the night before the massacre had treated the wounds of friends injured in the Muslim uprising on the West Bank. That evening he had read to his two young daughters from the Book of Esther, which tells the story of the Jewish festival of Purim, which would be celebrated the next day. Purim celebrates the deliverance of the Jews in ancient Persia from a planned massacre at the hands of Haman, the minister to King Ahasuerus, in retaliation of the refusal of the Jew Mordechai to kneel before Haman and acknowledge the minister's authority over him. Through the intervention of Esther, Mordechai's niece, the king decides to hang Haman, and the Jews are saved and rise up and kill their would-be persecutors. While for most Jews it is a celebration of deliverance from their enemies, in the words of one of the settlers, "*Purim is a holiday to kill the people who are trying to kill the Jews.*"[3] Goldstein too saw Purim as a celebration of Jewish violence in the service of defensive aggression, a day of righteous wrath when "the Jews smote all their enemies with the stroke of the sword and with slaughter and destruction, and did what they would unto them that hated them" (Esther 9:1).

Goldstein went on to echo Israeli Prime Minister Menachem Begin's fiery motto of "Never Again," referring to the Holocaust, sentiments central to Kahane's concept of the fighting Jew: "*When the Jewish people is seen as weak, the God of Israel is seen as weak. When the Nazis were able to trample the Jews and stamp on the Jews with their boots, then the obvious question was: so where is your God? Jewish weakness is seen by the world as a symbol of God's weakness, and that's why I say it's a desecration of God's name.*"[4] Goldstein uttered these fighting words in 1988. In the intervening six years, the sentiments reflected in these words only intensified, culminating in the massacre at the Tomb of the Patriarchs.

Assassination of Yitzhak Rabin

Yigal Amir, the 27-year-old student at Bar-Ilan University who assassinated Israeli Prime Minister Yitzhak Rabin, was also responding to a religious psycho-logic. At his arrest he stated that he was acting alone: "*I acted alone on God's orders. I have no regret.*"[5] In referring to "*God's orders,*" he was responding to a body of reasoning circulating among the radical rabbinate that "*the judgment of the pursuer*" had been fastened to Rabin. At his interrogation, Amir called Rabin a "pursuer," referring to a verse from the Old Testament book of Leviticus frequently cited by Meir Kahane, "Thou shalt not stand idly by thy brother's innocent blood" (19:16).[6] The Talmudic interpretation of this verse is that if your innocent brother is being pursued by a killer, you are required to kill the killer to protect your brother. A perfectly sensible ethical principle, but as the radical rabbinate extended this to Israeli politics, by having participated in the Oslo Accords, Rabin was agreeing to place terrorist killers on the very borders of Israel, thus posing a mortal threat to Israel. Accordingly the "*judgment of the pursuer*" had been fastened to him and he deserved to die, so that Amir was following "*God's orders.*"

KILLING IN THE NAME OF JESUS: CHRISTIAN FUNDAMENTALIST TERRORISM

Pro-Life Extremist Violence Against Abortion Providers

At the extremity of the pro-life movement is a group of radicals whose religious psycho-logic drives them to strike out violently at women's clinics and doctors, nurses and health care workers providing abortions. Their logic, often drawing on the Holocaust, is compelling, likening the legalization of abortion to genocide, to a *"resurrection of the spirit of Nazism."* Former Roman Catholic priest David C. Trosch of Mobile, Alabama, who was threatened with excommunication and stripped of his clerical duties for his calls for violence against abortion providers, supplies a striking example of this logic. In effect, he likened abortions to the Holocaust, arguing that if you were walking down the main street of Auschwitz-Birkenau, the main killing camp of the Holocaust during the Holocaust, and you came across Dr. Mengele, an architect of the Holocaust, and killed him, you would not be a murderer because you were killing a perpetrator of the Holocaust, and by doing so, would be impeding the Holocaust. You would be a hero, he argued, and would deserve our reverent admiration. Reasoning by analogy, since a Holocaust is being perpetrated on the unborn children of this nation, anyone who kills a doctor, nurse, or health care worker participating in this Holocaust is not a murderer. He or she is a hero, and deserves our reverent admiration.

Declaring that such actions were "justifiable homicide," Trosch stated that *"[d]efending human life is not murder. You're comparing the lives of morally guilty persons against the lives of manifestly innocent persons. That's like trying to compare the lives of the Jews in the incinerators in Nazi Germany or Poland or whatever with the lives of the Gestapo."*[7]

Defensive Action is "a small group of about 30 pastors and church leaders from across the country who signed a declaration proclaiming the Godly justice of taking all action necessary to protect unborn life." Reverend Paul Hill, the leader of Defensive Action, asserted that *"executing abortion providers was a moral imperative."* His reasoning was clear. *"Abortion is murder, and murderers deserve to be executed."* The legalization of abortion, in Hill's view, *"requires a sin of omission, by forbidding people to intervene as mass murder is taking place."*[8] Eager for the limelight, Hill called the *Phil Donahue* show two days after Michael Griffin killed Dr. David Gunn at the women's clinic he directed and indicated that he supported the killing. In Hill's subsequent appearance on the show, echoing the argument advanced by Bishop Trosch, he compared killing Dr. Gunn to *"killing a Nazi concentration camp doctor.*" Believing that his God-assigned mission was to carry on the work of Griffin, Hill wrote "Why Shoot an Abortionist," which was published in the magazine of Advocates for Life Ministries. His reasoning, as exposited in the article, is interesting, in that he assigns himself divine powers: "*I realized that using force to stop abortion is the same means that God has used to stop similar atrocities throughout history. . . . It is not unwise, or inappropriate, thus, to use the means that God has appointed for keeping the Commandments.*"[9]

Persuaded by his own logic, Hill went on to follow the path of Griffin, shooting and killing Dr. John Bayard Britton and his security escort, James Barrett, in front of a women's clinic in Pensacola, Florida. Commenting on his act, Hill proudly observed, "*One thing's for sure, no innocent people will be killed in that clinic today.*" Given the premise that the fetus is a person, for Hill the beliefs and actions followed logically.[10]

The Aryan Nation and the Church of Jesus Christ, Christian

Several racist terrorist groups have conceptualized pseudo-Christian ideologies, in which they dehumanize their targets to justify violence in pursuit of their extremist goals. The Aryan Nation is the action arm of the Church of Jesus Christ, Christian, imbued with the principles of the Christian Identity movement. Why the Church of Jesus Christ, Christian? For this intensely anti-Semitic group, the notion that Christ could have been a Jew is inconceivable. The Christian Identity churches claim that the Bible teaches the racial superiority of Aryans. Its members denounce Jews and blacks, claiming that they are on the spiritual level of animals. In this pseudo-Christian belief system, Jews are depicted as the literal offspring of the devil. Jews, according to Jarah Crawford, proponent of the Christian Identity bible, are a "*half-breed, race-mixed, polluted people not of God. . . . They are not God's creation. [They are] the children of Satan, the serpent seed line.*"[11] Proponents of Christian Identity are apocalyptic in their rhetoric, calling on their fellows to fight in "*these final days.*"

Identity Christians trace a line of Jewish descent from the serpent, the devil in disguise, who seduced and impregnated Eve in the Garden of Eden. Cain was the first offspring of this union, so when Cain slew Abel, it was the prototype of the genocide of the white race planned by the Jews, the spawn of the devil. But the Jews could not do this alone. Students of the Old Testament will be surprised to know that the story of Adam and Eve in the Garden of Eden as told in Genesis was not God's first attempt at creation, at least according to the creative myth-makers of Christian Identity. It seems that God tried once before, and it was a failed attempt, from which emerged a subhuman group, blacks and people of color, known as the mud people. So in the final struggle, Jews, the spawn of the devil, will manipulate the subhuman mud people, and together they will attempt to eliminate the true chosen people, the Aryans. Thus the violence against Jews and people of color is defensive aggression.

This creative reinterpretation of the Book of Genesis leads in turn to imperatives for action. Identity Christians believe the "*Aryans are descendants of the lost tribes of Israel and are the true chosen people. They have a special calling and are on earth to do God's work. It is the God-given task of the Aryans to warn of the dangers represented by the Jews and the blacks and to destroy them.*"[12]

The Creedal Statement of the Aryan Nation and the Church of Jesus Christ, Christians, to which new members swear on joining, encompasses this ideology: "*We believe that there are literal children of Satan in the world today. These children are the descendants of Cain, who was a result of Eve's original sin, her physical seduction by Satan. . . . There is a battle and a natural enemy between the children of Satan and the children of the Most High God. . . . We believe that there is a battle being fought this day between the children of darkness (today known as Jews) and the children of light (God), the Aryan race, the true Israel of the Bible.*"[13]

Thus the tenets of Christian Identity provide a rich basis for paranoid political activists of the radical right to support an extreme political agenda. In their view, God's laws are absolute and the only ones that people are obligated to follow. Because His laws have been disregarded, the United States in on the brink of disaster and Armageddon is imminent. Loyalty is not owed to institutions that violate these laws. America's laws especially are invalid because the United States government is controlled by the Jews, "a Zionist Occupied Government" (ZOG). The news media and economic institutions are also directed by Jews. Because Jews are the children of the devil, they are responsible for all the evil that has occurred throughout history and are the spiritual and moral enemies of white Christians. Armageddon will be a military confrontation between God's chosen (the Aryan race) and the forces of Satan (Jews, blacks, and other minority groups).[14]

KILLING IN THE NAME OF SHIVA: SHOKO ASAHARA AND AUM SHINRIKYO

Attempting to Precipitate the Apocalypse

The March 20, 1995, sarin gas attack on the Tokyo subway by members of Shoko Asahara's millenarian cult, Aum Supreme Truth, was to be the first move of an elaborate plan to precipitate World War III. Because of problems with weaponization, the attack killed only 12 but injured 5,500. Although this was not the first case of chemical/biological terrorism by a religious cult—in 1984 the Rajneeshnees, followers of Bhagwan Shree Rajnees, attacked salad bars and coffee creamer in 10 restaurants in Oregon with salmonella bacteria in a bizarre attempt to influence a local election—it was the sarin gas attack that dramatically called international attention to the dangers of weapons of mass destruction terrorism. The sarin gas attack on the subway was followed two months later by a foiled attempt at mass cyanide poisoning, when bags of chemicals were found burning in Tokyo's Shinjuku station. Police said had the bags been properly ignited, they could have killed 10,000 people. This was to be the run-up to coordinated attacks in November on government buildings, the Diet, and the imperial palace. Police were astounded by what they found during their raid on Aum headquarters: weapons stockpiles; truckloads of chemicals that could be used to make, detect, and develop antidotes for sarin; and munitions factories. The group had recruited microbiologists who were working on biological weapons, including the deadly Ebola virus. Simultaneously other members were attempting to develop a nuclear capability. Asahara had recruited nuclear scientists from Moscow State University and purchased a ranch in Australia and acquired mining licenses to mine the holdings for its uranium deposits. One of the captured plans was for a 512-foot-long remote-controlled helicopter that would spread chemical or biological weapons over Tokyo and other Japanese cities.[15] Asahara's plans were truly cosmic in scale! The goal was to defeat Japan's Self-Defense forces and take over the country.

The psychology and motivations of Shoko Asahara, the paranoid and megalomaniacal guru of Aum Supreme Truth, were quite remarkable. Given his bizarre worldview and grandiose plans, what was particularly striking was his ability to recruit senior scientists, politicians, and security officials to his movement. The consummate pitchman, Asahara targeted alienated Japanese youth who sought greater meaning in their lives, and was highly effective in winning their support as well as significant support from members of the establishment.

New recruits were quickly separated from their worldly goods through a variety of scams; new members were required to sign over their real estate holdings to the cult. For $1,000 a liter, members drank water from a "miracle pond"—in reality, Asahara's bathwater—so that they could absorb the essence of the master. For a fee of $10,000, they could rent for a month a helmet with an electronic apparatus designed to align their brain waves with those of the master, the Perfect Salvation Initiation headset. For a "love donation" of $10,000, a member could drink what was said to be 36 trillion units of DNA—human genetic material—from Asahara's blood, containing magical properties.[16] Not a small closed cult, at its peak, Aum had about 50,000 members internationally, 10,000 members in Japan, and some 30,000 member in Russia, with offices in Bonn, Sri Lanka, Moscow and New York, and assets of some $1.4 billion.

In a speech in 1988, a year after the cult's founding (he had failed with two previous efforts to establish cults), Asahara predicted a war at the twilight of the twentieth century in which the United States would take over Japan. The adulation of his converts persuaded Asahara that he might yet win a seat in the Diet in the 1990 Japanese general election. His white-robed followers marched through the streets of Tokyo, wearing papier-mâché heads of Asahara, beating drums and chanting his name. The campaign was a total failure, with Asahara receiving only 1,700 votes out of roughly 500,000 cast.

Embittered by this electoral rebuff, Asahara turned increasingly to violence, predicting apocalypse, and accelerating his exploration of weapons of mass destruction. Asahara transformed the word *poa*, which means "a cleansing of the soul" to justify violence in the name of advancing his cause, terrorizing his followers, killing his enemies, purifying through death. He drew this principle from Tibetan Buddhism. As an example of the cleansing of the soul of *poa*, Asahara, who was fascinated by high tech, caught a couple who were attempting to defect from the Aum Shinrikyo compound and had them incinerated in his industry-size microwave oven.

In his book *The Land of the Rising Sun Is Headed Toward a Bitter Fate*, Asahara predicted a nuclear U.S. nuclear attack on Japan between 1996 and 1998, which could be survived only by following his teachings.[17] This knowledge, he claimed, derived from "*my astral vision, intuitive wisdom, and my knowledge inferred from Jnana Yoga.*"[18] He modestly claimed in his book *The Teachings of the Truth*[19] that he was the "*only person in Japan who had achieved the ultimate stage of satori.*"[20] In 1994, preceding the 1995 sarin gas attack and projecting his own paranoid psychology, Asahara claimed that U.S. jets were delivering gas attacks on his followers. He became increasingly preoccupied, not with surviving the coming war but with precipitating it—defensive aggression on a cosmic scale.

Asahara's own psychological course, and that in which he led Aum Shinrikyo, was increasingly messianic and grandiose. One of the difficulties with Buddhism from Asahara's perspective was its timelessness. An important development occurred when Asahara read the New Testament. Seeing the remarkable parallels between Christ and himself, he stated, "*I hereby declare myself to be the Christ!*" Warning against false prophets, he declared himself to be "*the last messiah of the century.*"[21] In 1992 he published a manifesto, *Declaring Myself the Christ.*[22] The Book of Revelations with its apocalyptic prophecy especially fit Asahara's destructive charismatic personality and added the urgency of the final days. Asahara became increasingly obsessed with weapons of mass destruction, and his scientists were simultaneously exploring chemical, biological, and nuclear weapons.

Was he still but a con man, now writ large? Early in his career Asahara was indeed a charlatan who was convicted of fraud; later, in the heady role of guru, with tens of thousands of adoring followers, Asahara increasingly became captive of his own rhetoric. Consumed by delusions of grandeur, he sought to precipitate the final apocalypse, after which only he and his "true believers" would be resurrected and reign supreme.

THE CHANGING FACE OF TERRORISM

CHAPTER 15

AL-QAEDA VERSION 2.0 AND THE GLOBAL SALAFI JIHAD

The Afghanistan intervention offensively hobbled, but defensively benefited al-Qaeda. While al-Qaeda lost a recruiting magnet and a training, command and operations base, it was compelled to disperse and become even more decentralized, "virtual" and "invisible."

—International Institute for Strategic Studies, 2004

AL-QAEDA IN THE POST 9/11 ERA

The unique and far-reaching transnational nature of al-Qaeda represents one of the greatest threats currently facing international security. Following the September 11 attacks, NATO, for the first time since its founding 52 years ago, invoked Article V, which states that an attack on one member state of NATO is considered an attack on all member states of NATO. A massive air and ground campaign was launched against al-Qaeda, its operational bases, and its Taliban supporters in Afghanistan. As a result of the campaign, al-Qaeda suffered severe losses, including the death and/or capture of several senior leaders. Despite these losses and the dispersal of members throughout the world, it is a testament to its organizational structure that al-Qaeda remains operationally intact—severely wounded, but certainly not destroyed.

For many al-Qaeda followers, the fall 2001 attacks in Afghanistan only served to reinforce their sense of righteous belief in their cause and their perception of the West as anti-Islamic aggressors. Although we have not seen a second large-scale al-Qaeda attack, there is nothing to suggest that al-Qaeda is no longer operational. Despite al-Qaeda's Afghan base having been destroyed and its leadership dispersed, its cellular structure remains intact with both active and sleeper cells throughout the world. It is possible that in setting the bar so high with 9/11, al-Qaeda did not wish to lower their sights, and the shift from a more centralized command and control to a more dispersed semiautonomous network, delayed plans in track. It is most likely, however, due to the highly-focused international attention, that the next wave of al-Qaeda attacks will be on a smaller scale and undertaken by cells operating semi-independently. Yet, as witnessed by the foiled 2006 British–based U.S.-bound airliner plot, in their new semiautonomous form, al-Qaeda and the *jihadi* network retains the capability of mounting a major coordinated attack, the hallmark of al-Qaeda operations.

With the U.S. tendency to personalize our enmities, there is a wistful hope that the death or capture of bin Laden will end the threat from al-Qaeda. It will not. In the event of bin Laden's death or capture, al-Qaeda's flat, dispersed organizational structure, the presence of a designated successor, the nature of bin Laden's and Zawahiri's leadership and charisma, and their enshrined religious mission, all indicate that the terrorist network would survive. Bin Laden's loss would assuredly be a setback, but since Zawahiri is already running al-Qaeda's daily operations, his transition to the top job would be virtually seamless. The organization's luster for alienated Muslims would dim, but within the organization, Zawahiri's considerable stature and charismatic attractiveness should permit him to carry on the network's mission. Osama bin Laden has not been seen in public since September 23, 2001, and he is believed by some to have been seriously wounded in the attack on Tora Bora. Bin Laden's death would surely lead to his designation as a martyr in the cause of Islam and might well precipitate terrorist actions. His capture could lead to retaliatory hostage-taking or other terrorist actions. In either event, al-Qaeda would survive.

While U.S. President George W. Bush and former British Prime Minister Tony Blair took pains to clarify that the War on Terrorism is not a war against Muslims, but a war against terrorism, bin Laden, in seeking to frame this as a religious war, has now laid claim to the title of commander-in-chief of the radical Islamic world, opposing the commander-in-chief of the Western world, President George W. Bush. Alienated Arab youth find resonance in bin Laden's statements, and see him as a hero. Al-Qaeda has become a catalyst for an international *jihadist* movement that will continue to grow, influenced and operationally facilitated by the original parent organization.

FROM AL-QAEDA VERSION 1.0 TO
AL-QAEDA VERSION 2.0

No good deed goes unpunished, and as a consequence of the 2001 war in Afghanistan, al-Qaeda has progressively morphed from what has been called al-Qaeda Version 1.0 into al-Qaeda Version 2.0, operating much more autonomously, out of hubs and nodes, but absent the prior centralized hierarchical control. Al-Qaeda 1.0, with centralized planning, staffing, command, and control, was basically destroyed in the campaign in Afghanistan. While retaining a broad-based organization, al-Qaeda 2.0 has become an ideology that provides inspiration for the global Salafi *jihad* movement. The form and function of al-Qaeda has significantly changed since 9/11, but more precisely since the retaliatory military attack was launched against al-Qaeda, its operational bases, and its Taliban supporters in Afghanistan in the fall of 2001. While bin Laden does not have a controlling autocratic leadership style, there was nevertheless centralized operational planning, financial management, training, and logistical support prior to this attack.

Contributing to the resilience of al-Qaeda is that it is an adaptive learning organization, regularly reviewing and pursuing lessons learned from both successful and failed operations, such as the inclusion of the lessons from Mossad in the al-Qaeda Training Manual. A less adaptive organization would have been destroyed by the focused attack in Afghanistan. But bin Laden had taken courses in business management at the university in Jeddah and learned about delegation of authority, flat organizations, and dispersal of organizational functions. He sent out a communiqué in the fall of 2002, which dispersed the organization and established a regional command structure, and said, in effect, we have shown you the way. From now on it is up to you to plan and fund your own operations.

Osama bin Laden's active leadership in formulating specific attacks post-9/11 was transferred to the growing global recruits, who were thereby granted the responsibility to carry on operations against the Western Infidel.[1] Yet bin Laden continued to maintain symbolic leadership control over the organization through his full praise and hailing of attacks by al-Qaeda-linked groups. In 2002, he embraced attacks in Bali, Yemen, and Moscow as a *"response to what happened to all Muslim brothers around the world . . . The incidents that have taken place since the raids on New York and Washington up until now—the recent operation in Moscow and some sporadic operations here and there—are only reactions and reciprocal actions. These actions were carried out by the zealous sons of Islam in defense of their religion and in response to the order of their God and prophet, may God's peace and blessings be upon him."* In the audiotape, bin Laden speaks on behalf of all the *mujahedin* fighters, but more broadly, the nation of Islam: *"The Islamic nation, thanks to God, has started to attack you at the hands of its beloved sons, who pledged to God to continue jihad, as long as they are able, through words and weapons, to establish right and expose falsehood."*[2]

While the string of attacks in the last few years by al-Qaeda-linked groups were in response to bin Laden's guidance and affirmed by him, and, at least in the case of the British-based attacks, were operationally facilitated by al-Qaeda. They added to the luster of al-Qaeda rather than being portrayed as a reflection of bin Laden's and al-Qaeda's eroding influence and a lack of organizational coherence.

This was true of the March 2004 attack on the Madrid train station. A December 2003 posting on al-Qaeda websites called for terrorist attacks against Spain on the eve of the election, indicating it would either force the regime to withdraw from Iraq, or would lead to a socialist victory at the polls and the new party would then pull out.[3] In this way al-Qaeda could legitimately lay claim to inspiring the major March 2004 attack, just before the election, that led to the fall of the government and the decision of the successor socialist government to remove troops from Iraq. The Abu Hafs al-Masri Brigade, a European jihad group linked to al-Qaeda, claimed responsibility for the Istanbul, Turkey bombings in August 2004, stating that the attack in *"Istanbul was only the beginning. . . . [A] group of mujahedeen . . . did the first attack after all of them [European nations] have refused the truce that was offered by our sheikh,"*[4] referring to bin Laden's advice to European states to reject the U.S. war on terror. (This is an interesting example of the transfer of blame so characteristic of terrorist groups.) This sustained control over the reins of the organization illustrate his ultimate preeminence as leader of al-Qaeda while embracing an emerging generation of new blood to carry on the attacks and replace the killed and captured.

Abu Musab al-Zarqawi, leader of al-Qaeda in Mesopotamia, in an October 2004 audiotape, communicated the importance of the new generation to continue on the fight to resist the Infidel: *"Oh, young men of Islam, here is our message to you. If we are killed or captured, you should carry on the fight. Don't betray God and His Prophet."*[5]

COOPTING POTENTIAL RIVALS: THE CASE OF ABU MUSAB AL-ZARQAWI

Part of al-Qaeda's leadership genius under bin Laden and Zawahiri is not to focus on differences, but to coopt and embrace potential rivals. A striking example was that of Abu Musab al-Zarqawi, whose silent power and barbaric militant ways captivated audiences and proved to rival bin Laden on many levels.

The decision by bin Laden and Zawahari to forge relations with Zarqawi exemplifies the essence of the new global threat of terror—shifting alliances, changing mission, and resources. While sheer differences in vision and leadership were apparent, arguably combining resources benefited the overarching *jihad* mission of al-Qaeda and its need for decentralized leadership. Captivating media audiences around the world, Zarqawi's violent unbounded approach to waging war against the infidels on the battlefield of Iraq, including Shi'a brethren, provided a stark contrast to the deeply ideological principles of Islamic Jihad as espoused by bin Laden. In October 2004, Zarqawi swore allegiance *"to the sheikh of the mujaheddin, Osama bin Laden,"* and thereby recognized bin Laden as the "Emir" in Iraq.[6] But this was in words only, and by no means did Zarqawi hand over control. *"[This is] a cause [in which] we are cooperating for the good and supporting jihad."*[7]

Bin Laden recognized the need to provide Zarqawi relative autonomy to carry out operations in Iraq while attempting to retain influence over the *jihad*, which was diverging from the path of bin Laden's al-Qaeda, as it emphasized sectarian violence and threatened competition as more fighters flocked to Zarqawi's charismatic banner.

A letter intercepted by U.S. forces, dated July 2005, from Zawahiri to Zarqawi attempts to reassert al-Qaeda's priorities in Iraq by calling into question Zarqawi's lack of foresight and planning. This was in part due to the extent of the sectarian violence that Zarqawi was leading, with Sunni Muslims killing Shi'ite Muslims, raising questions about the religious justification for the escalating violence. *"We are extremely concerned, as are the mujahedeen and all sincere Muslims, about your Jihad and your heroic acts until you reach its intended goal. Therefore, I stress again to you and to all your brothers the need to direct the political action equally with the military action, by the alliance, cooperation and gathering of all leaders of opinion and influence in the Iraqi arena."*[8]

Zawahiri attempts to inject an element of reality into Zarqawi's *jihadist* thinking, which fostered sectarian violence and killing of supporters of the Infidel, and he demonstrates an acute awareness of the power of the media: *"Among the things which the feelings of the Muslim populace who love and support you will never find palatable—also—are the scenes of slaughtering the hostages. . . . And your response, while true, might be: Why shouldn't we sow terror in the hearts of the Crusaders and their helpers. . . . However, despite all of this, I say to you: that we are in a battle, and that more than half of this battle is taking place in the battlefield of the media. And that we are in a media battle in a race for the hearts and minds of our Umma."*

The Zawahiri letter captured the prevailing frustration at the highest levels of leadership to contain Zarqawi's deviations, which they felt were threatening the reputation of al-Qaeda, and in particular were counterproductive for al-Qaeda's reputation in the Muslim world.[9]

But Zarqawi did not change his indiscriminate tactics. Shortly after the letter surfaced, Zarqawi's al-Qaeda in Iraq claimed responsibility for three suicide attacks in Amman, Jordan, in November 2005, that left many Muslims dead, demonstrating that Zarqawi was by no means influenced and certainly was not deterred by the firm tone of Zawahiri's letter.

Despite Zarqawi's defiance, in a June 2006 audio speech eulogizing Zarqawi after his death, bin Laden offers up great respect for "*one of our best knights, an Emir who was one of the best Emirs.*" While the eulogy appears to be an effort to defend Zarqawi's role in sectarian violence in Iraq, in fact it is also an opportunity to reassert al-Qaeda's priorities in Iraq and set the record straight. "*To those who accuse Abu Musab al-Zarqawi of killing some segments of the Iraqi people, I say . . . Abu Musab, may God have mercy upon his soul, had clear instructions [implicitly, from bin Laden] to focus his fighting on the occupying invaders, led by the Americans, and not to target whoever wanted to be neutral, but whoever insisted on fighting along with the Crusaders against Muslims should be killed, regardless of their sect or tribe. Supporting the infidels against Muslims is one of the 10 things that nullify Islam, as stipulated by scholars.*"[10]

One of the difficulties in moving from centralized command and control to a more dispersed, decentralized organization is maintaining overall control and not having actions by assertive, competitive leaders threaten the organization's overall direction and reputation. This was the dilemma for bin Laden in containing the ambitious Zarqawi, whose sectarian excesses were leading to Muslim criticism of the *jihad* and undermining bin Laden's authority. This problem is exacerbated as the organizational shape of al-Qaeda has progressively evolved into the global *jihad* movement—how to maintain influence, if not control, and yet claim credit for actions to demonstrate the movement has not left the leader behind.

Some would go so far as to say that al-Qaeda now provides an overarching ideology for groups and organizations operating independently. The organizational form of Hamas and Hezbollah is much tighter and more authoritarian, with followers in action cells having little say in the conduct of operations. In contrast to these other radical Islamist terrorist organizations, which are quite hierarchical in organizational style, al-Qaeda has a much looser organizational form, with distributed decision making, reflecting the leadership style of bin Laden.

AL-QAEDA RECONSTITUTED[11]

In fact, early estimates that the 2001 conflict in Afghanistan had dealt a crippling blow to al-Qaeda and marked the beginning of the end of the end for the organization have proven to be overly optimistic and insufficiently to have considered the adaptive resilient nature of the organization. There is substantial reason to believe al-Qaeda central has largely been reconstituted. Because of its redundant leadership structure, the significant numbers of senior leaders that have been killed or captured have been replaced by longtime al-Qaeda members with demonstrated loyalty to bin Laden and Zawahiri. There is now a new generation of al-Qaeda senior leaders.

Many of the senior leaders have as a central responsibility serving in liaison roles to associated organizations. The resurgence of the Taliban did not occur spontaneously but represents major al-Qaeda influence. Moreover, as exemplified by the London transit bombings of July 2005 and the foiled U.S.-bound airline attack of August 2006, al-Qaeda's role was more than inspirational. In fact, further investigation by British authorities of these plots carried out by British citizens with Pakistani roots have clarified that these plots were ordered by al-Qaeda deputies, training was provided in Pakistan by al-Qaeda to the operational leaders, and Abu Obaidah al-Masri, the current chief of external operations, reportedly was extremely active in assisting with the August 2006 plot to place explosives aboard U.S.-bound airliners out of Heathrow. This showed a much firmer guiding hand than earlier believed. The reconstituted leadership is playing active roles in recruitment, training, and finance. Particularly impressive is their enhanced communication ability; their media arm al-Sahab, has proven to be extremely effective in getting the al-Qaeda message out.

THE GLOBAL SALAFI JIHAD

One of the more alarming developments, which poses profound counterterrorism challenges, is the increase in recruitment to the global Salafi *jihad* of second generation émigrés to Europe, as exemplified by the March 11, 2004 Madrid train station and the July 7, 2005 London transit bombings as well as the foiled August 2006 coordinated attack on U.S.-bound planes from Heathrow airport outside of London. Throughout Europe, there is an increased radicalization and recruitment of terrorists from second- and third-generation émigrés to the global Salafi *jihad*, with estimates reaching as high as 87 percent of the new recruits coming from the diaspora. Although most Muslim immigrants and refugees are not stateless, many suffer from an existential sense of loss, deprivation, and alienation from the countries where they live. Their families had emigrated to Western Europe to seek a better life, but they and their offspring had not been integrated within the recipient society. They are then exposed to extreme ideologies that increasingly radicalize them and can foster entering the path of terrorism.

Be it in Germany, where Atta and his 9/11 colleagues attended a radical mosque in Hamburg; in Great Britain, where both the 2005 London transit bombing and the 2006 foiled U.S.-bound airliner plot were carried out by Pakistani-British citizens; or the assassination of Dutch playwright Theo van Gogh for mocking the prophet, there is a growing population of discontented Muslim émigrés who have been secondarily radicalized within their host country, from whose culture they feel excluded and alienated. The Madrid train station bombing of 2004 was conducted by Muslim émigrés and members of the Muslim diaspora originally from countries in North Africa. The London transport bombings of 2005 were carried out by Muslim youth with Pakistani family roots, living in a Muslim diasporic community in Leeds, England. The Muslim diaspora in the Netherlands is mainly of Moroccan origin. Thus there is not a monolithic Muslim diaspora, but rather a pastiche of Muslim diasporic communities.[12]

These events raise concerns about so called "homegrown terrorists": young second- and even third-generation residents of Western countries driven by alienation and possibly inspired by the global Salafi *jihad* but carrying out these attacks independently of it. Recent events, however, show that "homegrown" may be too simple a characterization, as exemplified by the British individuals of Pakistani descent who planned the summer 2006 plot to hijack and blow up 10 U.S.-bound airliners. The leaders had traveled back to Pakistan, where apparently they were in contact with al-Qaeda members for training in explosives. Dame Eliza Maningham-Butler, the director-general of MI-5, Britain's security service, stated they had identified nearly 30 plots that "often have links back to al-Qaeda in Pakistan and through those links al-Qaeda gives training and guidance to its largely British foot soldiers here." She also stated that Spain, France, Canada, and Germany faced similar threats.[13] So while there is a looser control, al-Qaeda continues to play a significant role in influencing and guiding the global *jihad*. The influence and involvement of al-Qaeda (which in a sense is also a transnational diasporic entity), suggests that the group inspired and facilitated acts of the disaffected among Muslim British citizens.

Grounded in the everyday experience of secular Muslim émigrés to Western Europe, European social conditions promoted feelings of alienation among young Muslims who felt excluded from the rigid European social structure. Not particularly religious, they drifted back to the mosque to find companionship, acceptance, and a sense of meaning and significance. This in turn made them vulnerable to extremist religious leaders and their radicalization within Muslim institutions. Based on his study of *jihadi* networks, Marc Sageman sees one possible path in the movement as moving toward a global leaderless *jihad*.[14] The challenge for bin Laden, Zawahiri, and the founding generation of al-Qaeda will be to continue to provide both inspiration and direction to the *jihad* under their overall influence. And, given the semi-autonomous functioning of the radical cells within the diasporic communities, this poses a profound challenge to international counterterrorism.

CHAPTER 16

TACTICS OLD AND NEW: SUICIDE TERRORISM AND WEAPONS OF MASS DESTRUCTION TERRORISM

Suicide terrorism is by no means a new technique. In the modern era of terrorism, Hezbollah's truck bombing of the U.S. and French embassies and of the U.S. marine barracks in 1983 promoted the Shi'ite terrorist group to the first rank of terrorist groups, and other groups were to emulate Hezbollah's innovative techniques.

And the tactic of suicide terrorism has been so refined and incorporated into terrorist strategy that today it has proven to be the most difficult tactic to counter.

In the insurgencies in Iraq and Afghanistan and in the Israeli-Palestinian conflict, suicide terrorism has been the central equalizing tactic, which the militarily superior American, British, and Israeli armies have not been able to counter. The perpetrators are not crazed fanatics. In the Palestinian territories, they have been set on this course early in life. On radical Islamist websites, there are pictures of infants with toy suicide bomb belts, of a girl no more than two and a half years old, with a diamond earring, holding a hand grenade. In the mosques, sermons celebrate the glory of the *shahids* (martyrs). Friday sermons aired on Palestinian Authority television (PATV) in the summer of 2001 by Dr. Muhammad Ibrahim Madi are instructive. One stated: "*Shame upon he who does not educate his children of Jihad . . . blessings upon he who dons a vest of explosives on himself or his children and goes into the midst of the Jews and says: Allah Akbar* [God is Great]."

A few months later, Dr. Madi recounted a conversation he had with a 14-year-old boy who wanted to blow himself up and kill Jews. His sermon broadcast, on PATV, August 3, 2001, went:

> *I was uplifted when a youth said: "Oh, Sheikh, I am 14 years old. I have more than 4 years and then I will blow myself up among Allah's enemies, I will blow myself up among the Jews." I said to him, "Oh young child, may Allah let you merit Shahada [martyrdom] and let me merit Shahada. . . ."*
>
> *All the weapons must be aimed at the Jews, Allah's enemies, the cursed nation in the Koran, whom Allah describes as monkeys and pigs, worshippers of the calf and idol worshippers. . . . Nothing will deter them except the color of blood in their filthy nation . . . unless we blow ourselves up, willing and as our duty, in their midst.*

In interviews with incarcerated Palestinian terrorists, almost all indicated they first heard of the manner in which their parents' property had been taken in the mosque, and were set early on the path of terrorism and martyrdom. The signs on the walls of the Hamas-run kindergartens read: *"The children of the kindergarten are the shahids of tomorrow."* This theme is incorporated into all levels of school. At an Islamic school in Gaza City run by Hamas, an 11-year-old student states: *"I will make my body a bomb that will blast the flesh of Zionists, the sons of pigs and monkeys. . . . I will tear their bodies into little pieces and cause them more pain than they will ever know."*[1]

According to the June 26, 2001, *USA Today* article that reported the episode, the boy's classmates responded *"Allah akbar."* The teacher, demonstrating that the entire system is deeply involved, yelled, *"May the virgins give you pleasure,"* referring to one of the rewards awaiting martyrs in paradise, while the principal smiled and nodded his approval. The value of martyrdom continues to be emphasized throughout students' education, continuing into university. Signs in the classroom at Al-Najah University in the West Bank and at Gaza's Islamic University state, *"Israel had nuclear bombs. We have human bombs."*

The Israeli terrorism expert Ariel Merari, who teaches at Harvard Law School, made a revealing comment to me in the fall of 2004. "As I walk around Harvard Square," he said, "I am struck by the fact that teenagers are teenagers the world around." He went on to explain that when he entered a pizza parlor off the square, he would find the teenagers talking excitedly about their favorite team, the New England Patriots (this was during their run-up to the Super Bowl title). They were talking admiringly about their heroes on the team, such as the quarterback Tom Brady. And when they grew up, they wanted to be professional football players like their heroes. "Same thing," he said, "in the Palestinian refugee camps. Only their favorite team is Hamas. Their heroes are the shahids (the martyrs) and when they grow up, which they won't, they want to be a shahid like their heroes." It was a chillingly normal remark.

The suicide bomber assembly line, described by Merari, has now changed. In many ways, these new terrorists shatter the profile of Palestinian suicidal terrorists developed by Israeli terrorism experts who conducted suicide postmortems—that is, reconstruction of the lives of individual who committed suicide—of 93 suicide bombers. The subjects of the early studies were the first wave of Hamas suicide bombers that occurred in 1993–1994 in an attempt to undermine the Oslo negotiations. Young men, 17 to 22 years old, uneducated, unemployed, unmarried, the Palestinian suicide bombers were dispirited unformed youth, looking forward to a bleak future, when they decided to volunteer. The process was a gradual one, moving through stages as described earlier, including religious indoctrination, to full commitment. The suicide bomb commanders did not "brainwash" their eager young recruits but helped them come to closure to volunteer for a martyrdom operation. They told the recruits that they were looking forward to a dismal life. Unemployment rates ranged between 40 and 70 percent in the camps, especially for uneducated young men. The youth were led to believe that by carrying out a suicide bombing, which they called martyrdom operation bombing, they would be doing something significant with their lives and they would find an honored place in the hall of martyrs. Moreover, their parents would win status and would be financially rewarded. From the time they were recruited, the group members never left their sides, leaving the young recruits no opportunity of backing down from their fatal choice.

The statistics have changed now. The age range is 13 to 55, with women as well as men volunteering, and some are older adults with families. Moreover, they volunteer sometimes only hours before the bombing. The new recruits grew up in a culture of martyrdom and were eager for the task ahead. The socialization is occurring largely within society, so that by the time volunteers enter the cell, they require very little indoctrination, only technical training.

Nasra Hassan, a Pakistani Muslim journalist with the United Nations who has conducted extensive interviews with terrorist officials and with the "human bombs" and their families, reported that a Hamas leader told her: *"Our biggest problem is the hordes of young men who beat on our doors, clamoring to be sent. It is difficult to select only a few. Those whom we turn away again and again, pestering us, pleading to be accepted."*[2]

In the extended interview with Hassan Salame, the most prolific suicide bomb commander in the history of Palestinian terrorism in Israel, made clear how many people were involved in planning an operation and how easy it was to obtain recruits for the suicide bomb missions.[3]

In 1996, after [the Israelis] killed Yehya Ayash (the engineer), the former commander in chief of the military wing of Hamas, . . . who took over as commander, decided to avenge Ayash's death with a major armed action . . . I was made commander of the operation. . . .

In Hebron I made contact with Hamas activists from my time in jail. I also made contact with Saliman, whom I had met during my visit to the Marj Zahour camp in Lebanon. I asked him to help me find youngsters prepared to carry out suicide bombings. . . . The head of the Islamic faction came to me with the news that he had found two people willing to carry out suicide missions. I met the two young men and took them to my safe house in Abu Dis. I prepared two charges, each with 12 kilos of TNT, half a kilo of nails of different sizes, and round metal pellets. I put everything into nylon bags and attached batteries and detonators. Then I put each explosive charge into a bag. I explained to the two men how to activate the charges, and when to prime them. I left them in Abu Dis with orders to carry out the bombings the next day, and made my way to my safe house in Ramallah.

The next day, one of the suicide bombers was taken into Jerusalem by one of the members of the Jerusalem cell, where he got onto a no. 18 bus with the explosive charge. Within minutes he detonated the bomb, killing himself and some of the pas- sengers. In the bombing, more than 25 people were killed. As the first bomber was going to bus 18, the second was taken by the other member of the Jerusalem cell to the Ahkelon junction by car. There he was instructed to wait at a soldier's pick-up point and to blow himself up. In the bombing, a woman soldier was killed and many others wounded.

Three days after the two bombings, I met the head of the Islamic Faction at the teach- ers' seminary, and asked him to recruit another bomber. He told me there was another young student ready to carry out a suicide mission, and we agreed that he would bring him to me the next day. . . . After I had met the young man and he had expressed his willingness to carry out the mission, I put him up in [a] safe house. There I assembled another explo- sive bag and taught the young man how to operate it. . . . Everything went according to plan, and about a week after the first two bombings, there was another bus bombing, in which about 20 people were killed.

I present this in great detail both to show how well organized the operations were, with many members each playing their assigned role, and to emphasize how eager these recruits were to participate in a martyrdom opera- tion. Salame only provided technical training in how to detonate the charges. "Brainwashing" and manipulation were not required. These human bombs were already primed and ready to explode. Today there is no shortage of volun- teers for these missions.

Ismail Abu Shanab, a Hamas leader who is also head of the Society of Engineers in Gaza, has a theory about the correlation between militants' personalities and the weapons they choose. *"While in prison, I tried to figure out whether there is any particular personality type that gets involved in various kinds of military operations. I found that those who use knives tend to have nervous personalities. Usually they become violent as a direct reaction to an incident. The person who uses a gun in well trained. The person who explodes a bomb does not need a lot of training— he just needs to have a moment of courage."*[4]

Mia Bloom has played an important role in interviewing suicide bombers and their trainers. In her book, *Dying to Kill: The Allure of Suicide Terror*, she quotes one trainer, Munir al-Makdah, as saying, *"Jihad and the resistance begin with the word, then with the sword, then with the stone, then with the gun, then with planting bombs, and then transforming bodies into human bombs."*[5]

Writing in the *Palestinian-Israeli Journal*, Iyad Sarraj has tried to explain the desperation that has driven the Palestinian people to such extremes:

> The Palestinians have been driven to a state of hopelessness and despair, the kind of despair that comes from a situation that keeps getting worse, a despair where living becomes no different from dying. Desperation is a very powerful force—it is not only negative, but it can propel people to actions or solutions that would have previously been unthinkable. . . . The rapid Israeli military deployment and its immediate shoot-to-kill policy have deepened the sense of victimization, helplessness and exposure of the Palestinian masses. . . . Suicide bombing is an act of ultimate despair, a horrific reaction to extremely inhuman conditions in a seriously damaged environment of hopelessness. Suicide bombing is the ultimate cry for help.[6]

An art history student explained why she was preparing for a suicide bombing, *"At the moment of executing my mission, it will not be purely to kill Israelis, the killing is not my ultimate goal. . . . My act will carry a message beyond to those responsible and the world at large that the ugliest thing for a human being is to be forced to live without freedom."*[7]

As to how they justify killing civilians, Ahmed quotes two Palestinian interview subjects:

> *If it is considered moral and justifiable for the Israeli army to kill over 19 Palestinian civilians, including many children, and destroy houses on top of their heads just to kill a wanted Palestinian activist, why is it not OK for Palestinians to go after settlers and soldiers while other Israelis stay indifferent as we are getting slaughtered on a daily basis?*

> *We do not have highly-advanced weaponry with which to face a regular army. All we are in control of are our bodies. We do not like or want to die. But if this is what it takes to terrorize them as they brutalize us all the time, why not do it?*[8]

But there are pragmatic, strategic reasons as well. As Bloom observes, "as the Hamas training manual notes: *"it is foolish to hunt the tiger when there are plenty of sheep around."*[9] Nura Karmi, the coordinator of women's programs for Sabeel, the Ecumencial Liberation Theology Center in Jerusalem, explains, *"What the Palestinian suicide bombers are doing with these acts is telling the Israelis that we can reach anywhere. We are there. As long as you don't recognize us and don't want us to have a state, Israel can claim that it's establishing security, but they must also know that we can reach them anywhere. This is what Palestinian suicide bombers are demonstrating by their actions. Israelis will not have security as long as they don't want to give us our state."*[10]

How do these Islamist terrorists, who profess to be killing in the name of Allah, justify suicidal terrorism when the Koran specifically proscribes terrorism as well as taking the life of innocents? Elaborating on the verse in the Koran that specifically prohibits suicide—"And do not kill yourself, for God is merciful to you"—according to Islamic tradition, the suicide perpetrator is condemned to repeat in hell eternally the act by which he took his life, as represented in this *hadith:* "Whoever kills himself with an iron weapon, then the iron weapon will remain in his hand and he will continually stab himself in the belly with it in the fire of hell eternally, forever and ever; whoever kills himself by drinking poison will eternally drink poison in the hellfire, and whoever kills himself by falling off a mountain will fall forever in the fire of hell."

Ayatollah Fadlallah, the spiritual mentor of Hezbollah, ingeniously reinterpreted Koranic verses that proscribe suicide in order to justify it and other prohibited acts, such as kidnapping and hostage taking by observing that extreme circumstances permit, indeed require, taking extreme acts.[11] In fact, as Mohammad Hafez has observed, suicide terrorism violates three proscriptions: that against suicide, against the killing of innocents, and against the killing of Muslims.[12]

In our interviews with incarcerated Hamas, Islamic Jihad, Hezbollah, and Al-Aqsa Martyr Brigades terrorists, we had the opportunity of interviewing a number of suicide bomb commanders.[13] "You say you are carrying these acts out in the name of Allah. How," we asked, "can you justify suicide terrorism, when the Koran specifically proscribes suicide?" One Hamas respondent became quite angry: *"This is not suicide. Suicide is weak, it is selfish, it is mentally disturbed. This is istishhad"* (martyrdom or self-sacrifice in the name of Allah).

Thus the clerical authorities have reframed the suicide bombings into martyrdom operations. Asked the same question, Salame said, *"A martyrdom operation bombing is the highest level of jihad, and highlights the depth of our faith. The bombers are holy fighters who carry out one of the more important articles of faith."* According to another suicide bomb commander, *"It is martyrdom attacks which earn the most respect and elevate the bombers to the highest possible level of martyrdom."*

Another suicide bomb commander, not quite so prolific as Salame (he is only serving 26 consecutive life sentences while Salame is serving 46), in discussing a planned operation made it clear just how normal the act was in their culture.

> I asked Halil what it was all about and he told me that he had been on the wanted list for a long time and did not want to get caught without realizing his dream of being a martyrdom operation bomber. He was completely calm and explained to the other two bombers, Yusuf and Beshar, how to detonate the bombs, exactly the way he had explained things to the bombers in the Mahane Yehuda attack [suicide bombing at shopping mall in Tel Aviv]. I remember that besides the tremendous respect I had for Halil and the fact that I was jealous of him, I also felt slighted that he had not asked me to be the third martyrdom operation bomber. I understood that my role in the movement had not come to an end and the fact that I was not on the wanted list and could operate relatively freely could be very advantageous to the movement in the future.

That the respondent's feelings are hurt that he wasn't asked to be the third martyrdom operation bomber reminded me of the shame I felt in the sixth grade during recess when I was the last person chosen to be on the pickup baseball team. His feelings are hurt that he wasn't asked to be on the pickup suicide bomb team!

Hafez emphasizes the theme of redemption and concern for the Palestinian people, which regularly appear in bombers' last wills and testaments as well as in interviews with potential suicide bombers. "Suicide bombing is not only an opportunity to punish an enemy and fulfill God's command to fight injustice but also a privilege and a reward to those most committed to their faith and their values. To be selected for 'martyrdom operations' is akin to receiving a stamp of approval or a certificate of accomplishment from one's peers. It is a form of endorsement of one's moral character and dedication."[14]

Another theme that Hafez stresses is helping the Palestinian people, reflected in these quotes from interviews with failed female suicide bombers conducted by Nicole Argo, whose interviews have also enriched terrorism scholarship. According to one would-be bomber, *"I did this because of the suffering of the Palestinian people. The falling of shuhada [those martyred by Israeli forces] . . . and the destruction everywhere in Palestine. . . . I did this for God and the Palestinian people."* Another said, *"I believe the operation the operation would hurt the enemy. . . . Also [a] successful mission greatly influences society. It raises the morale of the people; they are happy, they feel strong."*[15]

The extremity of their situation required acts of martyrdom, which is a value deep within the society. But there is a difference between public and private attitudes. While in public, parents will speak with pride and celebrate the death of their son, the martyr, in private it can be quite another matter. There is, as Hassan emphasizes, a public expectation of celebrating with pride the gift of one's child to the cause. But in private, losing a child is always painful, no matter how glorious the cause. Hassan asked the mother of Ribhi Kahlou, a young man in the Gaza Strip who had blown himself up in November 1995, what she would have done if she had known what her son was planning to do. The woman said: "I would have taken a cleaver, cut open my heart, and stuffed him deep inside. Then I would have sewn it up tight to keep him safe."[16]

The impact of the new media has magnified the impact of Israeli attacks on the population. Argo relates this statement by a leader of the Popular Front for the Liberation of Palestine:

> *The difference between the first intifada and the second is television. Before, I knew when we were attacked here, or in a nearby camp, but the reality of the attacks everywhere else was not so clear. Now, I cannot get away from Israeli attacks—the TV brings them into my living room. When they are not in my camp, they are in Rafah, Gaza City, Ramallah, Jenin. . . . And you can't turn the TV off. How could you live with yourself? At the same time, you can't ignore the problem—what are you doing to protect your people? We live in an internal struggle. Whether you choose to fight or not, every day is this internal struggle.*[17]

The manner in which Muslim clerics—both Shi'ite and Sunni—have reframed the Koran to justify "martyrdom operations" and have contributed to Muslim children being set on the path of suicide terrorism from childhood on has been described. It is a value broadly represented within Islamic society, with few opposing voices.

But the tactic of suicide terrorism, which began in Lebanon with the 1983 Hezballah attacks on the U.S. and French embassies and the U.S. marine barracks, has spread to other countries.[18] Active implementers of this technique are three nationalist-separatist groups—the Tamil Tigers of Tamil Eelam in Sri Lanka (LTTE), who perfected the suicide bomb belt; the Kurdistan Workers Party

(PKK) in Turkey; and the Chechen separatists in Russia. And for these groups the tactic is not justified by appealing to a reframing of the Koran.

How can youth who willingly give their lives for the cause be explained when it is not justified on religious grounds? A feature in common among these three quite diverse movements is the presence of a charismatic leader-follower relationship, so that the leader of the cause is ascribed godlike status and the cause itself is treated as a matter of faith.[19] In the desperate situations of the Kurdish people and for the Tamils, devoting oneself entirely to the cause and being a follower of Ocalan of the PKK or Prabhakaran of the LTTE or Shamil Basayev of the Chechen separatists becomes the dominant identification for the members, transcending their individuality so that if the leader decrees that this act will advance the cause, the committed member willingly follows this directive.

Even after the apparent compromise of his career-long goals following his capture, Ocalan of the PKK, who had been seen as the very embodiment of the Kurdish cause, retained for some his godlike heroic stature. A 14-year-old Kurdish girl, Nejla Coskun, set herself on fire in central London protesting Ocalan's arrest in February 1999. The image in the story by Nik Fleming of the *Guardian* is vivid: "With flames leaping from her back and shoulders, she dashed through a crowd of startled demonstrators in central London. As the fire melted the skin on her neck and her hair began to burn, she clenched her teeth and ran faster, stretching out her arms, her hands curled into defiant victory symbols."[20]

Interviewed three years later, Coskun spoke without regret, "*I felt so strongly that I was willing to die,*" she said. "*I thought, 'What can I do to help change something?'*" Despite her permanent deformity and the multiple painful reconstructive surgeries she had to endure, her resolve was undiminished. She said:

> I'm glad I did it. It was worth it because Kurdish people are dying, burning daily. Before, when I told people I was Kurdish they did not understand. But the TV, magazines and newspapers have done interviews and talked about the situation, and now people know who the Kurds are and what they are fighting for. . . . I would do it again.[21]

Shorn of the religious justification, Coskun's motivations and rationalizations sound very similar to those of the Muslim suicide bombers. Bloom cites an interview with Vasantha, a young Tamil Tiger, whom she asked why he was prepared to contemplate such a drastic action. The boy had a simple answer, "*This is the most supreme sacrifice I can make. The only way we can get our Eelam [homeland] is through arms. That is the only way anybody will listen to us. Even if we die.*"[22] Another respondent replied, "*The harassment that I and my parents have suffered at the hands of the army makes me want to take revenge. . . . It is a question of Tamil pride, especially after so much sacrifice. There is no escape.*"[23] Reminiscent of the manner in which children in the Palestinian refugee camps idolize their heroes, the *shahids*, so do the Tamils. Bloom observes that "young Tamils know the names of the martyrs [and] . . . what they have done."[24]

Prabhakaran's forcible personality has already been described. Bloom cites his 1993 Black Tiger Day speech as demonstrating the charismatic force of his leadership. Demonstrating the powerful impact of Prabhakaran's leadership on his followers, one member related, "*We are given moral support by our leader and we have reached this position only because of him.*"[25]

Women are disproportionately represented among LTTE suicide bombers. For some of them, this is because they are trying to redeem their honor. "According to Hindu faith, once a woman is raped she cannot get married nor have children. Fighting for Tamil freedom may be the only way for such a woman to redeem herself.[26] This idea of sacrifice is ingrained in Tamil culture. "Tamil mothers make great sacrifices for their sons on a daily basis; feeding them before themselves or the girl children, serving on them and so on. Acting as a human bomb is an understood and accepted offering for a woman who will never be a mother. Family members often encourage rape victims to join the LTTE."[27]

This is also true for the so-called Chechen black widows. There is a deep cultural tradition within Chechen society concerning the role of widows, whose future is bleak. By carrying out an act of violence against the Russians responsible for their husbands' death, they can exact a measure of revenge as well as redemption. Anne Speckhard has addressed the issue of societal trauma leading to a value on suicidal terrorism not previously present:

> Suicide terrorism had no place in Chechen history but during the last two wars Chechen individuals and Chechen society as a whole increasingly found themselves devastated by meaningless traumas. In response to this many sought out, embraced and constructed, individually and as groups, ideologies that empowered, made meanings from and expressed their pain while fighting back against enemies much more powerful than themselves. Indeed the entire phenomena of suicide terrorism in Chechnya as in all the places it has migrated to since its modern-day appearance in Beirut has begun as a psycho-social phenomena in reaction to traumatic stress, a besieged mentality, social marginalization, alienation or other perceived or real sufferings—and in this response some segment of society has embraced and promoted the ideologies that breathed life into it as tactic for fighting back.[28]

Speckhard observed the manner in which the act of martyrdom released the traumatized Chechen from her psychological pain:

> A Chechen respondent recalls how her cousin became withdrawn and depressed following the killing of her brother by Russians, but just before going on her suicide mission this girl became euphoric falsely announcing her need to travel to Moscow in order to prepare for marriage. The cousin recalls, "*I believed her because she really was very much excited in those days, and a shine appeared in her eyes.*" Indeed just as with normal suicides who have committed to die, her depression likely lifted as she began contemplating release from psychic pain and she unconsciously activated the dissociative defense necessary to carry it out.[29]

The issue of revenge for the death of a sibling or friend is regularly encountered as motivation for entering the path of suicide terrorism in all the groups discussed.

While suicide terrorism is an old tactic that has been refined in the modern era of terrorism and incorporated into a devastating strategy, in the next section we turn to another major tactic. High-level concern has been given to the prospect of weapons of mass destruction terrorism. Indeed, one of the stated motivations for the war in Iraq was the concern that Saddam Hussein would provide weapons of mass destruction to terrorist organizations.

WEAPONS OF MASS DESTRUCTION TERRORISM[*]

Just as suicide terrorism traces its roots in ancient history, so too for weapons of mass destruction terrorism. In the feast of Passover, which Jews celebrate each spring to commemorate the release of the Jews from bondage to Pharaoh and their passage to the Holy Land as related in the Book of Exodus, the 10 plagues

---

[*] The term "weapons of mass destruction terrorism," usually employed to refer to chemical, biological, radiological, or nuclear weapons (CBRN) is semantically confusing, for conventional weapons, such as the fertilizer bomb used by Timothy McVeigh at the Alfred P. Murrah Federal Building in Oklahoma City, can produce mass destruction. Similarly, the coordinated attacks on the U.S. embassies in Nairobi, Kenya, and Dar es Salaam, Tanzania, and the coordinated attacks on New York and Washington, D.C., produced mass destruction and mass casualties but were conventional terrorism, with truck bombs in the former bombings and with hijacked airliners in the latter attacks. And the so-called weapons of mass destruction, especially biological and chemical weapons, can be employed with exquisite discrimination to produce low-level casualties, to the point of being employed for assassination of lone individuals. In the run-up to a November 2004 election in the Ukraine, Viktor Yushchenko was the victim of dioxin poisoning, which he survived but which left him permanently disfigured. The November 2006 death in London of former KGB agent and critic of Russia Alexander Litvinov, from polonium-210, for which he blamed the Russian government, is another example.

visited upon the Egyptians to force the Pharaoh to release the Jews, including locusts, boils, and the death of the firstborn son, play a prominent role. Moses, who confronts Pharaoh with the plagues that will befall the Egyptians until he liberates the Jews, can be considered the first bioterrorist.

The Black Death of the fourteenth century can be traced back to Tartars who catapulted plague-infected corpses into besieged fortresses in the Crimea. British commanders planned to infect the local Indian population in North America with smallpox by giving them disease-infected blankets from a military hospital.[30]

It was the sarin gas attack on the Tokyo subway in 1995 by Aum Shinrikyo that for the first time focused the international community on the dreaded prospect of chemical and biological terrorism. Investigation of the group revealed extensive efforts by leaders of this millennial cult to recruit PhD scientists—microbiologists, virologists, organic and inorganic chemists, nuclear physicists, and nuclear engineers—to develop chemical, biological, and nuclear weapons. This revelation led to high-level attention to the prospect of weapons of mass destruction terrorism, and in the United States, major resources were put into preparing first responders. As former secretary of defense William Cohen put it in a number of speeches on the topic, "*It isn't a question of 'if', but 'when'.*"[31]

In fact, there is a major disconnect between the weapons technology community and the community of academic terrorism experts. The former are focused on vulnerabilities of our society and what might happen in terms of technological possibilities, while the latter, who study terrorist motivation and decision making, are under-whelmed by the probability of such an event, having concluded that weapons of mass destruction terrorism would not be in the interest of most terrorist groups and organizations. Numerous Department of Defense, intelligence community, and Department of Homeland Security conferences have focused on weapons of mass destruction terrorism, with learned presentations by virologists, microbiologists, infectious disease experts, and chemical warfare experts, devoted to what might happen, what terrorists could do, what our societal vulnerabilities are, with little or no attention being given to the group motivations, that is, which groups might do it and why and, as important, why not.

To remedy this defect, I will summarize understandings of the differentiated psychology of terrorism developed earlier in this book and how it applies to the prospect of weapons of mass destruction terrorism. For this acknowledged high consequence–low probability class of acts, such an examination can further reduce the uncertainty and better focus on the source of danger.

Reviewing the spectrum of terrorist groups in terms of motivation, incentives and constraints, for nearly all groups, the feared catastrophic chemical/biological/radiological/nuclear (CBRN) super-terrorism, against the prospect of which the United States is zealously—and expensively—preparing, would be highly counterproductive.[32] The constraints are particularly severe for large-scale mass casualty terrorism for groups that are concerned with their constituents—social revolutionary and nationalist-separatist terrorists—although discriminate* low-level attacks, that is, attacks that do not endanger constituents—are less constrained. Nationalist-separatist and social revolutionary groups that are operating within their nation are particularly sensitive to the responses of their internal constituency as well as their international audience. This sensitivity provides a constraint against acts that are so violent or extranormal as to offend their constituents.

These groups will be significantly constrained from acts that indiscriminately involve mass casualties and will negatively affect their reputation with their supporters. But discriminate acts against their adversary, in areas where their constituents are not present, can be rationalized. Just as the rash of suicide bombings in Tel Aviv and other predominantly Jewish cities in Israel was implemented by absolutist Palestinian groups (some of which were radical Islamists as well) in order to reverse the peace process, the prospect of tactical chemical/biological weapons (CBW) in such areas is quite conceivable, although unlikely in Jerusalem, where there is a significant Islamic population. Similarly, social revolutionary terrorists could rationalize discriminate CBRN acts against government or symbolic capitalist targets.

Because of their tendency to dehumanize their victims and delegitimate the federal government, right-wing extremists, including individuals who are members of the right-wing virtual community of hatred, represent a distinct danger for low-level discriminate attacks against their demonized targets: Jews, blacks, and ethnic minorities, as well as federal buildings. Many of the case studies in *Toxic Terror* were committed by individuals hewing to a right-wing ideology but not belonging to a formal group or organization per se. Timothy McVeigh, responsible for the bombing of the Alfred P. Murrah Federal Building in

---

* Writing in *Disorders and Terrorism: Report of the Task Force on Disorders and Terrorism* 30 years ago, Mengel (1977) distinguished between random or indiscriminate targeting and what he called discriminate target selection. Random or indiscriminate targeting is associated with the motivation to cause social paralysis or inflict mass casualties. Discriminate target selection can be used in support of bargaining or to make a political statement. Discriminate acts do not alienate supporters or endanger constituents, usually taking place outside the regional base/home territory.

Oklahoma City is an exemplar of such individuals for mass casualty terrorism using conventional weapons. Individuals in this category are a significant threat for low-level CBW attacks; because of resource limitations, they probably do not represent a threat of mass casualty CBW terrorism. The perpetrator of the anthrax letter bomb attacks after 9/11 is believed by security officials to fall into this category.

Religious fundamentalist terrorist groups, who follow the dictates of charismatic religious leaders, are not constrained by their audience on earth, as their acts of violence are given sacred significance. They are more at risk for mass casualty attacks, although to the degree they have a constituency, they are also constrained. Should other nontraditional groups resembling Aum Shinrikyo emerge, they would be at great risk; most millennial cults, however, are not led by religious belligerents but rather passively await the final days.

Al-Qaeda and its allies have shown a willingness to perpetrate acts of mass casualty terrorism, as exemplified by the bombings of Khobar Towers in Saudi Arabia, the U.S. embassies in Kenya and Tanzania, and the 9/11 attacks on the World Trade Center and the Pentagon. Osama bin Laden, responsible for the embassy bombings and the attacks of 9/11, has actively discussed the use of weapons of mass destruction in public interviews. In an interview with Jon Miller of ABC News in May 1998, bin Laden first discussed such weapons. In a follow-up interview with *TIME* magazine, in January of 1999, when asked "The U.S. says you are trying to acquire chemical and nuclear weapons. How would you use these?" bin Laden replied, "*Acquiring weapons for the defense of Muslims is a religious duty. If I have indeed acquired these weapons, then I thank God for enabling me to do so. . . . It would be a sin for Muslims not to try to possess the weapons.*" Whether this was psychological warfare or represented genuine intent is not entirely clear. Bin Laden and al-Qaeda are not seen as constrained against carrying out CBRN attacks, including attacks against the defined major enemy, the United States.

Among the incarcerated Islamist terrorists we interviewed, most said something to the effect of "*Just give me a good Kalishnikov.*" While the majority was not averse to using a weapon that could kill 10,000 of their enemies, many had not even considered it. But some raised reservations. One spoke of his fear of "*the silent death,*" concerns about dangers from handling poisons or bacteria. Another quoted the Koran and its prohibitions against poisoning the creatures of the earth.

The role of the Internet in propagating the ideology of right-wing extremist hatred is of concern, for isolated individuals consumed by hatred can find common cause in these websites, feel they are not alone, and be moved along the pathway from thought to action, responding to the extremist ideology of the virtual community. Similarly there is a virtual community for Islamist militancy. Individual members of this virtual community of hatred who have never met face to face could be moved by the extremist messages on the estimated 4,800 militant Islamist extremist websites to attempt small-scale CBW attacks, but would have difficulties because of the resources required and the difficulties in weaponization mounting a large scale attack.

CHAPTER 17

CHALLENGES AND IMPLICATIONS: THE WAY AHEAD

There's no way to break the system of terror in the West bank, because the system is now in the minds of the people, in the minds of the teenagers, and what we're doing by this operation [Defensive Shield] is giving them more reasons to build that system.

—Israeli reserve solider

You start at kindergarten so by the time he's 22, he's looking for an opportunity to sacrifice his life.

—Roni Shaked, an Israeli terrorism expert and former officer in Israel's Shin Bet secret service

IT'S A MATTER OF TIME

One of the most daunting implications of the understandings of terrorist psychology conveyed in this book is the extended time frame during which individuals enter and move along the path to terrorism. When hatred is bred in the bone, it is not easy to change the righteous rage that has been fermenting since childhood; it is a heady brew. Pictures circulate on radical Islamist websites of children in the garb of martyrs. We have already lost the current generation, and what will be required to counter and reduce the terrorist threat is a campaign that will be sustained for decades, a process that must be put in place and be continued from one presidential administration to the next. Culture changes slowly, and altering deeply held attitudes will not be easy. It will indeed, in the words of the 2005 Quadrennial Defense Review of the Department of Defense, be "a long war."

In her book *What Terrorists Want*, Louise Richardson devotes the penultimate chapter to "Why the War on Terror Cannot Be Won." Defining this as a war has had some very negative consequences. For it is not a war that can be won, any more than the war on poverty or the war on drugs can be won. While the strong words on the heels of 9/11 were stirring for the American public, they promoted Osama bin Laden's stature for his alienated Muslim constituency. And despite President Bush attempting to make it clear that this was not a war on Islam but a war on terrorists, bin Laden was promoted to the world's number one terrorist and became, in effect, commander in chief of the world of radical Islam against the commander in chief of the West, President George W. Bush, and his deputy commander, British Prime Minister Tony Blair.

Defined as a war, this struggle will never end. As Israeli Prime Minister Rabin dolefully remarked during the fitful peace process negotiations with the Palestinian Authority, what a strange peace process this was where one act of an idealistic teenager could stop it. The concept of winning a war conveys the end of conflict, with a winner and a defeated enemy, and a surrender ceremony on the deck of a battleship. But terrorism can never be totally eliminated. There will always be an idealistic teenager ready to give his or her life for the cause. The goal rather must be reducing the extent of terrorism so that it interferes as little as possible with our open western way of life.

Reducing the frequency of terrorism to as low a degree as possible is very different from eliminating it. Terrorism cannot be eliminated altogether without eliminating democracy. The junta in Argentina tried this during the so-called "dirty war." The leaders invented a new form for the verb "disappear," where enemies of the state—those who disagreed with the leadership—were being "disappeared" by being thrown out of airplanes over open seas. A healthy democracy must be able to tolerate dissent. One of the reasons there has been so little domestic terrorism in this "buzzing, blooming confusion of a democracy" we live in is that disagreement is not disloyalty, and there are multiple channels for open disagreement without having to go underground.

A major conclusion of the Committee on the Psychological Roots of Terrorism that I chaired for the Madrid Summit on Terrorism, Security and Democracy was: "The 'war on terrorism' is a war unlike other wars, and will require concerted efforts over decades to counter. It is important to recognize that global terrorism can never be totally eliminated. Whereas all efforts should be made to reduce terrorism, it must not be at the cost of curtailing civil liberties, for that would weaken liberal democracy."[1] When civil liberties are degraded in the service of counter-terrorism, the terrorists have won.

Another conclusion of the Madrid Terrorism Summit was: "Because there is a growing number of vulnerable at risk individuals in émigré and diaspora communities, interventions that respect cultural differences while helping to integrate the refugees with the recipient society will be important." At the present time, an impossible choice exists in a number of European countries. When young Muslim girls were prohibited from wearing their *hijab* (head scarves) to school, the message Muslim émigrés in the slums surrounding Paris and other large French cities received was: in order to be accepted as French, you must give up your Muslim culture. Second-generation Muslim émigrés to Great Britain, the Netherlands, Belgium, Germany, and Spain experience the same sense of rejection by the host society. Mohammad Atta, the commander of the 9/11 attacks, and two of his colleagues were radicalized in a mosque in Hamburg, Germany, where they were graduate students in the Technology Institute. The July 7, 2005, London transit bombing and the foiled August 2006 coordinated attacks on U.S.-bound airline attacks from Heathrow Airport were by second-generation Pakistani Muslim émigrés to Great Britain. The Finsbury Park mosque in London is notorious for its radical sermons; its Imam, Abu Hamza, was sentenced to seven years in a top-security prison in South London for inciting murder and radical hatred. Our committee recommendation at the Madrid Summit was twofold: to incorporate programs helping new émigrés be integrated into the recipient society while preserving and respecting the émigrés' culture. It was recommended that joint committees be established to work collaboratively with émigré community leaders to identify growing tensions early and seek remedies.

How can the goal of reducing the frequency of terrorism be accomplished? If for every terrorist killed or captured, there are 10 more in line waiting to take his or her place, however successful we may be in killing or capturing terrorists, we will not stem the tide.

If one accepts the premise that terrorism is a vicious species of psychological warfare, waged through the media, with violence as communication, one does not counter psychological warfare with smart bombs and missiles. One counters psychological warfare with psychological warfare.

For the most part, we have not even entered the arena of strategic communications, let alone developed a strategy for countering the highly effective media strategy developed and refined by our terrorist adversaries. The major terrorism organizations have media committees whose main task is to get their message out quickly and effectively, putting their own spin on events, playing optimally both to their external and internal audiences. They are adroit at portraying themselves as victims whose actions were defensive and were required by their enemy's actions. In not countering their extremist messages, we have permitted extreme distortions to be accepted as fact, justifying, indeed requiring, defensive aggression.

How can we alter the extreme attitudes that are being shaped and that are now, for many, fixed?

ELEMENTS OF AN INTEGRATED STRATEGIC INFORMATION OPERATIONS PROGRAM

Four major elements of a psychological program designed to counter terrorism are:

1. Inhibiting potential terrorists from joining terrorist groups in the first place
2. Producing dissension within the group
3. Facilitating exit from the group
4. Reducing support for the group and its leaders

Earlier I stressed the centrality of the group and "collective identity." A group focus is central to the programmatic elements described. These elements are components of a strategic psychological operations program that must be conducted over decades.

Vladimir Lenin conveyed that "the goal of terrorism is to terrorize." When bin Laden's spokesman, in the wake of 9/11, warned observant Muslims not to live or work in high-rise buildings or to fly, because there were swarms of Muslim youth seeking death who would attack the weak Americans clinging to life, the goal was not to provide kindly advice to observant Muslims but to propagate terror throughout the country. And it was highly effective. The flying public was so terrified that several major airlines went into bankruptcy and still have not recovered. This point suggests a fifth element of a sustained campaign of strategic psychological operations:

5. Insulating the target audience, the public, from the intended goals of the terrorist to terrorize

These five elements of a sustained strategic psychological operations campaign deserve a closer look.

Inhibiting Potential Terrorists from joining the Group

The first element, inhibiting potential terrorists from joining terrorist groups and organizations, is the most important and complex of the five. Once an individual is in a group or organization, especially an underground group, powerful group dynamics will enforce his or her psychological commitment to its goals. From childhood there is a normalization and social value attached to joining a terrorist group, especially in the constituencies of particular concern to Israel. In the Palestinian terrorist research project described in chapter 2, it was clear that the major influence was the social setting.[2] As one terrorist remarked, *"Everyone was joining."* Individuals from strictly religious Islamic backgrounds were more likely to join Islamist groups, while those with no religious background might join either a secular or a religious group. Peers were of great influence and often recruited the subjects. For the secular groups the social environment centered on schools and clubs, while for Islamists the mosque, religious organizations, and religious instruction dominated.

One of the remarkable findings of the research project was the intensity of hatred towards Israelis expressed by the subjects given that most of the interview subjects had never met an Israeli.

> You Israelis are Nazis in your souls and in your conduct. In your occupation you never distinguish between men and women, or between old people and children. You adopted methods of collective punishment, you uprooted people from their homeland and from their homes and chased them into exile. You fired live ammunition at women and children. You smashed the skulls of defenseless civilians. You set up detention camps for thousands of people in subhuman conditions. You destroyed homes and turned children into orphans. You prevented people from making a living, you stole their property, you trampled on their honor. Given that kind of conduct, there is no choice but to strike at you without mercy in every possible way.

But what kind of interventions can help counter such powerful attitudes that are being shaped so early in life? Combating such deeply ingrained attitudes will be difficult. Yet failing that, there will be a growing stream of terrorists to replace those killed or arrested. Particularly problematic is schooling. The virulent anti-West brand of Islam being taught in the radical madrassas of Pakistan is a case in point. What steps might ameliorate the poison being dispensed? How can moderate clerics be encouraged to temper the curricula?

Youth taught by hate-mongering leaders and seeing a bleak future are impelled to violence out of despair. What can be done to open pathways for ambitious young people within their society? Support to programs that encourage economic development and opening of societies, whether in Egypt, Pakistan, or Saudi Arabia, can shrink the reservoir of dispirited youngsters who now see no recourse other than to strike out in despair. But this in turn will require diplomatic influence on the leaders of these nations, who in fact are the major target of the radical fundamentalists who seek to establish fundamentalist Islamist governments throughout the Middle East. Bin Laden, in shifting the primary target away from modernizing Muslim nations—the *"enemy that is near,"* Egypt, Saudi Arabia, Jordan, and Morocco—to the *"enemy that is afar,"* —the United States—in effect was saying "Yes, yes, of course our goal is to get rid of these apostate leaders and establish Islamic states governed by Sharia.* But who is propping up these leaders? It is the United States, and so we must attack them."

To break this out further, it is important to provide alternate pathways for redressing grievances. All too many bright ambitious, economically disadvantaged youth are unable to succeed in societies that offer few opportunities; in response, they strike out in despair. How can we assist in opening up autocratic societies? One way is to encourage moderate secular education that permits their youth to compete in a globalizing economy and does not expose them to radical ideology. A college classmate, Tom Moorehead, as undersecretary of labor for international affairs, provided a $25 million grant to Pakistan to combat child labor to develop a network of moderate curriculum secular schools. It costs $80 annually to educate a child in Pakistan. Every child educated in one of these moderate schools is one that is not being educated in a radical madrassa, who is not being exposed to extremist Islamist ideology. This is effective counter-terrorism. And it is important to de-romanticize the terrorists. These are not martyrs, but murderers. The Islamist militants violate provisions of the Koran. These are not heroic role models to emulate.

Both measures—educational support and economic programs—require funding by government or nongovernmental organizations, but the investment would go a long way toward reducing the population that strikes out in despair for it sees no other path. When one considers the mammoth expenditures in military operations in conducting the Global War on Terror, funding programs that could reduce the reservoir of terrorists by promoting hope for succeeding

---

* Sharia is the body of Islamic law. In societies governed by sharia, such as Afghanistan under the Taliban, all aspects of public life and many aspects of private life are strictly governed by Muslim principles of jurisprudence drawn from the Koran (Qur'an) and hadiths (the words and deeds of the Prophet Muhammad).

within these now rigid societies would be valuable investments. Hope is the enemy of despair.

The extremist anti-Western ideology calling for *jihad* against the destroyers of Islam is being spread through the radical madrassas, the radical mosques, and the "new media": both the 24/7 cable news channels, such as al-Jazeera, and the Internet—and, a crucial deficiency in our counter-terrorism policy, it is not being effectively countered. It is important to emphasize that one can subscribe to this ideological framework without ever committing a terrorist act. But being part of a supporting community, and providing financial and/or moral support, can encourage the passage of frustrated alienated Islamic youth into this pathway of terrorism, especially when there is wide-spread support in the community and no voice of moderation being raised in criticism of this extremism.

Assuredly my own research interviewing incarcerated Islamist terrorists supports the notion that the broader social context is critical in shaping individuals very early in life to enter the pathway of terrorism.[3] The mosque was consistently cited as the place where most members were initially introduced to the Palestinian/Israeli conflict, including members of the secular groups. Islamist fundamentalist terrorists have emerged from the culture of radical Islamism, which is shaping individuals from childhood on.

It is that broader radical Islamist culture which generates a continuing supply of recruits to the extremity of terrorism, including suicide terrorism, what Ariel Merari has called a "suicide bomber production line."[4] To counter the growing threat of Islamist terrorism, "truth" propagated through the information channels—the radical madrassas, the radical mosques, and the new media—must be countered, and the vulnerability of the alienated Islamic youth to the siren song of hatred must be reduced.

Creating Dissension within the Group

The second element is to produce dissension within the group. Terrorist organizations are often hothouses of tension. When they are attacked, internal tensions disappear, and it becomes them against the world. What would magnify tension, sow distrust, recast the image of the leader or pretenders to the throne, or weaken the already stressed climate and paralyze the group? Injecting such influences into a closed body is by no means easy, but it would reduce cohesion and efficiency. It is important to foster paranoia and organizational paralysis by injecting rumors in the ranks. It is especially important to alienate followers from leaders. From a distance, leaders are often idealized. Up close and personal, they can be experienced as—and should be portrayed as—arrogant, self-concerned, and corrupt.

The July 9, 2005, letter from Ayman al-Zawahiri to Abu Musab al-Zarqawi recognized the risk that the wave of hostage taking, beheadings, and sectarian violence had departed from al-Qaeda's focus on the "far enemy" and risked losing support among the Muslim community: *"the strongest weapon which the mujahedeen enjoy—after the help and granting of success by God—is popular support from the masses in Iraq, and the surrounding Muslim countries. So, we must maintain this support as best we can and we should strive to increase it. . . . In the absence of this popular support, the Islamic mujahed movement would be crushed in the shadows. . . . Therefore the mujahed movement must avoid any action that the masses do not understand or approve."*[5]

The letter was designed to bring Zarqawi back in line. Such signs of fissures and tensions within the adversary need to be swiftly exploited so that they can be magnified, promoting disunity within the adversary. In the event just described, the U.S. psychological operations mechanism was not able to rapidly respond and exploit this opportunity.

Facilitating Exit from the Group

The third element, facilitating exit from the group, exposes a danger of becoming a terrorist: once one has made that choice, it is hard to turn back, for an early hurdle for full acceptance is to carry out a terrorist action, which can lead to a criminal sanction. Yet a number of governments countering terrorism have instituted creative amnesty programs, akin to the U.S. protected witness program; amnesty is given in return for cooperation and information. The bargain includes financial support for a new life and can extend to resettlement in other countries and even plastic surgery, as Spanish authorities provided ETA defectors. The Italian *pentiti* (penitents) program was instrumental in breaking the back of the Red Brigades. In return for promises of having their sentences reduced or entirely forgiven for their cooperation, there was a wave of defectors, including "Antonio Savasta, who had been in charge of kidnapping General Dozier and Valerio Murucci who provided details on the Aldo Moro kidnapping, arrest and murder. As a consequence, there were about 300 hundred arrests and even more recantations. This change of mind among the Italian terrorists was brought about by not only promises, but also as a result of internal dissent."[6] Information developed by defectors can be fed back to the group to strengthen option 2, producing internal dissension.

Reducing Public Support for the Group and Delegitimizing the Leader

The fourth element is information operations directed against the group to reduce public support. An exemplar of this goal is al-Qaeda. For years Osama bin Laden has been unchallenged in the arena of marshalling opinion to his view of Islam and the West. The virulent brand of Islam he has championed and the violence he has justified with his extreme interpretation of the Koran are consistent with those of Hamas and Islamic Jihad leaders and have not been countered. Al-Qaeda has attracted alienated Muslim youth sensitized in the madrassas and mosques. In the 2001 trial of the al-Qaeda bombers of the U.S. embassies in Tanzania and Nairobi in Federal court in New York, I served as expert witness during the death penalty phase and spent many hours with one of the lower-level participants of the bombing in Dar es Salaam as well as with one of the senior participants. The roles of the madrassa and the mosque were particularly noteworthy. In the madrassa in Zanzibar, the participant was taught never to question learned authorities, especially those with religious credentials. In the mosque in Dar es Salaam, where he felt welcomed as a member of the *umma* (the community of observant Muslims), he heard of the obligation to help other Muslims wherever they were. He was shown films of Muslim mass graves in Bosnia and the bodies of Muslim women and children in Chechnya.

Alone and isolated except for the mosque, he vowed, in his words, to become a soldier for Allah and defend these innocent victims against the soldiers of Serbia and Russia. When he gave voice to these sentiments, he was informed by a spotter for al-Qaeda that to be a soldier for Allah he must get training; so, using his own money, he went to Pakistan to be screened and was sent to a bin Laden training camp in Afghanistan. After seven months there, he was offered the opportunity to participate in the conflict in Kashmir, which was irregular conflict, rather than fighting uniformed soldiers in either Bosnia or Chechnya. He had envisaged himself in uniform fighting soldiers who had taken up the sword against Muslims. He returned to Dar es Salaam and resumed his menial life as an assistant grocery clerk. Still participating at the mosque, he received the call to take part in a *jihad* three years later. He responded immediately. His pious wish to defend Muslim victims was bent into participating in an act of mass casualty terrorism. As he was confronted with the consequences of the bombing, in contrast to other terrorists, he was overwhelmed with the death of innocents, which he saw as inconsistent with his views of jihad: "*Their jihad is not my jihad.*" Nor is it the jihad of the majority of mainstream Muslims, yet they have been remarkably mute, allowing the extremists free rein to steer alienated youth into violence in the name of Islam. Osama bin Laden's justifications, as spelled out in the al-Qaeda terrorism manual, are inconsistent with the Koran, yet to the alienated youth they are justification for killing in the name of God.

To counter these religiously based arguments, moderate Islamic clerics and leaders must reclaim their hijacked religion and depict Osama bin Laden and his ilk as distorting the meaning of the Koran and violating the spirit of Islam in the service of self-aggrandizing motivations. The goal is to make the group not a mainstream path for alienated youth but a deviant path, to have the terrorist leaders seen not as romantic heroes but as preachers of a perverted Islam. Doing this requires activating voices not now heard, for these changes must come from within Islam, and at present the extremist view is uncontested.

Reducing support among the public at large would also reduce the recruitment pool. In the long run, this is the only way to diminish the terrorist threat, for new recruits are the lifeblood of a terrorist group. Marginalizing the group and reducing its appeals must be a key goal of an effective counterterrorism program over time, and this in turn will be facilitated by delegitimizing its leaders.

This overarching goal, of reducing support for the organization and delegitimizing its leader, is consistent with one of the key recommendations of Richardson, to separate the terrorists from their community.[7] As long as the Islamist militants are seen as acting on behalf of the community, the reservoir of potential terrorists will be inexhaustible. At the present time, al-Qaeda and the global Salafi *jihad* are perceived as powerful organizations to join; for alienated Muslim youth joining is an opportunity to find others sharing their frustrations and find a collective remedy for their shame and humiliation. And Osama bin Laden is a heroic figure, whose directions are followed uncritically.

AL-QAEDA EMBRACES AND SUPPORTS SOUTHEAST ASIAN ISLAMIC TERRORIST GROUPS

But, in fact, bin Laden does not have religious credentials, and an analysis of the al-Qaeda Terrorism Manual reveals that the more extreme acts that are called for are justified with verses from the Koran and *hadith* that are taken out of context.[8] For the "true believers" attracted to his charismatic banner, bin Laden's declaration that Allah has justified an act is sufficient. A challenge is to mobilize moderate Muslim clerics to not permit these distorted extremist interpretations to stand unchallenged. It is, after all, their religion that has been hijacked and is being stigmatized. But taking such a role is risky. Recall the courageous Muslim clerics with bullhorns in an open car in Baghdad during the wave of hostage taking and beheading. They were shot through the head for their troubles. But, in fact, the beheadings had promoted considerable concern in the broad Muslim community, and that negative reaction has inhibited its continuation. The indiscriminate nature of the violence diminished the reputation of the *jihadists*, in this case al-Qaeda of Mesopotamia with Zarqawi orchestrating this campaign, for the hostage taking and beheadings were seen as violating the tenets of the Koran.

Need to Counter al-Qaeda Exploitation of the New Media

The new media have played a major role in making bin Laden a godlike hero and in making al-Qaeda and the global *jihad* movement romantic and empowering. As observed in the discussion of al-Qaeda Version 2.0, the organization has a clear media strategy, including instructions to "Muslim Internet professionals" "*to spread and disseminate news and information about the Jihad through e-mail lists, discussion groups, and their own websites.*" They are warned that they will be held to account on judgment day if they do not so. This strategy is explicitly designed to render ineffective attempts to shut down the originating sites and to ensure that "*this way, even if our sites are closed down, the material will live on with the Grace of Allah.*"

Al-Qaeda has a well-organized program for conducting information warfare, and sees this as central to its mission, as emphasized in the previously referred to letter of July 9, 2005 from Zawahiri to Zarqawi. In the letter, he chides Zarqawi for his reckless actions, which he sees as risking disaffecting Muslim support, and states, "*I say to you that we are in a battle, and that more than half of this battle is taking place in the battlefield of the media. And that we are in a media battle, in a race for the hearts and minds of our Umma.*"[9]

Merely blocking or technologically taking down these radical sites will not work, as the messages migrate and proliferate very rapidly. But right now the extremist messages are not even being countered. There are no alternate messages in the information space. Any alternate messages generated by the United States, such as the government financed Arabic language program Al-Hurrah based in Springfield, Virginia, are automatically discounted by many. Yet this effort does have its adherents, seeking better to understand what is happening in their country and region, and, as with Voice of America, to the extent that the station presents news objectively, and is not merely counter-propaganda, its audience will grow.

A strategic information campaign needs a coordinated information policy so statements from the White House or the Department of State are in sync with the message campaigns coming out of the operational units in the Department of Defense and the Central Intelligence Agency. Indeed, public diplomacy statements designed to reassure the domestic constituency too often undermine the information goals of those conducting psychological operations. It is difficult in a large bureaucracy to integrate and coordinate information campaigns among key elements of government.

Insulating the Public from the Goals of the Terrorists to Terrorize

Addressed thus far is a fourfold approach to countering terrorism by reducing the attraction to the group and confronting and undermining internal cohesion, but as important is the fifth element: defending against the central goal of terrorism—to terrorize. If the act of one extremist youth can derail fragile movement toward dialogue and reconciliation, terrorism is being rewarded. Sustained public education is needed to reduce public susceptibility to fear and terror. Israel has shown remarkable resilience in the face of a campaign of chronic terrorism. We need better to understand resilience and how to promote it. If the goal of terrorism is to terrorize, and the public is immunized from terror, then this is the ultimate counterterrorism. But, as evidenced by the paralyzing effects of the so-called Beltway sniper attacks in Washington, D.C., Virginia, and Maryland in October 2002, in which 15 were killed, the United States has far to go.

In sum, coordinated information operations are an underutilized but critical weapon in combating terrorism. A five-pronged strategy has been specified for strategic psychological operations. Further elaboration of some of the themes described above follows, including two themes of consuming importance to the policy community, countering suicide terrorism and weapons of mass destruction terrorism.

COUNTERING SUICIDE TERRORISM

Chapter 16 addressed suicide terrorism in its refined modern form. As Mohammad Hafez has emphasized, there are three prohibitions against suicide terrorism in the Koran: the prohibition against suicide, the prohibition against killing innocents, and the prohibition against killing Muslims.[10] Yet the radical clerics of al-Qaeda and Hamas and the imams in the radical mosques in Europe in which the disaffected Muslim émigrés are being socialized, have reframed the act as a sacred obligation, *istishhad*, martyrdom in the service of Allah. These distortions of the Koran need to be addressed from within the Muslim community.

But the most daunting challenge is how very early children are being placed on the path of terrorism and are being socialized to seek martyrdom. The earlier they have been exposed to these unchallenged, continually reinforced sacred commands, the harder it is, to break youth out of this mind-set. They have been socialized to blame all of their difficulties on the West and/or Israel and also to dehumanize the blamed enemy. It is much easier to kill a subhuman devil than a fellow human being. This suggests the need for early intervention before these attitudes are crystallized. The Seeds of Peace is a prime example of early intervention. This non-profit organization, founded by John Waller, brings together in a camp setting Jewish children and teenagers from Israel with Muslim children from the "occupied" Palestinian territories, Jordan, and Egypt; Catholic and Protestant children from Northern Ireland; and Serbian, Croatian, and Muslim children from Bosnia and Kosovo. They sleep together in the same bunkhouses, play together on the same sport teams, work together on projects. The friendships formed make it more difficult to sustain a stereotyped hatred of the other.

The role of parents is important as well. It was, after all, the mothers of Plaza Major who ultimately by their silent vigil over "the disappeared" played a crucial role in bringing down the military junta controlling Argentina that was responsible for state terror. The contrast between public and private attitudes by the parents toward losing children has been mentioned. How can parents be mobilized to inhibit their children's entrance to the path of martyrdom?

What themes are important to emphasize in strategic communications to inhibit those who may be ambivalent about their act of martyrdom? Here research with the growing population of failed suicide terrorists will be important. The thoughts that have led some to turn away at the last moment could be important to emphasize in strategic communications. Others on the path of suicide terrorism might be induced to turn away.

COUNTERING WEAPONS OF MASS DESTRUCTION TERRORISM

The prospect of weapons of mass destruction terrorism, acknowledged to be low probability—high consequence, has mobilized a major effort. Most incarcerated

Middle Eastern terrorists had not thought about using weapons of mass destruction but were enthusiastic at the prospect of being able to kill thousands. But two responses from the terrorists deserve emphasis in strategic communication campaigns. One concerned the fear of these weapons, of "the silent death," of infectious microbes, deadly toxins, and radioactivity. Not everyone wishes to be a martyr, and the danger of handling these deadly chemical, biological, and radiological materials should be emphasized. The second theme was the proscription in the Koran against mass casualties, including killing innocents, and the requirement to not poison the earth and living things. This too is worthy of emphasis in a strategic communication campaign.

STRATEGY DERIVING FROM SYSTEMATIC INTERVIEWS

The recommendations for themes to emphasize in strategic communications programs designed to counter weapons of mass destruction terrorism emerged from a program of semi-structured interviews with incarcerated Middle Eastern terrorists. Similarly the understanding of the culture that fosters suicide terrorism was drawn especially from interviews with human bombs, their families, and their commanders. As the population of failed suicide bombers—both those that were thwarted as well as those who backed down at the last moment— grows, a systematic interview program can greatly assist in refining the psychological themes to emphasize in strategic communications programs.

Other terrorisms are of importance, and systematic interview programs can aid in refining counterterrorist techniques and programs. There are now, for example, some 4,000 demobilized FARC insurgents. This is a potential treasure trove of information not only about the FARC leadership and decision making, but also about the social psychology of the FARC soldiers. After all, unlike al-Qaeda and Hamas, many of them have been conscripted, and many joined not for ideological but for monetary reasons. What led them to leave? How many others are there ready to follow their path? How might Colombia appeal to them? Sensitive interviewing—eliciting information by playing to the ego of the interview subjects, not interrogation—can provide rich information that can add to our understanding of the psychological dynamics within terrorist groups and organizations, ranging from radicalization, to recruitment, to carrying out violent acts, and to disillusion and defection.

Conducting sophisticated strategic psychological operations campaigns requires nuanced research and analysis of the history, politics, and culture of potential enemies, and in particular of their leadership and strategic culture.

As is implicit in these recommendations, the programs called for go well beyond psychological operations and strategic information campaigns. Words without deeds will ring hollow. The damage done by the Abu Ghraib prison scandal photos, as they have been exploited by radical Islamist media specialists, has been incalculable. In suggesting elements of a program to inhibit potential terrorists from joining the group in the first place, the recommendations include reforming education systems and helping autocratic leaders to open up societies so that ambitious educated individuals can look forward to succeeding within the system and are not driven to strike out in despair. Doing this will require diplomacy and significant increases in aid programs. But such programs can begin to reduce the currently inexhaustible reservoir of youth in despair who continually replenish the ranks of terrorists. Hope is the antidote to despair. It is only when youth begin to be hopeful about their future and fully participate in their societies that we will see the plague of terrorism decline. And that will take a comprehensive program sustained over decades to alter these deep-seated attitudes, for when hatred is bred in the bone, it does not easily yield.

NOTES

CHAPTER 1

1. A TWA flight from Frankfurt bound for New York, a Swissair flight, a PanAm flight, the attempted but foiled hijacking of a New York-bound El Al flight, and the next day another PFLP hijacking of a U.S.-bound British jumbo jet, blowing up first the PanAm plane in Cairo, and the subsequent destruction of the other three airliners in a field outside of Beirut. All passengers were released.
2. Alex P. Schmid, *Political Terrorism: A Research Guided* (New Brunswick, NJ: Transaction Books, 1983).
3. BBC News, "Al-Qaeda Statement," 14 October 2001. http://news.bbc.co.uk/2/low/middle_east/1598146.stm.
4. Frederick Hacker, *Crusader Criminals and Crazies: Terror and Terrorism in Our Time* (New York: W. W. Norton, 1976).
5. Martha Crenshaw, "The Causes of Terrorism" *Comparative Politics* 13 (1981): 379–399.
6. C. R. McCauley and M. E. Segal, "Social Psychology of Terrorist Groups" in *Group, Organizational and Intergroup Relations, Annual Review of Social and Personality Psychology*, Vol. 9, ed. C. Hendrick (Beverly Hills, CA: Sage, 1987).
7. John Horgan, *The Psychology of Terrorism* (New York: Routledge, 2005).
8. Jerrold Post, "The Psychological Roots of Terrorism," in *Addressing the Causes of Terrorism: The Club de Madrid Series on Democracy and Terrorism* (Madrid: Club de Madrid, 2005), Vol. 1, pp. 7–12.
9. Bruce Hoffman, *Inside Terrorism* (New York: Columbia University Press, 1998), p. 25.
10. Jillian Becker, *Hitler's Children: The Story of the Baader-Meinhof Gang* (London: Panther Books, 1978).
11. Martha Crenshaw, ed., *Terrorism in Context* (University Park: Pennsylvania State University Press, 1995).
12. Jerrold Post, "The Psychological Roots of Terrorism."

SECTION I

1. Post, J., E. Sprinzak and L. Denny 2003 "The Terrorists in their Own Words: Interviews with 35 Incarcerated Middle Eastern Terrorists," *Terrorism and Political Violence*, Vol. 15, #1 pp. 171–184, Spring 2003.
2. Walter Laqueur, *The Age of Terrorism* (Boston: Little, Brown, 1987), p. 251.

CHAPTER 2

1. Jerrold Post, "Murder in a Political Context: Profile of an Abu Nidal Terrorist," *Bulletin of the Academy of Psychiatry and the Law*, Spring, 2000.

2. With the exception of the interview with Leila Khaled cited in note 3, the details of her life story and subsequent quotes are all drawn from Leila Khaled, *My People Shall Live: An Autobiography of a Revolutionary* (London: Hooder and Stoughton, 1973).
3. Katharine Viner, "Leila Khaled," *The Guardian*, 26 January 2001.
4. This research was conducted with support of the Smith Richardson Foundation. A report of the findings can be found in Jerrold Post, Ehud Sprinzak, and Laurita Denny, "The Terrorists in their Own Words: Interviews with 35 Incarcerated Middle Eastern Terrorists," *Terrorism and Political Violence* 15, no. 1 (2003): 171–184.
5. This psychobiographic portrait draws principally on four sources: Alan Hart, *Arafat, Political Biography* (Bloomington: Indiana University Press, 1989); Janet Wallach and John Wallach, *Arafat: In the Eyes of the Beholder* (New York: Birch Lane Press, 1997); Barry Rubin and Judith Colp Rubin, *Yasir Arafat: A Political Biography* (New York: Oxford University Press, 2003); and Shaul Kimhi, Shmuel Even, and Jerrold Post, eds., "Yasser Arafat: Psychological Profile and Strategic Analysis," International Disciplinary Center, Herzliya, and the American Jewish Committee, 2003.
6. Rubin and Rubin, *Yasir Arafat*, pp. 15.
7. Wallach and Wallach, *Arafat*, pp. 110–111.
8. Ibid.
9. Rubin and Rubin, *Yasir Arafat*, pp. 70–72.
10. Jerrold Post, S. Kimhi, and S. Even, eds., "Yasser Arafat: Psychological Profile."
11. See Jerrold Post and Robert Robins, *When Illness Strikes the Leader: The Dilemma of the Captive King* (New Haven, CT: Yale University Press, 1993), chapter 5, "Sitting Crowned Upon the Grave: Effects of Terminal Leadership on Political Behavior," pp. 121–158.

CHAPTER 3

1. Paul Foote, *Ireland* (London: Chatto & Windus, 1989), p. 5.
2. "The Historic Hedge Schools of Ireland," *Ye Hedge School*, September 3, 2006; www.hedgeschool.homestead.com/Irishhistory.html.
3. This section is drawn for the most part from a book written by Connolly's daughter. Nora Connolly O'Brien, *James Connolly: Portrait of a Rebel Father* (Dublin: Four Masters Press, 1975).
4. Terry Golway, *For the Cause of Liberty* (New York: Touchstone Press, 2000), p. 226.
5. C. Desmond Greaves, *The Life and Times of James Connolly* (New York: International Publishers, 1961), p. 135.
6. Ibid., p. 227.
7. O'Brien, *James Connolly*, pp. 235–236.
8. "The Forgotten Hunger Strikers," *Lark Spirit*, 19 September 2003; http://larkspirit.com/hungerstrikes/forgotten_strikes.html.
9. Tim Pat Coogan, *The IRA: A History* (Niwot, CO: Roberts Rinehart Publishers, 1994), p. 14.
10. Patrick Pearce, cited in Walter Laqueur, *The Age of Terrorism* (Boston: Little, Brown and Company, 1987), p. 236.
11. Richard English, *Armed Struggle: The History of the IRA* (New York: Oxford University Press, 2003), p. 6.
12. O'Brien, *James Connolly*, pp. 325–326.
13. Liam MacGowan, "Ballad of James Connolly," *Pearse Com*, www.pearsecom.com/Ireland/rebelsongs/connollysong.htm.

14. This section is drawn particularly from his biography written by Brendan Anderson, *Joe Cahill: A Life in the IRA* (Dublin: The O'Brien Press, 2004).
15. Ibid., p. 17.
16. Ibid.
17. Ibid., pp. 23–24.
18. Ibid., p. 48.
19. Thomas Hennessey, *A History of Northern Ireland* (New York: St. Martin's Press, 1997), p. 98.
20. Anderson, *Joe Cahill*, pp. 116–117.
21. Robert White, *Provisional Irish Republicans* (Westport, CT: Greenwood Press, 1993), p. 41.
22. Foote, *Ireland*, p. 32.
23. Margie Bernard, *Daughter of Derry* (London: Pluto Press, 1989), p. 85.
24. White, *Provisional Irish Republicans*, p. 70.
25. Bernard, *Daughter of Derry*, p. 58.
26. Bernard, *Daughter of Derry*, p. 69.
27. English, *Armed Struggle*, p. 102.
28. Chris Ryder, "Joe Cahill," *The Guardian*, 26 July 2004; http://politics.guardian.co.uk/politicsobituaries/story/0,,1269121,00.html#article_ continue.
29. Quoted in White, *Provisional Irish Republicans*, p. 64.
30. Anderson, *Joe Cahill*, p. 191.
31. J. Boywer Bell, *The Secret Army: The IRA*, 3rd ed. (Somerset: Transaction Publishers, 1997).
32. "Freedom Songs," *Ireland First*, www.eirefirst.com/f.html#f031.
33. "Irish Soldier Boy," *Ireland First*, www.eirefirst.com/i.html#i003.
34. Bernard, *Daughter of Derry*, p. 14.
35. Ibid., p. 94.
36. Ibid., p. 99.
37. Anderson, *Joe Cahill*, p. 241.
38. English, *Armed Struggle*, p. 183.
39. Harvey Kushner, *Encyclopedia of Terrorism* (Thousand Oaks, CA: Sage Publishing, 2003), 183.
40. Anderson, *Joe Cahill*, p. 325.
41. "Bobby Sands," *Lark Spirit*; http://larkspirit.com/hungerstrikes/bios/sands.html.
42. Ibid.
43. English, *Armed Struggle*, p. 198.
44. "The Diary of Bobby Sands," *Lark Spirit*, http://larkspirit.com/hungerstrikes/diary.html
45. "Joe McDonnell," *Ireland First*, http://www.eirefirst.com/j.html#j003.
46. Bernard, *Daughter of Derry*, p. 154.
47. "The Diary of Bobby Sands," *Lark Spirit*, http://larkspirit.com/hungerstrikes/diary.html.
48. English, *Armed Struggle*, p. 200.
49. Anderson, *Joe Cahill*, p. 329.
50. *Agreement Reached in the Multi-Party Negotiations*, 10 April 1998. www.dfa.ie/uploads/documents/good%20friday%20agreement.doc.
51. "IRA 'Has Destroyed All It's Arms,' " BBC News Online, 26 September 2005, http://news.bbc.co.uk/2/hi/uk_news/northern_ireland/4282188.stm.
52. Anderson, *Joe Cahill*, p. 376.

53. Alan Cowell and Eamon Quinn, "Power Sharing Beings in Northern Ireland," *New York Times*, May 8, 2007.

CHAPTER 4

1. The Basques, now a society of 3 million, live in four provinces of Spain, including the former kingdom of Navarre, and three territories across the French border. The Basque Spanish territory, however, accounts for 86 percent of all Basqueland and 91 percent of the Basque population. Fernando Reinares, "Nationalism and Violence in Basque Politics," *Conflict* 8, nos. 2–3 (1988): 141.

2. Drawn from Goldie Shabad and Francisco José Llera Ramo, "Political Violence in a Democratic State: Basque Terrorism in Spain," in *Terrorism in Context*, ed. Martha Crenshaw, (University Park: Pennsylvania State University Press, 1995), and from Leonard Weinberg and Ami Pedahzur, *Political Parties and Terrorist Groups* (New York: Routledge, 2003), 79.

3. "Citas de Sabino Arana," *Fundacion Para La Libertad* (November 2003), www.paralalibertad.org/modules.php?op=modload&name=News&file=article&sid=3854.

4. "History of Basque Nationalism: Historical Background," *Euskal Herria Journal*, www.ehj-navarre.org/navarre/na_history_pnv.html (accessed March 10, 1996).

5. "The Basque Town at the End of the Century XIX: Sabino of Arana and Goiri," *Fundacion Sabino Arana Kultur Elkarcoa*, www.sabinoarana.org/es/sabino.htm (accessed 10 March 2006).

6. "Sabina Arana," Sabine Text.org, www.sabinetxea.org/ingles/cronologia/cronologia/cronologia5.html.

7. Arana Goiri, "Bizkaya por su Independeci," in *Comparative Politics* by Milton da Silva, "Modernization and Ethnic Conflict: The Case of the Basques" Vol. 7, No. 2, 227–251 (January 1975).

8. "Sabina Arana," *Periódico Bizkaitarra*, no. 29, www.answers.com/topic/sabino-arana (accessed 22 February 2006).

9. "The Basque Town at the End of the Century XIX."

10. "Sabina Arana," *Periódico Bizkaitarra*, no. 27, www.answers.com/topic/sabino-arana (accessed 22 February 2006).

11. "The Basque Town at the End of the Century XIX."

12. Fernando Reinares, in a March 21, 2007 personal communication, emphasized that the Basque response to the Franco civil war was by no means uniform.

13. This was mainly symbolic, for since the Middle Ages, the majority of Basques had spoken not Euskera but rather Castilian (current Spanish).

14. Paddy Woodworth, "Why Do They Kill? The Basque Conflict in Spain," *World Policy Journal* 18, no. 1 (2001), www.worldpolicy.org/journal/sum01-1.html.

15. Shabad and Llera Ramo, "Political Violence in a Democratic State," p. 422.

16. Goldie Shabad, personal communication, 13 April 2007.

17. Fernando Reinares, "Who Are the Terrorists? Analyzing Changes in Sociological Profile among Members of ETA," *Studies in Conflict and Terrorism* 27 (2004): 465–488.

18. Ibid., p. 475.

19. Ibid., p. 467.

20. Ibid., p. 468.

21. Ibid., p. 472.

22. Ibid., pp. 477–478.

23. Ibid., p. 485.

24. Franco Ferracuti and F. Bruno, "Psychiatric Aspects of Terrorism in Italy," in *The Mad, the Bad, and the Different*, ed. I. L. Barak-Galantz and C. R. Huff (Lexington, KY: Lexington Books, 1981), pp. 199–213.

25. Robert Clark, "Patterns in the Lives of ETA Members," *Terrorism* 6, no. 3 (1983): 423–454.

26. "Leader's Death Won't End Movement, Basques Say," *Washington Post*, 24 April 1973.

27. Ibid.

28. Shabad and Llera Ramo, "Political Violence in a Democratic State," pp. 410–472.

29. Peter Merkl, "Approaches to the Study of Political Violence," in *Political Violence and Terror: Motifs and Motivations*, ed. Peter Merkl (Berkeley: University of California Press, 1986), p. 3.

30. Jerrold Post, Ehud Sprinzak, and Laurita Denny, "The Terrorists in Their Own Words: Interviews with 35 Incarcerated Middle Eastern Terrorists," *Terrorism and Political Violence* 15, no. 1 (2003): 171–184.

31. "ETA Members in Spain Told to 'Put Bodies on the Table,' " *El Pais*, 17 February 2005.

32. Ibid. Capitals in original.

33. Reinares, "Who Are the Terrorists?" p. 486.

34. Ibid.

35. Ibid., p. 471.

36. "ETA Targets Former Leaders for Attack," *El Mundo*, 9 November 2005.

37. "Ex-political leader of ETA calls for an end to terror campaign," Agence France-Presse, 11 June 1998.

38. Stephen E. Atkins, "ETA (Euskadi ta Askatasuna)," in *Encyclopedia of Modern Worldwide Extremists and Extremist Groups* (Westport, CT: Greenwood Press, 2004), p. 88.

39. Shabad, personal communication.

40. Richard Gillespie, "Peace Moves in the Basque Country," *Journal of Southern Europe and the Balkans* 1, no. 2 (1999): 135.

41. Ibid., p. 124.

42. "ETA: 'We have a real opportunity to achieve a truly democratic situation,' " *Berria*, 27 September 2005, www.berria.info/english/print.php?id=1813.

43. "ETA: 'New Opportunities, but Also Risks,' " *Gara*, 26 September 2005, www.gara.net/english/weekly/20050926/art134002.php.

44. ETA announced a permanent cease-fire on 22 March 2006. A translation into English of its statement, originally written in Basque, can be found at www.berria.info/english/engdokumentuak/dokumentua15.pdf.

CHAPTER 5

1. "Ocalan Declares a Cease-Fire (1998), retrieved on 7 October 2005 from www.xs4all.nl/~kicadam/pers/oud/staakt9.html.

2. Mesut Yegen, *Devlet Soyleminde Kurt Sorunu* (Istanbul: Itelisim, 1999), pp. 555–561.

3. Chris Kutschera, "Mad Dreams of Independence: The Kurds of Turkey and the PKK," *Middle East Report* 189 (1994): 12.

4. Abdula Ocalan, "Declaration of the Democratic Solution of the Kurdish Question: Part IV," *My Personal Status* (1999). Retrieved on 27 October 2005 from www.xs4all.nl/~kicadam/declaration/status.html.
5. Ibid.
6. Chris Kutschera, "The Middle East Talks to Abdullah Ocalan," *Middle East* 289 (1999): 9.
7. Ocalan, "Declaration."
8. Ibid.
9. Associated Press, "Ocalan Used Charisma plus Guns and Bombs in Deadly Struggle," 29 June 1999.
10. K. Kirisci and G. Winrow, *The Evolution of the Kurdish Question and Turkey: An Example of a Trans-state Ethnic Conflict*, (Portland, OR: Frank Cass and Co., 1997), p. 108.
11. Dogu Ergil, personal communication, 18 February 2007.
12. Dogu Ergil, "The Kurdish Question in Turkey," *Journal of Democracy* 11, no. 3 (2000): 122–135.
13. Ergil, personal communication.
14. Kirisci and Winrow, *The Evolution of the Kurdish Question and Turkey*, p. 110.
15. Henri Barkey, "Turkey and the PKK: A Pyrrhic Victory?" in *Democracy and Counterterrorism: Lessons From the Past*, eds. R. Art and L. Richardson, 348 (Washington, DC: United States Institute of Peace, 2007).
16. Ergil, "The Kurdish Question in Turkey," p. 127.
17. R. A. Hudson and H. C. Metz, "The Sociology and Psychology of Terrorism: Who Becomes a Terrorist and Why," report prepared under an interagency agreement by the Federal Research Division (Washington, DC: Library of Congress,1999), www.intellnet.org/documents/1000/090/1091.htm.
18. Turkish Grand National Assembly record, 18 October 1994, p. 401, cited in Barkey, "Turkey and the PKK," p. 376.
19. Chris Kutschera, "Disarray Inside the PKK," *Middle East*, 301 (2000): 18.
20. Final Statement, 17 June 1999, posted by *Kurdish Struggle*, www.kurdstruggle.org/defence/final.html.
21. Chris Kutschera "Kurdistan Turkey: PKK Dissidents Accuse Abdullah Ocalan," 2005. Retrieved on 15 October 2005 from www.chris-kutschera.com/A/pkk_dissidents.htm.
22. Ibid.
23. B. Witschi, "Who Is Abdullah Ocalan?" CNN.com (1999). Retrieved on 10 October 2005 from www.cnn.com/SPECIALS/1999/ocalan/stories/ocalan.profile.
24. M. Gunter "Abdullah Ocalan: 'We Are Fighting Turks Everywhere,'" *Middle East Quarterly* 5, no. 2 (1998): 85.
25. Ocalan, "Declaration."
26. Kutschera, "The Middle East Talks to Abdullah Ocalan."
27. Ocalan, "Declaration."
28. Witschi, "Who Is Abdullah Ocalan?"
29. D. Korn, "Interview with PKK Leader Abdullah Ocalan," 1995, retrieved on 7 October 2005 from www.etext.org/Politics/Arm.The.Spirit/Kurdistan/Articles/apo-korn-interview.txt.
30. Human Rights Watch, "Turkey and War in Iraq: Avoiding Past Patterns of Violation," March 2003.
31. Gunter, "Abdullah Ocalan," p. 82.

32. D. Ergil, "Suicide Terrorism in Turkey," *Civil Wars* 3, no. 1 (2000): 51.

33. C. Morris, "Turkey's Kurds Tell Their Story," 1999, retrieved on 16 October 2005 from http://news.bbc.co.uk/1/hi/world/europe/263523.stm.

34. Ergil, "Suicide Terrorism in Turkey," p. 45.

35. "The Kurdish People Are Prepared to Continue the Struggle," 1999, retrieved on 15 October 2005 from www.etext.org/Politics/Arm.The.Spirit/Kurdistan/PKK.ERNK.ARGK/pkk-mizgin-interview-1999.txt.

36. Statement from PKK Central Committee Member Nizamettin Tas on the Deportation of Abdullah Ocalan, 1999, retrieved on 7 October 2005 from www.ainfos.ca/99/feb/ainfos00155.html.

37. Witschi, "Who Is Abdullah Ocalan?"

38. L. Hevidar, "Kongra Gel Engulfed by Troubles—Again," *KurdishMedia*, 12 June 2004, www.kurdmedia.com/articles.asp?id=9659.

39. Peter Zemenides, interview with Iraqi Kurd in London, November 2005.

40. "I Would Do It Again," *The Guardian*, 18 February 2002.

41. "The Kurds Have Gone So Far that They Deserve Their Freedom," 1998, retrieved on 7 October 2005 from www.xs4all.nl/~kicadam/pers/oud/deserve.html.

42. Gunter, "Abdullah Ocalan," p. 3.

43. Dogu Ergil, personal communication, 18 February 2007.

44. Kutschera, "Disarray Inside the PKK," p. 18.

45. Jerrold Post, *Leaders and Their Followers in a Dangerous World: The Psychology of Political Behavior* (Ithaca, NY: Cornell University Press, 2004), pp. 239–258.

46. Drawn from both J. Brandon, "Mount Qandil: A Safe Haven for Kurdish Militants—Part 1," *Terrorism Monitor* 4, no. 17 (2006): 1–3, and L. Khalil, "Ocalan Culture Center, a PKK Contact Bureau, Opens in Baghdad," *Terrorism Focus* 3, no. 29 (2006): 3.

47. Drawn from both I. Torbakov, "Kurdish Unrest Escalates in Turkey's Southeast," *Terrorism Focus* 3, no. 17 (2006): 6–7, and L. Khalil, "Turkey's Mounting Concerns over PKK Incursions from Northern Iraq," *Terrorism Focus* 3, no. 28 (2006): 3.

48. Drawn from both Khalil, "Turkey's Mounting Concerns," and Khalil, "Ocalan Culture Center."

CHAPTER 6

1. David Little, *Sri Lanka the Invention of Enmity. Series on Religion, Nationalism, and Intolerance* (Washington, DC: United States Institute of Peace, 1994), pp. 3, 11.

2. Walter Laqueur, "Sri Lanka," in *The Terrorism Reader*, ed. David J. Whittacker, p. 85 (New York: Routledge, 2004).

3. Ibid.

4. Thomas Marks, "Sri Lanka and the Liberation Tigers of Tamil Eelam," in *Democracy and Counterterrorism: Lessons From the Past*, eds. R. Art and L. Richardson, pp. 484–485 (Washington, DC: United States Institute of Peace, 2007).

5. M. R. Narayan Swamy, *Inside an Elusive Mind: Prabhakaran: The First Profile of the World's Most Ruthless Leader* (Colombo: Vijitha Yapa Publications, 2003), p. 277.

6. Ibid.

7. Tamil National Leader Velupillai Pirapaharan's interview, "The Week," *Tamil Eelam Homepage*, March 1986. www.eelam.com/interviews/leader_march_86.html.

8. Ibid.

9. Vellupillai Prabhakaran, "How I Became a Freedom Fighter," *Tamil Nation*, April 1994. www.tamilnation.org/ltte/vp/interviews/94velicham.htm.

10. Alastair Lawson. "The Enigma of Prabhakaran," BBC News, 25 November 2003, http://news.bbc.co.uk/2/hi/south_asia/3236030.stm.

11. Swamy, *Inside an Elusive Mind: Prabhakaran*.

12. Ibid.

13. Greory Zilboorg and George Henry, *A History of Medical Psychology* (New York: W. W. Norton, 1941), pp. 405–406.

14. Vellupillai Prabhakaran, "How I Became a Freedom Fighter," April 1994.

15. Indeed, as Marks details *(Democracy And Terrorism,* pp. 487–488), an array of small radical groups steeped in Marxist-Leninist rhetoric existed at this time, all calling for "liberation from oppression." Included in this number was an international contingent of students abroad, the Eelam Revolutionary Organizations of Students (EROS), which sent representatives to the Palestine Liberation Organization for training, just as the People's Liberation Organization of Tamil Eelam (PLOT) forged links with the Marxist splinter group of George Habash, the Popular Front for the Liberation of Palestine (PFLP).

16. M. R. Narayan Swamy, *Tigers of Lanka: From Boys to Guerrillas* (Columbia, MO: South Asia Books, 1995), p. 69, cited in Marks, *Democracy And Terrorism*, p. 520, which refers to note 11 on p. 490.

17. Marks, *Democracy And Terrorism*, p. 522, note 20.

18. Ibid., p. 521, note 15.

19. Ibid., p. 523, notes 21 and 23.

20. Ibid., pp. 492–493

21. Swamy, *Tigers of Lanka*, p. 69 cited in Marks, *Democracy and Counterterrorism* p. 520.

22. Swamy, *Inside an Elusive Mind: Prabhakaran*, p. 29.

23. Sreeram Chaulia, "Book Review. Enigma Decryption: Inside an Elusive Mind," *Asian Times*, www.atimes.com/atimes/South_Asia/EJ04Df01.html.

24. Swamy, *Inside an Elusive Mind: Prabhakaran*, p. 36.

25. Ibid., p. 56.

26. Ibid., p. 34.

27. Marks, *Democracy and Counterterrorism*, p. 488.

28. Ibid., p. 499.

29. International Center for Political Violence and Terrorism Research, "Personality Profile of Velupillai Prabhakaran," 3 February 2005, www.Pvtr.org/database/13145_main_fr.html.

30. Swamy, *Inside an Elusive Mind: Prabhakaran*, p. 269.

31. Chaulia, "Book Review."

32. Swamy, *Inside an Elusive Mind: Prabhakaran*, p. 55.

33. Ibid.

34. Ibid., p. 267.

35. Ibid., p. 64.

36. Ibid., p. 65.

37. Ibid., pp. 69–70, 267

38. Ibid., p. 56.

39. Ibid., pp. 69–70.

40. Ibid., pp. 79–80.

41. Ibid., p. 81.

42. Ibid., p. 84.

43. Ibid., p. 269.

44. Marks, *Democracy and Counterterrorism*, pp. 501–502.

45. T. Manivannan, "The Road to Peace in Sri Lanka," BBC News Online, 16 September 2002, http://news.bbc.co.uk/2/hi/south_asia/2261863.stm.

46. Swamy, *Inside an Elusive Mind: Prabhakaran*, p. 223.

47. "We Killed Rajiv, confesses LTTE," *Times of India*, 28 June 2006, http://times ofindia.indiatimes.com/articleshow/1686574.cms.

48. Ibid.

49. "BBC Country Profile: Sri Lanka," http://news.bbc.co.uk/1/hi/world/south_asia/country_profiles/1168427.stm.

50. Tamil National Leader Velupillai Pirapaharan's interview, March 1986.

51. Andrew Perrin, "Tiger Country: Whatever the outcome of peace talks between Colombo and the separatist Tigers, a Tamil nation in all but law already exists in Sri Lanka's battle-scarred northeast," *Time*, 16 September 2002, www.time.com/time/asia/magazine/article/0,13673,501020923-351287,00.html.

52. Ibid.

53. Ibid.

54. Ibid.

55. Kevin Sites, "Ready to Kill, Willing to Die," Sri Lanka Archive, 14 June 2006, http://hotzone.yahoo.com/b/hotzone/blogs5836.

56. Swamy, *Inside an Elusive Mind: Prabhakaran* 2003, pp. 233 and 250.

57. Ibid., p. 26.

58. Sites, "Ready to Kill, Willing to Die."

59. *New York Times*, 29 May 1995, cited in Mia Bloom, *Dying to Kill: The Allure of Suicide Terror* (New York: Columbia University Press 2005), p. 71.

60. Swamy, *Inside an Elusive Mind: Prabhakaran*, p. 45.

61. B. Raman, "Split in LTTE—The Clash of the Tamil Warlords," South Asia Analysis Group, 3 August 2004, www.saag.org/papers10/paper942.html.

62. Ibid.

63. Bloom, *Dying to Kill*, p. 72.

64. Perrin, "Tiger Country."

65. C. Christine Fair, *Urban Battle Fields of South Asia: Lessons Learned from Sri Lanka, India, and Pakistan*, (Arlington, VA: RAND Arroyo Center, 2004), p. 25.

66. Marks, *Democracy and Counterterrorism*, pp. 504–505, 525, note 34.

67. Ibid., pp. 508, 526, note 42. (Punctuation and emphasis in original.)

68. Ibid., p. 511.

69. Ibid., p. 528, note 50, p. 529, note 53.

70. Dan Eggen and Scott Wilson, "Suicide Bombs Potent Tools of Terrorists: Deadly Attacks Have Been Increasing and Spreading Since Sept. 11, 2001," *Washington Post*, 17 July 2005, www.washingtonpost.com/wp-dyn/content/article/2005/07/16/AR2005071601363_pf.html.

71. Bloom, *Dying to Kill*, p. 160.

72. Amal Jayasinghe, "UN puts Sri Lanka Tigers on notice over child soldiers," *Agency France Presse*, 10 February 2005. www.un.org/special-rep/children-armed-conflict/Download/AgenceFrance-TamilTigersOnNotice.html.

73. Bloom, *Dying to Kill*, p. 65.

74. Perrin "Tiger Country."

75. Ibid.

76. Tamil National Leader Velupillai Pirapaharan's interview, "We Are Prepared to Pay for Freedom with Our Lives," *Tamil Eelam Homepage*, September–October 1985. www.eelam.com/interviews/leader_sept_85.html.
77. Perrin, "Tiger Country."
78. Marks, *Democracy and Counterterrorism*, p.524.
79. Swamy, *Inside an Elusive Mind: Prabhakaran*, p. 272.
80. Ibid., p. 275.
81. Tamil National Leader Vellupillai Pirapaharan's interview, "Frontline," *Tamil Eelam Homepage*, 30 December 1985. http://www.eelam.com/interviews/leader_december_85.html.
82. Sites, "Ready to Kill, Willing to Die."
83. Lawson, "The Enigma of Prabhakaran."
84. Swamy, *Inside an Elusive Mind: Prabhakaran*, p. 266.
85. Eggen and Wilson, "Suicide Bombs Potent Tools."
86. Swamy, *Inside an Elusive Mind: Prabhakaran*, pp. 277 and 266.

SECTION II

1. This section is informed by Walter Laqueur's *The Age of Terrorism* (Boston: Little, Brown, 1987), pp. 235–265, and a discussion of the fighting communist organizations by Dennis Pluchinsky and Yonah Alexander, in *Europe's Red Terrorists The Fighting Communist Organizations* (London: Frank Cass, 2001).
2. Pyotr Kropotkin, *The Spirit of Revolt*, first published in *Le Revolte* (Geneva, 1880), cited in W. Laqueur and Y. Alexander, *The Terrorism Reader* (New York: Meridian, revised edition 1987), p. 95.
3. John Most in *Freiheit, September 13, 1884*, cited in Laqueur and Alexander, *The Terrorism Reader*, p. 105.
4. Pluchinsky, in Pluchinsky, D., and Y. Alexander. *Europe's Red Terrorists: The Fighting Communist Organizations* (London: Frank Cass, 2001), pp. 17–50.
5. Karin Asbley, et al., "You Don't Need a Weatherman to Know Which Way the Wind Blows," *New Left Notes* (June 1969).
6. Bill Ayers, *Fugitive Days* (New York: Penguin Putnam, 2003), p. 168.
7. Weather Underground Organization. *Prairie Fire: The Politics of Revolutionary Anti-Imperialism* (San Francisco: Prairie Fire Organizing Committee, 1974).

CHAPTER 7

1. Robert Meade Jr., *Red Brigades: The Story of Italian Terrorism* (New York: St. Martin's Press, 1990), p. 1.
2. Ibid., p. 18.
3. Vittorfranco Pisano, *The Dynamics of Subversion and Violence in Contemporary Italy* (Stanford, CA: Hoover Institution Press, 1987), p. 19.
4. Meade, *Red Brigades*, p. 20.
5. Ibid., pp. xxiv–xxvii.
6. Ibid., p. 5.
7. Ibid., pp. 2–7.
8. Ibid., pp. 8–9.
9. Ibid., p. 10.

10. Ibid., pp. 7–8.
11. Alessandro Silj, *Never Again Without a Rifle: The Origins of Italian Terrorism* (New York: KARZ Publishers, 1979), p. 107.
12. Gian Carlo Caselli and Donatella Della Porta, "The History of the Red Brigades: Organizational Structures and Strategies of Action (1970–82)," in *The Red Brigades & Left-Wing Terrorism in Italy*, ed. Raimondo Catanzaro, p. 72 (New York: St. Martin's Press, 1991).
13. Ibid., p. 73.
14. Sergey Nechaev 1869 "Catechism of the Revolutinist" in *The Terrorism* Reader Walter Laqueur and Yonah Alexander (eds.) 1978, pp. 68–72.
15. Silj, *Never Again Without a Rifle*, p. 208.
16. Patrizio Peci, *I, The Contemptible One*, Worldwide Report Terrorism. Foreign Broadcast Information Service. JPRS-TOT-85-016-L, 20 March 1985: 55.
17. Ibid., p. 38.
18. Sidney Tarrow, "Violence and Institutionalization after the Italian Protest Cycle," in *The Red Brigades & Left-Wing Terrorism in Italy*, ed. Catanzaro, p. 52.
19. Chris Beck, Reggie Emilia, Lee Morris, and Ollie Patterson, *Strike One to Educate One Hundred: The Rise of the Red Brigades in Italy in the 1960s–1970* (Chicago: Seeds Beneath the Snow, 1986), p. 63.
20. Ibid., p. 113.
21. Ibid., p. 142.
22. Meade, *Red Brigades*, p. 58.
23. Beck, et al.,*Strike One to Educate One Hundred*, p. 154.
24. Meade, *Red Brigades*, p. 64.
25. Silj, *Never Again Without a Rifle*, p. 17.
26. Meade, *Red Brigades*, p. 64
27. Vittorfranco S. Pisano, *The Dynamics of Subversion and Violence in Contemporary Italy* (Stanford, CA: Hoover Institution Press, 1987), p. 39.
28. Meade, *Red Brigades*, p. 66.
29. Ibid., p. 73.
30. Silj, *Never Again Without a Rifle*.
31. Alison Jamieson, *The Heart Attacked: Terrorism and Conflict in the Italian State* (London: Marion Boyars, 1989), p. 117.
32. Meade, *Red Brigades*, p. 173.
33. Jamieson, *The Heart Attacked*, p. 179.
34. Peci, *I, The Contemptible One*, p. 12.
35. Ibid., p. 26.
36. Ibid., p. 11.
37. Ibid., p. 27.
38. Ibid., p. 139.
39. Ibid., p. 140.
40. Ibid., p. 143.
41. Ibid., p. 138.
42. Caselli and Della Porta, "History of the Red Brigades," pp. 100–101.
43. Jerrold Post, "Prospects for Nuclear Terrorism: Psychological Incentives and Constraints," in *Preventing Nuclear Terrorism*, eds. P. Leventhal and Y. Alexander (Lexington, KY: Lexington Press, 1987).
44. Dennis Pluchinsky, personal communication, 9 February 2007.
45. Meade, *Red Brigades*, p. 206.

CHAPTER 8

1. R. L. Merritt, "The Student Protest Movement in West Berlin," *Comparative Politics*, no. 1 (July 1969): 528.
2. Jillian Becker, *Hitler's Children: The Story of the Baader-Meinhof Terrorist Gang* (New York: J.B. Lippincott Company, 1977).
3. P. Lowenberg, *Decoding the Past: the Psychohistorical Approach* (Berkeley: University of California Press, 1985), pp. 240–280.
4. J. Post "When Hatred is Bred in the Bone: Psychocultural Foundations of Contemporary Terrorism," *Political Psychology*, Vol. 26, #4 pp. 615–636, August, 2005. Sanford Award Essay.
5. Klaus Wasmund, "The Political Socialization of West German Terrorists," in *Political Violence and Terror*, ed. Peter Merkl (Los Angeles: University of California Press, 1986), p. 194.
6. Becker, *Hitler's Children*, p. 39.
7. Ibid., p. 41.
8. Bommi Baumann, *Terror or Love? My Life as a West German Guerrilla* (New York: Grove Press, 1977), p. 31.
9. Peter Merkl, "West German Left-Wing Terrorism," in *Terrorism in Context*, ed. Martha Crenshaw (University Park: Pennsylvania State University, 1995), p. 185.
10. Wasmund, "Political Socialization of West German Terrorists," p. 215.
11. Stefan Aust, *The Baader-Meinhof Group: The Inside Story of a Phenomenon* (London: The Bodley Head, 1985), p. 51.
12. Wasmund, "Political Socialization of West German Terrorists," p. 197.
13. Baumann, *Terror or Love?* p. 32.
14. "The Concept Urban Guerrilla," attributed to Ulrike Meinhof, Baader-Meinhof.com, www.baader-meinhof.com/students/resources/communique/eng concept.html.
15. The use of the term "Urban Guerilla" demonstrates the influence of Latin American social-revolutionary doctrine, particularly Carlos Marighella's *Mini Manual of the Urban Guerilla*. June 1969. *www.marxists.org/archive/marighella-carlos/1969/06/minimanual-urban-guerrilla/index.htm*
16. This section is drawn from Jillian Becker, *Hitler's Children: The Story of the Baader-Meinhof Terrorist Gang* (New York: J.B. Lippincott Company, 1977), 68–173.
17. Ibid., p. 74.
18. Aust, *The Baader-Meinhof Group*, p. 53.
19. Ibid., p. 56.
20. Quotes in Hans Josef Horchem "European Terrorism: A German Perspective" *Terrorism: An International Journal* 6, no. 1 (1982).
21. *"Build up the Red Army! Manifesto for Armed Action"* Berlin 1970, http://home.att.net/~rw.rynerson/rafgrund.htm
22. Wasmund, "Political Socialization of West German Terrorists," p. 211.
23. "Baader-Meinhof Timeline," Baader-Meinhof.com, www.baader-meinhof.com/timeline/1974.html.
24. Becker, *Hitler's Children*, p. 180.
25. Peter Chalk, *West European Terrorism and Counter-Terrorism: The Evolving Dynamic* (New York: St. Martin's Press, 1996), p. 62.
26. Merkl, "West German Left-Wing Terrorism," p. 163.

27. Through the kindness and facilitation of the West German minister of the interior, in June 1979, I was able to interview nine of the social scientists who participated in this remarkable major interdisciplinary research project. They were involved in the research for Volume 2, *Life Course Analysis*, and Volume 3, *Group Process*, which helped inform understandings of the individual and social psychology, life course analysis, recruitment, and group dynamics of social revolutionary terrorist groups, and contributed to the generational matrix presented in chapter 1. See Ministry of the Interior, Federal Republic of Germany, *Analysen Zum Terrorismus 1–4* (Darmstadt: Deutscher Verlag, 1981, 1982, 1983, 1984) and H. Jager, G. Smidtchen, and L. Sullwold, eds., *Analysen Zum Terrorismus 2: Lebenslaufanalysen* (Darmstadt: Deutscher Verlag, 1981).

28. Wasmund, "Political Socialization of West German Terrorists," p. 203.

29. Ferracuti, Franco. "A Psychiatric Comparative—Analysis of Left and Right Terrorism in Italy." In World Congress of Psychiatry, *Psychiatry: The State of the Art*, 6. New York: Plenum, 1985.

30. Wasmund, "Political Socialization of West German Terrorists," p. 203.

31. Ibid., p. 205.

32. Ibid., p. 218.

33. Ibid.

34. Ibid., p. 214.

35. This anecdote was related to the author in June 1979 by Frau Baeyer-Kaette, who had interviewed the RAF recruit in connection with her research for Volume 3 of the Ministry of the Interior research project: W. von Baeyer-Kaette, D. Classens, H. Feger, and F. Neihardt (eds.) *Analysen Zum Terrorismus 3: Gruppenprozesse* (Darmstadt: Deutscher Verlag, 1982).

36. Merkl, "West German Left-Wing Terrorism," p. 191.

37. Ibid., p. 183.

38. Becker, *Hitler's Children*, p. 24.

39. "The Urban Guerrilla Is History . . ." Baader-Meinhof.com, www.baader-meinhof.com/students/resources/communique/engrafend.html.

CHAPTER 9

1. This chapter is substantially informed by revealing interview material and insightful analysis of Gustavo Gorriti, a Peruvian journalist who obtained remarkable access to Sendero's leadership and cadre. Particularly valuable are his definitive 1999 study *The Shining Path: A History of the Millenarian War in Peru* (Chapel Hill: University of North Carolina Press) and his 1992 chapter "Shining Path's Stalin and Trotsky," in *Shining Path of Peru*, ed. David Scott Palmer (New York: St. Martin's Press). Equally important are the insights and analysis of David Scott Palmer, especially his "The Revolutionary Terrorism of Peru's Shining Path" in Martha Crenshaw's *Terrorism in Context* and "Terror in the Name of Mao: Revolution and Response in Peru," in *Democracy and Counter Terrorism: Lessons from the Past*, ed. R. Art and L. Richardson (Washington, DC: United States Institute of Peace, 2007), as well as valuable personal commentary. Their scholarship has significantly contributed to the author's understanding of this Maoist organization and its charismatic leader.

2. "Abimael Guzman," information from Answers.com, www.answers.com/topic/abimael-guzm-n, accessed 28 September 2005.

3. *Encyclopedia of Modern Worldwide Extremists and Extremist Groups*, "Guzman, Abimael." (Westport, CT: Greenwood Press, 2004).
4. "Abimael Guzman," Biography Resource Center Online, Gale Group (1999). Thomson Gale, via Gale Group, http://galenet.galegroup.com.
5. "Exclusive Comments by Abimael Guzman," *World Affairs* 156, no.1 (1993). Foreign Broadcast Information Service (FBIS), via Find Articles, www.find articles.com.
6. Ibid.
7. Palmer, "Terror in the Name of Mao," pp. 197–198.
8. Gorriti, "Shining Path's Stalin and Trotsky," p. 155.
9. "Abimael Guzman (Comrade Gonzalo)," *Terrorism Reference Library*, ed. James L. Outman, Elisabeth M. Outman, Matthew May, and Diane Sawinski, Vol. 2, *Terrorism: Biographies*, p. 144 (Detroit: U*X*L, 2003).
10. "Exclusive Comments by Abimael Guzman."
11. Simon Strong, "Shining Path: A Case Study in Ideological Terrorism," *Conflict Studies*, no. 260 (London: The Research Institute for the Study of Conflict and Terrorism, 1993), p. 3.
12. Gorriti "Shining Path's Stalin and Trotsky," p. 157.
13. Ibid.
14. "Interview with Chairman Gonzalo," *El Diario*, 24 July 1988, www.blythe.org/peru-pcp/docs_en/interv.htm.
15. James F. Rochlin, *Vanguard Revolutionaries in Latin America: Peru, Colombia, Mexico* (Boulder, CO: Lynne Reinner Publishers, 2003), p. 32. Cite from Sendero Luminoso, "Linea internacional del PCP," n.d., translation by author.
16. "Abimael Guzman (Comrade Gonzalo)," p. 143.
17. Gorriti, "Shining Path's Stalin and Trotsky," p. 151.
18. Ibid.
19. Gorriti, *The Shining Path*, p.180.
20. Gorriti "Shining Path's Stalin and Trotsky," p. 158.
21. Gorriti, *The Shining Path*, pp. 182–183.
22. Ibid., p. 180.
23. Major James V. Huston, "Insurgency in Peru: The Shining Path," Marine Corps Command and Staff College, Marine Corps Combat Development Center, 11 May 1988, www.globalsecurity.org/military/library/report/1988/HJV.htm.
24. Palmer, "Terror in the Name of Mao," p. 203.
25. For more information on the various support groups, see Huston, "Insurgency in Peru."
26. As cited in Rochlin, *Vanguard Revolutionaries in Latin America*, p. 56. Cite from Sendero Luminoso, "Documentos fundamentals y programa," 1988, translation by author.
27. Rochlin, *Vanguard Revolutionaries in Latin America*, p. 39.
28. Gorriti, *Shining Path*, p. 91.
29. "Exclusive Comments by Abimael Guzman."
30. Cynthia McClintock, *Revolutionary Movements in Latin America* (Washington, DC: United States Institute of Peace Press, 1998), p. 276. Cite from Interview no. 32, Osores research team.
31. Ibid., Cite from Interview no. 6, Osores research team.
32. "Interview with Chairman Gonzalo." *El Diario*.
33. McClintock, *Revolutionary Movements in Latin America*, 275. Cite from Interview no. 18, Osores research team.

34. As cited in Huston, "Insurgency in Peru." Citation from Quehacer, September–October 1987, in FBIS 28 January 1988.
35. As cited in McClintock, *Revolutionary Movements in Latin*, 274. Cite from Interview no. 19, Osores research team.
36. Ibid.
37. Rochlin, *Vanguard Revolutionaries in Latin America*, p. 43.
38. Gorriti, *Shining Path*, pp. 34–35.
39. McClintock, *Revolutionary Movements in Latin*, pp. 230–231.
40. Strong, "Shining Path," p. 9.
41. "Interview with Chairman Gonzalo."
42. Strong, "Shining Path."
43. Ibid., p. 10.
44. *"Gloria al Día de la Heroicidad!"* (Lima: Ediciones Bandera Roja, 1987), p. 33; cited in McClintock, "Theories of Revolution and the Case of Peru," p. 249.
45. Strong, "Shining Path," p. 10.
46. "Interview with Chairman Gonzalo."
47. Huston, "Insurgency in Peru." Source information from Raúl Gonzáles, "Especial Sobre Sendero," *Quehacer* 30 (August–September, 1984), pp. 6–36.
48. Palmer, "Terror in the Name of Mao," p. 197
49. Rochlin, *Vanguard Revolutionaries in Latin America*, p. 57. Cite from Sendero Luminoso, "Somos los iniciadores," 19 April 1980.
50. Gorriti, *Shining Path*, p. 105.
51. Gorriti, "Shining Path's Stalin and Trotsky," p. 158.
52. Gorriti, *Shining Path*, p. 104.
53. Ibid., p. 105.
54. "Interview with Chairman Gonzalo," *El Diario*, 24 July 1988, p. 20. www.blythe.org/peru-pcp/docs_en/interv.htm. Located in Gorriti, *Shining Path*, p. 98. Cite from "Interview with Abimael Guzman, 'President Gonzalo,' " *El Diario*, 24 July 1988, p. 20.
55. As cited in Gorriti, *Shining Path*, p. 105.
56. Ibid.
57. As cited in Gorriti, *Shining Path*, p. 187. Quote from *El Pensamiento Militar del Partido* (December 1982): 13.
58. Gorriti, *Shining Path*, p. 246.
59. Ibid., p. 106.
60. "Profile: Peru's Shining Path," BBC News, http://news.bbc.co.uk/2/hi/americas/3985659.stm (accessed September 19, 2006).
61. As cited in Sonia Goldenberg, "Shining Path's American 'Friends,' " *The Nation* 256, no. 10 (1993): 335.
62. As cited in Huston, "Insurgency in Peru. Cite from Jeanne Dequine, "The Challenge of the Shining Path," *The Nation* 239 (December 1984): 610–6l3.
63. As cited in Billie Jean Isbell, "Shining Path and Peasant Responses in Rural Ayacucho" in *Shining Path of Peru*, ed. , p. 75. Cite from an interview by the author in Ayacucho in 1986.
64. Shawn Choy, "In the Spotlight: Sendero Luminoso," Center for Defense Information (2002), www.cdi.org/terrorism/sendero-pr.cfm (accessed on August 27, 2006).
65. As cited in Gorriti, *Shining Path*, pp. 253–254. Cite from Oficio No. 190-82-MP-Fiscalia Superior Departamental, 19 November 1982.

66. As cited in Huston, "Insurgency in Peru." Cite from an interview with a senior Peruvian officer.
67. United States Department of State, "Background Notes: Peru," Bureau of Western Hemisphere Affairs (2006), www.state.gov/r/pa/ei/bgn/35762.htm (accessed 19 September 2006).
68. "Guerrillas Insurgency, 1980–92," in *A Country Study: Peru. Federal Reserve Division*, Library of Congress, http://lcweb2.loc.gov/frd/cs/petoc.html (accessed 19 September 2006).
69. Jerrold Post, "Narcissism and the Charismatic Leader-Follower Relationship," pp. 187–199, in J. Post, *Leaders and their Followers in a Dangerous World* (Ithaca, NY: Cornell University Press, 2004).
70. As cited in Strong, "Shining Path," p. 1.
71. As cited in Rochlin, *Vanguard Revolutionaries in Latin America*, p. 32. Cite from Sendero Luminoso, "Historic Speech from the Dungeons of the Enemy," 24 September 1992.
72. Gary Leupp, "Sendero's New Trial: Guzman's Fist" *Counter Punch*, 11 November 2004, www.counterpunch.org/leupp11112004.html.
73. McClintock, *Revolutionary Movements in Latin America*, 275. Cite from Interview no. 33, Osores research team with additional reference to Interviews no. 4, 10, and 31.
74. "Abimael Guzman," information From Answers.com.
75. David Scott Palmer, personal communication, 2 March 2007.

CHAPTER 10

1. Interview with Commander Raúl Reyes, "Nivel de lucha cada vez más definitorio," Farcep.org, 4 May 2002, www.farcep.org/?node=2,765,1.
2. Steven Dudley, "On the Road with FARC." *The Progressive* (November 2003).
3. "House International Relations Committee, Summary of Committee Investigation of "IRA Links to FARC Narco-Terrorists in Colombia," Center for International Policy's Colombia Program, Committee on International Relations, U.S. House of Representatives, 24 April 2002, www.ciponline.org/colombia/02042401.htm.
4. Dudley, "On the Road with FARC."
5. Ibid.
6. "Colombia's Civil Revolutionary Armed Forces of Colombia (FARC)," Online NewsHour, 2003, http://cocaine.org/colombia/farc.html.
7. Thomas Marks, personal communication, 15 March 2007.
8. Constanza Vieria, *Colombia: Five Decades of a Struggle for Land that Became a War* (New York: Global Information Network, 2004).
9. Ibid.
10. Rex A. Hudson, *The Sociology and Psychology of Terrorism: Who Becomes a Terrorist and Why?* Report prepared under an interagency agreement by the Federal Research Division (Washington, DC: Library of Congress, 1999), p. 107.
11. "Entrevista con el Comandante Raúl Reyes," Farcep.org, 6 February 2006, www.farcep.org/?node=2,1880,1.
12. "FARC: We Don't Own Any Coca Fields," New Colombia News Agency (ANNCOL), www.anncol.org/uk/site/doc.php?id=253.
13. Thomas Marks, *Colombian Army Adaptation to FARC Insurgency* (Carlisle, PA: The Strategic Studies Institute, 2002), p. 4.
14. Interview with Commander Raúl Reyes, "Nivel de lucha cada vez más definitorio," Farcep.org, 4 May 2002.

15. Marks, *Colombian Army Adaptation to FARC Insurgency*, p. 7.
16. Ibid.
17. Marcela Sanchez. "Concern for Colombia's Little Guy," *Washington Post*, 24 June 2004.
18. Shannon McCaffrey, "Program to Battle Colombian Drug Trafficking Gets Fresh Scrutiny," Knight Ridder, 15 September 2005.
19. Marks, personal communication.
20. Commentary of Malcolm Deas, St. Anthony's College, Oxford, at Colombian Security Forum, "What Are FARC's Current Political and Military Strategies," 12 November 2003, summarized by Jay Cope, personal communication, 15 March 2007. Cope concurs with Thomas Marks that Marxist-Leninist ideology remains at the core of FARC's strategic goals.
21. Hudson, *Sociology and Psychology of Terrorism*, p.106.
22. "Child Soldier Use 2003: A Briefing for the 4th UN Security Council Open Debate on Children and Armed Conflict," Human Rights Watch (January 2003), http://hrw.org/reports/2004/childsoldiers0104/5.htm.
23. Hudson, *Sociology and Psychology of Terrorism*.
24. *Carlos A. Betancur López, Petitioner, v. Alberto González, Attorney General, Respondent. Petition for Review of an Order of the Board of Immigration Appeals*, United States Court of Appeals for the First Circuit,www.ca1.uscourts.gov/cgi-bin/getopn.pl? OPINION=05–2092.01A.
25. Hudson, *Sociology and Psychology of Terrorism*..
26. Marks, personal communication.
27. Hudson, *Sociology and Psychology of Terrorism*, p. 107.
28. Interview with Commander Raúl Reyes.
29. Ibid.
30. Marks, personal communication.
31. "Disarming, Bit by Bit," *The Economist*, 31 January 2004.
32. "An Encore for Uribe," *The Economist*, 24 May 2006.
33. Marks, personal communication.
34. "Nivel de lucha Cada vez más definitorio."
35. "Entrevista con el Comandante Raúl Reyes."
36. Jay Cope, personal communication, 15 March 2007.
37. Joaquin Villalobos, "Colombia: Expert Analyzes How FARC Is Losing Domestic Conflict," *Bogotá Semana*, 7 July 2003.
38. Ibid.
39. Jerrold Post, "'El Fenomeno Chavez': Hugo Chavez of Venezuela, Modern Day Bolivar," Monograph #39, Future Warfare Series (Maxwell Air Force Base, AL: USAF Counterproliferation Center, 2007).

SECTION III

1. David Rapoport (ed.), *Inside Terrorist Organizations* (New York: Columbia University Press, 1988).
2. Ibid., p. 13
3. Ahmad Hamzeh, *In the Path of Hizbullah* (Syracuse, NY: Syracuse University Press, 2004).
4. Robin Wright, *Sacred Rage: The Wrath of Militant Islam* (New York: Linden Press, 1985), p. 42.

CHAPTER 11

1. Robin Wright, *Sacred Rage: The Wrath of Militant Islam* (New York: Linden Press, 1985), 58.
2. Ibid.
3. Al-Musawi, "Min Antum Hizbullah?," in *In the Path of Hizbullah*, ed. Ahmad Hamzeh (Syracuse, NY: Syracuse University Press, 2004), 25.
4. R. Robins and J. Post, *Political Paranoia: The Psychopolitics of Hatred* (New Haven, CT: Yale University Press, 1997), 285.
5. "Hezbullah," Special Information Report, June 2003, Intelligence and Terrorism Information Center at the Center for Special Studies, http://www.intelligence.org.il/eng/.
6. Amal Saad-Ghorayeb, *Hizbu'llah: Politics and Religion* (London: Pluto Press, 2002), 18.
7. Ibid.
8. Ibid., p. 12.
9. Jerrold Post, Ehud Sprinzak and Laurtia Denny, previously unpublished interview summarized in "The Terrorists in their Own Words: Interviews with 35 Incarcerated Middle Eastern Terrorists," *Terrorism and Political Violence* vol. 15, no. 1 (Spring 2003): 171–184.
10. Saad-Ghorayeb, *Hizbu'llah*, p. 70.
11. Walter Laqueur, *The New Terrorism: Fanaticism and the Arms of Mass Destruction* (Oxford: Oxford University Press, 1999), 136–137, 177.
12. Grant Wardlaw, *Political Terrorism: Theory, Tactics, and Counter-Measures, 2nd ed.* (Cambridge: Cambridge University Press, 1989), 155.
13. Hala Jaber, *Hezbollah: Born With a Vengeance* (New York: Columbia University Press, 1997), 184.
14. Martin Kramer, "The Oracle of Hezbollah: Sayyid Muhammad Husayn Fadlallah," in *Spokesmen for the Despised: Fundamentalist Leaders of the Middle East*, ed. R. Scott Appleby (Chicago: University of Chicago Press, 1997), 84.
15. Ibid., p. 89.
16. Martin Kramer, "The Moral Logic of Hizballah," in *Origins of Terrorism: Psychologies, Ideologies, Theologies, States of Mind*, ed. Walter Reich (Washington, D.C.: Woodrow Wilson Center Press, 1998), 131–157.
17. Ibid., p. 144.
18. Martin Kramer, "Hezbullah: The Calculus of Jihad," in *Fundamentalisms and the State: Remaking Politics, Economies, and Militance: The Fundamentalism Project, vol. 3*, eds. M. Marty and R. S. Appleby (Chicago: University of Chicago Press, 1993).
19. Fadlallah Friday sermon, *al-Ahd*, December 5 1985, cited in Martin Kramer, "The Moral Logic of Hizballah," p. 144.
20. Kramer, "The Moral Logic of Hizballah," p. 154.
21. Rex A. Hudson, *The Sociology and Psychology of Terrorism: Who Becomes a Terrorist and Why?* Report prepared under an interagency agreement by the Federal Research Division (Washington, DC: Library of Congress, 1999), pp. 178–179.
22. Laqueur, *The New Terrorism*, p. 136.
23. "Charismatic Leader Behind the Latest Middle East Crisis," *The Guardian, Beirut*, July 23, 2006.
24. Annia Ciezadlo, "Sheik Up," *The New Republic Online*, July 28, 2006, http://www.tnr.com/doc.mhtml?i=20060807&s=ciezadlo080706.

25. Scott Peterson, "The Sheikh Behind Hezbollah," *Christian Science Monitor*, August 9, 2006.

26. Robin Wright, "Inside the Mind of Hezbollah," *Washington Post*, July 16, 2006, B01.

27. James Forest, ed. *Teaching Terror: Strategic and Tactical Learning in the Terrorist World* (Lanham, MD: Rowman and Littlefield, 2006), 9, 98, 115. Hezbollah has used a video game titled "Special Force," which simulates combat against Israeli forces in South Lebanon. The game is designed to provide emotional disengagement, preparing potential recruits for killing enemies.

28. "Hezbullah," Special Information Report, June 2003, Intelligence and Terrorism Information Center at the Center for Special Studies, http://www.intelligence.org.il/env/.

29. Shibley Telhami, "Reflection in Lebanon, Israel, but not in U.S," *Baltimore Sun*, September 3, 2006, 23A.

30. "Hezbollah Bombs Israeli Warship," *Al-Jazeera Magazine*, July 15, 2006, http://www.aljazeera.com/me.asp?service_ID=11743.

31. Ghassan Bin-Jiddu, "Interview with Hezbollah Secretary General Hasan Nasrallah," *Al-Jazeera*, July 20, 2006, http://www.informationclearinghouse.info/article14152.htm.

32. *BBC News Online*, "Text: Hezbullah Leader Defiant," August 9, 2006, news.bbc.co.uk/2/hi/middle_east/4779757.stm.

33. Ibid.

34. Ibid.

35. Martin Asser, "Lebanon's Devastation Sightseers," *BBC News Online*, August 18, 2006. www.news.bbc.co.uk/2/hi/middle_east/5262832.stm.

CHAPTER 12

1. The goal of this chapter is to convey understandings of the psychology of Hamas leaders and followers, and to do this, an overview of the political and cultural context is necessary. There is no intent to develop a definitive political history of Hamas, and so there will not be an attempt to portray in detail the intricacies of Hamas's role since the 2006 election nor of its relationship to other militant Islamist groups such as the Palestinian Islamic Jihad or secular groups such as the Al-Aqsa Martyrs Brigade, which have also actively participated in the wave of suicide bombings.

2. Bruce Hoffman, *Inside Terrorism* (New York: Columbia University Press, 1998), 162.

3. Amal Saad-Ghorayeb, *Hizbu'llah: Politics and Religion* (London: Pluto Press, 2002), 73.

4. Quotations from the charter are taken from Taheri 1987.

5. "The Covenant of the Islamic Resistance Movement (Hamas)" August, 1988. The complete transcript provided by The Avalon Project at Yale Law School. http://www.yale.edu/lawweb/avalon/mideast/hamas.htm.

6. "Dealing with Hamas," *International Crisis Group Middle East Report, Number 21*. Amman/Brussels, January, 26, 2004, 7.

7. Ibid., p. 16.

8. Walter Laqueur, *The New Terrorism: Fanaticism and the Arms of Mass Destruction* (Oxford: Oxford University Press, 1999), 138–139.

9. Leaflet of the Islamic Resistance Movement (Hamas), January 1988. Reproduced in Charles D. Smith, *Palestine and the Arab-Israeli Conflict: a History with Documents,* 5th ed. (Boston, MA: Bedford/St. Martin's, 2004), 433–434.

10. James Forest, ed. *Teaching Terror: Strategic and Tactical Learning in the Terrorist World* (Lanham, MD: Rowman and Littlefield, 2006), 194–195.

11. "Biography of Ahmad Yassin," *Encyclopedia of Palestinians,* November 12, 2000, http://www.palestineremembered.com/Gaza/al-Jura/Story185.html.

12. Nasra Hassan, "An Arsenal of Believers: Talking to the 'Human Bombs,'" *New Yorker,* November 19, 2001.

13. "Dealing with Hamas," 3.

14. Interview, *Al-Nahar* (Jerusalem), April 30, 1989. Quoted in Abu Amr, *Islamic Fundamentalism,* cited in "Dealing with Hamas," 13.

15. International Crisis Group Interview with Rantisi, October 2002, cited in "Dealing with Hamas," 13.

16. *Al-Quds* (East Jerusalem), October 12, 1995, cited by Shaul Mishal and Avraham Sela, *The Palestinian Hamas: Vision, Violence, and Coexistence* (New York: Columbia University Press, 2000), 71.

17. Mishal and Sela, 51–52.

18. International Crisis Group Interview, Abu Shanab, August 5, 2003, cited in "Dealing with Hamas," 17.

19. Leaflet of the Islamic Resistance Movement (Hamas), January 1988. Reproduced in: Smith, 433–434.

20. Ibid.

21. Hamas is not the only militant Palestinian group engaging in suicide terrorism. The Palestinian Islamic Jihad is a militant Islamist group that also has a campaign of suicide bombing, but, unlike Hamas, does not sustain a web of social services. The success of the suicide bombing campaigns of Hamas and the Palestinian Islamic Jihad can be seen as requiring the secular militant group Fatah to develop a unit that would also engage in suicide bomb attacks, the Al-Aqsa Martyrs Brigade, in order for Fatah to compete organizationally with Hamas for new recruits. In addition to this discussion of Hamas suicide terrorism, an extended consideration of suicide terrorism will be found in Chapter 16, Tactics Old and New: Suicide Terrorism and Weapons of Mass Destruction Terrorism.

22. "Dealing with Hamas," 1.

23. John Horgan, *The Psychology of Terrorism* (New York: Routledge, 2005), 131.

24. For extended discussions of this social psychological observation, see Ariel Merari, "Social, Organizational, and Psychological Factors in Suicide Terrorism," in *Root Causes of Terrorism,* Tore Bjorgo, ed., (London: Routledge, 2005), 70–86; A. Merari, "Psychological Aspects of Suicide Terrorism," in *Psychology of Terrorism,* B. Bongar, L. Brown, L. Beutler, J. Breckenridge and P. Zimbardo, eds. (Oxford: Oxford University Press, 2007); and A. Merari, "Suicidal Terrorism," in *Assessment, Treatment, and Prevention of Suicidal Behavior,* R. I. Yufit and D. Lester, eds., (Indianapolis: Wiley, 2004), 431–453.

25. Forest, *Teaching Terror,* 198.

26. Horgan, *The Psychology of Terrorism,* 91.

27. Laqueur, *The New Terrorism,* 141.

28. "BBC Panel Interview with Mona Yousef," *BBC News Online,* September 13, 2006, news.bbc.co.uk/go/pr/fr/-/2/hi/talking_point/5339478.stm.

29. Horgan, *The Psychology of Terrorism*, 101. Based on survey by B. Barber, *Heart and Stones: Palestinian Youth From the Intifada* (New York: Palgrave, 2003).

30. J. M. Post, E. Sprinzak, and L. M. Denny, "The Terrorists in their Own Words: Interviews with 35 Incarcerated Middle Eastern Terrorists," *Terrorism and Political Violence* vol. 15, no. 1 (2003): 171–184.

31. Previously unpublished interview summarized in Post, Sprinzak, and Denny, "The Terrorists in their Own Words," 171–184.

32. Horgan, *The Psychology of Terrorism*, 102.

33. Post, Sprinzak, and Denny, "The Terrorists in their Own Words."

34. Previously unpublished interview developed in association with terrorist interview project summarized in Post, Sprinzak, and Denny, "The Terrorists in their Own Words."

35. Jessica Stern, *Terror in the Name of God: Why Religious Militants Kill* (New York: HarperCollins Publishers, 2003), 38.

36. Philip Jacobson, "Home-Grown Martyrs of the West Bank Reap Deadly Harvest," *Sunday Telegraph*, August 19, 2001, 20 as cited in Stern, *Terror in the Name of God*, 38.

37. Reported by Amit Cohen, "Hamas Dot Com," in Maariv Online, July 2, 2003, www.maarivenglish.com/tour/Hamas%20Dot%20Com.htm. Reprinted in Forest, *Teaching Terror*, 119.

38. Forest, *Teaching Terror*, 119–121.

39. "Dealing with Hamas," 14.

40. Ibid.

41. Forest, *Teaching Terror*, 199.

42. Shlomo Brom, "A Hamas Government: Isolate or Engage?" *U.S. Institute of Peace Briefing*, March 2006, 2.

43. "Profile: Hamas PM Ismail Haniya," *BBC News Online*.

44. Alan Johnston, "Palestinian Despair as Donors Meet," *BBC News*, September 1, 2006.

45. BBC Panel Interview with Majeda Al-Saqqa. BBC News Online, 09/13/2006, accessed via news.bbc.co.uk/go/pr/fr/-/2/hi/talking_point/5338842.stm.

46. "BBC Panel Interview with Fathi Tobail," *BBC News Online*, September 13, 2006, news.bbc.co.uk/go/pr/fr/-/2/hi/talking_point/5339478.stm.

47. "Enter Hamas: The Challenges of Political Integration," *International Crisis Group, Middle East Report, Number 49* (January 18, 2006), 7.

CHAPTER 13

1. There are varying reports about Osama bin Laden's exact location within the family, although being the seventeenth of 20 to 25 sons of 52 or 53 total children is the most consistent figure available. Example sources include: Christopher Dickey and Daniel McGinn, "Meet the bin Ladens," *Newsweek*, http://www.msnbc.com/news/639250.asp; John Dorschner, "Osama bin Laden: The Mastermind of Terror," *Knight Ridder Newspapers*, September 24, 2001. http://www.freep.com/news/nw/terror2001/osama24_20010924.html; John Miller, "ABC interview with Usama bin Laden," http://www.terrorism.com/documents/crs-report.shtml.

2. As noted, there is no single agreed-upon figure as to the inheritance of Osama bin Laden and reports vary. Sources include: Lisa Beyer, "The Most Wanted Man in the World," *Time.com*, http://www.time.com/time/covers/1101010924/wosama.html; Robert McFadden, "Bin Laden's Journey From Rich, Pious Boy to the Mask

of Evil," *New York Times*, September 30, 2001; John Dorschner, "A Shadowy Empire of Hate was Born of a War in Afghanistan," *Knight Ridder Newspapers*, September 24, 2001.

3. Nearly all reports refer to Osama bin Laden as the only child (or the only son) of his mother with Mohammed bin Laden. Following her divorce, Osama bin Laden's mother remarried and subsequently started a second family.

4. While some reports (see A. Robinson, *Bin Laden*. London: Mainstream Publishing, 2002) claim that Mohammed had Hamida removed from the family before Osama was a year old, other reports more consistently note that she was ostracized by the family but do not indicate that her departure from the family, following her divorce with Mohammed, was as early as Robinson indicates.

5. While most reports indicate that Osama did indeed obtain his civil engineering certificate and at least start his degree in Business Management, Rohan Gunaratna in his *Inside al-Qaeda: Global Network of Terror* (New York: Columbia University Press, 2002) states that, contrary to other reports, bin Laden did *not* study engineering.

6. A. Hashim, "Usama bin Laden's Worldview and Grand Strategy," paper presented to conference at Navy War College, November 19, 2001.

7. Eric Hoffer, *The True Believer: Thoughts on the Nature of Mass Movements* (New York: Perennial (HarperCollins), 1951 reissued 1989).

8. *Declaration of War (1)*, available at http://www.msanews.mynet.net/MSANEWS/199610/19961013.10.html.

9. There are four *jihads*: The greater *jihad*, the *jihad* of the heart, calls on Muslims to have a heart that is pure of vice and evil thoughts. The *jihad* of the tongue directs Muslims to give voice to the words of the prophet. The *jihad* of the deed directs Muslims to carry out good works for members of the *umma*, the community of observant Muslims, by such acts as teaching in Muslims schools or working in clinics. Finally, the *jihad* of the sword, directs Muslims to defend Islam when it is under attack.

10. See Jerrold M. Post, ed., *Declaration of Jihad Against the Country's Tyrants, Military Series: The al-Qaeda Terrorism Manual* (Maxwell Air Force Base: USAF Counterproliferation Center, 2005), in which, based on consultations with experts on Islam, I demonstrate how many of the verses used to justify acts of terrorism are in fact taken out of context or mean something quite different from that which the manual's author, probably Zawahiri, asserts.

11. Countries believed to have active al-Qaeda cells include: Britain, France, Germany, Bosnia, Croatia, Albania, Bosnia, Spain, Argentina, Brazil, Paraguay, Uruguay, Trinidad & Tobago, Australia, Papua New Guinea, Borneo, Brunei, Nauru, Fiji, Philippines, Indonesia, Malaysia, Singapore, Saudi Arabia, UAE, West Bank & Gaza, Egypt, Pakistan, Yemen, Somalia, Sudan, Comoros, Ethiopia, Kenya, Libya, South Africa, the United States, Canada, as well as a growing presence in South America. Ibid., p. 79.

12. Gunaratna, *Inside al-Qaeda*, 54–94.

13. Ibid., 58.

14. Ibid., 5–6.

15. Ibid., 96.

16. Ibid., 72.

CHAPTER 14

1. Quoted in A. Aran, "A Mystico-Messianic Interpretation of Modern Israeli History: The Six-Day War as a Key Event in the Development of Original

Religious Culture of Gush Emunim," *Studies in Contemporary Jewry* 4 (1988): 263–264.

2. See the statement of one of the radicals, Yehuda Etzion, as quoted in E. Sprinzak, "From Messianis Pioneering to Vigilante Terrorism: The Case of the Gush Emunim underground," *Journal of Strategic Studies*, 4 October 1987, p. 206.

3. R. Friedman, "An Unholy Rage," *New Yorker*, 7 March 1994, p. 54.

4. E. Osmer, "Did He Kill in Peace? Baruch Goldstein in His Own Words," *Multinational Monitor* (1988). Reprint, *Washington Post*, 6 March 1996.

5. S. Schmemann, "Police Say Rabin Killer Led Sect that Laid Plans to Attack Arabs," *New York Times*, 11 November 1995.

6. J. Greenburg, "Israeli Police Question Two Rabbis in Rabin Assassination," *New York Times*, 27 November 1995.

7. G. Niebuhr, "To Church's Dismay, Priest Talks of 'Justifiable Homicide' of Abortion Doctors," *New York Times*, 24 August 1995.

8. C. Allen Jr., "Pro-Life Hate: Violence in the Name of God," *Reform Judaism* 10–17 (Summer 1994):14.

9. Paul Hill, *I Shot an Abortionist: Defending the Defenseless*, 2003 http://www.armyofgod. com/PHill_ShortShot.html. (This is a revised version of a paper published in an anthology in the Current Controversies Series: *The Abortion Controversy*, Greenhaven Press, 2001.)

10. Ibid.

11. Cited in M. Barkun, *Religion and the Racists Right*, (Chapel Hill: University of North Carolina Press, 1994), 131.

12. Ibid., p. ix.

13. M. Barkun, *Religion and the Racist Right* (Chapel Hill: University of North Carolina Press, 1994.)

14. R. Wood, "Right-Wing Extremism and the Problem of Rural Unrest," in T. D. McDonald , R. A. Wood, and M. A. Flug (eds.), *Rural Criminal Justice* (Salem: Sheffield Publishing, 1996), pp. 218–219.

15. A. Spaeth, "Engineer of Doom," *Time*, 12 June 1995: 57.

16. R. Lifton, *Destroying the World to Save It* (New York: Henry Holt, 2000), p. 36.

17. S. Asahara, *The Land of the Rising Sun Is Headed Toward a Bitter Fate* (Shizuoka, Japan: Aum Publishing, 1995).

18. S. Asahara, "Supreme Initiation: An Empirical Spiritual Science for the Supreme Truth" (n.p., 1988).

19. S. Asahara, *The Teachings of the Truth* (Shizuoka, Japan: Aum Publishing,1992).

20. T. R. Reid, "The Doomsday Guru: Japanese Sect Leader Rose to Venerated Master After Failure as Acupuncturist, Tonic Vender," *Washington Post*, 24 March 1995.

21. David Kaplan and Andrew Marshall, *The Cult at the End of the World* (New York: Crown Publishers, 1996), p. 67.

22. S. Asahara, *Declaring Myself the Christ* (Shizuoka, Japan: Aum Publishing, 1992).

CHAPTER 15

1. David Johnston and David Sanger, "New Generation of Leaders Is Emerging for Al-Qaeda," *New York Times*, August 10, 2004.

2. "Bin Laden Tape Praises Bali Attack," *The Guardian*, November 13, 2002, http://www.guardian.co.uk/alqaida/story/0,,838943,00.html.

3. "Jihadi Iraq: Hopes and Dangers", al-Qaeda on-line manual, December 2003.

4. "Rival Groups Claim Turkey Blast," *CNN.com*, August, 10, 2004, http://www.cnn.com/2004/WORLD/europe/08/10/turkey.blasts.twoclaims/index.html.

5. Michele Catalano, "October Turkey," *The Command Post*, October 3, 2004, http://www.commandpost.org/oped/2_archives/015711.html.

6. "Zarqawi's Pledge of Allegiance to al-Qaeda: From Mu'asker al-Battar, Issue 21", *The Jamestown Foundation*, December 16, 2004.

7. "Letter from Zarqawi to bin Laden", January 2004. www.cpa-iraq.org/transcripts/20040212_zarqawi_full.html

8. "Letter from al-Zawahiri to al-Zarqawi," *GlobalSecurity.org*, July 9, 2005, http://www.globalsecurity.org/security/library/report/2005/zawahiri-zarqawi-letter_9jul2005.htm.

9. "Al-Qaeda in Iraq: Letter to al-Zarqawi Fake," CNN.com, October 13, 2005, http://edition.cnn.com/2005/WORLD/meast/10/13/alqaeda.letter/index.html.

10. "Bin Laden Seizes Opportunities in his June and July Speeches," *The Jamestown Foundation*, July 5, 2006, http://www.jamestown.org/news_details.php?news_id=186.

11. This section draws extensively from a summary review of the reconstituted al-Qaeda leadership by Craig Whitlock, "The New al-Qaeda Central," which appeared in the *Washington Post*, September 9, 2007, pp. A1, A21.

12. A detailed discussion of the alienated Muslim diasporas in Europe can be found in Post and Sheffer, "The Risk of Radicalization and Terrorism in American Muslim Communities" *Brown Journal of International Affairs*, 2007.

13. E. Sciolino and S. Gey, "British terror trial traces a path to militant Islam," *New York Times: Europe*, 2006, http://www.nytimes.com/2006/11/26/world/europe/26crevice.html?ex=1322197200&en=7340a3579b048d42&ei=5088&partner=rssnyt&emc=rss; accessed 1/12/2006.

14. Marc Sageman, *Understanding Terror Networks* (Philadelphia: University of Pennsylvania Press, 2004).

CHAPTER 16

1. Jack Kelley, "The Secret World of Suicide Bombers: Devotion, Desire Drive Youths to 'Martyrdom.' Palestinians in pursuit of paradise turn their own bodies into weapons." *USA Today*, 26 June 2001

2. Nasra Hassan, "An Arsenal of Believers: Talking to the 'Human Bombs,' " *The New Yorker*, 19 November 2001.

3. This previously unpublished interview material is from the interview project summarized in Jerrold Post, Ehud Sprinzak, and Laurita Denny, "The Terrorists in Their Own Words: Interviews with 35 Incarcerated Middle Eastern Terrorists," *Terrorism and Political Violence* 15, no. 1 (2003): 171–184.

4. Jessica Stern, *Terror in the Name of God: Why Religious Militants Kill* (New York: HarperCollins, 2003), pp. 39–40.

5. Mia Bloom, *Dying to Kill: The Allure of Suicide Terror* (New York: Columbia University Press, 2005), p. 27.

6. Iyad Sarraj, "On Violence and Resistance," *Palestine-Israel Journal* 10, no. 1 (2003): 36–40, found in Hisham Ahmed, "Palestinian Resistance and 'Suicide Bombing,' " in *Root Causes of Terrorism*, ed. Tore Bjorgo (London: Routledge, 2005), 97.

7. Bloom, *Dying to Kill*, p. 90.

8. An extract from an interview conducted by Ahmed in March 2003. The name of the interviewee is kept anonymous for security reasons at his request. Ahmed, "Palestinian Resistance and 'Suicide Bombing,' " p. 93.

9. Bloom, *Dying to Kill*, p. 34.

10. Ahmed, "Palestinian Resistance and 'Suicide Bombing,' " p. 95.

11. Martin Kramer has explicated the "moral logic" of Fadlallah and the manner in which he has reinterpreted to not only make permissible but to assign a higher moral value to acts that the Koran in fact proscribes. Martin Kramer, "The Moral Logic of Hezballah," in *Origins of Terrorism: Psychologies, Ideologies, Theologies, States of Mind*, ed. Walter Reich (New York: Cambridge University Press, 1990).

12. Mohammed Hafez, *Manufacturing Human Bombs: The Making of Palestinian Suicide Bombers* (Washington, DC: United States Institute of Peace, 2006).

13. Jerrold Post, Ehud Sprinzak, and Laurita Denny, "The Terrorists in Their Own Words: Interviews with 35 Incarcerated Middle Eastern Terrorists," *Terrorism and Political Violence* 15, no. 1 (2003): 171–184.

14. Hafez, *Manufacturing Human Bombs*, p. 44.

15. Ibid., p. 50.

16. Nasra Hassan, "An Arsenal of Believers."

17. Nicole Argo, "The Istish'handin," in *Manufacturing Human Bombs*, ed. Hafez, p. 49.

18. Anne Speckhard. "Understanding Suicide Terrorism: Countering Human Bombs and Their Senders" in *Topics in Terrorism: Toward a Transatlantic Consensus on the Nature of the Threat" (Volume I)* Eds. Jason S. Purcell & Joshua D. Weintraub Atlantic Council Publication 2005. http://www.uwmc.uwc.edu/alumni/news_items/speckhard/uanderstanding%20_suicide.pdf.

19. Jerrold M. Post, *Leaders and Their Followers in a Dangerous World: The Psychology of Political Behavior* (Ithaca, NY: Cornell University Press, 2004), p. 187–199.

20. Nik Fleming, "I Would Do It Again," *The Guardian*, 18 February 2002.

21. Ibid.

22. Bloom, *Dying to Kill*, p. 63.

23. Ibid., p. 64.

24. Ibid.

25. Ibid., p. 159.

26. Ibid., p. 160.

27. As cited in Bloom, *Dying to Kill*, p. 160.

28. Speckhard, "Understanding Suicide Terrorism," p. 3.

29. Ibid., p. 10.

30. Walter Laqueur, *The New Terrorism: Fanaticism and the Weapons of Mass Destruction* (New York: Oxford University Press, 1999), p. 61.

31. Peter Pringle, "A Deadly Cloud of Paranoia Drifts Across the U.S." *The Independent*, December 20, 1998.

32. For a detailed review of psychological incentives and constraints for weapons of mass destruction terrorism by terrorist group type, see Jerrold Post, testimony presented to the House of Representatives hearings on biological terrorism conducted by the Subcommittee on National Security, Veterans Affairs and International Relations, Committee of Government Reform, US House of Representatives, 12 October 2001; J. Post, "Prospects for Chemical/Biological Terrorism: Psychological Incentives and Constraints," in *Bioterrorism: Psychological and Public Health Interventions*, ed. Robert Ursano, A.E. Norwood, and C. S. Fullerton, pp. 71–86 (Cambridge: Cambridge University Press, 2004); and J. Post, "Psychological and

Motivational Factors in Terrorist Decision-Making: Implications for CBW Terrorism," in *Toxic Terror: Assessing Terrorists Use of Chemical and Biological Weapons*, ed. J. Tucker, pp. 271–290 (London: MIT Press, 2000).

CHAPTER 17

1. Jerrold Post, "The Psychological Roots of Terrorism." In *Addressing the Causes of Terrorism: The Club de Madrid Series on Democracy and Terrorism*, Vol. 1, 7–12. Madrid: Club de Madrid, 2005.
2. Jerrold Post, Ehud Sprinzak, and Laurita Denny, "The Terrorists in Their Own Words: Interviews with 35 Incarcerated Middle Eastern Terrorists," *Terrorism and Political Violence*15, no. 1 (2003): 171–184.
3. Ibid.
4. Ariel Merari, personal communication, 2004.
5. Letter from al-Zawahri to al-Zarqawi July 9, 2005. Released by the Office of the Director of National Intelligence, 11 October 2005. Available on the Office of the Director of National Intelligence Web site, www.dni.gov/press_releases/letter_in_english.pdf.
6. Walter Laqueur, *The Age of Terrorism* (Boston: Little, Brown , 1987), pp. 131–132.
7. Louise Richardson, *What Terrorists Want: Understanding the Enemy and Containing the Threat* (New York: Random House, 2006), pp. 215–224.
8. Jerrold M. Post (ed.), *Declaration of Jihad Against the Country's Tyrants, Military Series: The al Qaeda Terrorism Manual* (Maxwell Air Force Base, AL: USAF Counterproliferation Center, 2005).
9. Letter from al-Zawahri to al-Zarqawi July 9, 2005. Released by the Office of the Director of National Intelligence, 11 October 2005. Available on the Office of the Director of National Intelligence Web site, www.dni.gov/press_releases/letter_in_english.pdf.
10. Mohammed Hafez, *Manufacturing Human Bombs: The Making of Palestinian Suicide Bombers* (Washington, DC: United States Institute of Peace, 2006).

BIBLIOGRAPHY

Agreement Reached in the Multi-Party Negotiations, 10 April 1998. www.dfa.ie/uploads/ documents/good%20friday%20agreement.doc.

Ahmed, Hisham. "Palestinian Resistance and 'Suicide Bombing': Causes and Responses." In *Root Causes of Terrorism*, ed. Tore Bjorgo, 87–102. London: Routledge, 2005.

al-Ahd. "Fadlallah Friday Sermon," December 5, 1985, cited in Martin Kramer, "The Moral Logic of Hizballah," in *Origins of Terrorism: Psychologies, Ideologies, Theologies, States of Mind*, ed. Walter Reich, 131–157. Washington, DC: Woodrow Wilson Center Press, 1998: 144.

Ali, Farhana. "Rocking the Cradle to Rocking the World: The Role of Muslim Female Fighters." *Journal of International Women's Studies* 8, no. 1 (2006): 21–35.

Aljazeera Magazine. "Hezballah Bombs Israeli Warship," July 15, 2006. www. aljazeera.com/me.asp?service_ID=11743.

Allen, Charles Jr. "Pro-Life Hate: Violence in the Name of God." *Reform Judaism* 22, no. 4, (Summer 1994): 10–17.

Al-Musawi. "Man antum Hizbullah?" no. 1, April 3, 2000, 24–25, in Ahmad Hamzeh, *In the Path of Hizbullah*. Syracuse, NY: Syracuse University Press, 2004.

"Al-Qaeda Claims Jordan Attacks," BBC Online, November 10, 2005. http://news. bbc.co.uk/2/hi/middle_east/4423714.stm.

"Al-Qaeda in Iraq: Letter to al- Zarqawi Fake," CNN.com, October 13, 2005. http://edition.cnn.com/2005/WORLD/meast/10/13/alqaeda.letter/index.html.*al-Qaeda Manual*. "Jihadi Iraq: Hopes and Dangers" (December 2003).

"al-Qaeda Statement," BBC News Online, October 14, 2001. http://news.bbc. co.uk/2/low/middle_east/1598146.stm.

Amr, Abu. "Interview, Al-Nahar (Jerusalem)," *Islamic Fundamentalism*, 30 April 1989, cited in "Dealing with Hamas," *International Crisis Group Middle East Report*, no. 21, January 26, 2004: 13.

Anderson, Brendan. *Joe Cahill: A Life in the IRA*. Dublin: The O'Brien Press, 2004.

Aran, A. "A Mystico-Messianic Interpretation of Modern Israeli History: The Six-Day War as a Key Event in the Development of Original Religious Culture of Gush Emunim." *Studies in Contemporary Jewry* 4 (1988): 263–264.

Argo, Nicole. "The Istish'handin." In *Manufacturing Human Bombs: The Making of Palestinian Suicide Bombers*, ed. Mohamed Hafez, 49. Washington, DC: United States Institute of Peace, 2006.

Art, R., and L. Richardson (eds.). *Democracy and Counterterrorism: Lessons from the Past*. Washington, DC: United States Institute of Peace, 2007.

Asahara, Shoko. *Declaring Myself the Christ*. Shizuoka, Japan: Aum Publishing, 1992.

Asahara, Shoko. *The Land of the Rising Sun Is Headed Toward a Bitter Fate[0]*. Shizuoka, Japan: Aum Publishing, 1995.

Asahara, Shoko. *Supreme Initiation: An Empirical Spiritual Science for the Supreme Truth*. New York: AUM USA, 1988.

Asbley, Karin, B. Ayers, B. Dohrn, J. Jacobs, J. Jones, G. Long, H. Machtinger, J. Mellen, T. Robbins, M. Rudd, and S. Tappis. "You Don't Need a Weatherman to Know Which Way the Wind Blows." *New Left Notes* (June 1969).

Asser, Martin. "Lebanon's Devastation Sightseers," *BBC News Online*, August 18, 2006. http://news.bbc.co.uk/2/hi/middle_east/5262832.stm

Atkins, Stephen. "ETA (Euskadi ta Askatasuna)." *Encyclopedia of Modern Worldwide Extremists and Extremist Groups*. Westport, CT: Greenwood Press, 2004, 87–89.

Aust, Stefan. *The Baader-Meinhof Group: The Inside Story of a Phenomenon*. London: The Bodley Head, 1985.

Ayers, Bill. *Fugitive Days*. New York: Penguin Putnam, 2003.

Baader-Meinhof.com. "Baader-Meinhof Timeline," November 3, 2004. www.baader-meinhof.com/timeline/1974.html.

Baader-Meinhof.com. "The Urban Guerrilla Is History . . ." (March 1998). www.baader-meinhof.com/students/resources/communique/engrafend.html.

Baeyer-Kaette, W. von, D. Classens, H. Feger, and F. Neihardt (eds.). *Analysen Zum Terrorismus 3: Gruppenprozesse*. Darmstadt: Deutscher Verlag, 1982.

Barber, B. *Heart and Stones: Palestinian Youth from the Intifada*. New York: Palgrave, 2003.

Barkey, Henri. "Turkey and the PKK: A Pyrrhic Victory?" In *Democracy and Counterterrorism: Lessons from the Past*, ed. R. Art and L. Richardson, 343–382. Washington, DC: United States Institute of Peace, 2007.

Barkun, M. *Religion and the Racist Right*. Chapel Hill: University of North Carolina Press, 1994.

Baumann, Bommi. *Terror or Love? My Life as a West German Guerrilla*. New York: Grove Press, 1977.

"BBC Panel Interview with Fathi Tobail," BBC News Online, September 13, 2006. http://news.bbc.co.uk/go/pr/fr/-/2/hi/talking_point/5339478.stm,

"BBC Panel Interview with Majeda Al-Saqqa," BBC News Online, September 13, 2006. http://news.bbc.co.uk/go/pr/fr/-/2/hi/talking_point/5338842.stm.

"BBC Panel Interview with Mona Yousef," BBC News Online, September 13, 2006. http://news.bbc.co.uk/go/pr/fr/-/2/hi/talking_point/5339478.stm.

"Country Profile: Sri Lanka," BBC News Online, March 9, 2007. http://news.bbc.co.uk/1/hi/world/south_asia/country_profiles/1168427.stm.

Beck, C., R. Emilia, L. Morris, and O. Patterson. *Strike One to Educate One Hundred: The Rise of the Red Brigades in Italy in the 1960s–1970*. Chicago: Seeds Beneath the Snow, 1986.

Becker, Jillian. *Hitler's Children: The Story of the Baader-Meinhof Gang*. London: Panther Books, 1978.

Bell, J. Boywer. *The Secret Army: The IRA*, 3rd ed.. Somerset: Transaction Publishers, 1997.

Bernard, Margie. *Daughter of Derry*. London: Pluto Press, 1989.

Beyer, Lisa. "The Most Wanted Man in the World," Time.com. www.time.com/time/covers/1101010924/wosama.html.

Bin-Jiddu, Ghassan. "Interview with Hezbollah Secretary General Hasan Nasrallah." *Al-Jazeera*, July 20, 2006. www.informationclearinghouse.info/article14152.htm.

"Bin Laden Tape Praises Bali Attack," *The Guardian*, November 13, 2002. www.guardian.co.uk/alqaida/story/0,,838943,00.html.

Biography Resource Center Online, Thomas Gale Group. "Abimael Guzman," 1999. http://galenet.galegroup.com.

Bjørgo, Tore (ed.). *Root Causes of Terrorism*. London: Routledge, 2005.

Bloom, Mia. *Dying to Kill: The Allure of Suicide Terror*. New York: Columbia University Press, 2005.

Brandon, James. "Mount Qandil: A Safe Haven for Kurdish Militants—Part 1." *Terrorism Monitor* 4, no. 17 (2006): 1–3.

Brom, Shlomo. "A Hamas Government: Isolate or Engage?" *United States Institute of Peace Briefing* (March 2006): 1–4.

"*Build up the Red Army! Manifesto for Armed Action*" Berlin 1970, http://home.att.net/~rw.rynerson/rafgrund.htm.

Burns, John. "A Sri Lankan Evokes Pol Pot; Asia's Latest Master of Terror," *New York Times*, May 28, 1995.

Caselli, Gian Carlo, and Donatella Della Porta. "The History of the Red Brigades: Organizational Structures and Strategies of Action (1970–82)." In *The Red Brigades & Left-Wing Terrorism in Italy*, ed. Raimondo Catanzaro. New York: St. Martin's Press, 1991.

Catalano, Michele. "October Turkey," *The Command Post*, October 3, 2004. www.commandpost.org/oped/2_archives/015711.html.

Center for International Policy's Colombia Program. "U.S. House International Relations Committee: Summary of Committee Investigation of 'IRA Links to FARC Narco-Terrorists in Colombia,'" April 24, 2002. www.ciponline.org/colombia/02042401.htm.

Chalk, Peter. *West European Terrorism and Counter-Terrorism: The Evolving Dynamic*. New York: St. Martin's Press, 1996.

"Charismatic Leader Behind the Latest Middle East Crisis," *The Guardian, Beirut*, July 23, 2006.

Chaulia, Sreeram. "Book Review. Enigma Decryption: Inside an Elusive Mind." *Asian Times*, March 4, 2003. www.atimes.com/atimes/South_Asia/EJ04Df01.html.

Choy, Shawn. "In the Spotlight: Sendero Luminoso," Center for Defense Information, July 1, 2002. www.cdi.org/terrorism/sendero-pr.cfm.

Ciezadlo, Annia. "Sheik Up," The New Republic Online, July 28, 2006. www.tnr.com/doc.mhtml?i=20060807&s=ciezadlo080706.

Clark, Robert. "Patterns in the Lives of ETA Members," *Terrorism* 6, no. 3 (1983): 423–454.

Cohen, Amit. "Hamas Dot Com," Maarivenglish Online, July 2, 2003. www.maarivenglish.com/tour/Hamas%20Dot%20Com.htm.

"Colombia's Civil Revolutionary Armed Forces of Colombia (FARC)," Online NewsHour, 2003. http://cocaine.org/colombia/farc.html.

Coogan, Tim Pat. *The IRA: A History*. Niwot: Roberts Rinehart Publishers, 1994.

Cowell, A., and Quinn, E. "Power Sharing in Northern Ireland," New York Times, May 8, 2007.

Crenshaw, Martha. "The Causes of Terrorism," *Comparative Politics* 13, no. 4 (1981): 379–399.

Crenshaw, Martha (ed.). *Terrorism in Context*. University Park: Pennsylvania State University Press, 1995.

Dequine, Jeanne. "The Challenge of the Shining Path," *The Nation* 239 (December 1984): 610–613.

Dickey, C., and D. McGinn. "Meet the bin Ladens," *Newsweek*, October 15, 2001.

Dorschner, John. "A Shadowy Empire of Hate Was Born of a War in Afghanistan." Knight Ridder Newspapers, September 24, 2001.

Dorschner, John. "Osama bin Laden: The Mastermind of Terror," Knight Ridder Newspapers, September 24, 2001. www.freep.com/news/nw/terror2001/osama24_20010924.html.

Dudley, Steven. "On the Road with the FARC," *The Progressive* (November 2003). http://findarticles.com/p/articles/mi_m1295/is_11_67/ai_110737536.

"Disarming, Bit by Bit," *The Economist* 370, no. 8360, January 31, 2004.

"An Encore for Uribe," Economist.com, May 24, 2006. www.economist.com/agenda/displaystory.cfm?story_id=E1_GJGJNNS.

Egan, T. "Federal Uniforms Become Cause of Wave of Threats and Violence," *New York Times*, April 25, 1995.

Eggen, Dan, and S. Wilson. "Suicide Bombs Potent Tools of Terrorists: Deadly Attacks Have Been Increasing and Spreading Since Sept. 11, 2001," *Washington Post*, July 17, 2005. www.washingtonpost.com/wp-dyn/content/article/2005/07/16/AR2005071601363_pf.html.

"Encyclopedia of Palestinians: Biography of Ahmad Yasin," Palestine Remembered.com, November 12, 2000. www.palestineremembered.com/Gaza/al-Jura/Story185.html.

English, Richard. *Armed Struggle: The History of the IRA*. New York: Oxford University Press, 2003.

"Entrevista con el Comandante Raúl Reyes," Farcep.org, February 6, 2006. www.farcep.org/?node=2,1880,1.

Ergil, Dogu. "The Kurdish Question in Turkey," *Journal of Democracy* 11, no. 3 (2000): 122–135.

"ETA: 'New Opportunities, but also Risks," *Gara*, September 26, 2005. www.gara.net/english/weekly/20050926/art134002.php.

"ETA: 'We Have a Real Opportunity to Achieve a Truly Democratic Situation," *Berria*, September 27, 2005. www.berria.info/english/print.php?id=1813.

"ETA Members in Spain Told to 'Put Bodies on the Table," *El Pais*, February 17, 2005.

"Exclusive Comments by Abimael Guzman," *World Affairs* 156, no. 1 (1993).

"ETA Targets Former Leaders for Attack," *El Mundo*, November 9, 2005.

"Ex-Political Leader of ETA Calls for an End to Terror Campaign," Agence France-Presse, June 11, 1998.

Fair, C. Christine. *Urban Battle Fields of South Asia: Lessons Learned from Sri Lanka, India, and Pakistan*. Arlington, VA: RAND Arroyo Center, 2004.

"FARC: We Don't Own Any Coca Fields," New Colombia News Agency (ANNCOL), September 14, 2006. www.anncol.org/uk/site/doc.php?id=253.

Ferracuti, Franco. "A Psychiatric Comparative—Analysis of Left and Right Terrorism in Italy." In World Congress of Psychiatry, *Psychiatry: The State of the Art*, 6. New York: Plenum, 1985.

Ferracuti, Franco, and F. Bruno. "Psychiatric Aspects of Terrorism in Italy." In *The Mad, the Bad, and the Different*, ed. I. L. Barak-Galantz and C. R. Huff, 199–213. Lexington, KY: Lexington Books, 1981.

Fleming, Nik. "I Would Do It Again." *The Guardian*, February 18, 2002.

Foote, Paul. *Ireland*. London: Chatto & Windus Press, 1989.

Forest, James (ed.). *Teaching Terror: Strategic and Tactical Learning in the Terrorist World*. Lanham, MD: Rowman and Littlefield, 2006.

Friedman, R. "An Unholy Rage." *New Yorker*, March 7, 1994, p. 54.

Fundacion Para La Libertad. "Citas de Sabino Arana" (November 2003). www.paralalibertad. org/modules.php?op=modload&name=News&file=article&sid=3854.

Fundacion Sabino Arana Kultur Elkarcoa. "The Basque Town at the End of the Century XIX: Sabino of Arana and Goiri." www.sabinoarana.org/es/sabino.htm.

Gillespie, Richard. "Peace Moves in the Basque Country," *Journal of Southern Europe and the Balkans* 1, no. 2 (1999): 119–136.

Goiri, Arana. "Bizkaya por su Independeci," as cited in Milton da Silva, "Modernization and Ethnic Conflict: The Case of the Basques," *Comparative Politics* 7, no. 2 (January 1975): 227–251.

Goldenberg, Sonia. "Shining Path's American 'Friends,' " *The Nation* 256, no. 10 (1993).

Golway, Terry. *For the Cause of Liberty*. New York: Touchstone Press, 2000.

Gonzáles, Raúl. "Especial Sobre Sendero," *Quehacer* 30 (August-September, 1984): 6–36.

"The Good Friday Agreement 1998–1999," BBC News Online. http://bbc.co.uk/ history/timelines/ni/good_friday.html.

Gorriti, Gustavo. *The Shining Path: A History of the Millenarian War in Peru*. Chapel Hill: University of North Carolina Press, 1999.

Gorriti, Gustavo. "Shining Path's Stalin and Trotsky." In *Shining Path of Peru*, ed. David Scott Palmer, 167–188. New York: St. Martin's Press, 1992.

Greaves, C. Desmond. *The Life and Times of James Connolly*. New York: International Publishers, 1961.

Greenburg, J. "Israeli Police Question Two Rabbis in Rabin Assassination," *New York Times*, November 27, 1995.

Gunaratna, Rohan. *Inside al-Qaeda: Global Network of Terror*. New York: Columbia University Press, 2002.

Gunter, Michael. "Abdullah Ocalan: "We Are Fighting Turks Everywhere." *Middle East Quarterly* 5, no. 2 (1998): 79–85.

Hacker, Frederick. *Crusader Criminals and Crazies: Terror and Terrorism in Our Time*. New York: W. W. Norton, 1976.

Hafez, Mohammed. *Manufacturing Human Bombs: The Making of Palestinian Suicide Bombers*. Washington, DC: United States Institute of Peace, 2006.

Hamzeh, Ahmad. *In the Path of Hizbullah*. Syracuse, NY: Syracuse University Press, 2004.

Hart, Alan. *Arafat, Political Biography*. Bloomington: Indiana University Press, 1989.

Hashim, A. "Usama bin Laden's Worldview and Grand Strategy," paper presented to conference at Navy War College, November 19, 2001.

Hassan, Nasra. "An Arsenal of Believers: Talking to the 'Human Bombs,' " *The New Yorker* 77, no. 36, November 19, 2001, 36–41.

Hennessey, Thomas. *A History of Northern Ireland*. New York: St. Martin's Press, 1997.

Hevidar, Lorin. "Kongra Gel Engulfed by Troubles—Again," *KurdishMedia*, June 12, 2004. www.kurdmedia.com/articles.asp?id=9659.

Paul Hill, *I Shot an Abortionist: Defending the Defenseless*, 2003 http://www.armyofgod. com/PHill_ShortShot.html. (This is a revised version of a paper published in an anthology in the Current Controversies Series: *The Abortion Controversy*, Greenhaven Press, 2001.)

"History of Basque Nationalism: Historical Background," *Euskal Herria Journal*, March 10, 1996. www.ehj-navarre.org/navarre/na_history_pnv.html.

Hoffman, Bruce. *Inside Terrorism*. New York: Columbia University Press, 1998.

Horchem, Hans Josef. "European Terrorism: A German Perspective," *Terrorism: An International Journal* 6, no. 1 (1982): 27–51.

Horgan, John. *The Psychology of Terrorism*. New York: Routledge, 2005.

Hudson, R. A., and H. C. Metz. "The Sociology and Psychology of Terrorism: Who Becomes a Terrorist and Why," report prepared under an interagency agreement by the Federal Research Division (Washington, DC: Library of Congress, 1999). www.intellnet.org/documents/1000/090/1091.htm.

Human Rights Watch. "Child Soldier Use 2003: A Briefing for the 4th UN Security Council Open Debate on Children and Armed Conflict" (January 2003). http://hrw.org/reports/2004/childsoldiers0104/5.htm.

Huston, James V. "Insurgency in Peru: The Shining Path," *Global Security* 11 (May 1988). www.globalsecurity.org/military/library/report/1988/HJV.htm.

Intelligence and Terrorism Information Center at the Center for Special Studies. "Hezbollah, Special Information Report" (June 2003). www.intelligence.org.il/eng/.

International Center for Political Violence and Terrorism Research. "Personality Profile of Velupillai Prabhakaran," February 3, 2005. www.Pvtr.org/database/13145_main_fr.html

International Crisis Group. "Interview, Abu Shanab," August 5, 2003, cited in *Middle East Report*, no. 21, "Dealing with Hamas," January 26, 2004.

International Crisis Group. "Interview with Rantisi," October 2002, cited in *Middle East Report*, no. 21, "Dealing with Hamas," January 26, 2004.

International Crisis Group. *Middle East Report*, no. 49, "Enter Hamas: The Challenges of Political Integration," January 18, 2006.

"Interview with Chairman Gonzalo," *El Diario* (July 1988). www.blythe.org/peru-pcp/docs_en/interv.htm.

"IRA 'Has Destroyed All Its Arms,' " BBC News Online, September 26, 2005. http://news.bbc.co.uk/2/hi/uk_news/northern_ireland/4282188.stm.

Ireland First. "Freedom Songs." www.eirefirst.com/f.html#f031.

Ireland First. "Irish Soldier Boy." www.eirefirst.com/i.html#i003.

Ireland First. "Joe McDonnell." www.eirefirst.com/j.html#j003.

Isbell, Billie Jean. "Shining Path and Peasant Responses in Rural Ayacucho." In *Shining Path of Peru*, ed. David Scott Palmer, 77–100. New York: St. Martin's Press, 1992.

"I Would Do It Again," *The Guardian*, February 18, 2002. www.guardian.co.uk/The_Kurds/Story/0,,652055,00.html.

Jaber, Hala. *Hezballah: Born with a Vengeance*. New York: Columbia University Press, 1997.

Jacobson, Philip. "Home-Grown Martyrs of the West Bank Reap Deadly Harvest," *Sunday Telegraph*, August 19, 2001.

Jager, H., G. Smidtchen, and L. Sullwold (eds.). *Analysen Zum Terrorismus 2: Lebenslaufanalysen*. Darmstadt: Deutscher Verlag 1981.

Jamieson, Alison. *The Heart Attacks: Terrorism and Conflict in the Italian State*. London: Marion Boyars, 1989.

Jayasinghe, Amal. "UN Puts Sri Lanka Tigers on Notice over Child Soldiers." Agence France-Presse, February 10, 2005. www.un.org/special-rep/children-armed-conflict/Download/AgenceFrance-TamilTigersOnNotice.html.

Johnston, Alan. "Palestinian Despair as Donors Meet." *BBC News*, September 1, 2006.

Johnston, D., and D. Sanger. "New Generation of Leaders Is Emerging for Al-Qaeda," *New York Times*, August 10, 2004.

Kaplan, D., and A. Marshall. *The Cult at the End of the World*. New York: Crown Publishers, 1996.

Kelley, Jack. "The Secret World of Suicide Bombers: Devotion, Desire Drive Youths to 'Martyrdom.' " *USA Today*, June 26, 2001.

Khaled, Leila. *My People Shall Live: An Autobiography of a Revolutionary*. London: Hooder and Stoughton, 1973.

Khalil, Lydia. "Ocalan Culture Center, a PKK Contact Bureau, Opens in Baghdad." *Terrorism Focus* 3, no. 29 (July 25, 2006): 3.

Khalil, Lydia. "Turkey's Mounting Concerns over PKK Incursions from Northern Iraq." *Terrorism Focus* 3, no. 28, (July 18, 2006): 3.

Kirisci, K. and G. Winrow. *The Kurdish Question and Turkey: An Example of a Trans-state Ethnic Conflict*. Portland, OR: Frank Cass and Co., 1997.

Korn, D. "Interview with PKK Leader Abdullah Ocalan" (April 1995). www.etext.org/Politics/Arm.The.Spirit/Kurdistan/Articles/apo-korn-interview.txt.

Kramer, Martin. "Hezbullah: The Calculus of Jihad." In *Fundamentalisms and the State: Remaking Politics, Economies, and Militance: The Fundamentalism Project, vol. 3*, ed. M. Marty and R. S. Appleby, 539–556. Chicago: University of Chicago Press, 1993.

Kramer, Martin. "The Moral Logic of Hizballah." In *Origins of Terrorism: Psychologies, Ideologies, Theologies, States of Mind*, ed.Walter Reich, 131–157. Washington, DC: Woodrow Wilson Center Press, 1998.

Kramer, Martin. "The Oracle of Hezballah: Sayyid Muhammad Husayn Fadlallah." In *Spokesmen for the Despised: Fundamentalist Leaders of the Middle East*, ed. R. Scott Appleby, 83–181. Chicago: University of Chicago Press, 1997.

Kropotkin, Pyotr. *The Spirit of Revolt*, first published in *Le Revolte* (Geneva, 1880), cited in W. Laqueur and Y. Alexander, *The Terrorism Reader*. New York: Meridian, revised edition 1987.

"The Kurdish People Are Prepared to Continue the Struggle," *Arm the Spirit*, February 18, 1999. www.etext.org/Politics/Arm.The.Spirit/Kurdistan/PKK.ERNK.ARGK/pkk-mizgin-interview-1999.txt.

Kurdish Struggle. "Final Statement," June 17, 1999. www.kurdstruggle.org/defence/final.html.

Kurdistan Informatie Centrum. "The Kurds Have Gone So Far that They Deserve Their Freedom" (1998). www.xs4all.nl/~kicadam/pers/oud/deserve.html.

Kutschera, Chris. "Disarray Inside the PKK." *The Middle East Magazine* (May 2000). www.africasia.com/archive/me/00_05/mebf0502.htm.

Kutschera, Chris. "Kurdistan Turkey: PKK Dissidents Accuse Abdullah Ocalan." *The Middle East Magazine* (July 2005). www.chris-kutschera.com/A/pkk_dissidents.htm.

Kutschera, Chris. "Mad Dreams of Independence: The Kurds of Turkey and the PKK," *Middle East Report* 189 (1994): 12–15.

Kutschera, Chris. "The Middle East Talks to Abdullah Ocalan." *The Middle East* 289 (April 1999). www.kurdistanica.com/english/politics/analysis/analysis-046.html.

Lake, P. "An Exegesis of the Radical Right," *California Magazine* 10, no. 4 (April 1985).

Laqueur, Walter. *The Age of Terrorism*. Boston: Little, Brown and Company, 1987.

Laqueur, Walter. *The New Terrorism: Fanaticism and the Arms of Mass Destruction*. Oxford: Oxford University Press, 1999.

Laqueur, Walter. "Sri Lanka." In *Terrorism Reader*, ed. David J. Whittaker, 83—New York: Routledge, 2004.

Laqueur, Walter, and Y. Alexander (eds.), *The Terrorism Reader*, rev. ed. New York: Meridian, 1987.

Lark Spirit. "Bobby Sands." Originally published in *IRIS* 1, no. 2 (November 1981). http://larkspirit.com/hungerstrikes/bios/sands.html.

Lark Spirit. "The Diary of Bobby Sands." Originally published in *Skylark Sing your Lonely Song: An Anthology of the Writings of Bobby Sands*. Cork: The Mercier Press Limited, 1991. http://larkspirit.com/hungerstrikes/diary.html.

Lark Spirit. "The Forgotten Hunger Strikers," September 19, 2003. http://larkspirit.com/hungerstrikes/forgotten_strikes.html.

Lawson, Alastair. "The Enigma of Prabhakaran." BBC News, November 25, 2003. news.bbc.co.uk/2/hi/south_asia/3236030.stm.

"Leader's Death Won't End Movement, Basques Say," *Washington Post*, April 24, 1973.

"Letter from al-Zawahiri to al-Zarqawi," GlobalSecurity.org, July 9, 2005. www.globalsecurity.org/security/library/report/2005/zawahiri-zarqawi-letter_9jul2005.htm.

Leupp, Gary. "Sendero's New Trial: Guzman's Fist." *Counter Punch*, November 11, 2004. www.counterpunch.org/leupp11112004.html.

Lifton, Robert. *Destroying the World to Save It: Aum Shinrikyo, Apocalyptic Violence, and the New Global Terrorism*. New York: Henry Holt and Company, 2000.

Little, David. *Sri Lanka the Invention of Enmity: Series on Religion, Nationalism, and Intolerance*. Washington, DC: United States Institute of Peace, 1994.

Lowenberg, P. *Decoding the Past: The Psychohistorical Approach*. Berkeley: University of California Press, 1985.

MacGowan, Liam. "Ballad of James Connolly," Pearse Com. www.pearsecom.com/Ireland/rebelsongs/connollysong.htm.

Manivannan, T. "The Road to Peace in Sri Lanka." BBC News Online, September 16, 2002. http://news.bbc.co.uk/2/hi/south_asia/2261863.stm

Marks, Thomas. *Colombian Army Adaptation to FARC Insurgency*. Carlisle, PA: Strategic Studies Institute, 2002.

Marks, Thomas. "Sri Lanka and the Liberation Tigers of Tamil Eelam." In *Democracy and Counterterrorism: Lessons from the Past*, ed. R. Art and L. Richardson, 483–530. Washington, DC: United States Institute of Peace, 2007.

Marighella, Carlos. *Mini Manual of the Urban Guerilla*. June 1969. www.marxists.org/archive/marighella-carlos/1969/06/minimanual-urban-guerrilla/index.htm.

McCaffrey, Shannon. "Program to Battle Colombian Drug Trafficking Gets Fresh Scrutiny." Knight Ridder Newspapers, September 15, 2005.

McCauley, C. R., and M. E. Segal. "Social Psychology of Terrorist Groups." In *Review of Personality and Social Psychology*, ed. C. Hendrick, 231–256. Beverly Hills, CA: Sage, 1987.

McClintock, Cynthia. *Revolutionary Movements in Latin America*. Washington, DC: United States Institute of Peace Press, 1998.

McClintock, Cynthia. "Theories of Revolution and the Case of Peru." In *The Shining Path of Peru*, ed. David Scott Palmer, 225–240. New York: St. Martin's Press, 1992.

McFadden, Robert. "Bin Laden's Journey from Rich, Pious Boy to the Mask of Evil," *New York Times*, September 30, 2001.

Meade, Robert Jr. *Red Brigades: The Story of Italian Terrorism*. New York: St. Martin's Press, 1990.

Meinhof, Ulrike (attributed to). "The Concept Urban Guerrilla," Baader-Meinhof.com. www.baader-meinhof.com/students/resources/communique/engconcept.html.

Mengel, R. W. "Terrorism and New Technologies of Destruction: An Overview of the Potential Risk." In *Disorders and Terrorism: Report of the Task Force on Disorders and Terrorism*, ed. U.S. National Advisory Committee on Criminal Justice Standards and Goals. Washington, DC: U.S. Government Printing Office, 1977.

Merari, Ariel. "Psychological Aspects of Suicide Terrorism." In *Psychology of Terrorism*, ed. B. Bongar, L. Brown, L. Beutler, J. Breckenridge, and P. Zimbardo. Oxford: Oxford University Press, 2007.

Merari, Ariel. "Social, Organizational, and Psychological Factors in Suicide Terrorism." In *Root Causes of Terrorism*, ed. Tore Bjorgo, 70–86. London: Routledge, 2005.

Merari, Ariel. "Suicidal Terrorism." In *Assessment, Treatment, and Prevention of Suicidal Behavior*, ed. R. I. Yufit and D. Lester, 431–453. Indianapolis: Wiley, 2004.

Merkl, Peter. "Approaches to the Study of Political Violence." In *Political Violence and Terror: Motifs and Motivations*, ed. Peter Merkl, 19–60. Berkeley: University of California Press, 1986.

Merkl, Peter. "West German Left-Wing Terrorism." In *Terrorism in Context*, ed. Martha Crenshaw, 160–210. University Park: Pennsylvania State University, 1995.

Merritt, R. L. "The Student Protest Movement in West Berlin," *Comparative Politics* 1, no. 4 (July 1969): 516–533.

Miller, John. "*ABC Interview with Osama bin Laden*," May 1998. www.pbs.org/wgbh/pages/frontline/shows/binladen/who/interview.html.

Ministry of the Interior, Federal Republic of Germany. *Analysen Zum Terrorismus 1–4*. Darmstadt: Dueutscher Verlag, 1981, 1982, 1983, 1984.

Mishal, Shaul, and Avraham Sela. *The Palestinian Hamas: Vision, Violence, and Coexistence*. New York: Columbia University Press, 2000.

Morris, Chris. "Turkey's Kurds Tell Their Story." BBC News Online, February 17, 1999. http://news.bbc.co.uk/1/hi/world/europe/263523.stm.

Most, John, "Freiheit," September 13, 1884, cited in W. Laqueur and Y. Alexander, *The Terrorism Reader*, rev ed. New York: Meridian, 1987.

Murillo, Mario A. "Colombia's Indigenous Caught in the Conflict." *NACLA Report on the Americas*, 39, no. 4 (January–February 2006): 4–7.

Niebuhr, G. "To Church's Dismay, Priest Talks of 'Justifiable Homicide' of Abortion Doctors," *New York Times*, August 24, 1995.

"Nivel de lucha cada vez más definitorio," Farcep.org, May 4, 2002. www.farcep.org/?node=2,765,1.

O'Brian, Nora Connolly. *James Connolly: Portrait of a Rebel Father*. Dublin: Four Masters Press, 1975.

Ocalan, Abdullah. "My Personal Status." *Declaration of the Democratic Solution of the Kurdish Question: Part IV* (1999). www.xs4all.nl/~kicadam/declaration/status.html.

"Ocalan Declares Cease-Fire," MED TV Television, London, August 28, 1998. www.xs4all.nl/~kicadam/pers/oud/staakt9.html.

"Ocalan Used Charisma plus Guns and Bombs in Deadly Struggle," Associated Press, June 29, 1999.

Office of the Director of National Intelligence. "Letter from al-Zawahri to al-Zarqawi," October 11, 2005. www.dni.gov/press_releases/letter_in_english.pdf.

Osmer, E. "Did He Kill in Peace? Baruch Goldstein in His Own Words." *Multinational Monitor* (1988). Reprint, *Washington Post*, March 6, 1996.

Outman, James, E. Outman, M. May, and D. Sawinski (eds.). "Abimael Guzman (Comrade Gonzalo)," *Terrorism Reference Library, Vol. 2: Terrorism: Biographies*. Detroit: U*X*L, 2003.

Palmer, David Scott. "'Terror in the Name of Mao': Revolution and Response in Peru." In *Democracy and Counterterrorism: Lessons from the Past*, ed. R. Art and L. Richardson, 195–220. Washington, DC: United States Institute of Peace, 2007.

Paz, Reuven. "Sawt al-Jihad: New Indoctrination of Qa'idat al-Jihad." *PRISM (Project for the Study of Islamist Movements)* 1, no. 8 (October 2003). www.eprism.org/images/PRISM_no_9.doc.

Peci, Patrizio. *I, the Contemptible One.* Worldwide Report Terrorism. FBIS. JPRS-TOT-85-016-L, March 20, 1985.

Perrin, Andrew. "Tiger Country." *TIME*, September 16, 2002. www.time.com/time/asia/magazine/article/0,13673,501020923-351287,00.html.

Peterson, Scott. "The Sheikh Behind Hezballah." *Christian Science Monitor*, August 9, 2006.

"PKK Central Committee Statement on Abdullah Ocalan's Deportation," *Arm the Spirit*, February 16, 1999. www.ainfos.ca/99/feb/ainfos00155.html.

Pierce, William [Andrew McDonald, pseudo]. *The Turner Diaries*, 2nd ed. Washington, DC: National Alliance, 1980.

Pisano, Vittorfranco. *The Dynamics of Subversion and Violence in Contemporary Italy.* Stanford, CA: Hoover Institution Press, 1987.

Pluchinsky, D., and Y. Alexander. *Europe's Red Terrorists: The Fighting Communist Organizations.* London: Frank Cass, 2001.

Post, Jerrold M. (ed.). *Declaration of Jihad Against the Country's Tyrants, Military Series: The al-Qaeda Terrorism Manual.* Maxwell Air Force Base: USAF Counterproliferation Center, 2005.

Post, Jerrold. *"El Fenomeno Chavez": Hugo Chavez of Venezuela, Modern Day Bolivar.* Maxwell Air Force Base: USAF Counterproliferation Center, 2007.

Post, Jerrold. *Leaders and Their Followers in a Dangerous World: The Psychology of Political Behavior.* Ithaca, NY: Cornell University Press, 2004.

Post, Jerrold. "Murder in a Political Context: Profile of an Abu Nidal Terrorist." *Bulletin of the Academy of Psychiatry and the Law*, Spring, 2000.

Post, Jerrold. "Notes on a Psychodynamic Theory of Terrorism," *Terrorism* 7, no. 3 (1984): 241–256.

Post, Jerrold. "Prospects for Chemical/Biological Terrorism: Psychological Incentives and Constraints." In *Bioterrorism: Psychological and Public Health Interventions*, ed. Robert Ursano, A. E. Norwood, and C. S. Fullerton, 71–86. Cambridge: Cambridge University Press, 2004.

Post, Jerrold. "Prospects for Nuclear Terrorism: Psychological Incentives and Constraints." In *Preventing Nuclear Terrorism*, ed. P. Leventhal and Y. Alexander, 91–103. Lexington KY: Lexington Press, 1987.

Post, Jerrold. "Psychological and Motivational Factors in Terrorist Decision-Making: Implications for CBW Terrorism." In *Toxic Terror: Assessing Terrorists Use of Chemical and Biological Weapons*, ed. J. Tucker, 271–290. London: MIT Press, 2000.

Post, Jerrold. "The Psychological Roots of Terrorism." In *Addressing the Causes of Terrorism: The Club de Madrid Series on Democracy and Terrorism*, Vol. 1, 7–12. Madrid: Club de Madrid, 2005.

Post, Jerrold. "Terrorist Psycho-Logic: Terrorist Behavior as a Product of Psychological Forces." In *Origins of Terrorism*, ed. by Walter Reich, 25–40. Cambridge: Cambridge University Press, 1990.

Post, Jerrold. Testimony presented to the House of Representatives hearings on biological terrorism conducted by the Subcommittee on National Security, Veterans Affairs and International Relations, Committee of Government Reform, US House of Representatives, October 12, 2001.

Post, Jerrold. "When Hatred is Bred in the Bone: Psychocultural Foundations of Contemporary Terrorism," *Political Psychology*, Vol. 26, #4 pp. 615–636, August, 2005. Sanford Award Essay.

Post, Jerrold, S. Kimhi, and S. Even (eds.). *Yasser Arafat: Psychological Profile and Strategic Analysis*. The Inter-Disciplinary Center. Herzliya and the American Jewish Committee, 2002.

Post, Jerrold, and R. Robins. *Political Paranoia: The Psychopolitics of Hatred*. New Haven, CT: Yale University Press, 1997.

Post, Jerrold, and R. Robins. *When Illness Strikes the Leader: The Dilemma of the Captive King*. New Haven, CT: Yale University Press, 1993.

Post, Jerrold, E. Shaw, and K. Ruby. "From Car Bombs to Logic Bombs: The Growing Threat from Information System Terrorism." *Terrorism and Political Violence* (Summer 2000): 97–122.

Post, Jerrold, E. Sprinzak, and L. Denny. "The Terrorists in Their Own Words: Interviews with 35 Incarcerated Middle Eastern Terrorists," *Terrorism and Political Violence* 15, no. 1 (2003): 171–184.

Prabhakaran, Vellupillai. "How I Became a Freedom Fighter." *Tamil Nation* (April 1994). www.tamilnation.org/ltte/vp/interviews/94velicham.htm.

Pringle, P. "A Deadly Cloud of Paranoia Drifts Across the U.S." *The Independent*, December 20, 1998.

"Profile: Hamas PM Ismail Haniya," BBC News Online, December 14, 2006. http://news.bbc.co.uk/2/hi/middle_east/4655146.stm.

"Profile: Peru's Shining Path," BBC News Online, November 5, 2004. http://news.bbc.co.uk/2/hi/americas/3985659.stm.

Raman, B. "Split in LTTE—The Clash of the Tamil Warlords." *South Asia Analysis Group*, no. 942, August 3, 2004. www.saag.org/papers10/paper942.html.

Rapoport, David (ed.). *Inside Terrorist Organizations*. New York: Columbia University Press, 1988.

Reich, Walter. *Origins of Terrorism: Psychologies, Ideologies, Theologies, States of Mind*. Cambridge: Cambridge University Press, 1990.

Reid, T. R. "The Doomsday Guru: Japanese Sect Leader Rose to Venerated Master After Failure as Acupuncturist, Tonic Vender," *Washington Post*, March 24, 1995.

Reinares, Fernando "Nationalism and Violence in Basque Politics," *Conflict* 8, no. 2–3 (1988): 141–155.

Reinares, Fernando. "Who Are the Terrorists? Analyzing Changes in Sociological Profile among Members of ETA," *Studies in Conflict and Terrorism* 27, no. 6 (2004): 465–488.

Richardson, Louise. *What Terrorists Want: Understanding the Enemy and Containing the Threat*. New York: Random House, 2006.

"Rival Groups Claim Turkey Blast," CNN.com, August, 10, 2004. www.cnn.com/2004/WORLD/europe/08/10/turkey.blasts.twoclaims/index.html.

Robinson, A. *Bin Laden*. London: Mainstream Publishing, 2002.

Rochlin, James F. *Vanguard Revolutionaries in Latin America: Peru, Colombia, Mexico*. Boulder, CO: Lynne Reinner Publishers, 2003.

Rubin, Barry, and Judith Colp Rubin. *Yasir Arafat: A Political Biography*. New York: Oxford University Press, 2003.

Ryder, Chris. "Joe Cahill." *The Guardian*, July 26, 2004. http:// politics.guardian.co.uk/politicsobituaries/story/0,,1269121,00.html#article_continue.

Saad-Ghorayeb, Amal. *Hizbu'llah: Politics and Religion*. London: Pluto Press, 2002.

"Sabina Arana," *El periódico Bizkaitarra*, no. 27. www.answers.com/topic/sabino-arana.

"Sabina Arana," *El periódico Bizkaitarra*, no. 29. www.answers.com/topic/sabino-arana.

"Sabina Arana," Sabine Text.org. www.sabinetxea.org/ingles/cronologia/cronologia/cronologia5.html.

Sageman, Marc. *Understanding Terror Networks*. Philadelphia: University of Pennsylvania Press, 2004.

Sanchez, Marcela. "Concern for Colombia's Little Guy," *Washington Post*, June 24, 2004.

Sarraj, Iyad. "On Violence and Resistance," *Palestine-Israel Journal* 10, no. 1 (2003): 36–40, cited in Hisham H. Ahmed, "Palestinian Resistance and 'Suicide Bombing.' " In *Root Causes of Terrorism*, ed. Tore Bjorgo, 87–102. London: Routledge, 2005.

Scheuer, Michael. "Bin Laden Seizes Opportunities in his June and July Speeches," *Jamestown Foundation*, July 5, 2006. www.jamestown.org/news_details.php?news_id=186.

Schmemann, S. "Police Say Rabin Killer Led Sect that Laid Plans to Attack Arabs," *New York Times*, November 11, 1995.

Schmid, Alex P. *Political Terrorism: A Research Guided*. New Brunswick, NJ: Transaction Books, 1983.

Sciolino, E., and S. Gey. "British Terror Trial Traces a Path to Militant Islam." *New York Times: Europe*, November 26, 2006. www.nytimes.com/2006/11/26/world/europe/26crevice.html?ex=1322197200&en=7340a3579b048d42&ei=5088&partner=rss nyt&emc=rss.

Shabad, G., and Francisco Jose Llera Ramo. "Political Violence in a Democratic State: Basque Terrorism in Spain." In *Terrorism in Context*, ed. Martha Crenshaw, 410–472. University Park: Pennsylvania State University Press, 1995.

Silj, Alessandro. *Never Again Without a Rifle: The Origins of Italian Terrorism*. New York: KARZ Publishers, 1979.

Singh, Jasvinder. "Tamil National Leader Velupillai Pirapaharan's Interview," *The Week* (March 1986). www.eelam.com/interviews/leader_march_86.html.

Sites, Kevin. "Ready to Kill, Willing to Die," *Yahoo: Sri Lanka Archive*, June 14, 2006. hotzone.yahoo.com/b/hotzone/blogs5836.

Smith, Charles D. *Palestine and the Arab-Israeli Conflict: A History with Documents*, 5th ed. Boston: Bedford/St. Martin's, 2004.

Spaeth, A. "Engineer of Doom," *TIME*, June 12, 1995, p. 57.

Speckhard, Anne. "Understanding Suicide Terrorism: Countering Human Bombs and Their Senders" in *Topics in Terrorism: Toward a Transatlantic Consensus on the Nature of the Threat" (Volume I)* Eds. Jason S. Purcell & Joshua D. Weintraub Atlantic Council Publication 2005. http://www.uwmc.uwc.edu/alumni/news_items/speckhard/uanderstanding%20_suicide.pdf

Speckhard, Ann. "Understanding Suicide Terrorism: Countering Human Bombs and Their Senders," *NATO Security through Science Series*, vol. 9 (2006): 158–175.

Sprinzak, E. "From Messianis Pioneering to Vigilante Terrorism: The Case of the Gush Emunim Underground," *Journal of Strategic Studies*, October 4, 1987, p. 206.

Stern, Jessica. *Terror in the Name of God: Why Religious Militants Kill*. New York: HarperCollins, 2003.

Strong, Simon. "Shining Path: A Case Study in Ideological Terrorism," *Conflict Studies* 260 (April 1993): 1–28.

Strong, Simon. *Shining Path: Terror and Revolution in Peru*. New York: Times Books, 1992.

Swamy, M. R. Narayan. *Inside an Elusive Mind: Prabhakaran: The First Profile of the World's Most Ruthless Leader*. Colombo: Vijitha Yapa Publications, 2003.

Swamy, M. R. Narayan. *Tigers of Lanka: From Boys to Guerrillas*. Columbia: South Asia Books, 1995.

Tarrow, Sidney. "Violence and Institutionalization after the Italian Protest Cycle." In *The Red Brigades & Left-Wing Terrorism in Italy*, ed. Raimondo Catanzaro, 44. New York: St. Martin's Press, 1991.

Telhami, Shibley. "Reflection in Lebanon, Israel, but Not in U.S.," *Baltimore Sun*, September 3, 2006.

"Text: Hezbullah Leader Defiant," BBC News Online, August 10, 2006. http://news.bbc.co.uk/2/hi/middle_east/4779757.stm.

Torbakov, I. "Kurdish Unrest Escalates in Turkey's Southeast," *Terrorism Focus* 3, no. 17 (May 2, 2006): 6–7.

United States Court of Appeals for the First Circuit. "*Carlos A. Betancur López, Petitioner, v. Alberto González, Attorney General, Respondent*. Petition for Review of an Order of the Board of Immigration Appeals," September 6, 2006. www.ca1.uscourts.gov/cgi–bin/getopn.pl?OPINION=05–2092.01A.

United States Department of State. "Background Notes: Peru," Bureau of Western Hemisphere Affairs (December 2006). www.state.gov/r/pa/ei/bgn/35762.htm.

Vieria, Constanza. *Colombia: Five Decades of a Struggle for Land that Became a War*. New York: Global Information Network, 2004.

Villalobos, Joaquin. "Colombia: Expert Analyzes How FARC Is Losing Domestic Conflict." *Semana*, July 7, 2003.

Viner, Katharine. "Leila Khaled," *The Guardian*, January 26, 2001.

Wallach, Janet, and John Wallach. *Arafat: In the Eyes of the Beholder*. New York: Birch Lane Press, 1997.

Wardlaw, Grant. *Political Terrorism: Theory, Tactics, and Counter-Measures*, 2nd ed. Cambridge: Cambridge University Press, 1989.

Wasmund, Klaus. "The Political Socialization of West German Terrorists." In *Political Violence and Terror*, ed. Peter Merkl, 191–228. Los Angeles: University of California Press, 1986.

Weather Underground Organization. *Prairie Fire: The Politics of Revolutionary Anti-Imperialism*. San Francisco: Prairie Fire Organizing Committee, 1974.

Weinberg L., and A. Pesahzur. *Political Parties and Terrorist Groups*. New York: Routledge, 2003.

Weimann, Gabriel. *Terror on the Internet: The New Arena, the New Challenges*. Washington, DC: United States Institute of Peace, 2006.

"We Killed Rajiv, Confesses LTTE," *Times of India*, June 28, 2006. http://timesofindia.indiatimes.com/articleshow/1686574.cms.

White, Robert. *Provisional Irish Republicans*. Westport, CT: Greenwood Press, 1993.

Witschi, B. "Who Is Abdullah Ocalan?" CNN (2001). www.cnn.com/SPECIALS/1999/ocalan/stories/ocalan.profile/.

Wood, R. "Right-Wing Extremism and the Problem of Rural Unrest." In *Rural Criminal Justice: Conditions, Constraints and Challenges*, ed. T. D. McDonald, R. A. Wood, and M. A. Flug. Salem, OR: Sheffield Publishing, 1996.

Woodward, Bob. "The World According to Rummy," *Washington Post*, October 8, 2006.

Woodworth, Paddy. *Dirty War, Clean Hands: ETA, the GAL and Spanish Democracy*. Cork: Cork University Press, 2001.

Woodworth, Paddy. "Why Do They Kill? The Basque Conflict in Spain," *World Policy Journal* 18, no. 1 (Spring 2001). www.worldpolicy.org/journal/sum01–1.html.

Wright, Robin. "Inside the Mind of Hezballah," *Washington Post,* July 16, 2006.

Wright, Robin. *Sacred Rage: The Wrath of Militant Islam.* New York: Linden Press, 1985.

Yegen, Mesut. *Devlet Soyleminde Kurt Sorunu.* Istanbul: Itelisim, 1999.

Ye Hedge School. "The Historic Hedge Schools of Ireland," September 3, 2006. www.hedgeschool.homestead.com/Irishhistory.html.

Zemenides, Peter. Interview with Iraqi Kurd in London, November 2005.

Zilboorg, Greory, and G. Henry. *A History of Medical Psychology.* New York: W. W. Norton, 1941.

INDEX

Previous Publications
Jerrold M. Post, M.D.

Declaration of Jihad Against the Country's Tyrants, Military Series:
The al-Qaeda Terrorism Manual (2005)

Leaders and their Followers in a Dangerous World:
The Psychology of Political Behavior (2004)

Political Paranoia: The Psychopolitics of Hatred (1997)
with Robert S. Robins

When Illness Strikes the Leader:
The Dilemma of the Captive King (1993)
with Robert S. Robins

※ ※ ※

Know Thy Enemy:
Leadership and Strategic Culture in an Asymmetric Security Environment
(2002; 2nd ed. 2003)
co-edited with Barry Schneider

The Psychological Assessment of Political Leaders
with Profiles of Saddam Hussein and Bill Clinton (editor, 2003)

Yasser Arafat:
Psychological Profile and Strategic Analysis (2002)
with S. Kimhi and S. Even, editors